THE REBIRTH OF THE
STATE OF ISRAEL—

Is It of God or of Men?

ARTHUR W. KAC, M.D.

MOODY PRESS
CHICAGO

U.S.A.
MOODY PRESS
820 NORTH LASALLE STREET
CHICAGO 10, ILLINOIS

LONDON
MARSHALL, MORGAN AND SCOTT, LTD.
1–5 PORTPOOL LANE
HOLBORN, E.C.1

CANADA
EVANGELICAL PUBLISHERS
241 YONGE STREET
TORONTO

AUSTRALIA
119 BURWOOD ROAD
MELBOURNE, E.13

SOUTH AFRICA
P.O. BOX 1720, STURK'S BUILDINGS
CAPE TOWN

PRINTED IN THE UNITED STATES OF AMERICA

FOREWORD

Since the beginning of the twentieth century, but especially since the end of the First World War, a large number of nations, including Israel, gained or regained political independence. With the exception of Israel all these nations lived in their respective countries at the time they acquired national sovereignty. The Jews in Palestine constituted a minority of Palestine's population when the State of Israel was established. The political independence which the Jews won in Palestine was accompanied by the liquidation of many centuries-old Jewish communities in various countries and the transfer of large numbers of Jews to Palestine. There is not another similar instance in the history of the world. What is the meaning of this extraordinary historical phenomenon? This work is an attempt to give an answer to this question.

The subject was approached from four points of view. Accordingly, this work consists of four divisions.

In the first division we are concerned with the question whether the Bible speaks of a final and permanent national restoration of the Jewish people.

In the second division we sought to explain the peculiar relationship which the rebirth of the State of Israel bears to the history of the Jewish people. In the many centuries of their forced separation from Palestine the Jews never ceased to mourn the loss of their National Homeland, and never gave up hope of a return to the land of their ancestors. The Prayer-Book of the Synagogue is replete with petitions for a speedy restoration of the Land of Israel. In the centuries of Jewish dispersion Palestine began to show the effects of the absence of the Jews from the country. Once a land flowing with milk and honey and supporting a population numbering between three to five million Palestine under the Arabs became a veritable wilderness. In the short time since the Jews returned to Palestine the country recovered much of its former fruitfulness.

The rebirth of the State of Israel stands also in an important

5

relationship to the religious crisis of Judaism. This crisis began—at least it became apparent—at the end of the eighteenth century. Jewish history is to a large extent the history of the Jewish religion. In the life of no other nation have religion and nationality been so inseparably intertwined as in the case of the Jewish people. Judaism owes its preservation to the Jews, and the Jews—humanly speaking—owe their preservation to Judaism. The decline of religious Judaism which set in at the end of the eighteenth century posed a serious problem to the national preservation of the Jews. Intermarriages and other forms of assimilationism threatened to submerge whole Jewish communities in Central and Western Europe. The resurgence of racial antisemitism in the middle of the nineteenth century came as a rude shock to the European Jews. The Jews at last began to realize that in spite of all their efforts to identify themselves fully with the environment in which they lived they were made to feel that they were not wanted. Zionism was the Jewish answer to the new situation. It was the revitalization of the age-long Jewish hope of national restoration in Palestine. It stepped into the breach created by the disintegration of religious Judaism. It rallied the Jewish people behind its banner and filled them with a determination to undertake a definite programme designed to re-establish themselves in the land of their forefathers.

The roots of the religious crisis of Judaism reach back to the first century A.D. The destruction by the Romans of Jewish Palestine at the end of the first century eliminated from Jewish religious life the sacrificial system of its worship centred in the Jerusalem Temple. The Jewish sages of that day assembled at Yavneh and laid the groundwork for a Judaism without sacrifices. The framers of this reconstructed Judaism based their work on the assumption that the Jewish people will remain in the world in a position of political subjection until the Messiah will come who will then terminate the exile and restore the Jews in Palestine. They did not—indeed they could not—foresee the mighty happenings of the eighteenth, nineteenth and twentieth centuries and the effect of these events on the destiny of the Jews. The American and French Revolutions freed the Jews of their political disabilities in many countries of Jewish residence; while the events of the two World Wars paved the way for the rebirth of the State of Israel. Both the Political Emancipation of the eighteenth and nineteenth centuries, and the re-establishment of the State of

Israel in the twentieth century came about without the Messiah. The Jews in the emancipated countries discovered that religious Judaism is in conflict with the duties of their newly found citizenship; while the Jews in the reconstituted State of Israel arrived at the painful conclusion that religious Judaism is incompatible with the functions of a modern State. Thus the Political Emancipation of the eighteenth century precipitated the great religious crisis of Judaism, while the rebirth of the State of Israel brought this crisis to a climax.

The last two chapters in the second division of this work are devoted to the problem of the Messiahship of Jesus. The history of the Jewish attitude to Jesus is one of the strangest historical phenomena. Having given Jesus to the world the Jews found themselves in the tragic position of opposing a spiritual movement which became the faith of the most civilized portion of the human race, and which to this day continues to give to millions of human hearts peace, hope and the answer to life's ultimate questions. Though the name of Jesus was for centuries adored and worshipped by hundreds of millions of Gentiles, the Jews have for centuries been trying to erase his name from their memory. The development which Rabbinic Judaism attained in the centuries following the destruction of the Second Temple was partly the result of an effort by the Synagogue to seal off the Jew from the influence of Jesus. But history, or rather God, the Lord of history, willed it otherwise. The destruction of European Jewry in World War Two has placed the vast majority of the world's remaining Jews in countries which for several centuries have been moulded by the spirit of Biblical Christianity; while the Jews who went to Palestine to rebuild the wastes of Zion went to the country where, according to the Bible, Jesus lived, suffered, died and rose again. In fact, the reconstitution of the State of Israel has placed the Jewish people there in a relationship to Christianity of such an intimate character as never existed since the destruction of the Jewish National Homeland in A.D. 70. Thus the Person of Jesus, whose name not many Jews up to a generation ago would even dare to mention, has come back to haunt the Jewish conscience. In recent years the Jews have displayed an unprecedented interest in the Person and message of Jesus. Jewish history is definitely moving to a complete reconciliation between the Jewish people and Jesus Christ. The rebirth of the State of Israel is an important step in this direction.

The third division of the book discusses the meaning of the
rebirth of the State of Israel in the light of current world events.
The general public probably does not realize that the present
world crisis goes back to World War One, if it does not actually
antedate it. The decline of Europe—the birthplace of Western
Civilization—certainly began with the outbreak of World War
One, if not before. The First World War brought home to many
people the startling realization that not all is well with Western
Civilization. Since Western Civilization became the civilization
of the world, the present crisis is world-wide in scope. Is it a pure
coincidence that in the same year of 1917, in which Europe was
approaching the end of its first war of self-destruction, Oswald
Spengler completed his work on "The Decline of the West",
while the British Government published the Balfour Declaration
in which it undertook to assist the Jewish people to re-establish
themselves in the land of their forefathers? Is it a mere coincidence
that the end of World War Two—in which the process of Europe's
decline was further advanced—saw the re-emergence of the State
of Israel? Is the destruction of European Jewry in World War
Two, the Jewish exodus from Europe, the "dwarfing" of Europe,
the reappearance of Israel on the eastern Mediterranean, and the
shift of the centre of world events to the Middle East—all without
some deeper significance? The fact is that in the Olivet Prophecy,
recorded in Matthew, Mark and Luke, Jesus Christ predicts
the end of Gentile civilization—the "Times of the Gentiles"—
and the restoration of the Jewish people as taking place in the
same era of world history.

In the last division of the book the subject of the rebirth of
Israel is presented in its relation to Israel's mission. Whatever
punitive element there is in Israel's suffering—and the Synagogue
does not deny it—its main object is to train Israel for her divinely
appointed mission to the nations. Israel could never discharge her
mission to the nations until she first regained for herself the status
of a nation. A people without statehood can have no first-hand
knowledge of the true nature of international problems. This is
the first time in over two thousand years that Israel is compelled
to deal with the nations of the world on an international level,
and this in a most stormy period of human history, and at a time
when the world has the largest number of politically independent
nations. Having resumed statehood at the same time with the
advent of the atomic era tiny Israel is quickly learning the salutary

truth that in a world as presently constituted there is no security for any nation. There is ample evidence that the thoughts of many in Israel are turning heavenward, that many of them are beginning to see a Messianic meaning in present-day events. To all of us whose faith is grounded in the Bible the rebirth of Israel should be a cause for much encouragement, and a sign that God is working out His eternal purposes even in these our times, and that the day may not be too far off when the Lord Jesus will come to rule and reign and to transform the kingdoms of men into the Kingdom of God.

ACKNOWLEDGMENTS

The writer wishes to make grateful mention of the following individuals for their part in the preparation and publication of this book:

Rev. Harcourt Samuel of London, England, and Jacob Peltz, B.D., Ph.B., of Chicago, Illinois, for their helpful service; N. J. Stone, A.B.Th.M., of Moody Bible Institute, for reading the manuscript and for his valuable assistance in many other ways; H. L. Ellison, B.A., B.D., of London, England, for compiling the Index; Mr. Kenneth N. Taylor, director of Moody Press, and Mr. A. H. Chapple, of Marshall, Morgan and Scott—for their helpful advice; my father-in-law, A. J. Kligerman, D.D., who placed at my disposal his useful library; last, but certainly not least, my beloved wife, who typed the manuscript.

GLOSSARY

The words below are spelled differently by different authors.

Kabbalah—Jewish mystic teachings concerning God and the universe.

Diaspora—All countries of Jewish residence outside of the land of Israel.

Galut—Exile, at times used in the same sense as Diaspora.

Halacha—The legal part of the Talmud.

Hassidism—A Jewish pietist movement which sprang up in South-East Europe in the eighteenth century.

Mishna—The oldest part of the Talmud.

Shulchan Aruch—Jewish Religious Code.

Talmud—A body of Jewish religious literature whose primary object was to interpret the law of Moses and its application in the daily life of the Jew.

Torah—The Law of Moses, but often used to denote all Jewish Religious Doctrine.

Biblical references used in this work were taken mostly from the American Standard Version. In most cases where there is a difference between the English and Hebrew texts the reference to the Hebrew text is added in parenthesis.

The author wishes to thank all publishers and owners of copyright material for permission granted to use excerpts in the following pages. If any acknowledgment has inadvertently been omitted apologies are offered.

CONTENTS

PART ONE

DOES THE BIBLE TEACH A PERMANENT NATIONAL RESTORATION OF THE JEWISH PEOPLE?

CHAPTER I

THE ELECTION OF ISRAEL

I. Its Objectives

    1. TO PROCLAIM THE EXISTENCE OF GOD

    2. TO PROCLAIM HIM AS JEHOVAH THE GOD OF REVELATION

    3. TO DEMONSTRATE THE BLESSING TO BE DERIVED FROM BELONGING TO GOD

    4. TO BECOME THE WRITERS AND PRESERVERS OF GOD'S REVELATION

    5. TO BECOME GOD'S NATION-PRIEST TO THE NATIONS OF THE WORLD

    6. TO BRING INTO THE WORLD THE WORLD'S REDEEMER

        a. The Redeemer's human origin

        b. His national origin

        c. A descendant of the tribe of Judah

        d. A descendant of the Royal house of David

        e. The place of the Redeemer's birth

        f. His Divine nature

II. The Fulfilment of the Objectives of the Election of Israel Rests on Two Premises:

    1. ISRAEL'S POSSESSION OF AND HER PRESENCE IN THE LAND OF ISRAEL

    2. THE FULL REALIZATION OF THE OBJECTIVES OF THE ELECTION OF ISRAEL WILL TAKE PLACE DURING THE REIGN OF THE MESSIAH

THE ELECTION OF ISRAEL

I. Its Objectives

The purpose of the election of Israel has for the first time been stated to Abraham: ". . . and in thee shall all the families of the earth be blessed", Genesis 12: 3. It has been restated to Isaac: ". . . and in thy seed shall all the nations of the earth be blessed", Genesis 26: 4. It has been declared again to Jacob: ". . . and in thee and in thy seed shall all the families of the earth be blessed", Genesis 28: 14. The same purpose has been reiterated on numerous occasions throughout the Bible.

An examination of these Biblical statements discloses the following objectives which the election of Israel was expected to achieve:

1. To proclaim to the world the existence of God: "This people have I formed for myself, they shall set forth my praise", Isaiah 43: 21.

2. To proclaim to the world that Jehovah, the God of Israel, is the one God of Revelation, the only one God who has revealed to Israel His purposes for the whole of mankind: "Hear, O Israel: Jehovah our God is one Jehovah", Deuteronomy 6: 4. It is by this name of Jehovah that God makes Himself known to Abraham when He made a covenant with him known as the Abrahamic Covenant: "And he said unto him, I am Jehovah that brought thee out of Ur of the Chaldees, to give thee this land to inherit it", Genesis 15: 7. When the time came for God to fulfil His promises to Abraham He revealed Himself to Moses again by the name of Jehovah. "And God said unto Moses, I Am That I Am; and he said, Thus shalt thou say unto the children of Israel, I Am hath sent me unto you. And God said moreover unto Moses, Thus shalt thou say unto the children of Israel, Jehovah, the God of your fathers, the God of Abraham, the God of Isaac, and the God of Jacob, hath sent me unto you: this is my name for

ever, and this is my memorial unto all generations", Exodus 3: 14–15.

3. To demonstrate to the world the blessing to be derived from belonging to God: ". . . Happy is the people whose God is Jehovah", Psalm 144: 15.

4. To become the writers and preservers of the Word of God: "Behold, I have taught you statutes and ordinances, even as Jehovah my God commanded me, that you should do so in the midst of the land whither you go in to possess it. Keep therefore and do them; for this is your wisdom and your understanding in the sight of the peoples, that shall hear all these statutes, and say, Surely this great nation is a wise and understanding people", Deuteronomy 4: 5–6. Notice what was to be Israel's most distinctive contribution in the world; "for this is your wisdom and your understanding in the sight of the peoples . . .". The apostle Paul expresses the same truth in the Roman letter: "What advantage then hath the Jew? or what is the profit of circumcision? [i.e. of the Abrahamic Covenant]. Much every way: first of all, that they were entrusted with the oracles of God", Romans 3: 1–2. Not only have the Jews been used to keep the record of God's revealed truth, but they have become the zealous guardians of His Word. On many occasions they have poured out their lives in its defence. They guarded it against corruption and against destruction. They have preserved it intact. The tremendous influence of the Bible upon the destiny of the nations of the world was made possible by the faithfulness with which the Jews have watched over it.

5. To become God's nation-priest to all other nations of the world, a channel by which God's blessings would flow to all nations of the earth: "Now, therefore, if you will obey my voice indeed, and keep my covenant, then you shall be a peculiar treasure unto me from among all peoples: for all the earth is mine. And ye shall be unto me a kingdom of priests, and a holy nation . . .", Exodus 19: 5–6.

6. To bring into the world the world's Redeemer. This is well expressed by the following two Talmudic utterances: "The world was not created but only for the Messiah", Sanh. 98b. "All the prophets prophesied not but of the days of the Messiah", Sanh. 99a.[1] The story of the Bible is primarily the story of God's plan for the redemption of mankind. Everything else in the Bible is subsidiary or incidental to this main theme. Even the story of

creation is of secondary importance. It is recorded chiefly
because the earth was to become man's dwelling-place. It is
merely introductory to the Bible's main subject. Consequently,
the creation story is condensed into two chapters, the first two
chapters, while the story of man's redemption begins in the third
chapter of Genesis and runs through the whole Bible to the very
end.

The following are a few Biblical passages describing the person
of this Redeemer.

   a. His human origin: "And I will put enmity between thee
and the woman, and between thy seed and her seed: he [the
woman's seed] shall bruise thy head, and thou shalt bruise his
heel", Genesis 3: 15. In an essay entitled "Universality of
Serpent-Worship" Professor W. G. Moorhead gives a most
interesting account of serpent-worship among the heathen nations
which throws much interesting light on the Genesis story. The
serpent was worshipped in Egypt, Babylon, Palestine, China,
India, America, England, France, Italy, Ireland, Scandinavia
(Sweden and Norway), Greece, Africa in its most savage parts—
in a word, all over the world.[2] "Deified as the serpent has been
all over the world, it has always been the emblem of the evil
principle in nature, and its worship was inspired rather to avert
evil than to express reverence or gratitude. A god it might
become in the perverted judgment of fallen men, but the feeling
of antipathy and aversion with which it was regarded has never
abated. It might be feared, but loved it never was nor could be.
Thus, we are told that while many Hindus pay religious homage
to the serpent at the present day, they regard it, notwithstanding,
'as a hideous reptile, whose approach inspires them with a secret
awe, and insurmountable horror'. Worshipped universally, the
serpent was still 'cursed above all and above every beast of the
field'."[3]

Here is a more recent comment on the meaning and implications of this deeply significant passage. "The serpent now is
obviously the snake. In our world of physical experience there
is nothing from which men have a more natural revulsion than
from the snake. It is secret and stealthy. It strikes without
warning and its bite has poison in it. Only a fool will walk care-
lessly where snakes lurk. Many men have come to their senses
when God has intervened to show the nature of sin, for then its
reality is unmistakably abhorrent. The evil that somehow is in

our world cannot be whistled off. It shall bruise man's heel. A man cannot think he will escape the fact of sin as if it were not there. It will strike at him and wound him. . . . Much contemporary religious thinking has emphasized anew the fact of sin and man's vulnerability to it. See the writings of Karl Barth and Emil Brunner and of most of the continental theologians and others deeply affected by the brutal aspect of our civilization in the twentieth century. Neither life nor civilization is an easy process. A generation ago some churches had on their bulletin board a statement of belief which included belief in 'the progress of man onward and upward forever'. We are not so shallow as to believe in automatic progress."[4]

The passage in Genesis 3: 15 predicts a Divinely inspired antagonism between the two groups of people, the godly ones, who are of the seed of the woman, and those who follow the guidance of the Evil One, who are here referred to as the seed of the Serpent. In the end, the conflict between the two will end with the complete defeat of the Evil One: "He [the seed of the woman] shall crush [or bruise] thy head." In striking man down the Tempter really aimed his blows in the direction of God. But since man fell victim to Satan's deceptions man shall contribute to Satan's final defeat.

b. His national origin: "Now Jehovah said unto Abram, Get thee out of thy country, and from thy kindred, and from thy father's house, unto the land that I will show thee. And I will make of thee a great nation, and I will bless thee, and make thy name great; and be thou a blessing. And I will bless them that bless thee, and him that curseth thee will I curse: and in thee shall all the families of the earth be blessed", Genesis 12: 1–3.

c. A descendant of the tribe of Judah: "The sceptre shall not depart from Judah, nor the ruler's staff from between his feet, until Shiloh come, and unto him shall the obedience of the peoples be", Genesis 49: 10.

d. A descendant of the royal house of David: "And there shall come forth a shoot out of the stock of Jesse [David's father], and a branch out of his roots shall bear fruit. And the Spirit of Jehovah shall rest upon him, the spirit of wisdom and understanding, the spirit of counsel and might, the spirit of knowledge and of the fear of Jehovah", Isaiah 11: 1–2. Another translation of the first verse in the above passage runs like this: "And there comes forth a twig out of the stump of Jesse, and a shoot from its roots brings forth fruit." The royal house of David has become like the stump of a felled tree, like a root without a stem, or branches. Out of this stump, out of the remnant of the royal family of David, there comes forth a twig, out of the roots covered with earth there appears a fresh green shoot. It is from this twig and from this shoot that the royal house of David becomes regenerated.

e. The place of the Redeemer's birth: "But thou, Bethlehem Ephrathah, which art little to be among the thousands of Judah, out of thee shall one come forth unto me that is to be ruler in Israel, whose goings forth are from of old, from everlasting", Micah 5: 2 (5: 1 Heb.). Bethlehem was a small insignificant place, not large enough to have a thousand families within its boundaries. It was this inconspicuous town of Bethlehem which God has appointed to be the birth-place of the Messiah, whose origin is from eternity.

f. His Divine nature: This was already implied in the prophecy of Micah cited above. The following statement in Isaiah is more explicit: "For unto us a child is born, unto us a son is given; and the government shall be upon his shoulder, and his name shall-be called Wonderful, Counsellor [or Wonderful Counsellor], Mighty God, Everlasting Father, Prince of Peace", Isaiah 9: 6.

II. The Fulfilment of the Objectives of the Election of Israel Rests on Two Premises

1. ISRAEL'S POSSESSION OF AND HER PRESENCE IN THE LAND OF ISRAEL

The realization of the objectives of Israel's election rests on two premises. One of these is the presence of Israel in her land. If we turn once again to those passages in Genesis already cited in the first section of this chapter and dealing with the Abrahamic Covenant we shall observe that Israel's mission to the world is inseparably linked with her possession of and her presence in the Land of Israel: "Now Jehovah said unto Abram, Get thee out of thy country, and from thy kindred, and from thy father's house, unto the land that I will show thee . . . and in thee shall all the families of the earth be blessed. And I will establish my covenant between me and thee and thy seed after thee throughout their generations for an everlasting covenant, to be a God unto thee and to thy seed after thee. And I will give unto thee, and to thy seed after thee, the land of thy sojournings, all the land of Canaan, for an everlasting possession; and I will be their God", Genesis 12: 1, 3; 17: 7–8.

These promises were confirmed to Isaac as seen from the following statement: "And Jehovah appeared unto him, and said, Go not down into Egypt; dwell in the land which I shall tell thee of. Sojourn in this land, and I will be with thee, and will bless thee; for unto thee, and unto thy seed, I will give all these lands, and I will establish the oath which I swore unto Abraham thy father. . . . And in thy seed shall all the nations of the earth be blessed", Genesis 26: 2–4.

The same promises were in due time reaffirmed by God in His dealings with Jacob: "And, behold, Jehovah stood above it, and said, I am Jehovah, the God of Abraham thy father, and the God of Isaac: the land whereon thou liest, to thee will I give it, and to thy seed . . . and in thee and in thy seed shall all the families of the earth be blessed. And, behold, I am with thee, and will keep thee whithersoever thou goest, and will bring thee again into this land; for I will not leave thee, until I have done that which I have spoken to thee of", Genesis 28: 13–15.

It is true that the uninterrupted possession of the Promised Land by Israel depended on Israel's faithfulness to God's covenant with her. But her ownership of the Land, her title to it, was never to be affected by her conduct. The Abrahamic Covenant was a contract between two parties, but, unlike a human contract, one of these parties was God Himself. The Abrahamic Covenant was, therefore, irrevocable: "For all the land which thou seest, to thee will I give it, and to thy seed forever. . . . And I will establish my covenant between me and thee and thy seed after thee throughout their generations for an everlasting covenant, to be a God unto thee and to thy seed after thee. And I will give unto thee, and to thy seed after thee, the land of thy sojournings, all the land of Canaan, for an everlasting possession; and I will be their God", Genesis 13: 15; 17: 7–8.

Israel was twice exiled from her land, once by the Babylonians, and a second time by the Romans. But she was forewarned in the Bible again and again that this will happen if she does not conform to the covenant which God had made with her. But the same God who had made these warnings also promised that He will bring her back to her land: "And yet for all that, when they are in the land of their enemies, I will not reject them, neither will I abhor them, to destroy them utterly, and to break my covenant with them; for I am Jehovah their God", Leviticus 26: 44. Nations and governments make agreements one day, and when circumstances change, or when it suits their interests, they tear up these promises. Not so with God: "For I am Jehovah their God."

In conclusion, let us also remember this, that for Israel to accomplish her mission to the world while being exiled from the Land of Israel is an utter contradiction. Israel can never fulfil her Divinely-appointed mission if she is not right with God. And to be exiled from the Land of Israel is for Israel, as a nation, to be exiled from God.

2. THE FULL REALIZATION OF THE OBJECTIVES OF THE ELECTION OF ISRAEL WILL TAKE PLACE DURING THE REIGN OF THE MESSIAH

This is the second premise on which the fulfilment of Israel's mission to the world rests. The subject will be discussed more thoroughly in the next chapter. Here we wish to make a few introductory observations. The earliest instance where this truth is taught in the Bible is recorded in Genesis 49 which we cite below:

"And Jacob called unto his sons, and said: Gather yourselves together, that I may tell you that which shall befall you in the latter days. Judah, thee shall thy brethren praise; thy hand shall be on the neck of thine enemies; thy father's sons shall bow down before thee. The sceptre shall not depart from Judah, nor the ruler's staff from between his feet, until Shiloh come, and unto him shall the obedience of the peoples be", Genesis 49: 1, 8, 10.

Elsewhere in this book the phrase "latter days" is discussed in great detail. Suffice it to say here that it points to the end of the Age, i.e. to the end of that phase of human history in which man is permitted to have his own way in the world, and the beginning of a new phase in the history of the world when the kingdoms of the earth will become the Kingdom of God, and God's Will will be done on earth as it is in heaven. In the forty-ninth chapter of Genesis we have a preview of Israel's history. But the thing which concerns us here most is what Jacob had to say with reference to the destinies of the tribe of Judah. In the

first place, we have a prediction of the ascendancy of Judah.
Judah shall attain to a position of leadership among the rest of
the tribes of Israel. For centuries it did not appear that this
prophecy would ever find fulfilment. Not even the first king of
Israel was of the tribe of Judah. When Saul died and David became king of Israel there was the beginning of the fulfilment of this
prophecy. But after the death of Solomon, David's son, a division
set in and the larger part of the nation—ten tribes—rejected
Judah's leadership. And this was the state of affairs for many years
to come until the end of the eighth century B.C., when the Northern
Kingdom of Israel was destroyed and its people carried off to
exile never to be heard from. From then on until this day—for
about 2,700 years—the history of Israel, the history of the Jewish
people, is the history of the tribe of Judah. "Judah, thee shall thy
brethren praise . . . thy father's sons shall bow down before thee."
God may at times appear to move very slow, but He is nevertheless sure to perform all He promised to do.

The second thing which Jacob declared concerning Judah is
that he will remain a sovereign nation until Shiloh's appearance.
Rashi (Rabbi Solomon ben Yitzchak), one of the greatest Jewish
Bible commentators in the Middle Ages, interprets Shiloh to
mean "king Messiah to whom belongs the kingdom". Now,
Jacob declares that not only will Judah gain pre-eminence in
Israel, but that he will be a sovereign nation until the very time
when Messiah arrives and takes over the kingdom. Judah was a
sovereign nation until 586 B.C. when its kingdom was destroyed
by the Babylonians. After seventy years the exiles returned from
Babylon and rebuilt their country. But they remained subservient
first to Persia, later to Alexander the Great, and after the death
of Alexander the Great Jewish Palestine passed into the hands
of one of his successors.

About the middle of the second century B.C. the Second Jewish
Commonwealth regained political independence under the
leadership of the Maccabees. This, however, was of short duration; for in 63 B.C. the Romans extended their power over Palestine. The Jewish wars against Rome, first in A.D. 66–70, then in
A.D. 132–135, resulted in the destruction of the Jewish National
Homeland, and the world-wide dispersion of the bulk of the
Jewish people. From then on until 1948, for about nineteen
centuries, the Jewish people had no country of their own, and no
status as a sovereign nation. In her long and chequered history

Israel stood many a time on the brink of total national annihilation. During the many centuries of Israel's dispersion among the Gentiles it must have often appeared that something had gone wrong with that part of Jacob's prophecy which declares that Judah was to remain a sovereign nation until Shiloh comes. But the events since 1948 have thrown fresh light on the prophetic character of Genesis 49: 10. Israel is back in the land of her forefathers and is in possession of all the attributes of a sovereign nation in the world. "The sceptre shall not depart from Judah, nor the ruler's staff from between his feet, until Shiloh come."

The third revelation which Jacob uttered before his death concerned the destiny of the nations of the world: "And unto him [i.e. Shiloh] shall the obedience of the peoples be", Genesis 49: 10. Unto Shiloh, whó, according to the Jewish Bible commentator Rashi, is King Messiah, the nations of the world will render willing obedience. Thus the ingathering of the nations, the transformation of the kingdoms of the nations into the kingdom of God, which is the aim and end of the election of Israel and Israel's mission, will only take place when Messiah comes.

If Jacob's prophecy were an isolated passage this fact would not in the least invalidate the truths set forth in it. The marvellous thing, however, is that far from standing alone, it is the beginning of a whole body of teachings in the Old Testament emphasizing the same fact in no uncertain terms. This is especially true of the prophetic writings. Let us take for an example the passage in Isaiah 11: 1, 10, part of which was quoted already in the first section of this chapter. "And there shall come forth a shoot out of the stock of Jesse, and a branch out of his roots shall bear fruit. And it shall come to pass in that day, that the root of Jesse, that stands for an ensign of the peoples, unto him shall the nations seek. . . ." We have selected the first and last verse of this passage for lack of space. To appreciate the Messianic character of this prophecy the whole passage should be read. It speaks of the cessation of war and universal peace—something which has never taken place as yet in the history of the world. For our purpose we wish to call the reader's attention to the contents of the tenth verse. Complete and repeated destruction and devastation of the Land of Israel was predicted in chapter six. This will leave the royal house of David in a state likened to a tree whose stem and branches were felled and only the root-stump remained. In chapter eleven we are informed that at the appointed time a descendant of the Davidic line will arise and will cause the regeneration of the royal house of David.

This event will be of world-wide significance. For this descendant of the Davidic royal family who will restore the Davidic monarchy will at the same time become the rallying point for all the nations of the earth and usher in an era of international justice and world peace. Reading the prophecy of Jacob together with the prophecy in Isaiah, chapter eleven, we arrive at the following conclusions: Whatever history may have in store for Israel, at the time of the end she will be a nation in her own land, and in possession of full political independence. The Davidic monarchy, however, will not be restored until Shiloh, the shoot out of the root-stump of David, will come, and under His leadership the nations of the earth will turn to God, and the objectives of Israel's election will be fully achieved.

NOTES TO CHAPTER 1

1. Quoted by Alfred Edersheim, *The Life and Times of Jesus the Messiah* (Longmans, Green & Co.: London, 1899), Eighth Edition, Revised, vol. 1, p. 1.
2. Prof. W. G. Moorhead, "Universality of Serpent-Worship", essay printed in *The Old Testament Student*, Wm. R. Harper, Editor, Chicago (September 1884–June 1885), vol. 4, p. 207.
3. Ibid., p. 206.
4. Walter Russell Bowie, *The Interpreter's Bible* (Abingdon-Cokesbury Press: New York and Nashville), vol. 1, pp. 508–9. Copyright 1952 by Pierce and Smith. By permission of Abingdon Press.

THE SIX-FOLD ASPECT OF
ISRAEL'S NATIONAL RESTORATION

CHAPTER 2

THE SIX-FOLD ASPECT OF
ISRAEL'S NATIONAL RESTORATION

In the attached Chart we have tabulated a number of Biblical passages according to whether they emphasize one or another of the several aspects of Israel's restoration. We have not attempted to present an exhaustive list of these teachings, but we have included the more familiar ones. The impressive number of these Bible citations merely proves that the restoration of Israel is not a stray teaching. The reader interested in the subject may use the chart as a guide and check these references in his own Bible. We shall give below, under each heading, a few representative portions from the Bible as compiled in our Chart.

I. A PERMANENT AND/OR FULL RESTORATION

Let the reader note that the characteristic feature common to all Bible passages which follow is the permanent and/or universal aspect of Israel's restoration.

Joel 3: 20 (4: 20 Heb.): "But Judah shall abide forever, and Jerusalem from generation to generation."

Amos 9: 15: "And I will plant them upon their land, and they shall no more be plucked up out of their land which I have given them, saith Jehovah thy God."

Micah 4: 6–7: "In that day, saith Jehovah, will I assemble that which is lame, and I will gather that which is driven away, and that which I have afflicted. And I will make that which was lame a remnant, and that which was cast far off a strong nation: and Jehovah will reign over them in mount Zion from henceforth even for ever."

Zephaniah 3: 14–15: "Sing, O daughter of Zion; shout, O Israel; be glad and rejoice with all the heart, O daughter of Jerusalem. Jehovah hath taken away thy judgments, he hath cast out thine enemy; the King of Israel, even Jehovah, is in the midst of thee; thou shalt not see evil any more."

Isaiah 60: 18, 21: "Violence shall no more be heard in thy land, desolation nor destruction within thy borders; but thou shalt call thy walls Salvation, and thy gates Praise. Thy people also shall be all righteous; they shall inherit the land forever, the branch of my planting, the work of my hands, that I may be glorified."

Jeremiah 32: 37–40: "Behold, I will gather them out of all the countries, whither I have driven them in mine anger, and in my wrath, and in great indignation; and I will bring them again unto this place, and I will cause them to dwell safely. And they shall be my people, and I will be their God. And I will give them one heart and one way, that they may fear me for ever, for the good of them, and of their children after them. And I will make an everlasting covenant with them, that I will not turn away from following them, to do them good; and I will put my fear in their hearts, that they may not depart from me."

Ezekiel 37: 21, 25: "And say unto them, Thus saith the Lord Jehovah: Behold I will take the children of Israel from among the nations, whither they are gone, and will gather them on every side, and bring them into their own land. And they shall dwell in the land that I have given unto Jacob my servant, wherein your fathers dwelt; and they shall dwell therein, they and their children, and their children's children, for ever; and David my servant shall be their prince for ever."

II. The Physical Aspect of Israel's Restoration

The second column in the Chart contains a number of Bible teachings which speak of the physical aspect of Israel's ingathering. The emphasis here is on the return of the people to the land of their forefathers and the reconstruction of the Homeland. Following below are a few representative examples taken from the second column.

Amos 9: 11, 13–14: "In that day will I raise up the tabernacle of David that is fallen, and close up the breaches thereof; and I will raise up its ruins, and I will build it as in the days of old. Behold, the days come, saith Jehovah, that the plowman shall overtake the reaper, and the treader of grapes him that soweth seed; and the mountains shall drop sweet wine, and all the hills shall melt. And I will bring back the captivity of my people Israel, and they shall build the waste cities, and inhabit them; and they shall plant vineyards, and drink the wine thereof; they shall also make gardens, and eat the fruit of them."

Source of Reference	Permanent and/or Full	The Physical Aspect	The Spiritual A.
Leviticus		26: 44–5	
Numbers			
Deuteronomy	30: 3–5		30: 6
Joel	3: 20 (4: 20 Heb.)	2: 18–27	2: 28–9 (3: 1–2 3: 17 (4: 17 Heb
Amos	9: 15	9: 14	
Hosea			2: 19–20 (2: 21–2 Heb.)
Micah	4: 6–7	2: 12	7: 18–19
Nahum	1: 9–12b		
Zephaniah	3: 15	3: 14–20	3: 10–13
Daniel			
Obadiah		1: 17–21	
Haggai			
Zechariah	14: 10–11	8: 7; 10: 6–12; 12; 13; 14	8: 8; 12: 10–14; 13: 1, 9; 14: 20–2
Malachi			
Isaiah	43: 1–7; 51: 11, 21–3; 52: 1; 54: 6–10; 60: 15, 18–22; 61: 7–9; 62: 4, 8–9; 65: 18–19, 22–25; 66: 22	11: 11–12; 14: 1–3; 27: 12–13; 35: 1–10; 49; 14–26; 51: 3; 52: 3–12; 54: 1–17; 60: 4–22; 61: 4–5	4: 2–6; 10: 20–3; 35: 8; 60: 18–2!; 61: 6, 9–10; 62: 1–2, 12
Jeremiah	16: 14–16; 23: 3–4, 7–8; 24: 5–6; 30: 8–9; 31: 10–12 (31: 9–11 Heb.); 31: 38–40 (31: 37–9 Heb.); 32: 40–1; 46: 27	30: 1–11, 18–22; 31: 7–12 (31: 6–11 Heb.); 31: 27–8 (31: 26–7 Heb.); 32: 37–8; 33: 6–13; 46: 27; 50: 18–20	24: 7; 31: 31–4 (31: 30–3 Heb.); 32: 38–40; 33: 8; 50: 20
Ezekiel	34: 11–12, 22, 28; 36: 8–15; 37: 25, 28; 39: 28–9	11: 17; 28: 25–6; 34: 11–16; 37: 12, 21; 39: 25–9	34: 22–5; 36: 24 37: 14, 23–8; 39: 29
Matthew	24: 31		
Luke		21: 24	
The Acts		15: 13–16	
Romans			11: 25–7

The Messianic Aspect	Universal Judgment of the Nations	The Conversion of the Nations
5-24	24: 15-24	
	2: 30-1 (3: 3-4 Heb.); 3: 1-2, 11-16 (4: 1-2, 11-16 Heb.)	2: 32 (3: 5 Heb.)
I		9: 12
-5		
(5: I Heb.)	4: 11-13	4: 1-4
	3: 8	3: 9
	2: 44-5	
	1: 15-16	
	2: 20-3	2: 1-9
0-11 (2: 14-15 Heb.); -9; 6: 12-15; -10; 12: 10-14	1: 18-21 (2: 1-4 Heb.); 10: 11; 12: 1-9; 14: 3, 12-15	2: 11 (2: 15 Heb.); 8: 20-3; 14: 16
-3; 4: 1-6 : 19-24 Heb.)		1: 11
-7 (8: 23; 9: 1-6 Heb.); -12; 49: 1-13; -3; 61: 1-3	24: 12-23; 26: 20-1; 34: 1-17; 49: 25-6; 63: 1-6; 66: 15-16	2: 1-4; 11: 9-10; 25: 7-8; 49: 6; 51: 4-5; 52: 10; 60: 3; 61: 11; 66: 18-20, 23
5-6; 33: 14-17	30: 23-4	
23-4; 37: 24-5	36: 1-7; 38: 39	36: 23; 38: 23; 39: 21
	25: 31-46	
		15: 13-18
		11: 15

Isaiah 35: 1, 6, 10: "The wilderness and the dry land shall be glad; and the desert shall rejoice, and blossom as the rose. Then shall the lame man leap as an hart, and the tongue of the dumb shall sing; for in the wilderness shall waters break out, and streams in the desert. And the ransomed of Jehovah shall return, and come with singing unto Zion; and everlasting joy shall be upon their heads; they shall obtain gladness and joy, and sorrow and sighing shall flee away."

Jeremiah 30: 18: "Thus saith Jehovah: Behold, I will turn again the captivity of Jacob's tents, and have compassion on his dwelling-places; and the city shall be built upon its own hill, and the palace shall be inhabited after its own manner."

Ezekiel 28: 25-26: "Thus saith the Lord Jehovah: When I shall have gathered the house of Israel from the peoples among whom they are scattered, and shall be sanctified in them in the sight of the nations, then shall they dwell in their own land which I gave to my servant Jacob. And they shall dwell securely therein; yea, they shall build houses, and plant vineyards, and shall dwell securely, when I have executed judgments upon all those that do them despite round about them; and they shall know that I am Jehovah their God."

III. THE SPIRITUAL ASPECT OF ISRAEL'S RESTORATION

The theme of the preceding section was the physical aspect of the restoration of Israel, i.e. the reconstruction of the Land of Israel by the returned Remnant. In this section we shall cite several representative portions from the third column in our Chart which emphasize the spiritual character of the Restoration.

Hosea 3: 4-5: "For the children of Israel shall abide many days without king, and without prince, and without sacrifice, and without pillar, and without ephod or teraphim. Afterward shall the children of Israel return, and seek Jehovah their God, and David their king, and shall come with fear unto Jehovah and to his goodness in the latter days." Notice the phrase "latter days" with which this prophecy ends, and remember what we have said in the first chapter about the significance of this phrase in connection with our discussion of Jacob's prophecy as recorded in Genesis 49.

Isaiah 62: 11-12: "Behold, Jehovah hath proclaimed unto the end of the earth, Say ye to the daughter of Zion, Behold thy salvation cometh; behold, his reward is with him, and his recompense before him. And they shall call them The holy people, the redeemed of Jehovah; and thou shalt be called Sought out, A city not forsaken."

Jeremiah 31: 31–34 (31: 30–33 Heb.): "Behold, the days come, saith Jehovah, that I will make a new covenant with the house of Israel, and with the house of Judah. Not according to the covenant that I made with their fathers in the day that I took them by the hand to bring them out of the land of Egypt, which my covenant they brake, although I was a husband unto them, saith Jehovah. But this is the covenant that I will make with the house of Israel after those days, saith Jehovah; I will put my law in their inward parts, and in their heart will I write it; and I will be their God, and they shall be my people. And they shall teach no more every man his neighbour, and every man his brother, saying, Know Jehovah; for they shall all know me, from the least of them unto the greatest of them, saith Jehovah; for I will forgive their iniquity, and their sin will I remember no more."

Zechariah 8: 7–8: "Thus saith Jehovah of hosts: Behold, I will save my people from the east country, and from the west country. And I will bring them, and they shall dwell in the midst of Jerusalem; and they shall be my people, and I will be their God, in truth and in righteousness."

Romans 11: 25–27 [Paul's letter to the Christians in Rome]: "For I would not, brethren, have you ignorant of this mystery, lest ye be wise in your own conceits, that a hardening in part hath befallen Israel, until the fulness of the Gentiles be come in. And so all Israel shall be saved: even as it is written, There shall come out of Zion the Deliverer; He shall turn away ungodliness from Jacob. And this is my covenant unto them, when I shall take away their sins."

IV. The Messianic Aspect of Israel's Restoration

There are some Messianic teachings which stand in the Bible by themselves, as, for example, the already mentioned Jacob prophecy of Genesis 49 where the Restoration factor is either absent or not discernible. The fourth column in the Chart entitled "Messianic Aspect" is a compilation of Bible teachings in which the Messianic and Restoration elements are inseparable. The following are a few representative passages.

B

Isaiah 9: 6-7: "For unto us a child is born, unto us a son is given; and the government shall be upon his shoulder: and his name shall be called Wonderful, Counsellor, Mighty God, Everlasting Father, Prince of Peace. Of the increase of his government and of peace there shall be no end, upon the throne of David, and upon his kingdom, to establish it and to uphold it with justice and with righteousness from henceforth even for ever. The zeal of Jehovah of hosts will perform this."

Jeremiah 23: 5-6: "Behold, the days come, saith Jehovah, that I will raise unto David a righteous Branch, and he shall reign as king and deal wisely, and shall execute justice and righteousness in the land. In his days Judah shall be saved, and Israel shall dwell safely; and this is his name whereby he shall be called: Jehovah our righteousness."

Ezekiel 37: 24-25: "And my servant David shall be king over them; and they all shall have one shepherd: they shall also walk in mine ordinances, and observe my statutes, and do them. And they shall dwell in the land that I have given unto Jacob my servant, wherein your fathers dwelt; and they shall dwell therein, they, and their children, and their children's children, for ever: and David my servant shall be their prince for ever."

V. DIVINE JUDGMENT OF THE NATIONS

There is such a thing as historical judgment which is a process continually operating in history. By this is meant that human sin and evil bear in themselves the seed of their own punishment. Every historical era witnesses the operation of this inexorable principle. But just as human wickedness will reach its highest degree in the "Time of the End" phase of human history, so will the full weight of God's judgment fall upon the evil-doers of that time. It is this judgment with which we are here concerned. We have below some familiar Biblical statements taken from the fifth column in the Chart.

Joel 2: 30-31 (3: 3-4 Heb.); 3: 1-2, 11-16 (4: 1-2, 11-16 Heb.): "And I will show wonders in the heavens and in the earth: blood, and fire, and pillars of smoke. The sun shall be turned into darkness, and the moon into blood, before the great and terrible day of Jehovah cometh. For, behold, in those days, and in that time, when I shall bring back the captivity of Judah and Jerusalem, I will gather all nations, and will bring them down into the valley of Jehoshafat, and I will execute judgment upon them there for my people and for my heritage of Israel, whom they have scattered among the nations, and they have parted my land. Haste ye, and come, all ye nations round about, and gather yourselves together; thither cause thy mighty ones to come down, O Jehovah. Let the nations bestir themselves, and come up to the valley of Jehoshafat; for there will I sit to judge all the nations round about. Put ye in the sickle, for the harvest is ripe; come, tread ye; for the winepress is full, the vats overflow; for their wickedness is great. Multitudes, multitudes in the valley of decision! for the day of Jehovah is near in the valley of decision. The sun and the moon are darkened, and the stars withdraw their shining. And Jehovah will roar from Zion, and utter his voice from Jerusalem; and the heavens and the earth shall shake: but Jehovah will be a refuge unto his people, and a stronghold to the children of Israel."

Isaiah 26: 20–21: "Come, my people, enter thou into thy chambers, and shut thy doors about thee: hide thyself for a little moment, until the indignation be overpast. For, behold, Jehovah cometh forth out of his place to punish the inhabitants of the earth for their iniquity; the earth also shall disclose her blood, and shall no more cover her slain."

Isaiah 34: 1–2, 8: "Come near, ye nations, to hear; and hearken, ye peoples: let the earth hear, and the fulness thereof; the world, and all things that come forth from it. For Jehovah hath indignation against all the nations, and wrath against all their host: he hath utterly destroyed them, he hath delivered them to the slaughter. For Jehovah hath a day of vengeance, a year of recompense for the cause of Zion."

Jeremiah 30: 23–25: "Behold, the tempest of Jehovah, even his wrath, is gone forth, a sweeping tempest: it shall burst upon the head of the wicked. The fierce anger of Jehovah shall not return, until he have executed, and till he have performed the intents of his heart: in the latter days ye shall understand it."

Zechariah 12: 2–3: "Behold, I will make Jerusalem a cup of reeling unto all the peoples round about, and upon Judah also shall it be in the siege against Jerusalem. And it shall come to pass in that day, that I will make Jerusalem a burdensome stone for all the peoples; all that burden themselves with it shall be sore wounded; and all the nations of the earth shall be gathered together against it."

In the New Testament the Divine judgments which are to visit the nations in the "Time of the End" era are described especially in the book of Revelation.

VI. The Conversion of the Nations

The destruction of the ungodly world powers is not an end in itself. God's great purpose is to win mankind to Himself, and the aim and end of the election of Israel is to transform the kingdoms of this world into the Kingdom of God. This subject is dealt with in a body of Bible teachings some of which are found in the last column in the Chart. We will cite below several of these passages.

Joel 2: 32 (3: 5 Heb.): "And it shall come to pass, that whosoever shall call on the name of Jehovah shall be delivered; for in mount Zion and in Jerusalem there shall be those that escape, as Jehovah hath said, and among the remnant those whom Jehovah doth call."

Isaiah 2: 2–4: "And it shall come to pass in the latter days, that the mountain of Jehovah's house shall be established on the top of the mountains, and shall be exalted above the hills; and all nations shall flow unto it. And many peoples shall go and say, Come ye, and let us go up to the mountain of Jehovah, to the house of the God of Jacob; and he will teach us of his ways, and we will walk in his paths; for out of Zion shall go forth the law, and the word of Jehovah from Jerusalem. And he will judge between the nations, and will decide concerning many peoples; and they shall beat their swords into plowshares, and their spears into pruning-hooks; nation shall not lift up sword against nation, neither shall they learn war any more."

Isaiah 66: 18–19, 23: "For I know their works and their thoughts: the time cometh, that I will gather all nations and tongues; and they shall come, and see my glory. And I will set a sign among them, and I will send such as escape of them unto the nations, to Tarshish, Pul, and Lud, that draw the bow, to Tubal and Javan, to the isles afar off, that have not heard my fame, neither have seen my glory; and they shall declare my glory among the nations. And it shall come to pass, that from one new moon to another, and from one Sabbath to another, shall all flesh come to worship before me, saith Jehovah."

Zechariah 8: 22–23: "Yea, many peoples and strong nations shall come to seek Jehovah of hosts in Jerusalem, and to entreat the favour of Jehovah. Thus saith Jehovah of hosts: In those days it shall come to pass, that ten men shall take hold, out of all the languages of the nations, they shall take hold of the skirt of him that is a Jew, saying, We will go with you, for we have heard that God is with you."

VII. Do the Restoration Teachings Apply to the Return from Babylon?

What is the relation of the Restoration teachings of the Bible to the Return from the Babylonian Exile? Is it perhaps true that the Restoration promises in the Bible have all had the Babylonian Exile in view? A careful analysis of the Restoration teachings as classified in our Chart or as written out in the discussion of the various subdivisions of the Chart will supply the answer to this question.

1. THE RETURN FROM BABYLON WAS NOT A UNIVERSAL INGATHERING

Note in the following passages how the emphasis is placed on the universal character of Israel's ingathering.

Isaiah 11: 11: "And it shall come to pass in that day, that the Lord will set his hand again the second time to recover the remnant of his people, that shall remain, from Assyria, and from Egypt, and from Pathros, and from Cush, and from Elam, and from Shinar, and from Hamath, and from the islands of the sea." Here we have the two great powers which at the time of Isaiah affected the destiny of Israel: Assyria and its surrounding territories to the north of Israel, and Egypt and its surrounding dominions to the south of Israel. We have the same political picture today. Israel's relations with the Arabs are bound to be influenced by its relations with Egypt to the south and Assyria (Iraq) to the north. Notice the sentence "the Lord will set his hand again the second time to recover the remnant of his people that shall remain". It implies two scatterings and two ingatherings. The sojourns of the Hebrews in Egypt was not a scattering. They settled in Egypt voluntarily and remained there some four hundred years. Egypt was their home, and if not for the adoption of a hostile policy towards them by one of the later Egyptian governments the Hebrews would have never thought of leaving the country. The first dispersion of the Jewish people was accomplished by Babylon and the first Return had taken place at the end of the Babylonian Exile. The passage cited above speaks of a second ingathering and it implied a second dispersion.

Notice also the universal character of the second ingathering: from the countries to the south and from the countries to the north of Palestine, and "from the four corners of the earth" (Isaiah 11: 12). Notice, especially, the phrase "from the islands of the sea" (Isaiah 11: 11) by which are meant "the islands and coastland of the Mediterranean, together with the whole of the insular continent of Europe".[1] There is no evidence that the return from the Babylonian Exile included Jews from the European continent, nor even that Jews lived there at that time.

Jeremiah 16: 14-16: "Therefore, behold, the days come, saith Jehovah, that it shall no more be said, As Jehovah liveth, that brought up the children of Israel out of the land of Egypt. But, as Jehovah liveth, that brought up the children of Israel from the land of the north, and from all the countries whither he had driven them. And I will bring them again into their land that I gave unto their fathers. Behold, I will send for many fishers, saith Jehovah, and they shall fish them up; and afterward I will send for many hunters, and they shall hunt them from every mountain, and from every hill, and out of the clefts of the rocks." No such ingathering has ever taken place after the Babylonian Exile.

Finally this remarkable passage from Ezekiel which speaks of a universal, total, complete and permanent ingathering.

Ezekiel 34: 11-12; 39: 28: "For thus saith the Lord Jehovah: Behold, I myself, even I, will search for my sheep, and will seek them out. As a shepherd seeketh out his flock in the day that he is among his sheep that are scattered abroad, so will I seek out my sheep; and I will deliver them out of all places whither they have been scattered in the cloudy and dark day. And they shall know that I am Jehovah their God, in that I caused them to go into captivity among the nations, and have gathered them unto their own land; and I will leave none of them any more there."

2. THE RETURN FROM BABYLON WAS NOT A PERMANENT INGATHERING

It was followed by a second, truly world-wide, dispersion after the destruction of the Jewish National Homeland by the Romans.

Not only do the Restoration teachings of the Bible speak of a universal Restoration, they dwell on the fact that it is to be a permanent one. The reader's attention is invited to the Biblical statements tabulated in the first column of our Chart. Read them again and see how they emphasize the permanent aspect of Israel's Restoration. The Restoration following the Babylonian Exile was certainly not a permanent regathering. It is true that certain Restoration teachings apparently have the Babylonian Exile in view. See, for example, Jeremiah 24: 5–6; 25: 11–12; 29: 10–14. But it is clear from the plain meaning of these predictions that the promises which they hold out never found fulfilment after the conclusion of the Babylonian Exile. Notice this statement from one of Jeremiah's utterances apparently dealing with the regathering after the Babylonian Exile.

Jeremiah 24: 5–6: "Thus saith Jehovah, the God of Israel: Like these good figs, so will I regard the captives of Judah, whom I have sent out of this place into the land of the Chaldeans, for good. For I will set mine eyes upon them for good, and I will bring them again to this land: and I will build them, and not pull them down; and I will plant them, and not pluck them up." They were certainly pulled down and plucked up by the Romans some four hundred years later.

3. THE RETURN FROM BABYLON WAS NOT A POLITICAL
   RESTORATION

Reference to the Biblical citations as listed in the Chart will convince us that the Restoration of which the Bible speaks is the reconstitution of a fully independent sovereign State. No such thing had come into being when the Babylonian Exile was over. The decree issued by Cyrus gave the Judean exiles permission to return to Judea and to rebuild the Temple in Jerusalem. "Thus saith Cyrus king of Persia, All the kingdoms of the earth hath Jehovah, the God of heaven, given me; and he hath charged me to build him a house in Jerusalem, which is in Judah. Whosoever there is among you of all his people, his God be with him, and let him go up to Jerusalem, which is in Judah, and build the house of Jehovah, the God of Israel (he is God), which is in Jerusalem," Ezra 1: 2-3. "All the kingdoms of the earth", says Cyrus, "hath Jehovah, the God of heaven, given me." He was the political master of the world, including Palestine. To his Jewish subjects he granted the privilege of returning to Judea in order to rebuild the Temple which was the centre of the Jewish religion. In other words, the Jewish exiles were permitted to re-establish a religious community in Palestine and nothing else. Politically the Jewish community in Palestine in the era of the Second Commonwealth was an appendage of one of the great world powers in that era: first of Persia, then of Alexander the Great, and finally of Rome. True, towards the end of this era the Jews in Palestine regained political independence under the leadership of the Maccabees. But this development was made possible by the unsettled state of the world at that time, and when Rome had completed consolidating her gains in Asia Palestine reverted to the status of a political dependency. The political subjection of the Second Commonwealth is well described in these words: "Behold, we are servants this day, and as for the land that thou gavest unto our fathers to eat the fruit thereof and the good thereof, behold, we are servants in it", Nehemiah 9: 36.

4. THE PRAYER OF DANIEL

In the ninth chapter of his book Daniel relates that from the writings of Jeremiah the prophet he was led to believe that the desolations of Jerusalem were to end after seventy years. Daniel became deeply disturbed when the seventy years were up and the city of Jerusalem continued in a desolate state. To relieve himself of his burden and perplexities he poured out his heart in fervent prayer. In it he confessed his and his people's unrighteousness, and pleaded for God's mercy and pardon. In response to this heart-breaking intercessory prayer Daniel was granted a new revelation recorded in the last part of the ninth chapter and beginning with the following words: "Seventy sevens are decreed upon thy people and upon thy holy city, to finish transgression, and to make an end of sins, and to make reconciliation for iniquity, and to bring in everlasting righteousness, and to seal up vision and prophecy, and to anoint the most holy", Daniel 9: 24.

God did promise through Jeremiah that the desolation inflicted upon Jerusalem by the Babylonians is to terminate after seventy years. And he was determined to keep His promises. But what He wished his faithful servant Daniel to know was that the end of the Babylonian Exile was not going to bring about Israel's complete delivery. This was to come not after seventy years but after seventy sevens or 490 years. We are not here concerned with the full exposition of the so-called vision of the "seventy sevens". We mention this only to show that Daniel was told that the return from the Babylonian Exile was not exactly the kind of Restoration spoken of by the prophets.

5. THE PROPHECY OF ZECHARIAH 8: 7–8

Zechariah 8: 7–8: "Thus saith Jehovah of hosts: Behold, I will save my people from the east country, and from the west country. And I will bring them, and they shall dwell in the midst of Jerusalem; and they shall be my people, and I will be their God, in truth and in righteousness." The significance of this prophecy lies in the fact that it was written by Zechariah, one of the three prophets who lived in Palestine following the termination of the Babylonian Exile. Babylon is not even mentioned here. This prediction of a Return from the East and the West, coming as it did after the ingathering of the Babylonian Exile had already taken place, certainly implies another Restoration.

6. THE RETURN FROM BABYLON WAS NOT ATTENDED BY A UNIVERSAL JUDGMENT OF THE NATIONS

A perusal of the Biblical teachings in the last two columns in our Chart amply proves the important place which Divine judgment upon the nations followed by the conversion of the nations occupies in the Restoration of Israel teachings. No such judgment and no such universal conversion of the nations to God have taken place after the Babylonian Exile.

VIII. THE TIME RELATIONSHIP BETWEEN THE PHYSICAL REHABILITATION OF THE LAND OF ISRAEL AND THE SPIRITUAL REGENERATION OF THE PEOPLE OF ISRAEL

A careful analysis of the Restoration passages in the Bible brings to light the following pertinent facts: Some of them are concerned exclusively or predominantly with the physical rehabilitation of the country; while others deal chiefly with the spiritual rebirth of the people of Israel. In some of the Restoration teachings no attempt is made to state the time relationship between the physical reconstruction of the Land of Israel and the spiritual rebirth of the people of Israel. In others this time element is definitely emphasized. Where the time factor is clear and certain a definite time relationship is seen to exist between the two phenomena: the physical rehabilitation of the Land of Israel comes first; this is followed by the spiritual rebirth of the people of Israel. The following are a few Restoration passages in which this time relationship is quite evident.

Joel 2: 18–29 (2: 18–27; 3: 1–2 Heb.). Read the whole passage, only several sentences will be quoted here: "Then was Jehovah jealous for his land, and had pity on his people. Fear not, O Land, be glad and rejoice; for Jehovah hath done great things. Be not afraid, ye beasts of the field; for the pastures of the wilderness do spring, for the tree beareth its fruit, the fig-tree and the vine do yield their strength. Be glad then, ye children of Zion, and rejoice in Jehovah your God; for he giveth you the former rain in just measure, and he causeth to come down for you the rain, the former rain and the latter rain, in the first month" (Joel 2: 18, 21–23). Following this description of the physical reclamation of the Land of Israel comes this declaration of the spiritual rebirth of the nation. "And it shall come to pass afterward, that I will pour out my Spirit upon all flesh; and your sons and your daughters shall prophesy, your old men shall dream dreams, your young men shall see visions. And also upon the servants and upon the handmaids in those days will I pour out my Spirit" Joel 2: 28–29; (3: 1–2 Heb.).

Isaiah 4: 2–3: "In that day shall the branch [or shoot] of Jehovah be beautiful and glorious, and the fruit of the land shall be excellent and comely for them that are escaped of Israel." Following the description of the total destruction of the country in the preceding chapter, Isaiah paints a picture of the Restoration in Chapter Four. In the second verse he speaks first of the physical aspect of the Restoration. Then comes the spiritual phase of the Restoration: "And it shall come to pass, that he that is left in Zion, and he that remaineth in Jerusalem, shall be called holy, even everyone that is written among the living in Jerusalem."

Jeremiah 33: 6–9: "Behold, I will bring it health and cure, and I will cure them; and I will reveal unto them abundance of peace and truth. And I will cause the captivity of Judah and the captivity of Israel to return, and will build them, as at the first." This prediction of the physical reconstruction of the land is followed in the next two verses by a declaration of the spiritual rebirth of the people. "And I will cleanse them from all their iniquity, whereby they have sinned against me; and I will pardon all their iniquities, whereby they have sinned against me, and whereby they have transgressed against me. And this city shall be to me for a name of joy, and for a praise and for a glory, before all the nations of the earth, which shall hear all the good that I do unto them, and shall fear and tremble for all the good and for all the peace that I procure unto it." This state of affairs has never come into existence after the Babylonian Exile.

Ezekiel 36: 24-26: "For I will take you from among the nations, and gather you out of all the countries, and will bring you into your own land." The return of the people to their land depicted here is followed by a spiritual transformation of the nation as seen from the following sentences. "And I will sprinkle clean water upon you, and ye shall be clean: from all your filthiness, and from all your idols, will I cleanse you. A new heart also will I give you, and a new spirit will I put within you; and I will take away the stony heart out of your flesh, and I will give you a heart of flesh."

Ezekiel 37: 1-14: "The hand of Jehovah was upon me, and he brought me out in the Spirit of Jehovah, and set me down in the midst of the valley; and it was full of bones. And he caused me to pass by them round about: and, behold, there were very many in the open valley; and, lo, they were very dry. And he said unto me, Son of man, can these bones live? And I answered, O Lord Jehovah, thou knowest. Again he said unto me, Prophesy over these bones, and say unto them, O ye dry bones, hear the word of Jehovah. Thus saith the Lord Jehovah unto these bones: Behold, I will cause breath to enter into you, and ye shall live. And I will lay sinews upon you, and will bring up flesh upon you, and cover you with skin, and put breath in you, and ye shall live; and ye shall know that I am Jehovah.

"So I prophesied as I was commanded: and as I prophesied, there was a noise, and, behold, an earthquake; and the bones came together, bone to its bone. And I beheld, and lo, there were sinews upon them, and flesh came up, and skin covered them above; but there was no breath in them. Then said he unto me, Prophesy unto the wind, prophesy, son of man, and say to the wind, Thus saith the Lord Jehovah: Come from the four winds, O breath, and breathe upon these slain, that they may live. So I prophesied as he commanded me, and the breath came into them, and they lived, and stood up upon their feet, an exceeding great army.

"Then he said unto me, Son of man, these bones are the whole house of Israel: behold, they say, Our bones are dried up, and our hope is lost; we are clean cut off. Therefore prophesy and say unto them, Thus saith the Lord Jehovah: Behold, I will open your graves, and cause you to come up out of your graves, O my people; and I will bring you into the land of Israel. And ye shall know that I am Jehovah, when I have opened your graves, and caused you to come up out of your graves, O my people. And I will put my Spirit in you, and ye shall live, and I will place you in your own land: and ye shall know that I, Jehovah, have spoken it and performed it, saith Jehovah."

Let us set down a number of the deeply significant truths which this extraordinary prophecy proclaims. In the first place, Israel's physical and spiritual regeneration is the work of God. "Can these bones live?" the prophet was asked. Humanly speaking these bones cannot live—was Ezekiel's implied answer. This assertion is emphasized at the end of the prophecy. "And ye shall know that I, Jehovah, have spoken it and performed it, saith Jehovah." Man is merely God's agent, but God is the motivating force. Israel's restoration is first and last the work of God.

What is the state of the nation in this vision of the dry bones? They are buried among the Gentiles (see verse 21). They are a disunited, disjointed, formless, mass of people living under the flags of many nations without a national awareness of their own. In the national and spiritual sense they are a mass of scattered, dry, i.e. dead bones.

The purpose of the Divine message to Ezekiel is to inform him —and us—that God will accomplish the seemingly impossible: He will cause the dead bones to live (verse five). Let us now carefully note the method or order or steps in which this reawakening of Israel will be accomplished: "And I will lay sinews upon you, and will bring up flesh upon you, and ye shall live, and ye shall know that I am Jehovah" (verse six). The remainder of the prophecy is an elaboration of the contents of verse six. The first phase in the work of the Restoration of Israel is of a physical nature. They develop a national consciousness and begin to leave the various countries of their dispersion: "And I beheld, and, lo, there were sinews upon them, and flesh came up, and skin covered them above" (verse eight). The state of the Jewish people in the last 150 years is a remarkable fulfilment of this passage. In the years following the so-called Political Emancipation many Jews in the various European countries began to look upon themselves not as Jews but as nationals of their respective countries differing from their Gentile fellow citizens only in religion. They called themselves Germans of the Mosaic Persuasion in Germany, and Poles of the Mosaic Persuasion in Poland, and the same in the other countries. When the Zionist Organisation sprang into existence aiming to secure a Jewish National Home in Palestine many of these assimilationist Jews bitterly and vehemently denounced the whole movement on the grounds that the Jews are not a nation but a religious community. This, in spite of the fact that many of these assimilationist Jews had very little religion, if any at all. When the Palestine Mandate was issued granting the Jewish people the right to establish a Jewish National Home in Palestine the League of Nations called for the creation of a Jewish Agency representing all Jews willing to assist in the work of rebuilding the National Home. Weizmann relates in his memoirs that seven years were spent in an effort to induce these so-called non-Zionist Jews to become members of the Jewish Agency. Even then they were anxious to make it clear that their association with the Agency is on purely humanitarian grounds. Whatever the motives of the various Jewish groups represented in the Agency, Jews of various political, economic and sociological convictions, representing world Jewry, rallied behind the banner of Zionism. "All sections of the Jewish people", says Weizmann, "were represented and every community of any size. . . . The Jewish Agency brought together as distinguished a group of Jews as we have witnessed in our time; all classes and fields of achievement were represented, from Léon Blum, the great socialist leader, to Marshall and Warburg on the right; from Lord Melchett, one of England's leading industrialists, to Albert Einstein the scientist and Chaim Nachman Bialik, the poet."[2] "And I beheld, and, lo, there were sinews upon them, and flesh came up, and skin covered them above."

But, significantly, as the prophet gazes at the miraculous change which has come over the disjointed, disunited mass of the Jewish people he observes that one thing was lacking—"but there was no breath in them" (verse eight). "Then said he [God] unto me, Prophesy unto the wind, prophesy, son of man, and say to the wind, Thus said the Lord Jehovah: Come from the four winds, O breath, and breathe upon these slain, that they may live. So I prophesied as he commanded me, and the breath came into them, and they lived, and stood up upon their feet, an exceeding great army" (verses nine to ten).

The same time relationship between the physical and the spiritual aspects of Israel's Restoration is taught in Zechariah, who, as mentioned above, was one of the three prophets who lived and laboured in Palestine after the Return from the Babylonian Exile. Read the twelfth, thirteenth and fourteenth chapters.

Zechariah 13: 8–9: "And it shall come to pass, that in all the land, saith Jehovah, two parts therein shall be cut off and die; but the third shall be left therein. And I will bring the third part into the fire, and will refine them as silver is refined, and will try them as gold is tried. They shall call on my name, and I will hear them: I will say, It is my people; and they shall say, Jehovah is my God." We shall conclude our discussion of the time relationship between the physical and spiritual character of Israel's Restoration with the following statement by the apostle Paul: "Howbeit that is not first which is spiritual, but that which is natural; then that which is spiritual", I Corinthians 15: 46.

NOTES TO CHAPTER 2

1. Franz Delitzsch, *Biblical Commentary on the Prophecies of Isaiah* (Wm. B. Eerdmans Publishing Co.: Grand Rapids, Mich., 1949), vol. 1, p. 289.
2. Chaim Weizmann, *Trial and Error* (The Jewish Publication Society of America: Philadelphia, 1949), vol. 2, pp. 313–14. Used by permission of Harper & Brothers, New York, N.Y.

CHAPTER 3

CHRISTIAN OPINION CONCERNING THE NATIONAL
RESTORATION OF THE JEWS IN PALESTINE

CHRISTIAN OPINION CONCERNING THE NATIONAL RESTORATION OF THE JEWS IN PALESTINE

The wide diffusion of a knowledge of the Bible brought about by the Protestant Reformation has led to a growing belief among Christian people of the eventual restoration of the Jewish people to Palestine. This belief was especially strong in Great Britain. "Interest in the return of the Jews to Palestine had long captured the imagination of Christians in England. In a despatch to Lord Ponsonby, then the British Ambassador to the Porte, Lord Palmerston had written on the 11th August 1840: 'There exists at present among the Jews dispersed over Europe a strong notion that the time is approaching when their nation is to return to Palestine, and, consequently, their wish to go thither has become more keen, and their thoughts have been bent more intensely than before upon the means of realising their wish.' Even before the end of the seventeenth century at least twelve publications had appeared in England advocating the return of the Jews to Palestine, mainly on religious grounds. In the minds of many British Christians this return was looked on as a fulfilment of prophecy, and linked with the Second Coming of Christ. Many anticipated a simultaneous conversion of the Jews to Christianity. During the nineteenth century humanitarian motives strengthened religious conviction."[1]

In an article entitled "Christian Pioneers of Zionism" published in the *Hebrew Christian Alliance Quarterly* the writer lists a number of leading Christians in England and America who have championed the cause of Zionism.[2] Of those living in the seventeenth century mention is made of Paul Knell who in 1648 published a book on the subject of Zionism; John Milton, one of England's greatest poets, who believed that all twelve tribes will some day be restored to the Land of Israel; Oliver Cromwell, the devout Puritan leader of England; John Sadler, Town Clerk of London and a friend of Oliver Cromwell; Edmund Bunny, Isaac de La Peyrère, Thomas Draxe, Isaac Vossius, Hugo Grotius, Gerhard John Vossius, David Blondel and Paulus Felgenhauer.

Thomas Brightman, a Bible exegete, in his exposition of Revelation 15: 12 published in 1641, referring to the Jews, says: "What! Shall they return to Jerusalem again? There is nothing more certain: the prophets do everywhere confirm it!"

James Durham and Vasovor Powel called attention to the many passages in the Bible pertaining to the subject of Israel's return to Palestine.

Roger Williams, the great spokesman for religious liberty and the founder of Rhode Island, was an ardent believer in the restoration of Israel.

In the eighteenth century, Bishop Thomas Newton of Bristol, Edward King, William Whiston, Bishop Robert Lowth of London, Philip Dodridge, John Gill, Henry Porter and John Scott—all have given their support to the idea of Israel's restoration.

Thomas Witherby (1760–1820) called for the emancipation of the Jews in all countries of their residence and for the restoration of the Jewish Commonwealth in Palestine.

John Scott (1777–1834), mentioned above, in his book *The Destiny of Israel* published in 1813 makes the following statement: "But wherefore are the Jews thus preserved? Is it only as monuments of divine vengeance, and to bear testimony to others of blessings which they shall never taste themselves? 'Hath God' forever 'cast off His people'? 'Have they stumbled that they might fall', to rise no more? God forbid! All the facts before us, and particularly their preservation, might well raise hopes in our minds that mercy was still in reserve for Israel!"

John Adams (1735–1826), the second President of the United States (1797–1801), in a letter to Major Mordecai Manuel said: "I really wish the Jews again in Judea, an independent nation. . . ."

In the nineteenth century, among the staunchest British champions of the cause of Israel's restoration were Lord Shaftesbury, A. G. H. Hollingsworth, Thomas Clarke, James Finn, who was British Consul in Jerusalem, Edward Cazalet and Laurence Oliphant. In 1838 and 1839 Lord Shaftesbury vigorously and indefatigably upheld the Zionist cause. He published his ideas in *The Times*, London, and appealed to Queen Victoria on behalf of Israel's restoration. In his diary he made the following entry in 1854: "There is a country without a nation, and God now, in His wisdom and mercy, directs us to a nation without a country." [3]

Two other English names which deserve notice are those of the poet Lord Byron (1788–1824) and George Eliot (Mary Ann Evans, 1819–1880). Byron's kindly feelings to the Jewish people found expression in his literary production entitled *Hebrew Melodies*, where the following lines, taken in part from the New Testament, are among the most touching: "The wild dove hath her nest, the fox his cave, Mankind their country, Israel but the grave."

In the forty years of his dealings with British statesmen and those prominent in British public life Chaim Weizmann came to realize that there was a connection between their positive attitude to Zionism and their religious spirit. In 1904 Weizmann had an interview with Lord Percy who was then in charge of African affairs and who was acquainted with the nature of the Uganda proposal which the British Government had made to the Zionist Organization as a possible place for Jewish colonization. As we know, the Zionists declined to accept this project. Weizmann describes Lord Percy's attitude to the Uganda idea in the following words: "Himself deeply religious, he was bewildered by the thought that the Jews could even entertain the idea of any other country than Palestine as the centre of their revival; and he was delighted to hear from me that there were so many Jews who had categorically refused. He said: 'If I were a Jew I would not give a half-penny for this proposition!'" [4]

Relating to Mrs. James de Rothschild his conversation with Weizmann in December 1914 Lloyd George remarked: "When Dr. Weizmann was talking of Palestine he kept bringing up place names which were more familiar to me than those on the Western Front." [5] On November 11, 1918, the day on which the fighting in the First World War ceased, Weizmann was invited to lunch with Lloyd George. When he arrived at 10 Downing Street he found the Prime Minister reading the Psalms; "he [the Prime Minister] was moved to the depths of his soul", Weizmann remarks, "and was, indeed, near to tears". [6]

Orde Wingate, famous in the Second World War for his exploits in the Burma campaign, was another intensely religious Christian who supported wholeheartedly the idea of the Jewish National Homeland in Palestine. Weizmann says of him that "he showed himself a fanatical Zionist, and he had come to his views not under any personal influence or propaganda, but by the effect of Zionist literature on his deep and lifelong study of the Bible".[7]

Of men like Balfour, Lloyd George, Churchill, Lord Milner, and General Smuts, Weizmann says that they "were deeply religious, and believed in the Bible, that to them the return of the Jewish people to Palestine was a reality, so that we Zionists represented to them a great tradition for which they had enormous respect".[8] "Those British statesmen of the old school, I have said, were genuinely religious. They understood as a reality the concept of the Return [the return of the Jews to Zion]. It appealed to their tradition and their faith."[9]

On March 5, 1891, Wm. E. Blackstone, a great student of the Bible, presented to President Harrison a memorandum signed by over five hundred clergymen, Federal, State and city government officials, newspaper editors, prominent industrialists and businessmen. The petitioners asked the President and the Honourable James G. Blaine, Secretary of State, to call a conference of the European powers, including Turkey, "to consider the condition of the Israelites and their claims to Palestine as their ancient home". "Why not give Palestine back to them again?" we read in this memorandum. "According to God's distribution of nations it is their home—an inalienable possession from which they were expelled by force. Under their cultivation it was a remarkably fruitful land, sustaining millions of Israelites, who industriously tilled its hillsides and valleys. They were agriculturists and producers as well as a nation of great commercial importance—the centre of civilization and religion. Why shall not the powers which under the treaty of Berlin, in 1878, gave Bulgaria to the Bulgarians and Servia to the Servians now give Palestine back to the Jews? For over seventeen centuries they have patiently waited for such a privileged opportunity. . . . We believe this is an appropriate time for all nations, and especially the Christian nations of Europe, to show kindness to Israel. . . . Let us now restore to them the land of which they were so cruelly despoiled by our Roman ancestors."

Attached to this memorandum was Blackstone's personal statement to the President in which he relates that in 1889 he had spent several weeks in Palestine and Syria and carefully studied contions there. He believed "that the land of Palestine is capable of remarkable development both agriculturally and commercially.

Its geographical situation, as the half way house between Europe and Asia, is unequalled.... That he has special reasons for believing such sentiment [restoration of Palestine to the Jews] already prevails, to a large extent, in Great Britain, and it seems to appeal to all classes of Christians as a magnificent humanitarian movement.... That there seem to be many evidences to show that we have reached the period in the great roll of the centuries, when the everliving God of Abraham, Isaac and Jacob, is lifting up His hand to the Gentiles (Isaiah 49: 22), to bring His sons and His daughters from far, that He may plant them again in their own land, Ezekiel 34, etc. Not for twenty-four centuries, since the days of Cyrus, King of Persia, has there been offered to any mortal such a privileged opportunity to further the purposes of God concerning His ancient people. May it be the high privilege of your Excellency, and the Honourable Secretary, to take a personal interest in this great matter, and secure through the Conference, a home for these wandering millions of Israel, and thereby receive to yourselves the promise of Him, who said to Abraham, 'I will bless them that bless thee', Genesis 12: 3".[10]

Several months later Blackstone published an article in which he analysed Israel's right to Palestine. In this article Blackstone states: "No other people can boast of such high authority for the title to their earthly inheritance. It is rooted in the Holy Word, which all Christian nations receive as the foundation of their religion, and the rule of their practice. Israel gave this word to us; and in it God says 'I will lift up my hand to the Gentiles, and they shall bring my sons in their arms'. Does not the present dire extremity of Israel, and the quickening of their national sentiment, and the expression of Gentile sympathy, and the providential openings toward the land, all point to the uplifted hand of God?"[11]

Rabbi Stephen S. Wise relates the important part President Wilson had played in the Zionist movement. On one occasion President Wilson said to him: "I am the son of the manse, son of a Presbyterian clergyman, and therefore I am with you completely and am proud to think that I may in some degree help you to rebuild Palestine."[12]

In addition to those referred to above, there have been large numbers of Christian theologians, ministers and Bible teachers, who have been teaching and preaching the certainty of Israel's restoration to Palestine in fulfilment of the teachings of the Bible.

To conclude this discussion we will mention this rather amusing incident. Dr. Philip Hitti, first Arab witness to appear before the Anglo-American Committee of Inquiry on Palestine, told the members of the Committee "that there was actually no such entity as Palestine—never had been; it was historically part of Syria", but 'the Sunday Schools', he declared, 'have done a great deal of harm to us because by smearing the walls of classrooms with maps of Palestine, they associate it with the Jews in the mind of the average American and Englishman.'[13]

NOTES TO CHAPTER 3

1. Quoted by S. A. Morrison, *Middle East Survey* (S.C.M. Press: London, 1954), p. 25. Permission for use in U.S.A. granted by Harper & Brothers, New York, N.Y.
2. Elias Newman, "Christian Pioneers of Zionism", article in the *Hebrew-Christian Alliance Quarterly* (Hebrew Christian Alliance of America: Chicago), Summer 1949.
3. Quoted by S. A. Morrison, op. cit., p. 25.
4. Quoted by Chaim Weizmann, *Trial and Error* (The Jewish Publication Society of America: Philadelphia, 1949), vol. 1, p. 89.
5. Ibid., vol. 1, p. 152.
6. Ibid., vol. 1, p. 239.
7. Ibid., vol. 2, p. 398.
8. Ibid., vol. 1, p. 157.
9. Ibid., vol. 1, p. 178.
10. Wm. E. Blackstone, "Palestine for the Jews", memorandum presented to President Harrison on March 5, 1891.
11. Wm. E. Blackstone, "May the United States Intercede for the Jews?", article in *Our Day*, vol. viii, October 1891, No. 46.
12. Quoted by Bartley C. Crum, *Behind the Silken Curtain* (Simon and Schuster: New York, 1947), pp. 15–16.
13. Quoted by Bartley C. Crum, ibid., pp. 20–1.

PART TWO

THE REBIRTH OF THE STATE OF ISRAEL IN THE CONTEXT OF JEWISH HISTORY

CHAPTER I

PALESTINE IN JEWISH HISTORY, LIFE AND FAITH

CHAPTER I

PALESTINE IN JEWISH HISTORY, LIFE AND FAITH

I. THE HISTORICAL ASSOCIATION OF THE JEWISH PEOPLE WITH PALESTINE

The ancient State of Israel, sometimes referred to as the First Commonwealth, came to an end with the capture of Jerusalem and the destruction of the First Temple by the Babylonians. Seventy years later the exiles obtained permission from Persia— the successor to the Babylonian Empire—to return to Jerusalem and to rebuild the Temple. Only some 49,000 Jews returned. A large part, if not the majority, of the exiles remained in the Persian Empire. With the exception of a brief interval under the Maccabees towards the end of the B.C. Era there was no politically independent Jewish State after the destruction of the First Commonwealth by the Babylonians. Palestine had a succession of political overlords consisting of Babylon, Persia, Alexander the Great and his successors, and finally Rome.

But while Jews had no real or lasting political independence after the return from the Babylonian Exile, Palestine was nevertheless the National Home of the Jews. The great majority of the people in Palestine were Jews. At least once a year during the Passover Jews from all parts of Palestine and from the Jewish communities outside Palestine went to Jerusalem to worship God in the Temple in accordance with the instructions of the Law of Moses. No matter where they lived Jews considered Palestine their National Home. Whenever a Jew wished he could go to Palestine and take up his residence there.

This Jewish National Homeland came to an end after the destruction of Jerusalem and the Second Temple by Rome in A.D. 70 and especially after the suppression of the uprising in A.D. 132–135 The Jew living now in the various parts of the Roman Empire was painfully aware of the fact that he had no National Home. And by this time the great bulk of the nation lived outside of

Palestine. With the loss of the Jewish National Home in A.D. 70 the long exile actually began, and the Jews became wanderers over the face of the earth, a people without a country.

But the Jew was only bodily in the lands of his dispersion, his heart remained in the Land of Israel. Many a Jew could say with the great medieval Jewish poet Yehudah Halevi: "I am in the West, but my heart abides in the East." The Land of Israel continued to dominate his thoughts, his prayers, study, and the activities of his daily life.

This same Yehudah Halevi, twelfth century A.D., taught that the Land of Israel has retained its holiness, and this holiness has not become affected by the various vicissitudes of history; that the Jew can serve God fully only in the Land of Israel, that not merely perfection of the deed but perfection of the soul are possible only in the Holy Land. [1]

Rabbi Liva ben Bezalel, the great sage of Prague, who lived in the sixteenth century, believed that it was the holiness of Palestine which enabled the Patriarchs to attain to their high level of holiness, and that Israel as a nation can serve God fully and perfectly only in Palestine. [2]

This was fundamentally the belief of Rabbi Nachman of Brazlav, the great grandson of the Baal-Shem-Tov, founder of Hasidism. "Holiness", he taught, "has its sole dwelling place in Palestine", and the Jew can gain holiness by establishing contact with Palestine. [3]

The Jewish people share their destiny in common with the Land of Israel. When Israel suffered, the Land of Israel suffered also. Even while separated from each other, the people and Land experience the same fate. [4] The land waits for the Jewish people to return from exile, and only through the return of the exiles can the Land be renovated physically and regenerated spiritually. [5] "The world can be redeemed only by the redemption of Israel and Israel can be redeemed only by reunion with its land." [6] There is no other kind of liberation for the Jewish people but a return to the Land of Israel. [7]

Moses Hess, the Jewish religious socialist and author of *Rome and Jerusalem*, also believed that outside of Palestine it is impossible for the Jewish nation as such to discharge fully its religious duties, many of which presuppose the existence in Palestine of an organized political and social pattern of life. [8]

Not only in the religious thinking of the Jew, but also in his worship and religious study Palestine occupied the centre of things. Three times daily, while reciting his prayers, he would turn his face towards Jerusalem. During the winter he prayed for rain, and in the summer for dew—for the Land of Israel, in accordance with the climatic conditions of Palestine. On the fifteenth day of the month of Shvat, which marks the first day of spring in Palestine, he would participate in the celebration of spring even though it may still be winter in the country of his sojourn.

The days of fasting and mourning on the Jewish calendar were days set aside to commemorate tragic events in the history of Palestine. The major festivals were in some manner all associated with the national history of the Jews in Palestine. The Prayer Book of the Synagogue is replete with prayers for the speedy termination of the exile and restoration of Zion. A large part of the Talmudic studies were concerned with matters which were of no relevance outside of Palestine, and were based on the unshakable conviction of the eventual reconstitution of the Jewish people in their ancient homeland. The great ambition of many a pious Jew was to go to Palestine, if not to live there, then, at least, to die there; and if this was impossible, then he would have a sack containing some soil imported from Palestine and placed under his head in the grave.

Nor was this Jewish attachment to Palestine a matter of sentiment only. Again and again, practically in every century, there were efforts to get back to the Land of Israel. This intense Jewish longing for Palestine was in some respect exploited by certain individuals who represented themselves as Messiahs, and are referred to in Jewish history as pseudo-Messiahs. There is no doubt that some of these pseudo-Messiahs were upright though misguided or deluded men. On the top of the list stands Bar-Kochba in the first third of the second century who led the Jews of Palestine in a rebellion against Rome. Hundreds of thousands of Jews lost their lives and the uprising completed the destruction of the Jewish National Homeland.

In the fifth century Moses of Crete promised to lead the Jews dryshod through the Mediterranean to Palestine. He gained many followers who left their possessions on Crete and subsequently drowned in the sea.

In the seventh century Persian Jewry was stirred by a Messianic movement headed by Abu-Isa who led his adherents against the existing authorities. The adventure ended in the death of many of his followers. Judah Yudghan of Hamadan, Persia, in the eighth century; Serene of Syria, eighth century, and David Alroy of Baghdad in the twelfth century, were other pseudo-Messiahs who attempted to free the Jews from Mohammedan oppression.

Abraham Abulafia of Spain was influenced by mystical teachings of the Jewish Cabbala, and became the pseudo-Messiah of the thirteenth century. He proclaimed the year of 1290 as the date of Israel's redemption.

In the sixteenth century David Reubeni presented himself in Italy as the brother of a certain Joseph who was supposed to have been the ruler of a Jewish kingdom in North Arabia. He claimed to have been sent by his brother to enlist the help of the Christian world against the Turks. The favourable impression which he had made on the Pope gained for him many followers among the Jews. Finally the Emperor Charles V ordered the arrest of both Reubeni and Solomon Malko, his disciple, both of whom had been seeking to interest the Emperor in their mission. They were delivered to the Inquisition which consigned Malko to the fire at the stake, while Reubeni died in prison.

Of all the pseudo-Messiahs since Bar-Kochba none created such a world-wide excitement as Sabbatai Tzvi of Smyrna in the seventeenth century. Whole Jewish communities made preparations to leave and follow him to Palestine. Even the Gentile world became aroused and many Gentiles were led to believe that the end of the world was approaching. In the end, in order to save his life, Sabbatai Tzvi accepted the Moslem religion, causing widespread disillusionment among the Jewish masses.

The eighteenth century saw the rise of another pseudo-Messianic movement by Jacob Frank, many of whose followers later accepted Catholicism.

This readiness with which the Jewish people responded to the reckless claims of one pseudo-Messiah after another, in spite of repeated disappointments, testifies to the ardent yearnings for national redemption. Some of the most astute and balanced Talmudic authorities busied themselves with computing the actual date of the coming of the Messiah.[9] In the eighteen centuries following the destruction of the Jewish Homeland the Jews living in the Dispersion never considered themselves as having "a place in the permanent fabric of the societies among which they dwelt. The part they were permitted to play in those societies might, in its degree, be useful or even dignified. But through good and evil days alike, Palestine remained the desire of their hearts. In the ease and security of Andalusia, hardly less than in the gloomy recesses of the Ghetto, they stretched out their hands to Palestine —sang of it, prayed for it, wept for its fallen majesty, and patiently awaited the hour of redemption".[10]

II. THE ERA OF POLITICAL EMANCIPATION

Towards the middle of the eighteenth century, which marks the end of the Middle Ages for the Jews, the degradation of European Jewry reached its worst. It was the cumulative effect of centuries of inhuman oppression. From this time on there began a general improvement in the condition of Europe's Jews, and within one century the Jews of Central and Western Europe became emancipated, receiving. in some countries full civic and political equality.

This new turn in the affairs of the European Jews was the outgrowth of profound changes which had taken place in the world in the preceding two centuries brought about by the extensive geographic discoveries, by the Protestant Reformation, and by the French and American Revolutions. In the religious sphere these events spelled religious liberty. Organized religion was deprived of the support of the state in enforcing its particular brand of belief. Religious faith was to be based on the conviction of the believer, rather than on blind obedience to external authority. The emphasis in religious matters was shifted from the masses to the individual. For Christianity this meant a return to the principles of the first three centuries of the Christian era and to the Bible as the source of the believer's faith and conduct.

Even before the crumbling of the Ghetto walls traditional Judaism began to feel the effects of these profound changes in Christendom. Like medieval Christianity Judaism behind the Ghetto walls was also a religion based on the unquestioned allegiance to external authority. What made the problem of Judaism especially complex at this juncture of human history was the national and communal character of the Jewish religion in which the Jew as an individual, apart from the congregation of Israel, had no religious standing. For the first time in seventeen centuries Judaism was confronted with a crisis threatening its very existence. The gravity of this spiritual crisis may be judged from the fact that it has not been resolved to this very day.

The effects of the Political Emancipation on Jewish life were far-reaching. One of these goes under the name of "Assimilation". This is a relatively new term in the Jewish vocabulary and it denotes a process by which the Jew strives to become fully integrated into and identified with the political, economic and cultural life of his non-Jewish surroundings. The changed political and economic conditions in Europe, and the removal of the Jewish civic and political disabilities, encouraged the Jew to leave his Ghetto isolation and enter into the general stream of the life of the country of his residence. He began to dress like the Gentiles, speak their language, attend their schools and mix and mingle with them. He renounced his Jewish tradition, deserted the Jewish schools and became part and parcel of his Gentile environment. This development began first in Central and Western Europe and from there it has spread to Eastern Europe. There it proceeded at a slower pace due to the greater concentration of Jews in that area and the slower tempo with which the progressive ideas of Western Europe seeped into East European countries. The Jew ceased to look upon himself as an alien in a foreign land, and began to consider himself a member of the nation of the country of his birth or adoption. The word "exile" began to lose its meaning, and the age-long dream of a return to Palestine was losing its hold upon the Jewish mind. The country of his domicile was now his Zion.

These changes in the legal status, language, occupation, and education of the Jew were beginning to affect also his attitude to his religion. His departure from the Ghetto surroundings often meant a departure from the faith and world outlook of traditional Judaism. With many Jews this change in attitude led to a complete break with Judaism. Intermarriages and baptisms have made deep inroads into the Jewish communities of the emancipated countries. "There was hardly a Jew of any standing in Berlin at the beginning of the nineteenth century who adhered to his inherited faith."[11] In the nineteenth century about 205,000 Jews adopted Christianity all over the world.[12] In Hungary over 12,000 Jews were baptized in the 1919–1929 period.[13] In the beginning of the twentieth century many Jews in Germany and Austria left the Jewish community without affiliating with any other religious community.

Another factor of disturbing significance to the problem of Jewish survival was the decreasing birth-rate among the Jews.

While the size of the world's Jewish population had gone up considerably in the nineteenth century, this increase began to level off in the twentieth century. The Jewish birth-rate in the emancipated countries is the lowest of any people. "We are simply dying out."[14] In Great Britain, of the 10,000 Jews who lived there in 1840 only about 5,000 of their descendants remain. If not for the influx of East European Jews and their influence British Jewry might have gone out of existence. It is stated that Hitlerism has not caused the disappearance of the German Jews, it merely hastened the process. Even if left alone German Jewry would have died a natural death in due course of time. The same may be said of the Jewish communities in the other emancipated countries of Europe. As to American Jewry, its phenomenal growth is mainly due to immigration. With no new Jewish arrivals to the United States the best one can hope is that American Jewry will hold its own, which even the optimists do not believe to be possible.

III. The Liberal Movement in Judaism

The Reform Synagogue came into existence in response to the need of putting a stop to the dangerous drift away from Judaism. It recognized the fact that the changes which had taken place in the world following the French Revolution made traditional Judaism obsolete. Judaism had to be reformulated, reconstructed, redefined and reinterpreted so as to enable it again to serve the spiritual needs of the Jew. To this end a series of far-reaching innovations were introduced into the Synagogue ritual. Hebrew was replaced by the vernacular. The references in the Prayer-Book to a return to Palestine were omitted. Some synagogues—or temples as they were now called—substituted Sunday services in place of Saturday. Choir singing was instituted and the sermon by the Rabbi assumed a prominent place in the worship. The outward appearance of the Synagogue and the form of worship have undergone significant alterations designed to beautify the religious services in accordance with the aesthetic taste of the modern Jew.

To instil a greater respect for the Jewish heritage of the past a group of German Jews organized the so-called Science of Judaism whose object it was to bring traditional Judaism into greater harmony with modern thought. The founder of this movement was Leopold Zunz (1794–1886). Among those banded together with him in this work were J. M. Jost (1793–1860), the first modern historian of the Jews; Abraham Geiger (1810–1874); Heinrich Graetz, the author of a great work on the history of the Jews. Two Jews from Galicia of enormous learning, Nachman Krochmal and S. J. Rappoport, were also associated with this movement. This society did excellent work in the critical investigation and scientific presentation of Jewish history and literature.

From Germany the Liberal Synagogue movement spread to other European countries and to America. It proved most successful among the cultured and well-to-do Jews of the emancipated lands. By abolishing many of the old customs, by rejecting many Jewish observances, by revising the Prayer-Book and by eliminating from it the references to a national restoration of the Jewish people in Palestine, Liberal Judaism made the emancipated Jew feel that he is a full-fledged member of the country of his birth or adoption. In this respect the so-called Frankfort Declaration of 1843 is significant. This Declaration was issued by the members of the Frankfort (Germany) Reform Society. They formulated five principles in which they attempted to re-define Judaism. They declared: "(1) that they consider the Mosaic religion capable of continuous development; (2) that they do not consider binding the various ritual, dietary, and other laws concerned with bodily practices that emanated from the ancient policy; (3) that they do not consider circumcision binding either as a religious act or a symbol; (4) that they do not recognise the Talmud as authoritative; and (5) that they do not expect or long for a Messiah who will lead the Jews back to Palestine, but regard the country to which they belong either by birth or citizenship as their only fatherland."[15] This was not only a sharp departure from Jewish tradition, but also a denial of the millennial Jewish hope for a national restoration in Palestine. While in subsequent years, under the pressure of changing events, liberal Judaism modified the position taken by its founders with respect to Jewish observances and Jewish nationalism, it has never become a potent religious force in Jewry, and it has failed to revitalize the religious life of the Jew.

Another movement was born in Germany in the era of emancipation, and it was the outgrowth of the activities of Moses Mendelssohn, a brilliant German Jew, who did more than any other Jew of his generation for the intellectual and social regeneration of the Jewish people. A profound philosophical thinker and excellent German stylist, Mendelssohn translated the Old Testament into German but transcribed into Hebrew characters. To his German translation he added a Hebrew commentary. The result of this achievement was threefold: it helped shift the interest of the Jews back to the Bible; it contributed to a revival of the Hebrew tongue; while the German language became the means of introducing the Jews into the intellectual and cultural movements of that day. The revival of the Hebrew language gave birth to the so-called Haskalah movement or Jewish Enlightenment. The publication of the Hebrew periodical *Hameasef* (*The Collector*) became the rallying point of a group of Neo-Hebraists in Germany, Austria and Poland. This movement became especially active in Eastern Europe where it brought about a rejuvenation of the Hebrew tongue with a considerable output of works on literary and scientific subjects. Among the creators or recreators of modern Hebrew the most important names are those of Abraham Mapu (1808–1867), Leon Gordon (1831–1892) and Perez Smolenskin (1842–1885).

In an incredibly short time—in the space of one generation—many Jews whose parents, or who themselves, were born in the degrading Ghetto surroundings, had risen to places of distinction in all walks of life including science, art, literature and politics. In Germany of 1848 the Jew Gabriel Riesser, a grandson of a Lithuanian Rabbi, became a Vice-President of the German Parliament of that year and a member of its deputation which offered the crown of the German empire to Frederick William IV. In the same year Adolphe Cremieux became a member of the Provisional Government of France, and a second time a member of the Government of National Defence, in 1870–1871. Benjamin Disraeli was one of England's greatest empire builders. In Italy three Jews attained to places of high influence in that period: Giuseppe Ottolenghi—general of the Italian army; Luigi Luzatti—prime minister of Italy; while Ernesto Nathan was chief magistrate of Rome itself. The Rothschilds and other Jewish bankers played an important part in the financial life of Europe, while two Jews, Karl Marx and Ferdinand Lassalle, became the founders of modern socialism. In Berlin some Jewish homes were the cultured meeting-places frequented by some of the leading German intellectuals of that day. The Jews of the emancipated countries were certain that they were standing on the threshold of a golden era, as it were, in the history of the world.

IV. THE RISE OF MODERN ANTISEMITISM

The process of emancipation of the Jews in Germany had hardly been completed when a wave of new Jew-hatred struck in the last quarter of the nineteenth century and in time overflowed to countries outside the German borders. Why this new anti-semitism originated in Germany can be explained in a number of ways. It coincided with the birth of a fanatical, chauvinistic German nationalism, which placed itself in opposition to the liberal ideas which had penetrated German life under the influence of the French Revolution. While the clock of progress could not be set back German reaction was determined to eliminate from the new order what it considered its undesirable aspects. The emancipation of the Jew was, from the point of view of German chauvinism, such an undesirable feature. While the physical Ghettos of pre-revolutionary days could not be restored, the Jew nevertheless had to be eliminated from German society and German culture.

Germany's international position in the second half of the nineteenth century played an important part in the shaping of this German reactionary movement. While Germany had been broken up into a number of self-governing units, the strong nations of Europe, like England, France, Holland and others, carved out for themselves colonial empires. When Germany did become a unified country in the second half of the nineteenth century there was little opportunity for her to become a colonial power of significance. She could now expand only at the expense of her European neighbours. But this would have led to a disturbance of the European balance of power. Unable to expand inside or outside of Europe Germany was, as it were, hemmed in within her borders ever seeking for an opportunity to break out.

In the eyes of the German people the Jew came to symbolize the foreigner in general. Moreover, the rapid progress which the German Jew had, so soon after his emancipation, made in all walks of life, competing successfully with his German neighbours in the professions, industry, commerce, science, literature and the arts, gave the lie to German theories of the racial superiority of the German people. Hatred of the Jew was probably a disguised form of hatred of the world outside Germany which blocked Germany's march to world dominion.

What distinguished this neo-antisemitism from the one in the pre-Emancipation era was its secular and racial character. While Medieval Jew-hatred wore a religious garb, the neo-antisemitism of the nineteenth century was racial and secular in content. The Jew was to be hated not on account of his religion but because of his racial origin. To the German antisemite the Jew, whatever his religious belief, or absence of belief, is an inferior being because of his race. The change from religious to the racial antisemitism had its roots in the changed religious atmosphere and secularization of life in Europe of that day. The Christian Church, as a result of the Reformation of the sixteenth century, had undergone —and was still undergoing—a process of spiritual purification. A feeling of repentance set in with reference to its relation to the Jewish people. A number of Christian societies sprang up inside and outside the Church with the object of ridding the Church of anti-Jewish feeling, of fostering a better appreciation of God's purpose in and through Israel, and of approaching the Jewish people in the spirit of Christian love and tolerance. Moreover, the "blood and soil" basis of neo-antisemitism could not but encounter stiff opposition from the Christian Church which recognized no such distinctions. The Church knows only two kinds of people, depending on whether they are for or against Jesus Christ. This new spirit within Christianity on the one hand, and the secularization of European life together with the emergence of German national chauvinism on the other hand, were undoubtedly important factors in the origin of the modern racial antisemitism in Germany in the last quarter of the nineteenth century. Thus the foundation was laid for the antisemitism of German Nazism of the twentieth century which led to the extermination of the bulk of European Jewry in World War Two.

The two more immediate consequences of this virulent antisemitism, which were to have far-reaching effects on the destiny of the Jews, were the outbreak of atrocities against the Jews in Russia in 1882, putting an abrupt end to a decade of tolerance and liberalism under Tzar Alexander II, and the Dreyfus affair in France in 1894 in which Dreyfus, a Jewish officer, was falsely accused of treason, in an attempt of French antisemites to oust the Jews from the higher ranks in the French Army, and to detract the attention of the French masses from the real nature of the problem besetting France of that day.

V. The Jewish Reaction to Post-Emancipation
Antisemitism

This new antisemitism left the Jews stunned, especially in Germany whose Jews have done everything in their power to conform to the ways of their German neighbours, only to find in the end that they were not wanted. Undoubtedly many German Jews sought to solve their predicament by a more thorough obliteration of their Jewishness. But there were many others who began to question whether this so-called political emancipation has effected any real improvement in the status of the Jewish people, and whether this was the real solution of the Jewish problem.

The mood of these Jews is best expressed by Moses Hess, a German Jew born in Bonn in 1812 of orthodox Jews, but who devoted a large part of his most active years to the liberal movement in Germany. After the failure of the revolution in 1848 he was forced to leave his native land and took refuge in Paris. "A thought," he states, "which I believed to be forever buried in my heart, has been revived in me anew. It is the thought of my nationality, which is inseparably connected with the ancestral heritage and the memories of the Holy Land, the Eternal City, the birthplace of the belief in the divine unity of life, as well as the hope in the future brotherhood of men."[16] "The European nations," Hess declares in another place, "have always considered the existence of the Jews in their midst as an anomaly. We shall always remain strangers among the nations. They may tolerate us and even grant us emancipation, but they will never respect us as long as we place the principle *ubi bene ibi patria* [my country is wherever I fare well] above our own great national memories."[17]

"The civic emancipation of Jewry," writes Leo Pinsker, a Russian Jew, in 1882, "was the utmost that we wrung from the nineteenth century. It is clear by now that civic emancipation did not lead to social emancipation. The granting of legal equality has utterly failed to normalize the position of the Jew within the structure of society. For it must not be forgotten that the emancipation of Jewry was justified by reason, by considerations of abstract justice, and by an enlightened self-interest. It was never the spontaneous expression of a human sentiment."[18]

"We," declares Theodor Herzl, "have honestly endeavoured everywhere to merge ourselves in the social life of surrounding communities and to preserve the faith of our fathers. We are not permitted to do so. In vain are we loyal patriots, our loyalty in some places running to extremes; in vain do we make the same sacrifices of life and property as our fellow citizens; in vain do we strive to increase the fame of our native land in science and art, or her wealth by trade and commerce. In countries where we have lived for centuries we are still cried down as strangers, and often by those whose ancestors were not domiciled in the land where Jews had already had experience of suffering."[19]

"The nineteenth century," says Nordau, "was the epoch of the decomposition of the Jewish people which, in exchange for its apparent acceptance into the European family of nations, was prepared to give up its past, its future, its very self."[20] "The last quarter of the nineteenth century was marked by a sudden and catastrophic change. From one end of Europe to another there flared up a burning antisemitism unparalleled since the Middle Ages. With desperate amazement the Westerners of Jewish faith watched their Christian fellow-citizens as individuals and as social groups retract that equality which their political entity, the state, had conferred. Above all, Jews were once more denied the very capacity of patriotic feeling; once more they were called strangers and treated as such. And that was the sorest hurt that could be inflicted upon them. Zealously and even angrily had they denied the very existence of a Jewish people; they had violently denied any solidarity with Jewish foreigners; they had bartered away light-heartedly enough all hope of a national future for their people, all desire for one. And now they were strangers again."[21] In another passage of his pamphlet Max Nordau presents a picture of the various reactions of the emancipated Jews to the new outburst of antisemitism which threatened to rob them of their newly-won position in their countries. Some acted as if nothing happened, they pretended not to see anything unusual. Others, again, organized campaigns and drives against the antisemites and made frequent complaints to the Government authorities about every antisemitic act or utterance. Still others became Jew-haters themselves. "But," Nordau continues, "this new moral expulsion from their fatherlands and from European society had an effect of a far different kind upon one part of Western Jewry. It is but a small part as yet, but an important part, since it comprises that Jewish youth which unites character to intellect. Tens of thousands of young Jews of high culture and ideals have returned to the great historic traditions of their people; they have revivified within themselves the Jewish past and have awakened to a faith in the Jewish future as an incentive to vigorous action." [22]

The growth of industry in Europe in the nineteenth century brought into existence in Eastern Europe a sizeable Jewish working class. The vast majority of Jewish labourers and tradesmen were employed in Jewish establishments. With the rise of modern socialism in Europe there sprang up also Jewish socialist parties which confined their activities to the Jewish labouring masses. The approach to the Jewish problem on the part of the Jewish socialists reflected the general attitude of socialism to the Jewish question. The socialists believed that antisemitism, if not a child of the capitalist system, is at least being utilized by the capitalists to divert the attention of the working men from the fundamental failures inherent in the capitalist system; that when capitalism will be supplanted by the new socialist order antisemitism will vanish as the snow melts away with the arrival of spring. Needless to say that large numbers of young Jewish idealists in Eastern Europe fell for this sort of propaganda. The miseries of the Jewish people, the wretched condition of the Russian peasant, and the lack of civic and political freedom in Tzarist Russia provided a fertile soil for socialist teachings.

However, because of its materialistic conception of human history in general, socialism failed to see and could not, or would not, probe into the real cause underlying the Jewish problem. There was no room in its dogmatic system for the millennial national aspirations of the Jewish people. Admittedly, the Jewish problem would be solved in a socialist order, but it would be solved by the complete disappearance of the Jew from the face of the earth. This is the policy which "socialist" Russia has been pursuing, and to all appearances she is doing a good job of it.

Some of the Jewish immigrants from Eastern Europe transplanted the Jewish brand of Eastern European socialism among the Jewish immigrants in America. A Jewish press, and a number of Jewish publications were created, and they carried on an extensive cultural and labour-union activity. But the political freedom and the structure of the American economy exerted a moderating influence on the Jewish labour movement which in time has grown quite conservative. The Jewish socialist parties in Eastern Europe have disappeared: those in Soviet Russia, because of the opposition to it on the part of Soviet Communism, and those in Poland were wiped out by the Nazis together with millions of other Jews. As to Jewish socialism in America it is dying a natural death. The extermination of the East European Jews eliminated the source from which Jewish socialism used to receive its human replenishments, while the Jewish labour group in America is disappearing as a separate distinct group. The descendants of the Jewish labour immigrants seldom choose their parents' occupations, and if they become members of a union at all, it is not bound to be a Jewish union. Deprived of a distinctly Jewish labouring class Jewish socialism in America has no future.

Thus Jewish socialism born in the post-emancipation era, and upon which large numbers of oppressed Jews pinned their hopes for a better future, has ceased to be an important factor in Jewish life in the Dispersion. The anti-Zionist policy pursued by the Russian Communist Government almost from the moment of its accession to power, and the downright hostile attitude to Jewish Palestine on the part of the late Mr. Bevin, secretary for foreign affairs in the Labour cabinet which ruled England right after World War Two, have made the Jewish people wary of socialism in general.

Modern antisemitism has led some Jews to seek a solution of the Jewish problem in resettlement of large numbers of Jews in some part of the world where they could live an autonomous political life. This movement became known by the name of Territorialism. Several places were suggested among which were East Africa, South America, the island of Cyprus, and the Sinai peninsula. The most practical of these projects was that offered by England and consisting of a territory of 6,000 square miles in the Guas Ngishu plateau in East Africa. The Zionist Organizations to whom the offer was made refused to accept it on the grounds that it is concerned solely with the resettling of Jews in Palestine.

There were other schemes aiming to settle Jews on land, the most important of which were the labours carried on by the Jewish Colonization Association founded in 1891 by Baron Maurice de Hirsch with an initial fund of two million pounds, subsequently increased to some nine million pounds. The purpose of this society was to assist Russian Jews to resettle in non-European countries. It established a number of agricultural settlements in Argentina. In 1900 it extended its activities to Palestine. The colonies in Argentina became in time thriving agricultural communities but the project was not of too great significance in the over-all picture. It did not prove a lasting success even in Argentina, as the children of the settlers tend to leave the farms for city life in accordance with the general country-to-city trend. Thus the territorialistic movement failed to accomplish the goals marked out by its founders.

VI. THE RISE OF MODERN ZIONISM

"If I forget thee, O Jerusalem, let my right hand forget her cunning. Let my tongue cleave to the roof of my mouth if I remember thee not; if I prefer not Jerusalem above my chief joy", Psalm 137: 5–6. Throughout the many ages of the great Dispersion the Jews never forgot Zion. The return to Zion was their consuming passion. Their whole life was conditioned by the conviction and hope of their eventual return to the land of their forefathers.

A definite change in this mood came with the ushering in of the Era of Emancipation. The accelerated rate of scientific progress, the industrial revolution of the nineteenth century with its many opportunities for economic betterment, the civic and political liberties which the Jews were granted in a number of European countries, drew Jews and Gentiles closer together in many spheres of life, and wrought a profound change in the attitude of the Jew to Zion. He began to consider himself as belonging to the country of his birth or citizenship and wished to contribute his best and his most to its welfare.

But the Jew was not destined to enjoy indefinitely peace and happiness in the lands of his dispersion. In spite of his best efforts to identify himself closely with the country of his domicile, he discovered that he is still regarded as a stranger. Many of them went to the extreme in their desire to erase their Jewishness and to convince the Gentiles of their patriotic feelings only to find that they are being rebuffed and repelled.

Modern Zionism was born, or reborn, in response to the realization which the generation of the Emancipation was gradually gaining that the Jew was still unwanted in spite of all the social, economic and political changes of the preceding two centuries. Modern Zionism was the Jewish people's reaction to the disintegrating forces within Jewry and to the rise of racial antisemitism in the nineteenth century. As medieval religious Judaism was conditioned by the religious antisemitism of the Middle Ages, so

Zionism was the answer of national Judaism to the racial anti-semitism of the nineteenth and twentieth century.

This reawakening of the Zionist idea, after a lapse of about a century, gave birth to the so-called "Chibat Zion" ("Love of Zion") movement which was organized in Russia about 1880 with its headquarters in Odessa from where the movement spread to other countries. The chief aim of this organization was to help Jewish colonization work in Palestine.

The greatest contribution to the development of the modern Zionist movement was made by the activities of Moses Hess and Rabbi Zevi Hirsh Kalisher, who may be regarded as the ideological forerunners of modern Zionism. Moses Hess was born in Bonn, Germany, in 1812, of orthodox parents. In his younger days he broke away from the tenets of traditional Judaism and became absorbed in the intellectual activities of his native land of that day. For a time he collaborated with Karl Marx, the founder or systematizer of modern socialist thought. But Hess was apparently unhappy about Marx's materialistic conception of history and he broke with him in the end. "Much as he [Hess] recognizes the importance of social conditions for the development of social ideas, he nevertheless considers it essential that socialism should be based not on the economic and technical stage of development alone but also on that of the spirit. For him social freedom is 'either a result of spiritual freedom, or it is without foundation and turns over into its opposite'; he sees the heart of the social movements of our time proceeding 'not from the needs of the stomach but from the needs of the heart' and from 'ideas'."[23]

Already in 1840, some twenty-two years before the production of his *Rome and Jerusalem*, Hess began to experience a change of heart about the destiny of the Jewish people. The false ritual murder accusation in Damascus in 1840—the so-called Damascus Affair—was the immediate cause for Hess's changed attitude to his people. The effect of this affair was to pour a feeling of dismay and agony into the hearts of the European Jews. "Then," Hess declares, "it dawned upon me for the first time, in the midst of my socialistic activities, that I belong to my unfortunate, slandered, despised and dispersed people."[24]

In *Rome and Jerusalem* written in 1862 and in his other utterances he analysed the unique position and destiny of the Jewish people, and laid down a programme for the rebirth of Israel and its restoration in Palestine along lines in which the modern Zionist movement, born some thirty years later, has been proceeding ever since. Hess's thoughts on the subject of Israel's national rebirth were as follows:

(1) The Jewish people and Palestine are inseparable. (2) The national rebirth of the Jewish people is impossible without a return to the soil and the full normalization of Jewish life in Palestine. (3) The ultimate aim of the Jewish national rebirth is the setting up on earth of the Messianic Kingdom of God, but this cannot take place until the Jewish people have regained first their national State in Palestine. (4) Hess predicted the founding of Jewish colonies in Palestine, when the political conditions became ripe, "under the protection of the great powers of Europe". (5) The founding of Jewish settlements will be preceded by the acquisition of land in Palestine which land should become the common possession of the Jewish people. (6) The establishment of Jewish societies for agriculture, industry and commerce in accordance with the principles of Mosaic law. (7) The revival of the Hebrew language in Palestine.[25] He also spoke with great significance of the restored State of Israel as a link between East and West. It is remarkable how much of the programme of the Zionist movement has been fulfilled exactly as foreseen by Hess.

The significance of Rabbi Kalisher's efforts on behalf of the modern Zionist movement lies in a different direction. He was a highly educated Rabbi, born in the German part of what was originally a Polish province. He was steeped in Rabbinic lore and secular subjects. The importance of Rabbi Kalisher's pro-Zionist activities lies in the effect of his labours on Orthodox Judaism. Orthodox Judaism clung to the belief that the restoration of the Jewish people in the land of their forefathers will take place only through the agency of the Messiah. For Jews to try to rebuild Palestine by themselves was considered by orthodox Jews as forcing the issue before the appointed time and therefore bound to fail. The tragic way in which the many pseudo-Messianic movements of the past have ended may have strengthened Orthodox Judaism in this belief. Rabbi Kalisher set out to break down this passive, defeatist attitude of his orthodox brethren. In his writings he sought to prove from the Bible and Rabbinic sources that not only is it God's will that the Jews should re-establish themselves in their ancient Homeland but that the Messiah would not come until the Jews had first prepared the way for Him by rebuilding the land to which He is to come. Rabbi Kalisher pointed out that the Bible teaches that there will be two returns to Palestine, the first to consist of a small group of pioneers who will prepare the way for a later return of the whole nation. In consequence of the many years of self-sacrificing work on the part of this venerable and deeply religious Rabbi "a new spirit of hope and labour was breathed into the dormant body of a people hibernating through the centuries of persecution in the hollow log of tradition and faith".[26]

Three external events were the immediate precursors of the birth of the modern Zionist movement: (1) The resurgence of the spirit of Jew-hatred under the name of racial antisemitism in Germany; (2) intimately associated with this event was the renewal of anti-Jewish policies in Russia which culminated in the pogrom of 1882; (3) the plot against the Jews in France which was one of the underlying factors of the Dreyfus Affair in 1894.

The insecurity and essential abnormality of the Jewish position in the modern world impressed themselves deeply on Theodor Herzl, a Viennese Jew, during the trial of Captain Dreyfus in Paris which he covered as a correspondent for the *Neue Freie Presse*. Herzl became convinced that the only solution for the centuries-old suffering of the Jewish people is its reconstitution in a country of its own. In 1897 he published his *Judenstaat* (*The Jewish State*), in which he gave expression to his convictions, and laid down a plan for the re-establishment of the Jews as an independent nation. In what country Jewish national existence should be organized did not interest Herzl at the beginning of his labours on behalf of the Jewish people. But the violent opposition which arose among the Zionists to the Uganda project of Britain soon convinced Herzl that the Jewish people would never consent to the establishment of the Jewish State in any country but Palestine.

The publication of Herzl's *The Jewish State* with the directness, clarity, precision and daring manner with which he deals with the whole problem of the Jews stirred the whole Jewish people from one end of the world to the other. In 1897 Herzl convened a Congress in Basle, Switzerland, to consider his project. The Basle Congress formed the Zionist Organization and adopted the following programme:

"Zionism strives to create for the Jewish people a home in Palestine secured by public law. The Congress contemplates the following means to the attainment of this end:

1. The promotion on suitable lines of the Colonization of Palestine by Jewish agricultural and industrial workers.
2. The organization and binding together of the whole of Jewry by means of appropriate institutions, local and international, in accordance with the laws of each country.
3. The strengthening and fostering of Jewish national sentiment and consciousness.
4. Preparatory steps towards obtaining Government consent where necessary to the attainment of the aim of Zionism."[27]

Thus Political Zionism was born. It made articulate the millennial Jewish hopes and aspirations for a restored Zion. It brought the whole question out into the open and laid it at the doorstep of the Gentile world. Since the Gentile world did not want the Jew in its midst it was up to this same Gentile world to help the Jew find a place in this world and this place is no other than Palestine. World War One freed Palestine from Turkey. In 1917, twenty years after the First Zionist Congress, the British Government issued the Balfour Declaration in which it solemnly promised to assist the Jews to secure a National Home in Palestine. This Declaration became the basis of the British Mandate over Palestine under the League of Nations, ratified separately by the United States Government. Thus the rebuilding of Jewish Palestine was guaranteed by America and the nations belonging to the League of Nations.

Political Zionism encountered some opposition from certain Jewish segments. The assimilationists, denying the whole idea of a Jewish nation, were afraid that it will provide the antisemites with more fuel for their anti-Jewish activities on the ground of Jewish disloyalty to the countries of their domicile. The Jewish socialists opposed Zionism because they were against all nationalism. Orthodox Jews were against it for reasons already discussed above. But the events between the two World Wars, especially the destruction of European Jewry by Nazism, have practically wiped out all opposition to Zionism within Jewry. Assimilationism, Orthodox Judaism, socialism—all these failed. Zionism became the unifying factor and the rallying point for all Jewry, and in May 1948 the centuries-old dream of a restored Zion became a reality with the proclamation of the reconstitution of the State of Israel.

VII. Conclusion

When the Jewish State was destroyed by the Romans and the Jewish people were dispersed all over the world, Palestine was not left without Jews. A small group remained in the Holy Land and clung doggedly to the country, being reinforced from time to time by immigrants from the Dispersion. Thus a Jewish community was in existence through all the centuries of the Great Dispersion, dwelling amidst the ruins and desolations of the country, but holding on—a link between the past and the future—until the exile would come to an end, and the dispersed would return home.

"During all this period of nearly two thousand years, Palestine was not even a name on the political map of the world. It was a portion of a larger province, whether Roman, Byzantine, Arab or Turkish; and its people were never conscious of themselves as a national unit, nor did they ever attempt, as they had done in early and later Israelite days, to form an independent kingdom."[28] At no time in the whole recorded history of Palestine was the country one independent political state except under the Jews. Palestine's political identity was destroyed when the Jewish National Homeland was destroyed. When at the end of the nineteenth century the Jews began to return to the country with a renewed determination to rebuild their National Homeland, Palestine once more re-emerged from obscurity. And when in 1948 the State of Israel became re-established Palestine became again, after a lapse of some two thousand years, an independent State.

NOTES TO CHAPTER 1

1. Martin Buber, *Israel and Palestine* (East and West Library: London, 1952), pp. 69–70.
2. Ibid., pp. 87–8.
3. Ibid., p. 94.
4. Ibid., p. 74.
5. Ibid., p. 88.
6. Ibid., p. 77.
7. Ibid., p. 88.
8. Ibid., p. 118.
9. T. W. Rosmarin, "Nation or Religion—What are the Jews?", article in the *Jewish Spectator* (New York), November 1945.
10. Leonard Stein, *Zionism* (Adelphi Co.: New York, 1926), p. 20. By permission of Greenberg Publisher.

11. Arthur Ruppin, *The Jews in the Modern World* (Macmillan and Co.: New York, 1934), p. 328. Used by permission of St. Martin's Press, New York.

12. De La Roi, *Judentaufen im 19. Jahrhundert*; quoted by Arthur Ruppin, op. cit., p. 328.

13. Arthur Ruppin, op. cit., p. 329.

14. J. Litvin, "The Galuth must be Liquidated", article in the *Jewish Spectator* (New York), October 1948.

15. David Philipson, *The Reform Movement in Judaism* (Macmillan and Co.: New York, 1931), p. 118. By permission of the publishers.

16. Moses Hess, *Rome and Jerusalem*, English translation by M. Waxman (Bloch Publishing Co.: New York, 1918), p. 43.

17. Ibid., p. 74.

18. Leo Pinsker, *Auto-emancipation*; quoted by Ludwig Lewisohn, *Rebirth* (Harper and Brothers: New York, 1935), pp. 18–19.

19. Theodor Herzl, *The Jewish State*, 1896 (English translation published by the American Zionist Emergency Council, 1946), p. 76.

20. Max Nordau, *The Tragedy of Assimilation*; quoted by Ludwig Lewisohn, op. cit., p. 42.

21. Max Nordau; quoted by Ludwig Lewisohn, op. cit., p. 40.

22. Max Nordau; quoted by Ludwig Lewisohn, op. cit., pp. 41–2.

23. Martin Buber, op. cit., p. 112.

24. Moses Hess, op. cit., p. 68.

25. Martin Buber, op. cit., pp. 120–1.

26. Joshua Stampfer, "The Religious Zionism of Kalisher", article in *Judaism* (New York), July 1953.

27. Leonard Stein, op. cit., p. 88.

28. James Parkes, *A History of Palestine* (Victor Gollancz: London, 1949), p. 13. Permission for use in the United States and Canada granted by Oxford University Press, Inc., New York, N.Y.

Chapter 2

JEWISH VIEWS OF THE SIGNIFICANCE OF THE PRESENT NATIONAL RESTORATION

JEWISH VIEWS OF THE SIGNIFICANCE OF THE PRESENT NATIONAL RESTORATION

The following are a few representative Jewish pronouncements on the subject of the significance of the present national restoration of the Jewish people in Palestine. As would be expected some dwell on one, others on another aspect of the situation.

I. IT ASSURES THE NATIONAL SURVIVAL OF THE JEWS AND OF JEWISH CULTURE

"The rebuilding of Palestine is for us Jews not a mere matter of charity or emigration: it is a problem of paramount importance for the Jewish people. Palestine is first and foremost not a refuge for East European Jews, but the incarnation of a reawakening sense of national solidarity." "It is for me beyond any shadow of doubt that in present circumstances the rebuilding of Palestine is the only object which has a sufficiently strong appeal to stimulate the Jews to effective corporate action. . . . Palestine will become a cultural home for all Jews, a refuge for the worst sufferers from oppression, a field of activity for the best among us, a unifying ideal and a source of spiritual health for the Jews of every country."—Albert Einstein. [1]

"For Zionism means infinitely more than the building or rebuilding of the Jewish National Home. It means the Jewish will to live Jewishly versus the wish to survive Jewishly or un-Jewishly, to create a Jewish centre in the Judea of history whence shall radiate Jewish stimulus and inspiration to Jews wherever they may dwell. Zionism is the Jewish answer to cowardly counsels of Jewish suicide. Zionism is the collective will of the Jewish people to endure and to create."—Stephen S. Wise. [2]

II. It Normalizes Jewish Life

"But Zionism is not a refugee-movement. It is not a product of the second world war, nor of the first. It is a product of our millennial national homelessness since our dispersion, and its sole correct solution. Were there at present no displaced Jews in Europe and were there free opportunities for Jewish immigration in other parts of the world at this time, Zionism would still be an imperative necessity. There were many opportunities for immigration in the last decades of the nineteenth century and first decade of the twentieth when our movement was organized and developed. All the centuries of Dispersion and the recurrent incidents of persecution . . . have persuaded the Jewish people that in order to normalize its position in the world and to gain a measure of security, it needs a country of its own."—Abba Hillel Silver.[3]

"Ever since the inception of political Zionism the realization has matured in our midst that the situation of the Jewish people is fundamentally anomalous. To remove the anomaly of our existence by the restoration of Israel to its historic homeland has been the Zionish goal."—E. Berkovits.[4]

"The only remedy for antisemitism is the 'normalization' of Jewish life: the restoration of the Jewish people to its own soil in order to enable it fully and freely to unfold its physical and mental abilities in all fields of human productive activity."—Josef Heller.[5]

"All that we desire in Palestine comes to this, that we create with our own hands all that constitutes life; that with our own hands we perform all the work and labour that is needed from the highest and most complicated and easiest down to the coarsest and hardest and most contemptible, and that we thus come to feel and think and experience all that labouring human beings in the performance of all these varied tasks can come to feel and think and experience. Only when we do that will we possess a culture because only thus will we have a life of our own."—A. D. Gordon.[6]

"A people unadapted to political existence has established a State, and that State stands firm. A people that had not engaged in a war of its own for sixty generations has set up an army, and that army has proved itself capable and courageous. . . . We have set up some 350 new villages, and Jews are being transformed into farmers; indeed, some of them show promise of becoming very good farmers."—Eliezer Livneh. [7]

"For seventy years they came, these pioneers, from Hungary, from the Old City of Jerusalem, from the Western Hemisphere, discerning truly that in a return to the soil lay national revival. In seventy years we founded 290 farm settlements, we cultivated 700,000 dunams or 10,000 every year, and settled all told, 100,000 Jews on land. In the two years since the State, we have founded 240 new settlements, settled 82,000 on the land, brought 2,100,000 new dunams under the plough. Just think! Thirty times as many settlements, seventy times as much cultivation, thirty times as many settlers, all this, almost incomparably creative as it is, done by Jews from the Yemen, Morocco, Turkey and Eastern Europe, at it on the land and in the factories, building villages and towns, planting forests, making roads, repeopling the Negev, restoring Jaffa, Lydda and Ramleh, Beersheba and Beisan. Many cannot read or write, but they learn quickly. Those of military age receive their Jewish and general education in the Army; the others in evening classes or from their children. Good soldiers these and fine workers."—David Ben Gurion. [8]

All the hopes of Zionism with regards to normalizing Jewish life have become a living reality in the Jewish National Homeland. Outside of the State of Israel the economic position of the Jews is abnormal. The Jews in the land of the Diaspora favour certain occupations and shun others. They flock to certain professions, and choose certain lines of business. They are not sufficiently represented in the trades and they shun the industries. Only in the State of Israel do the Jews have a normal economic structure. There they till the soil, and work in the factories. There they operate the mines and build the roads, and do all kinds of construction work. There the fishermen are Jews, the firemen are Jews and the policemen are Jews. There they run the railroads, ply the ships at sea and pilot the planes in the sky. There alone are they fully identified with the whole economic structure of the country.

III. It Enhances the National Dignity of Diaspora Jewry

"But its [i.e. Zionism's] greatest achievement was this: to countless scattered Jews and Jewish families things Jewish ceased to seem, as under alien pressure they had hitherto done, subtly ignoble."—Arnold Zweig. [9]

"Through the return of Jews to Palestine, and so to a normal and healthy economic life, Zionism involves a creative function, which should enrich mankind at large. But the main point is that Zionism must tend to enhance the dignity and self-respect of the Jews in the Diaspora."—Albert Einstein.[10]

"On us depend the prestige, self-respect and dignity of all Jewries."—David Ben Gurion.[11]

"The mere existence of the restored Jewish home will beneficially influence the psychological, political and social situation of those Jews who remain outside the national home."—Josef Heller.[12]

". . . an ideal Israel, where all is as it should be, increases the self-esteem of the Diaspora Jew and strengthens his position among the non-Jewish population. . . . It provides the Diaspora Jew with a distinguished 'Old Country': no longer is he a mere shadow, but a person with an authentic mooring."—Eliezer Livneh.[13]

IV. THE SPIRITUAL, PROPHETIC AND MESSIANIC ASPECTS OF THE PRESENT RESTORATION

"The Zionists seek to establish this home in Palestine because they are convinced that the undying longing of the Jews for Palestine is a fact of deepest significance. . . . They believe that there only can the Jewish spirit reach its full and natural development."—Louis D. Brandeis.[14]

"Classical Judaism is grounded in a very strong foundation: God and Torah. Israel has been chosen to embody the Revelation in its life. Not to conquer or destroy has Israel been selected, but to educate humanity and to restore the image of God to man. But Israel is also the people of God per se. Irrespective of its task to carry God's light to the world, Israel must return to its soil to complete its task and become what its destiny calls for it to be, a holy people, a people of God."—David S. Shapiro.[15]

"The Jewish problem is therefore not only a national-ethical, but, first and foremost, a spiritual-religious problem with a national and an international aspect, and the aim of Zionism is not merely the establishment of a Jewish Commonwealth in the Land of Israel, but to pave the way for a rebirth of the spirit of the Prophets and for the revival of Judaism. . . . The task of reviving the Middle East, of bridging the cultural gap between Europe and the eastern shore of the Mediterranean, which was the cradle of human civilization, and of mediating between the Christian and the Islamic circles of nations, can be achieved neither by the European states nor by the reawakening peoples of the Arab world alone. The Jewish people, which in the Middle Ages acted as the intermediary between the Arab and the Christian civilizations, seems to be predestined for this great task . . .

"The highest value of Zionism lies, however, not in the material and political sphere, but in its spiritual meaning for the Jews and for the world. It is this moral and spiritual effect of the development of a free Jewish community in the land of the Prophets which paves the way for the final settlement of the Jewish question. . . . Zionists hope and believe that the land of Israel will again become a source of spiritual life for the Jews and for the non-Jewish world alike."—Josef Heller.[16]

"The State of Israel was also destined to foster and develop in freedom and self-respect the great moral and cultural heritage of our forefathers, our law-givers and our prophets, and enthrone it in modern, civilized garb, with the aid of modern science and technology."—David Ben Gurion.[17]

" 'I will surely assemble, O Jacob, all of thee; I will surely gather the remnant of Israel.' In our sight and in our days the scattered people is homing from every corner of the globe and every point of the compass, out of all the nations among which it was cast away, and it is coursing over its Land, over Israel redeemed." "We live and die for a messianic ideal, the advance-guard of universal redemption." "Through generations untold we, and no other people, believed in the vision of the last days. It cannot be that a vision which for so long inspired a people's faith, its hope and patient expectancy will disappoint it now of all times, when the miracle which is the State of Israel has come to pass." "Today, as we renew our independence, our first concern must be to build up the Land, to foster its economy, its security and international status. But these are the whereby not the end. The end is a State fulfilling prophecy, bringing salvation, to be guide and exemplar to all men. In the words of the Prophet is for us a truth perpetual: 'I will give thee for a light to the Gentiles, that thou mayest be my salvation unto the end of the earth'."—David Ben Gurion.[18]

"We are witnessing today the wondrous process of the joining of the tribes of Israel, bone to bone and flesh to flesh, the merging of them into one nation. . . . I pray that the Rock and Redeemer of Israel may prosper our ways, and that in our days Judah may be saved and Israel dwell securely."—Isaac Ben-Zvi, second President of the State of Israel.[19]

". . . We share as Americans and Jews, the unforgettable memory that this [the land of Israel] is the Holy Land. Of yore there came forth the three great faiths that have dominated our Western thinking and our Western way of life. There is the knowledge that the ancient State of Israel, while it never attained military or economic might, exercised its influence through the spiritual, moral, ethical, and religious values that it gave to mankind. All of us here—all of us everywhere realize the great strides that man has made in the recent past in the mechanical, the material, and the scientific, but we are affrighted when we realize that these may be used for our destruction and not for our salvation. May we not turn our hearts, hopes, and thoughts to the new State of Israel and may we not believe, and believing affirm, that this new state has not come into being by historical accident, but that it represents the will of Providence; that in our own day and our own time new spiritual and moral messages may come from this land that will be for our blessing and will enable us to use the great gains we have made in the material for our salvation, not for our destruction.

"Yes; Israel is a secular state with all the economic and political and social problems that beset others. It has, however, a history and a memory and a tradition like no other. Here we were told that no word of the Lord returns void unless it shall have accomplished that which He intended. Thus we as Jews and Zionists and with the help of our America shall resolutely maintain our courage and our faith and our conviction that great moral, spiritual, and ethical truths are going to come from this land in the days that lie ahead.

"Scripture asserts: 'The Lord was passing by and a great and mighty wind was rending the mountains and shattering the rocks, but the Lord was not in the wind but in the sound of a still small voice.' May we not believe that this small voice, the voice of the Lord, shall in our own day and our own time be heard coming from Jerusalem. The world awaits this voice; it will surely hear it when it comes forth. Let us then rededicate ourselves to all the various material tasks involved; let us too believe that Israel will once again in good character vindicate the ways of God to man."—Mortimer May.[20]

"What has secured the survival of the Jewish people throughout the generations, and led to the creation of the State is the Messianic vision of the prophets of Israel, the vision of redemption for the Jewish people and for all humanity. . . . The ingathering of the exiles, that is the return of the Jewish people to its land, is the beginning of the realization of the Messianic vision."—David Ben Gurion.[21]

If the above statements concerning the Messianic significance of the re-establishment of the State of Israel constitute individual expressions the two passages cited below reflect the convictions of the Chief Rabbinate of the State of Israel. They are found in the Order of Prayer compiled with the approval of the Chief Rabbinate of the State of Israel and which are recited with other prayers on Independence Day, i.e. on the anniversary of the proclamation of the reconstitution of the State of Israel. One of these prayers is recited on Independence Day eve following one blast of the trumpet, and it reads like this: "May it be Thy will, O Jehovah our God and the God of our fathers, that as we have been granted the dawn of redemption, so may we be granted to hear the trumpet of the Messiah."

The second petition is from the selection of prayers read at the morning service of Independence Day celebration, and it runs like this: "He who performed miracles for our fathers and for us and who redeemed Israel from servitude to freedom, may He speedily redeem us with a complete redemption and gather our dispersed ones from the four corners of the earth, and we shall sing before Him a new song. Hallelujah."[22]

NOTES TO CHAPTER 2

1. Albert Einstein, *About Zionism: Speeches and Letters, 1931*; see Ludwig Lewisohn, *Rebirth* (Harper and Brothers: New York, 1935), pp. 208, 212, 213.
2. Stephen S. Wise; see Ludwig Lewisohn, op. cit., p. 237.
3. Abba Hillel Silver, "The Zionist Road Ahead", article in *The Jewish Spectator* (New York), December 1945.
4. E. Berkovits, "A Strategy for the Galut", article in *The Jewish Spectator* (New York), April 1947.
5. Josef Heller, "Zionism and the Jewish Problem", symposium on *The Future of the Jews*, edited by J. J. Lynx (Lindsay Drummond: London, 1945), p. 72.
6. A. D. Gordon; see Ludwig Lewisohn, op. cit., pp. 76–7.

7. Eliezer Livneh, "The Meaning of Zionism", article in *The Jewish Spectator* (New York), June 1954.

8. David Ben Gurion, *Rebirth and Destiny of Israel* (Philosophical Library: New York, 1954), p. 536.

9. Arnold Zweig; see Ludwig Lewisohn, op. cit., p. 165.

10. Albert Einstein, *About Zionism: Speeches and Letters, 1931*; see Ludwig Lewisohn, op. cit., p. 207.

11. David Ben Gurion, op. cit., p. 528.

12. Josef Heller, op. cit., p. 82.

13. Eliezer Livneh, idem.

14. Louis D. Brandeis, *The Jewish Problem: How to Solve It* (Cleveland, 1934); see Ludwig Lewisohn, op. cit., p. 229.

15. David S. Shapiro, "Whither, American Judaism?", article in *The Jewish Spectator* (New York), January 1946.

16. Josef Heller, op, cit., pp. 73, 74, 76, 82.

17. David Ben Gurion, "Israel's Achievements", article in *The Jewish Spectator* (New York), May 1954.

18. David Ben Gurion, *Rebirth and Destiny of Israel* (Philosophical Library: New York, 1954), pp. 360, 397, 399, 437.

19. Excerpt from the inaugural address of Isaac Ben-Zvi, second President of the State of Israel; quoted in *The Jews in the News* (Grand Rapids, Michigan), January 1953.

20. Mortimer May, formerly President of the Zionist Organization of America. Excerpt from an address delivered in New York City on November 18, 1954 entitled "A Report on Israel". This address was, at the suggestion of Senator Kefauver, printed in the Appendix of the Congressional Record, November 30, 1954.

21. David Ben Gurion, "Israel and Judaism", address at the Zionist General Council, published in *The Jewish Agency's Digest of Press and Events* (The Jewish Agency: Jerusalem and New York, July 25, 1957) vol. 10, No. 47, p. 1339.

22. *Tikun Yom Ha'Atzmaut* (The World Zionist Organization: Jerusalem, 5716), pp. 28, 47.

CHAPTER 3

THE STATE OF ISRAEL AND THE JEWISH RELIGIOUS CRISIS

Chapter 3

THE STATE OF ISRAEL AND THE JEWISH RELIGIOUS CRISIS

I. The Religious Crisis in the Diaspora

1. INTRODUCTORY REMARKS

The religious crisis in Jewry, a matter of increasing concern to many Jews, is not a recent development. It is over one hundred and fifty years old; indeed, its roots reach all the way back to the destruction of the Temple and Second Commonwealth in the year A.D. 70 and the Great Dispersion which followed it. However, a number of phenomena of far-reaching consequences have combined in recent years to add to this crisis an air of great urgency and importance. We will name only three of these: (1) the downward trend of the Jewish birth-rate and the upward trend of intermarriages; (2) the destruction of a third of world Jewry in World War Two; (3) the emergence of the State of Israel.

The decreasing birth-rate began among the Jews in Western Europe some time before World War One. This fact together with the high intermarriage rate would have resulted in the eventual disappearance of West European Jewry even had Hitlerism never come to Europe. The periodic migrations of Jews from East to West Europe kept West European Jewry temporarily alive. But with the closing of the immigration doors the extinction of West European Jewry was only a matter of time. But even among the great masses of East European Jews the birth-rate began to fall soon after World War One. Thus even before World War Two the natural increase of the Jewish population in the world as a whole ceased.[1]

The destruction of the great Jewish centres in Europe in World War Two has reduced the Jewish people by more than one-third. It has at the same time eliminated the last stronghold of traditional Judaism which up to World War Two was still firmly entrenched in the countries of East and South-east Europe. As a result of this disaster the English-speaking Jews, i.e. those living in America and the British Empire, have now come to represent the great majority of the Jews in the Diaspora. By "Diaspora" we refer to Jewish communities in the various countries of the world outside the Land of Israel. While prior to World War Two the English-speaking Jewries looked to East European Jewry for guidance in religious matters, at the end of World War Two it suddenly found itself deprived of the source from which it had been drawing much of its religious nourishment.

The third event which has served to deepen the Jewish religious crisis is, strangely enough, the sudden appearance of the State of Israel. This aspect of the problem we will consider further on in this chapter. In this section we wish to examine the crisis as it affects the Jews in the Diaspora. Since, as was mentioned above, the English-speaking Jewries constitute now the bulk of the Diaspora we will limit the discussion of the religious problem of the Diaspora to the American scene. The Jews in America are by far the largest English-speaking Jewish community, and conditions among the English-speaking Jewries are on the whole the same.

In general, investigators of the Jewish religious question may be divided into two groups. Those representing the position of Orthodox or traditional Judaism take, by and large, a pessimistic view of the present religious state of the Jewish community. As recently as June 1953 it was stated in *The Jewish Spectator* that "there is little faith in God in the American Jewish Community".[2] This should not be taken to mean that most of American Jews are actually atheists. It is probably more correct to say that "the American Jew is not an atheist, and has a positive belief in God, yet hardly feels the need to call upon Him".[3]

Large masses of the Jewish people—we are informed—are strongly indifferent to all things of a Jewish religious nature. They know little and care less for the traditions of their past. They are ignorant of the God of Judaism and the nature of Jewish belief. They have no knowledge of the Biblical or Rabbinic teachings with regard to the basic things of human life.[4]

There is a growing secularization of Jewish life in general. A Jew can now lead an active Jewish life and remain entirely outside the Synagogue. He can be a Zionist, a member of the Anti-defamation groups to combat antisemitism, he may contribute generously to charitable organizations or for the State of Israel; he can do all these things, and consider himself a good Jew, and yet have no connection with the Synagogue.[5]

Notwithstanding this gloomy picture, there are others who discern signs of religious stirrings in the Jewish community. Many new synagogues have sprung up, many more of the old ones are engaged in expanding building programmes. A number of new Jewish social centres have arisen. Attendance at synagogue services has improved, and more young people are seen at the services than in former years.

To be sure, even today less than a third of the American Jews are affiliated with the Synagogue, and the great majority of those who are affiliated attend the services mostly three days a year, on the High Holidays. Many Jewish religious leaders feel that this mushrooming and expansion of Jewish organizational forms is nothing but an attempt to compensate for the inner impoverishment of Jewish life,[6] while the unpleasant truth remains that on the whole Jewish life in the Diaspora is experiencing a spiritual decline. Nevertheless, there are signs of a spiritual hunger among Jews today and a real concern about their spiritual condition. "There is a religious revival under way among American Jews today."[7] This change is probably related to the tragic experiences of the Jews in Europe in World War Two, to the rise of the State of Israel, and to man's plight in the present stage of human history.

And yet the Jew struggling his way back to God finds his path littered with great obstacles. "The Jew [of the past] living before God, knew both crisis and fulfilment, anguish and exaltation. But there was one problem he did not know—whereas we know it only too well: the situation of a man before the leap into faith. . . . Can one choose religious existence at will? Can one decide to believe in God? Can one on one's own volition 'accept the yoke of the Kingdom of Heaven'? . . . But no man can force the leap into faith; he can merely remove the obstructions. He can understand that existence [religious experience] is open, not closed, and can make himself ready to listen and to answer."[8]

We will now proceed with the discussion of the religious crisis in its relation to the various component parts of the Jewish community.

2. THE RABBINATE

The American Rabbinate consists of three groups: Orthodox, Conservative and Reform. There are fewer Rabbis among American Jews, proportionately speaking, than religious leaders among the non-Jewish religious groups.[9] The Rabbinate does not appear to attract enough young men who would want to dedicate their lives to it. The peculiar position which the Rabbi holds in the Jewish community and the meagre achievements of his labours discourage many from entering the Rabbinate.[10]

In a book entitled *Disciples of the Wise* the writer presents the results of a study by which he endeavoured to ascertain the social and religious views of the American Rabbinate. We will only cite some of the theological opinions of the Rabbis as presented in this study.[11]

(1) *Definition of God*. Most American Rabbis believe that God is "the sum total of forces which make for greater intelligence, beauty, goodness".

(2) *The Bible*. More than two-thirds of the Rabbinate do not accept the view attributing the authorship of the Pentateuch to Moses. More than half of those who replied to the questionnaire reject the literal interpretation of the Biblical story of creation.

(3) *Prayer*. The great majority of the Rabbinate do not believe that the function of prayer is to bring Divine aid to the suppliant.

(4) *Sin*. Only a minority of those that answered the questions conceive of sin as originating in the base impulses of human nature. The great majority "believe that the concept of sin which needs greatest emphasis in our age is to be expressed in social terms, either as: (*a*) harm to neighbours, friends and business associates; (*b*) harm to society; (*c*) support of or acquiescence to accepted institutions which are socially harmful".

(5) *Salvation*. Salvation according to some of the interrogated Rabbis is "achievement of an integrated personality", according to others in the group it is "participation in efforts for social progress".

One of the criticisms levelled against the Rabbinate is that it has ceased to be a teacher and interpreter of Jewish religion. The average Rabbi is a lecturer on literature or politics, an administrator, or a meddler in psychiatry. "In brief, I have found talented rabbis, but no rabbinic rabbis. The rabbis, while they may be a powerful influence in the life of the community, have no acceptance in the community as rabbis. They carry weight in all fields where, whatever their rights as men, they have no claim from the standpoint of their life's vocation."[12]

In a review of Rabbi Steinberg's book *Basic Judaism*, Irving Kristol remarks that the book is an effort to accommodate Judaism to the American scene of the New Deal variety. "What is worse, this accommodation represents not merely Rabbi Steinberg's state of mind, but also the state of mind of a large section of the American rabbinate, and much of the American Jewish community in general. It results in the perversion of the Jewish religion into a doctrine of social (and sociable) principles, the transformation of Messianism into a shallow, if sincere, humanitarianism, plus a thoroughgoing insensitivity to present day spiritual problems."[13]

At the fifty-third annual convention held in Atlantic City, many of the two hundred Conservative Rabbis assembled there confessed that much of their work is a failure. Addressing the assembled Rabbis Professor Abraham J. Heschel of the Jewish Theological Seminary spoke the following heart-searching words. "There are many who can execute and display many magnificent fireworks: but who knows how to kindle a spark in the darkness of the soul? . . . Ours is a great responsibility. We demand that people come to the synagogue instead of playing golf, or making money, or going on a picnic. Why? Don't we mislead them? People take their precious time off to attend services. Some even arrive with profound expectations. But what do they get? . . . Sometimes even the rabbi sits in his chair wondering: 'Why did all these people flock together?'" Concluding the discussion on how to revitalize prayer in the Synagogue, Dr. Heschel said: "I spoke in sincerity, in wholeheartedness, out of my deep respect and affection for the members of the Rabbinical Assembly. I spoke in the spirit of self-criticism. . . . I have been deeply bothered all my life by my own failure in obtaining *kavanah* [spiritual concentration] when I pray myself. I have a great many difficulties, doubts. I do not oversimplify the religious situation. But let us stop avoiding the issue by overrating the periphery: prayer is not the main issue. The issue of prayer is God. And the problem is not synagogue attendance—it is spiritual attendance. It is not how to fill buildings, how to attract bodies to enter a space of a temple, but how to inspire souls to enter an hour of spiritual concentration in the presence of God."[14]

In a conversation with the editor of *The Jewish Spectator* an Orthodox Rabbi made the following heart-searching confession: "I feel so very inadequate in the rabbinate at times. I feel I have nothing to give to my people. How can I make God real to them? How can I make them believe that God really hears their prayers—when I myself am not quite certain? Of course I believe in God, otherwise I could not get up in front of my congregation. But there is uncertainty in my belief. I am not even sure that my prayers are being heard. I have no clear conception of God. But how can one place implicit trust in God when one is not utterly certain of Him and His concern for men . . . I lack certainty [in the Divine origin of the Law] and because of this I am ineffective."

Concluding this conversation with the Rabbi, Dr. Rosmarin informs us that over the years she has met many Rabbis who unburdened their worries and anxieties to her. Many have spoken of their inadequacy and ineffectiveness in their Rabbinical work. From these experiences she has learned that "the doubts and fears of the Rabbi of Middle City are shared, to a larger, lesser or equal extent, by virtually all 'American type' rabbis. The solution? I have none to suggest—none at all".[15]

3. THE SYNAGOGUE

Profound changes have taken place in the status of the Synagogue in the Jewish community. These changes are especially evident in the following three areas:

The Synagogue ceased to occupy a central position in the Jewish community. Not even that small percentage of Jews who identify themselves with the Synagogue all the year round place it in the centre of their life's interests. The major activities of Jewish life, both individual and communal, are all carried on outside the Synagogue's sphere of influence. This is an important departure from the past when the Synagogue was at the heart of all things Jewish.

The second important change which the Synagogue is experiencing is its increasing secularization. Not only the practice of Jewish religious observances is now rare among the Synagogue members, but not even belief in God may be taken for granted. "To put it plainly, the Synagogue in America no longer represents

D

a community of believers. . . . It is becoming an institution in which religion is no longer indispensable. . . . Indeed, is there not some warrant for the assertion, often made, that many a synagogue has become so completely secularized that it is neither a centre for teaching, study, and worship, nor a community of believers, but simply a large institution entangled in a multiplicity of external activities without religious content and meaning?"[16]

The estrangement of the Jewish people from the Synagogue is the third development affecting the Synagogue's position in Jewish life. Most of the Synagogues are empty except on three days during the year. One source states that only ten per cent of American Jews are affiliated with the Synagogue.[17] Synagogue attendance during the year centres around the recitation of the Kaddish prayer for the dead. Many of the men who do not believe in the Kaddish prayer or who for one reason or another do not wish to discharge this responsibility to their departed relatives hire professional Kaddish reciters for that purpose.[18]

The two groups of Jews who have no connection with the Synagogue, especially with its religious programme, are the Jewish labour class and the intellectuals. The Jewish labour unionists have inherited the anti-religious attitude of the Jewish immigrants from Eastern Europe. In this country the Jewish workers have built up impressive communities, with their own newspapers or other publications, and even their educational systems. Religion is excluded from their institutions. The Synagogue has neither the inclination nor any hope of ever reaching this large and important segment of the Jewish population.[19] At the same time the Zionists and other Jewish organizations have gained among the Jewish workers many supporters for their particular cause.

4. THE JEWISH INTELLECTUAL

Professor Heinrich Graetz, probably the greatest Jewish historian since the days of Josephus Flavius, some sixty years ago complained about the Jewish intellectual's growing estrangement from Judaism. "How can Judaism maintain itself if its most distinguished sons, the cultured classes, turn their backs on it?"[20] In America—we are told—there is less interest in traditional Judaism among the intellectuals than among any other group of Jews.[21]

From another source we are informed that the bulk of the Jewish people, but especially those represented in the fields of science, have repudiated their belief in the authority and credibility of the Jewish religious law. [22]

The situation is not radically different in other parts of the Diaspora as may be noted from the following statement about the status of the Jewish intellectual group in Britain: "Within it are many already completely lost to Jewry. Others we still flatter ourselves that we possess, although perhaps only their names indicate any connection." [23]

In 1932 Rabbi Marvin Nathan wrote a book entitled *The Attitude of the Jewish Student in the Colleges and Universities Towards His Religion*. The material in the book is based on the answers to a questionnaire sent out to fifteen hundred Jewish students from fifty-seven colleges and universities. In addition, Dr. Nathan personally interviewed over one hundred students at the University of Pennsylvania and Temple University, and participated in many group discussions at several institutions of higher learning.

This book furnishes much useful information relative to the spiritual state of the Jewish college student of twenty years ago. Two-thirds of the students confessed that they no longer entertained the personal concept of God. One third declared themselves sceptics, agnostics or atheists. About three-fifths of the students—according to this study—displayed doubt, confusion or indifference with reference to their religion. Three-fourths of the students had never recited their prayers at home or had given up that practice. Two-thirds had never attended or had ceased to attend synagogue services. One of the most revealing facts brought out in this study was that of the three religious groups— the Orthodox, Conservative and Reformed—a larger percentage of the Orthodox group gave up the religious practices than either of the other two groups.

In commenting on the findings of his study Rabbi Nathan states, among other things, that the religious education which the student received had a negative effect upon him: he either rejected the things he learned or assumed an antagonistic attitude toward them. "The religious life of our youth is in an unhealthy state. This is clearly evident. That these symptoms, however, indicate that the malady is widespread, that it reaches to the very heart of our faith, we do not fully understand nor willingly acknowledge." [24]

This was in 1932. Has the situation changed in the last twenty years?

5. THE RELIGIOUS RESURGENCE IN THE POST-WORLD WAR TWO ERA

The attitude of the Jewish community of the pre-Emancipation era to the inherited religious beliefs and ideas of Judaism was one of complete and unquestioned loyalty. The internal crisis of Judaism commenced with the emergence of the Jew from the Ghetto towards the end of the eighteenth century.[25] Doubts in the validity of much in Jewish beliefs and practices were assailing the Jew from all sides. In time the Reform movement sprang up in Germany from where it spread to the other countries of the West and America. The Reform Synagogue relegated much of the ritual and ceremonial part of Judaism to the periphery of Jewish life. It declared as obsolete and unessential many of the laws and practices which for centuries controlled and regulated the daily life of the Jew. This was the first serious schism in the Jewish community since the Karaite movement in the early Middle Ages.*

In Eastern Europe where the Jewish population never received full civic liberties until after World War One, and even then not to the same extent as in the West, the Reform Synagogue never gained the same place of importance as in the West. But even here traditional Judaism was put on the defensive; and in the course of time the Jewish people residing in the lands of Eastern Europe lost its organic communal unity which it had enjoyed in the previous centuries. The Haskalah (Jewish "Enlightenment" or "Rationalism"), Zionism, and the Jewish Labour Movement, slowly, but relentlessly, were displacing Orthodox Judaism from its position of dominance in the Jewish community. However much these new movements differed among themselves in their approach to the problem of remaking Jewish life, they were united in their negative, if not outright hostile, attitude to Orthodox Judaism.[26]

Since World War Two two significant developments have taken place in the Jewish attitude to the religious problem. One of these has to do with the Synagogue. There is evidence of a relaxation of the past rigid attitude on the part of the Orthodox and Liberal

---

* Karaism—a movement whose members reject the authority of tradition and accept the authority of the Bible as the only binding rule for Jewish life.

branches of the Synagogue to Jewish religious observances. Until a few years ago Orthodoxy presented a solid front of no compromise with those groups in the Jewish community which deviated from the basic tenets of traditional Judaism. In recent years many Orthodox leaders have abandoned this uncompromising attitude and a sustained clamour for revising Jewish religious law is now being heard in the ranks of Orthodoxy itself. Judaism is suffering from centuries of stagnation,[27] and "Make Lighter Our Yoke",[28] we now hear Orthodox representatives say. This phenomenon, fraught with great importance to the future of the Jewish religion, stems from two causes. One of these is the sudden re-establishment of the State of Israel; the aspect of this problem we will discuss in the second part of this chapter. The other factor responsible for this change in the Orthodox camp is the growing recognition of Orthodox leaders in the countries of the Diaspora of their total inability to halt the drift away from Jewish religious observances. There is an increasing indifference, even among Orthodox Jews, to Jewish religious practices for which Orthodox leadership knows no solution.

The Reform Synagogue, on the other hand, displays a trend in the opposite direction. ". . . Reform Jewish theology", we are told, "must attempt to explain Judaism in terms of the Jew's—and Israel's—encounter with God in the critical present. Sinai was a crisis to which the Torah was the answer. Jamnia* was a crisis to which Rabbinic Judaism was the answer; and the crisis of the individual Jew at whatever time or place defines the situation in which he confronts God and attempts to find an answer. This very confrontation of the religious man with a metaethical God, who is not an idea or abstraction but a living Person, is the old Judaism; yet it is the new. Without God, no Judaism; without modern thought, no Reform Judaism. . . . We have learned to appreciate Torah more fully, due in part to the influence of non-Jewish scholarship."

". . . It used to be fashionable for the Reform Jews to apologize for God or for a belief in Him. Our own age has taught us a great deal about the shallow rationalism that sometimes left its imprint on religious thought. No longer does any Reform Jew advocate a godless Judaism. Faith is regaining its place again. Reform Judaism, as a part of Judaism, renews and reaffirms the abiding

---

*Jamnia (or Yabneh)—a town in Palestine where religious Judaism was reconstituted after the destruction of the Jewish Homeland in A.D. 70.

faith of our forebears. Our founders had faith in God, in providence, in Israel, in Judiasm; many of them, indeed, were God-intoxicated personalities. We must match their faith, even though our interpretations of details may not gibe with theirs."[29]

At the same time there is a new attempt to re-emphasize the importance of the law and Jewish ritual in the faith of the Jew. "There is no Judaism without Halacha" [Religious Law]—we often hear at conventions of the Reformed Synagogue. "The traditions of Israel, as expressed not only in its ethic but in its ritual, must be respected. And these again are not merely folk-ways with a 'survival' value for the practitioners; they are marks of holiness, signs of distinctiveness of an *am olam* [eternal people] that lives its own life and that dare not lose its particularity as God's people living by Torah. . . . The task of Reform is to work out not only what Torah can mean to us, but how much of it—and there is much—that we can keep as Halakah. Leo Baeck and Samuel Cohon have shown us that halakahless Judaism is not authentic."[30]

In conclusion, we must add that this renewed interest in the significance of Jewish observances is not limited to Reform Jews. It has spread also to the secular-minded Jews who are either religiously indifferent or even frank atheists. Even these Jews have come to see the survival value of the Jewish religion for the Jewish people.

The second equally important development in Jewish life in the post-World War Two era is the unmistakable evidence of a growing religious concern among the younger generation of Jews, especially the college group. The tragic events of World War Two, the shattering of all human security with the ushering in of the atomic-bomb era, the dismal failure of the teachings of humanism and liberalism to provide a solution to man's perplexing problems, these and other things combined to generate in the younger Jewish generation a genuine religious stirring.

Will Herberg who had visted a number of American universities and colleges lecturing to, and holding group discussions with, various student groups, Gentile and Jewish, had this to say: "It seems to me that the first, and perhaps basic, aspect of the outlook of the 'returning' generation is a thirst for the 'metaphysical' that marks it off distinctly from its immediate predecessors. There is a wide dissatisfaction with the naturalistic and humanistic philosophies that only yesterday were the mark of the 'modern' mind; there is a demand for something deeper, for a philosophy that takes account of the full dimensions of human existence. There is a new feeling for depth and a new sense of realism."[31]

In the various universities which he has visited Herberg met "Jewish students deeply interested in religion and ready to implement their interest in various ways. A good deal in this respect depends on the outlook and preoccupations of the Hillel director [Jewish fraternity on college campuses]. But, of course, the real problem for the Jewish student is something that transcends institutions and activities, however worthwhile. The real problem is the meaning of his Jewishness and this problem raises for the Jew of the 'younger generation' a bundle of perplexities that his elders only dimly feel and that his non-Jewish contemporaries know little of.

"The paradox in which the Jewish student of today is gripped is characterized by the fact that at the very time when his self-affirmation as a Jew has become more assured, his Jewishness has grown more problematical. He knows, accepts, and affirms that he is a Jew—but then what does it mean to be a Jew?

"This is the question that, whether they fully realized it or not, seemed to plague the thinking young Jews I met. Wherever I addressed Jewish groups, and whatever happened to be the subject on which I spoke, the talk almost always, before it had gone very far, came round to this question. Clearly my audience could no longer accept, or even understand, the matter-of-fact, pre-critical Jewishness of their immigrant forebears, compounded as that had been of traditional folkways embedded in a rich Yiddish culture. They were, socially and culturally, too thoroughly American for that. . . . It was not hard to bring the profound dilemma of contemporary Jewish existence out into the open and draw its implications. The untenability, indeed the meaninglessness, of 'secular Judaism'—that is of the attempt to understand Jewishness in wholly non-religious terms was widely acknowledged, although sometimes rather reluctantly. . . .

"Institutional religion and ritual observance appeared to constitute a particular problem for many of the Jewish students whom I met. They found it very difficult to make any correlation between their religious concern and the kind of thing they encountered in the synagogues and temples they occasionally visited. They tended to attribute this to the stultifying effects of institutionalism as such. They did not absolutely deny the necessity of institutional forms of religious expression, but I do not think I met a single Jewish student who felt quite at home with them. Kashrut [dietary laws] and the Sabbath I found to be observed little if at all, but the problem of observance did bother a great many young men and women. Why should these ancient folkways be necessary today? How can the performance or non-performance of certain otherwise meaningless acts be essential to one's religious existence as a Jew? And what acts are essential—the entire Shulhan Aruch [Religious Code], or whatever each individual may pick and choose for himself?"[32]

6. THE FAILURE OF THE SYNAGOGUE TO SATISFY THE NEW RELIGIOUS QUEST

How does the Synagogue meet the new religious awakening on the part of many of the young generation of Jews? Let us hear what these "returning" Jews have to say about this. "This new concern with Jewishness and Jewish faith leads the 'returning' generation to the synagogue, and the statistics of institutional affiliation and membership bear witness to this 'return'. They enter the synagogue with eager anticipation, especially if it is for the first time; what they find there is often such as to disconcert and dishearten them in their search for a deeper understanding of their Jewish existence. I do not want to be unfair to the present-day American synagogue. Under pressure of its environment, it is called upon to perform a thousand and one tasks of which the old-time synagogue knew nothing, and it does most of them well; but in the one task of providing a significant and creative environment for the 'returning' generation, it is failing most deplorably. ... It remains a fact that only too frequently the first contact with the synagogue since childhood on the part of these 'returning' young men and women is a deeply disillusioning experience which many of them never really get over. ... What is wrong with the contemporary synagogue from the point of view of the 'returning' generation? To put the whole case in a nutshell, it is the essential secularism, the externalism, and the ingrained mediocrity of the contemporary synagogue, Orthodox, Conservative, and Reform alike, that render it so inadequate in meeting the needs of those who come to it with high, though often vague and ill-defined anticipations. ... The religion of the present-day American synagogue is not one but many. It may be a religion of 'Jewish values'. . . . Of it may be a religion of Jewish scholarship, in which acquaintance with texts becomes the vehicle of Jewish identification. It may be a religion of Zionist nationalism or a religion of Jewish folk-culture. . . . But whichever or whatever it may be, it is equally remote from the kind of faith the 'returning' generation is seeking, a faith that will yield some glimpse of the meaning of life in its ultimate terms and some way of living on the level of really significant existence."[33]

Orthodoxy is accused of being out of touch with the needs and problems of modern life,[34] of ignoring the conflict and evading the issues of modern civilization,[35] of pursuing "a way of thought" foreign to the twentieth-century mind.[36]

"Judaism, today, and especially liberal Judaism, despite the horrors of modern totalitarianism, seems unable to recognize sin when it sees it. It does see the evil of individual wickedly-minded men (or nations), but it refuses to assign to evil its full and menacing stature. . . . At a time when Judaism is in need of a world view, its perspective is still catastrophically narrow. . . . Judaism, at the present moment, seems shy of asking the important questions for fear its answers might be inadequate."[37]

In a symposium entitled *Under Forty* Lionel Trilling, one of the participants, speaking of the Jewish religion states that "its function is to provide, chiefly for people of no strong religious impulse, a social and rational defence against the world's hostility. A laudable purpose surely, but not a sufficient basis for a religion; and one has only to have the experience of modern Judaism trying to deal with a death ritual to have the sense of its deep inner uncertainty, its lack of grasp of life which must eventually make even its rational social purpose quite abortive."[38]

In an article entitled "The Plight of the Jewish Intellectual" Leslie A. Fiedler describes the situation of the Jewish Intellectual who, in search of a living faith, seeks to turn back to Judaism:

"What does the Intellectual, fumbling his way 'back' toward a Jewish faith discover in our Jewish institutions? In the orthodox shul [house of prayer] the hassidic* fire, the old unity of devotion are moribund beneath an emphasis on Kashruth, and the endless pilpul† long since turned into a substitute for any moving faith. In the Reform Temple, the glib young Rabbi, with his tags from

---

* Hassidism—a pietist movement which originated in the eighteenth century in South-eastern Europe.
† Pilpul—the legalistic, hair-splitting method of Talmudic studies.

Freud, his sociological jargon speaks his conviction that God is a 'cosmological blur'. Like the more debased Protestant Churches, the Temples have tended to substitute 'social service' for religion, felt to belong to the unenlightened past. These conditions do not prevail universally, of course, but in general American Judaism has made everything its centre but God." And if the Jewish Intellectual actually does return to Judaism, "his 'return' has only made him more than ever aware of his aloneness".[39]

"We may still speak of ourselves," declares Rabbi Nathan A. Barack, "as a religious people. The fact is: we were; we no longer are. Many of us look back nostalgically to our religious days; our longing does not restore them. Obviously, one is religious neither by the routine observance of Jewish customs nor by the mere attendance at Friday evening services. There can be no religion without faith and feeling. We lack both elements. Any sincere intelligent layman will readily admit the fact. To open-eyed rabbis, it is a painful reality in the pursuit of their daily duties.... Today, most Jews are no longer able to pray.... Our people do not pray because they cannot. One prays to God not by addressing Him verbally. One must know in one's heart to whom he prays. We do not."[40]

Speaking of the absence of genuine spiritual experience in present-day Jewish life Nathan Glazer states: "I think I do not exaggerate when I say there is nothing in American Jewish literature—and many rabbis have written their autobiographies —that might possibly find a place in any anthology of religious experience. I once asked one of our leading authorities on American Jewish history whether he knew of any autobiography published or in manuscript, by rabbi or layman, that described in detail a spiritual or religious experience—whether a conversion or a loss of faith. He could think only of the autobiography of a Jew who had been converted to Christianity.... In the biographies of American Jews, and of rabbis too, one will find passions engaged by the problems of Zionism, by politics and reform movements, by the conflict of different organizations within Jewish life —but the category of spiritual experience, as ordinarily defined, is absent."[41]

In an article "Has Judaism Still Power to Speak?" Will Herberg states the following: "We have long prided ourselves on being universally recognized as the People of the Book. What have we done to make the Book relevant to the perplexities of our age? What has been our response in terms of creative religious thinking, theological interpretation, or prophetic witness? What word has Judaism for mankind in agony? . . . The fact is that neither the world catastrophe nor the Jewish disaster, with which it is so inseparably linked, has evoked any creative response on the part of present-day Judaism."[42]

II. THE RELIGIOUS CRISIS IN THE STATE OF ISRAEL

With the reconstitution of the new State the Israeli Jews found themselves over night, as it were, citizens of a State for whose internal and external security and daily maintenance they became directly and solely responsible. For the first time in more than two thousand years Jews have had to assume the duties of citizens of their own State.

The reconstitution of the State of Israel has added a new and unexpected turn to the religious crisis of Judaism. The reason for this lies in the abiding Jewish belief in the essential and inseparable unity between the God of Israel, the people of Israel and the Land of Israel. Consequently, from the very beginning of the existence of this State the Jewish community in the State of Israel was faced with the question of the relationship between the Jewish religion and the Jewish State. To understand the true nature of this problem two factors must be clear in our mind. First, that the Jewish religion is a legalistic religion, designed to regulate the whole of the daily life of the Jew; second, that many of the observances which constitute the heart and foundation of the Jewish religion are incompatible with conditions of modern life. As long as the Jews lived behind Ghetto walls, shut off from the Gentile environment, and deprived of the normal duties and privileges of citizenship, observance of the many laws and commandments of the Jewish religion posed no problem. The difficulty began when political emancipation came toward the end of the eighteenth century. Many Jews for the first time became aware that it is impossible for them to live the life of normal citizens and at the same time to comply with the requirements of their religion. It was a matter of choosing one or the other way of life. The great majority gradually gave up the Jewish traditional way of life.

But the Jew, especially the religious Jew, never anticipated the probability of a similar conflict between his religion and modern life in the country of his forefathers. The re-emergence of the State confronted religious Jewry in the State of Israel with the fateful question: "Is the State of Israel merely a State where Jews happen to constitute the majority of the population, or is it the continuation of the Jewish State which existed prior to its destruction by the Romans in A.D. 70?" The answer of the vast majority of religious Jewry in Israel was that this State of Israel is the continuation of the Jewish State which existed prior to A.D. 70. The conclusion which Orthodoxy drew from this answer was that the Law of Moses which was the law of the Land prior to A.D. 70 must be the law of the Land now. The difficulty began when the question arose how to apply the Law of Moses in everyday life in this day and age. While the draft constitution of the State of Israel guarantees to· each person full religious freedom the "Religious Block" made up of certain religious parties voting as a unit in the Parliament, has succeeded in promulgating certain laws designed to impose on the country a way of life in harmony with the tenets of traditional Judaism. Such a policy is in step with the spirit of traditional Judaism which recognizes no separation or division between religion and the State. It is this factor, however, which has served to focus the attention of the State and its people on the religious problem, and make all Jews, both in Israel and in the Diaspora, acutely conscious of the basic conflict that exists between Judaism and modern life. Let us see how this policy is working out in everyday life.

I.   RELIGIOUS FREEDOM IN THE STATE OF ISRAEL

The State of Israel not only affirms the sanctity of life and the dignity of man, but guarantees freedom of individual conscience and full religious liberty. However, from the very inception of the State the "Religious Block", though representing a minority of the Jews in the country, has forced upon the country a number of religious laws which violate the very principle of freedom of conscience on which the state is founded. No non-Orthodox Rabbi has the legal right to officiate in the State of Israel. This means that any Jew, religious or not, wishing to avail himself of the services of a Rabbi in an official capacity must use the services of an Orthodox Rabbi. This infringement on individual liberty exists also in other spheres of life.

2. THE PROBLEM OF THE DIETARY LAWS

The dietary laws form an important part of Jewish religious life. For meat to be kosher it must come from a ritually clean animal, and the animal must be slaughtered in accordance with Rabbinic rules, and no flaws must be found in the slaughtered animal. Should some mishap take place in the process of the slaughtering, or a flaw found in the slaughtered animal, that animal is declared unfit for Jewish consumption. These factors serve to make kosher meat expensive. To make things worse the Orthodox group prevailed on the Government to forbid the importation of non-kosher meat. The Jew, therefore, in the State of Israel, if he wants to be a law-abiding citizen, must eat kosher meat at a high price or no meat at all.

Isaiah Leibowitz, lecturer in organic chemistry at the Hebrew University at Jerusalem and a religious Jew, relates an interesting incident pointing out Orthodox failings in the matter of kosher meat. When the siege of Jewish Jerusalem by the Arabs had begun there was a small supply of kosher food in the beleaguered city and a large stock of canned pork left by the British military authorities when the British garrison had evacuated Jerusalem. The Command of the Jewish Forces defending the city had planned to use first the kosher meat as long as it lasted, and later to utilize the canned pork food. But the Chief Rabbi of Jerusalem had besought the Israel Command to feed the kosher meat only to the "religious" soldiers and the pork to all other Jewish soldiers. When the Chief Rabbinate of Palestine was asked for a clarification of this matter it gave the impression of disassociating itself from the position taken by the Jerusalem Chief Rabbi, but it rendered no decision of how the Army Command should act. The plan suggested by the Jerusalem Chief Rabbi remained in force. The men in the army were divided up into "religious" and "non-religious"; the "non-religious" received pork in their rations, while the "religious" were eating kosher meat. Needless to say that this procedure aroused widespread resentment.[43]

3. THE MARRIAGE AND DIVORCE LAWS

In the State of Israel the administration of the laws dealing with marriage and divorce is under the jurisdiction of the Orthodox

Rabbinate. Intermarriages between Jews and Gentiles are forbidden. Even non-religious Jews who might prefer a civil marriage must submit to a religious ceremony performed by an Orthodox Rabbi.

Of special importance is the position of the Agunah, i.e. the deserted wife whose husband refuses to divorce her. Such a woman may not remarry unless the husband can be prevailed upon to grant her a divorce. The wife of a missing husband belongs in the same category. There are many women whose husbands were taken to the concentration camps in Germany and have never been heard of since. If their wives are unable to present clear evidence of their death they cannot remarry. A wife whose husband is insane cannot be divorced. So far, the Rabbinate has done nothing to modify the Rabbinic marriage and divorce rules in order to free the Jewish woman from these disabilities and hardships.

It should be noted that the Rabbinic marriage and divorce laws reflect the generally low status of the woman in Rabbinic Judaism. The Jewish male recites daily a prayer in which he thanks God for not having been created a woman, while the woman thanks God for having created her according to His Will. The "Religious Block" in the State of Israel did all in its power to prevent woman suffrage, but in 1951 the Israel Parliament overruled it and passed a bill granting women equal rights with men.

4. SABBATH OBSERVANCE

The Sabbath, i.e. the seventh day of the week, is the legal rest day in the State of Israel. Centuries of Rabbinic teachings have added considerably to the already stringent Biblical laws with reference to the observance of the Sabbath. Thus a Jew may not purchase things on the Sabbath, and he must not even touch money. He may not tear a piece of paper or write on paper. He cannot ride on the Sabbath. He may not carry any objects on the Sabbath.

In the Diaspora, especially under the conditions which prevailed in the days before the political emancipation, it was actually possible to practice Sabbath observance as prescribed by Rabbinic teachings. In part at least, the observance of the Sabbath was made possible by the utilization of the services of Gentile help which used to perform a number of domestic chores for the Jew, such as extinguishing the candles on Friday night, or starting the fire on Sabbath morning.

It is different, however, in the State of Israel where the Jews themselves must perform daily all those functions necessary for the maintenance of the State. Nothing has served to reveal the incompatibility between traditional Judaism and the State as the question of Sabbath observance in the State of Israel. The "Religious Block" recognizes the necessity of an uninterrupted supply of electric current in the State. It sanctions the use on the Sabbath day of certain mechanical devices which automatically turn on the electric-current supply. It is permissible for the Orthodox Jew to use electricity on the Sabbath in spite of the fact that other, non-Orthodox, Jews manufacture it.

An Orthodox Jew may not work on the Sabbath on the water-pumping station, but he may use tap water which is made available to him because the non-Orthodox Jew is operating the water-pumping station. The Orthodox Jew may work in the Police Force, but he must not work on the Sabbath day. Incidentally, not until the reconstitution of the State of Israel has religious Judaism taken the attitude that it is permissible for one group of Jews to break Jewish religious law while another group of Jews must observe it. Commenting on this strange behaviour of Orthodox Judaism in the State of Israel, Isaiah Leibowitz, already referred to above, states: "Here we have an example of parasitism elevated to the degree of a religious principle."[44]

There is the story of an Orthodox wireless operator working in a government department maintaining a twenty-four-hour communication service with the outside world. He sought Rabbinical dispensation to perform his duties on the Sabbath day. He found a Rabbi who granted him this dispensation but under the following conditions: he was instructed "to reverse his usual procedures, tapping out messages with his left hand instead of his week-day right, and transcribing them with Latin letters instead of the usual Hebrew."[45]

One of the highest religious authorities in the State of Israel was once questioned whether the electricity stations in Israel should cease operations on the Sabbath. He answered in the negative but added that "it is preferable that this work on the Sabbath should be performed by a non-Orthodox Jew". In his discussion of this attitude of the religious leaders in Israel Louis

I. Rabinowitz states: "I challenge the authors of that aberration from Judaism to point to one single instance in the whole of Jewish law suggesting that the Torah is not the heritage of 'the congregation of Israel', which applies to one Jew and not to another. Either something is permitted by Jewish law, in which case it is permitted to all Jews, or forbidden, in which case it is forbidden to all Jews."[46]

We are told that soon after the State of Israel came into existence an unofficial Orthodox committee approached the Israel Rabbinate recommending that it "sanction the performance of a limited number of essential public services on the Sabbath. The Rabbinate received the committee's recommendations, took fright, and shelved them precipitately—it was safer to behave as if no such problems existed."[47]

5. THE BEHAVIOUR OF ORTHODOXY DURING THE SIEGE OF JERUSALEM

When Jerusalem was besieged by the Arabs during the Arab-Jewish War, the entire population of Jewish Jerusalem participated in the defence of the city except the students of the Orthodox religious schools. The religious leaders prevailed on the Government to exempt the students of their schools from military service. Following one night bombardment fifty-five men, women and children were killed. The bodies of the dead were laid out in the courtyard of the Bikkur Cholim Hospital of Jerusalem. A request was addressed to the heads of the religious schools in the embattled city to instruct their students to stand watch over the dead bodies and to take care of their burial. This request was turned down on the ground that these Talmudical students are dedicated to the study of the Torah and, therefore, no other duties should be imposed on them. Dr. Leibowitz, in relating this incident, states that "the blood that was shed in the defence of Jerusalem stands today between that group and the people of Israel", the group of those "who demanded that other Jews die for them".[48]

6. EXEMPTION OF "RELIGIOUS" WOMEN FROM MILITARY SERVICE

With the consent of the majority of the Israel Parliament the government several years ago introduced a bill imposing on women the duty of military service. The religious parties in the

Parliament opposed the bill on the plea that this would be against the Torah principles of chastity as it might lead to immorality. When the government agreed to modify the bill by an amendment exempting "religious" women from the law the Orthodox members of the Parliament threw their support behind the bill. An incident is related of a girl who claimed exemption from military service on the ground of religious convictions and was found one day, on the Sabbath, working in a non-kosher restaurant. When she was hailed before a magistrate "the defence called an 'expert' witness on behalf of the Rabbinate, who declared that profanation of the Sabbath and the eating of non-kosher food did not invalidate the girl's right to claim exemption from military service on religious grounds."[49] Thus religious Jewry in Israel is perfectly satisfied to have other Jews send their daughters to the army even though from the Orthodox point of view this is dishonourable, as long as "religious" daughters are exempt from such service.

III. THE SPIRITUAL DILEMMA OF THE STATE OF ISRAEL

1. THE SPIRITUAL VACUUM

The founders of political Zionism were steeped in Western ideology. They have inherited the Western concept of religious liberty and separation of religion and state. Dr. Herzl, the father of modern Zionism, defined in his book *The Jewish State* the Zionist attitude to religion. "We shall keep our priests within the confines of their temples in the same way as we shall keep our professional army within the confines of their barracks."[50] Zionism, therefore, assumed from the very beginning a neutral attitude to religion. It believed that the Jewish problem will never be solved until the Jewish people will have become restored politically to the land of their ancestors. To achieve this goal Zionism sought to rally under its banner all Jews, irrespective of their religious beliefs. The young pioneers who answered the call of Zionism were secularized Jews. They were indifferent, if not actually antagonistic, to traditional Judaism, and hostile to the social injustice and economic inequality which existed in Eastern Europe from where most of them hailed. The ideals which inspired them to leave their homes and which sustained them under the most trying and heart-breaking conditions in the new land were the following: (1) To rebuild the country with a view to re-establishing the Jewish State; (2) the ingathering of the exiles, i.e. to create conditions in the country which would make it possible for every Jew, if he wished to do so, to settle in Palestine; (3) to develop a new economic and social life based on social justice and economic equality.

The rebuilding of the country, and the establishment of the State of Israel have brought fulfilment of all the above goals of Zionism. It is this realization of the hopes and aspirations of Zionism which has created a spiritual vacuum in the lives of many of the people of Israel. They are now discovering the existence of problems which Zionism or the State cannot solve, problems which belong in the realm of the spiritual. This is one of the elements in Israel's spiritual dilemma.

2. THE FAILURE OF RELIGIOUS JUDAISM TO MEET ISRAEL'S SPIRITUAL NEEDS

The fulfilment of Zionism's goals has left a spiritual void in the hearts of many young Israelis. Those who have a first-hand knowledge of Israel speak of the existence of a real yearning among many of the young Israeli for something with which to fill this void. We are told that this spiritual yearning is at the bottom of an increased interest on the part of some Israeli in the spiritual message of Christ.[51]

Symptomatic of this spiritual hunger are the various experiments aiming to find some satisfying form of religious expression. Thus we are told that in the agricultural settlement of Ramat Rachel a room was set aside for religious devotion. The room is empty except for a light suspended from the ceiling and a table in the centre containing a laver of water and bread. The water and bread are supposed to symbolize "the shew-bread" in the Temple. In this room members of the settlement gather for religious devotion consisting of silent meditation and the reading of a Psalm. Similar experiments—we are told—are being conducted in other places in Israel.[52]

Notwithstanding all this groping and searching for some spiritual foundation of life there is a growing estrangement of Israeli Jewry from the Synagogue. Large crowds of Israeli Jews walk the streets on Sabbath morning instead of going to the Synagogue. This, because, as one Israeli farmer said, they hear nothing in the synagogues that deals with the heart of their problems. As a matter of fact what young Israelis know of the Synagogue serves to repel them from it. To Rabbi Herbert Weiner who interviewed David Ben Gurion on the possibility of establishing in Israel a Liberal Synagogue, Ben Gurion made the following statement: "We need to have liberal Judaism in Israel. The state needs it for the sake of religious freedom and freedom of conscience. Come and set up a liberal synagogue. Let the youth here see something else besides them [i.e. Orthodox politicians] ... I tell you, I know them. Most of them don't have God in their hearts."[53]

Visitors to Israel are quick to sense a widespread and deep resentment on the part of the rank and file of the population against the Orthodox minority. "The Orthodox politicians," they say, "make our life miserable. They make our cafés close on Friday night, the movies on Saturday, and stop the inter-urban buses from running."[54] The Israeli attitude to Orthodox Judaism in Israel is well expressed in a passage from the writings of the Israeli poet Yitzhak Lamdan: "It is not a parodox to say that if there are enemies of religion in Israel, enemies of faith and of the lofty values of Torah, then these enemies are primarily the official leaders of our religion, and through their insensitivity, bad manners, and hypocritical tactics, and through their limited vision and striving for power, a striving which does not bother about means, they are the ones who more than any others drive away the younger generation."[55]

3. THE LINK BETWEEN RELIGION AND THE STATE

Probably the most important single element in the present spiritual crisis of Israel is the link between the State and organized religion fostered upon the State by the politicians of the minority "Religious Block" in the Israeli Parliament. The Israeli political scene with its multiple party system has so far made it practically impossible for any one party to win a clear working majority in the Parliament. Consequently, the government is not a single party government as for example in the United States and, normally, in England, but a coalition government composed of representatives of two or more of the major parties. This system affords the various political parties opportunities to gain concessions for their particular projects in exchange for their support of the coalition government.

It is in this way that the minority "Religious Block" composed of Orthodox Jews has carved out for itself a most privileged position and imposed on the non-Orthodox majority of the people of Israel a set of laws which are having a far-reaching effect. Thus the laws governing marriage, divorce, burial and inheritance have been placed under the jurisdiction of the Religious Courts. This development has created a most unusual situation. A case in point is the status of the Jewish women. For centuries the outmoded Rabbinic laws have kept the Jewish woman in the legal status of a minor. The Emancipation ushered in at the end of the eighteenth century, by granting the Jews civic and political equality, made the Jew, together with all other citizens, subject to the laws of the land. This freed the Jewish woman from the disabilities which she suffered under Jewish religious law. The link between the State and Religion in Israel placed the Jewish woman in Israel in much the same position in relation to the Jewish male in which she had been in the pre-Emancipation era. Will the Israeli women who enjoyed equal right with men before 1948, or will the Jewish women from the democratic West who may choose to settle in Israel, tolerate being placed in this inferior position?

There is yet another more general aspect to this problem. Since Judaism makes no definite or real distinction between the religious or believing and the non-religious or non-believing Jew, all Jewish citizens of Israel are required by law to submit to the authority of the Religious Courts in matters of marriage, divorce, burial, inheritance, etc. In the case of the Jew who is an atheist, an agnostic, or just un-Orthodox, this enforced practice is clearly a violation of the principle of freedom of conscience or religious liberty. Thus many in and out of Israel have come to believe that there is no full religious liberty in the State of Israel.

But this political victory of Israeli Orthodoxy bears the seeds of its own defeat. Orthodoxy itself is experiencing in Israel its most serious spiritual crisis. To convert Israel into a theocracy regulated along the lines of the Law of Moses is the ideal to which Orthodoxy aspires. But at the same time it is convinced that a modern State could not possibly be organized according to the Mosaic theocracy. An example in point is the question of Sabbath observance. The Law of Moses forbids all sorts of work on the Sabbath day. In the State of Israel many of the essential services, such as electricity, the water supply, the armed services, the police, and others are functioning on the Sabbath just the same as on any other day. While it realizes that the performance of these functions, so essential to the life of the State, is an infringement upon the Mosaic Law, Orthodoxy nevertheless avails itself of these services on the Sabbath day. While it refuses to sanction the work which makes the uninterrupted supply of these services on the Sabbath day possible it would not advocate the stoppage of this work on the Sabbath. However, it advises its Orthodox followers not to work on the Sabbath and to leave the operation of these essential services to the non-Orthodox Jews. This policy has exposed the weakness and inconsistencies of Jewish Orthodoxy in Israel and it exhibits its essential inability to cope with the daily realities of modern life. What little sympathy the Israeli Jews may have harboured for Orthodox Judaism is fast giving way to bitter contempt.

In the State of Israel there are at present (1957) 204,935 non-Jewish citizens. Most of them are Arabs, some of whom profess a form of Christianity, others the Moslem faith. In the whole 3,500 years of the history of the Jewish nation this is the first time that an independent Jewish State has within its borders a sizeable non-Jewish group. It is the presence of this group which highlights the spiritual crisis of Israel. To be sure there was a group of non-Jews in Palestine in the days of the Second Commonwealth, the so-called Samaritans who lived in the Samaria region of Palestine. They were brought into Palestine by the conquerors of the First Jewish Commonwealth to occupy the empty spaces created by the removal of the native Jewish population into the countries of the conquerors. These Samaritans in due time accepted the religion of Israel in a modified form. When the exiles returned from Babylon and began to rebuild the Temple the Samaritans offered their help. Apparently they wished to merge religiously with the Jewish people. But under the influence of Ezra they were rebuffed and rejected and relations between the two groups became strained and remained so throughout the days of the Second Commonwealth. It should be noted that with the exception of a brief period during the Maccabean era the Jews had no independent political life in Palestine during the Second Commonwealth. How the Jews would have solved the Samaritan problem had they been politically independent throughout the existence of the Second Commonwealth is somewhat uncertain.

It is unthinkable that they would have tolerated indefinitely a foreign group in their midst. One can safely say that, in accordance with the spirit of that particular era, the Samaritans would have gradually become absorbed by the Jews.

The situation in this respect is radically different in the modern State of Israel. The Arabs living within its borders are Israeli citizens and enjoy the same civic and political rights as the Israeli citizens of Jewish origin. In fact, economically, and even politically, they fare better than their brethren in the Arab countries. And yet there is a difference in the political or civic status of the Israeli citizens of the Jewish majority and the Israeli citizens of the Arab minority. This difference is rooted in the social concept of religious, especially Orthodox, Judaism, and it is being aggravated, intensified, and perpetuated by the link between the State and religious Judaism of the Orthodox variety. When the Jewish community in Palestine became an independent State in 1948 it had adopted "Israel" as the name of the reborn Jewish State. "Israel" is the national name of the State and the national name of all of its citizens, irrespective of their racial or religious character. A Gentile, whatever his religion may be, living in the State of Israel is an Israeli citizen in the same sense as a Jew residing in the State of Israel.

But the State of Israel is also a Jewish State. The basic laws adopted by the State have made the weekly Sabbath and the Jewish holidays days of rest for the whole population. But these legal holidays have a religio-national connotation for the Israeli citizens of the Jewish majority of the State of Israel. They have no such connotation for the non-Jewish minority group of Israeli citizens. In this respect the Israeli non-Jews are in a similar position as, for example, the Jewish citizens residing in the lands of Christendom, who are made to observe Sunday and the other Christian holidays as legal days of rest. But here is where the similarity ends. In the State of Israel there is a set of laws applicable only to the Israeli citizens of the Jewish majority. We refer to the laws of marriage, divorce, burial, inheritance, etc. which are the direct outgrowth of the link between the State and Orthodox Judaism. This union between the State and Orthodox Judaism distinguishes between two classes of Israeli citizens, those of the Jewish majority, and those of the non-Jewish minority. It has created a civic or political barrier between the two groups of citizens. All the efforts and strivings of the State to establish the non-Jewish Israeli citizens on an equal basis with their Jewish fellow-citizens will fail as long as the law of the land sanctions the existence of a double standard or status of Israeli citizenship. Under these existing conditions there is no room in the State of Israel for the Western concept of full equality before the law for all its citizens. Nor is it possible under the present circumstances to achieve in Israel "the kind of unity that would make for a Western democracy".[56]

To the Israeli Jew it appears that he has been thrown back to the pre-emancipation era of Jewish history when every Jew was a member of the Jewish community organized on a religious foundation and sanctioned by the law of the land. To the core of the surviving pioneer idealists who had gone to Palestine to remake Jewish life and to lay the groundwork for a new human society based on equality and justice, and to the young Israeli, who were trained in the principles of Western, especially American, democracy, "this turn of events was little short of tragic".[57] Prior to the establishment of the State of Israel the young pioneers, and then their children, were led to believe that to be a Jew meant to be a citizen of a Jewish State. Now they are discovering that being a Jew is not identical with being a citizen of a Jewish State, but it is a certain religious pattern of life which they, as Jews, are compelled to follow. Consequently they feel that they have been misled, deceived or betrayed. No wonder that they feel bitter not only about the minority of Orthodox politicians but also about Zionist leaders in Israel who helped the Orthodox bring about this state of affairs.

The situation is bad and fraught with great forebodings. To the better kind of Orthodox Jews in Israel the way out of this dilemma is to separate religion from the State, being persuaded that if the Israeli Jews are ever to be won back to Judaism, it will have to be done by persuasion rather than by coertion. This is said to be the hope of such outstanding Israeli Jews as Martin Buber, and Ernst Simon whose article "Are We Israeli Still Jews?" has evoked considerable interest in Israel.[58] To the question posed by Professor Simon in this article many of the Israeli Jews would unhesitatingly answer: "Of course we are not Jews!" The word Jew to them has a religious connotation only, and many of them do not profess Judaism. They are therefore determined to effect a complete separation between the two concepts, "Israeli" and "Jew", leaving the first of the two to apply to all citizens of the State of Israel, and the second to designate those, and only those, who of their own free will adhere to religious Judaism. The word "Jew" would then assume the meaning of religious or denominational affiliation. An "Israeli" would then correspond to "American", "British" or "German", while "Jew" would be equivalent to "Protestant", "Catholic" or "Moslem".

This trend among the Israeli Jews to a break with traditional Judaism is of increasing concern to the Jews outside of Israel. The most exaggerated, and probably distorted, expression of this tendency is represented by the so-called "Canaanites", a group of young Israelis who consider themselves as Hebrews but not Jews. This group considers Israeli Jews as having no connection with the Jews outside of Israel. They issue a publication named *Aleph* (the first letter of the Hebrew alphabet) which reflects the teachings of the group advocating a fresh start from the beginning by discarding the entire heritage of traditional Judaism of the last two thousand years.

Apart from the eccentric ideas of this group their attitude to the Jewish past is representative of the thinking of the majority of the young Israeli Jews. The reaction of the Jews outside of Israel to this Israeli trend may be seen from the following expressions:

"They [the younger generation] turn up their noses at everything that bears a Jewish label: Jewish prayer, Jewish customs, the Jewish Sabbath, Jewish charm, quotations from Yiddish literature, Jewish clothes."[59]

"There are today in Palestine several kinds of youth groups that desire to create a conscious separation between the old 'Jew' and the new 'Hebrew'."[60]

"Israel's greatest spiritual danger is that of a real break with the past while exhibiting a spurious re-established contact with it."[61] "This sundering from Diaspora Jewry, this severance of life-transmitting connections, is a pervasive thing . . . it is characteristic of Israel as a whole."[62]

Finally the following deeply significant observation: "What would be the effect on Jewish life in America of an Israel that would proclaim to Jews and all the world that the Jewish religion was irrelevant and outmoded? For wasn't this the meaning of what was going on in Israel? How long could the bustle of organization and the large membership lists of synagogues in America disguise the knowledge that at the centre of it all was a religion that was not meeting one of its greatest tests?"[63]

NOTES TO CHAPTER 3

1. L. Hersch, "The Downward Trend of Jewish Population", article in *Commentary* (New York), February 1949.
2. Samuel Dresner, "A Rabbi Looks at Jewish Leadership", article in *The Jewish Spectator* (New York), June 1953.
3. See Fritz A. Rothschild, "Conservative Judaism Faces the Need of Change", article in *Commentary* (New York), November 1953.
4. T. W. Rosmarin, "Converting Jews to Judaism", article in *The Jewish Spectator* (New York), March 1950.
5. Samuel Dresner, idem.
6. Will Herberg, "The Post-war Revival of the Synagogue", article in *Commentary* (New York), April 1950.
7. Ibid.
8. Emil L. Fackenheim, "The Modern Jew's Path to God", article in *Commentary* (New York), May 1950.
9. Louis Feinberg, "An Analysis of the Business of Judaism", article in *The Jewish Spectator* (New York), September 1948.
10. *Zionist Review*, London; see *The Jewish Spectator* (New York), November 1948.
11. Joseph Zeitlin, *Disciples of the Wise* (Teachers' College, Columbia University: New York, Second Printing, 1947), pp. 76–81.
12. "Returned Chaplain", "Why I Gave Up My Congregation", article in *Commentary* (New York), March 1948.
13. Irving Kristol, "How Basic is 'Basic Judaism'?", article in *Commentary* (New York), January 1948.
14. Quoted by Fritz A. Rothschild, idem.
15. See T. W. Rosmarin, "Perplexed Rabbis", article in *The Jewish Spectator* (New York), July–August 1949.
16. Will Herberg, idem.
17. T. W. Rosmarin, "Credits and Debits", article in *The Jewish Spectator* (New York), November 1946.
18. Ibid.
19. Will Herberg, idem.
20. Heinrich Graetz, "The Significance of Judaism for the Present and the Future", a lecture delivered at the Anglo-Jewish Historical Exhibition in 1887; quoted in *Contemporary Jewish Record* (New York), February 1943.
21. I. Jakobovits, "Judaism for the Twentieth Century", article in *The Jewish Spectator* (New York), December 1947.
22. Joseph Judis, "Is the Bible Relevant to Our Day?", article in *The Jewish Spectator* (New York), October 1953.

23. Barnet Litvinoff, "Britain's Jewish Intellectuals Look Ahead", article in *Commentary* (New York), May 1952.

24. Marvin Nathan, *The Attitude of the Jewish Student in the Colleges and Universities towards his Religion* (Bloch Publishing Company: New York, 1932), p. 10.

25. Eliezer Berkovits, "The Challenge of Destiny", article in *The Jewish Spectator* (New York), June 1952.

26. Herbert Parzen, "When Secularism came to Russian Jewry", article in *Commentary* (New York), April 1952.

27. See Jospeh Porton, Leeds, England, "Needed: Some Reforms", article in *The Jewish Spectator* (New York), January 1953.

28. T. W. Rosmarin, "Make Lighter Our Yoke", article in *The Jewish Spectator* (New York), June 1953.

29. Felix A. Levy, "Reform Judaism in America: Its Problems and Tasks", article in *Judaism* (New York), October 1952.

30. Ibid.

31. Will Herberg, "Religious Trends in American Jewry", article in *Judaism* (New York), Summer 1954.

32. Will Herberg, "The Religious Stirring on the Campus", article in *Commentary* (New York), March 1952.

33. Will Herberg, "Religious Trends in American Jewry", article in *Judaism* (New York), Summer 1954.

34. Will Herberg, "Rosenzweig's 'Judaism of Personal Existence'", article in *Commentary* (New York), December 1950.

35. Eliezer Berkovits, idem.

36. Fritz A. Rothschild, idem.

37. Irving Kristol, idem.

38. Lionel Trilling, "Under Forty—A Symposium on American Literature and the Younger Generation of American Jews", article in *Contemporary Jewish Record* (now *Commentary*), February 1944.

39. Leslie A. Fiedler, "The Plight of the Jewish Intellectual", article in *Congress Weekly* (New York), April 9, 1951.

40. Bernard Heller, "War and the Spirit of Israel", article in *Contemporary Jewish Record* (now *Commentary*), August 1942.

41. Nathan Glazer, "The Jewish Revival in America": II, article in *Commentary* (New York), January 1956.

42. Will Herberg, "Has Judaism Still Power to Speak?", article in *Commentary* (New York), May 1949.

43. Isaiah Leibowitz, "Religion versus State", article in *The Jewish Spectator* (New York), November 1953.

44. Ibid.

45. Judd L. Teller, "Religious Modernism Stirs in Israel", article in *Commentary* (New York), June 1953.

46. Louis I. Rabinowitz, "Problems of Halacha in Israel", article in *The Jewish Spectator* (New York), September 1953.

47. Judd L. Teller, idem.

48. Isaiah Leibowitz, idem.

49. Ibid.

50. Theodor Herzl, *The Jewish State*, English Translation, published by the American Zionist Emergency Council (New York), 1946, p. 146.

51. Herbert Weiner, "The Liberal Religious Impulse in Israel", article in *Commentary* (New York), July 1955.

52. Idem.

53. Quoted by Herbert Weiner, "The Liberal Religious Impulse in Israel": II, article in *Commentary* (New York), August 1955.

54. Judd L. Teller, idem.

55. Quoted by Herbert Weiner, "The Liberal Religious Impulse in Israel", article in *Commentary* (New York), July 1955.

56. Robert L. Lindsey, "Israel's Coming Crisis Over 'Jewishness'", article in *Commentary* (New York), July 1954.

57. Ibid.

58. Published in *Commentary* (New York), April 1953.

59. Quoted by Judd L. Teller, idem.

60. Ernst Simon, "Tomorrow's Jew in the Making", article in *Commentary* (New York), July 1948.

61. Maurice Samuel, "Why Israel Misunderstands American Jewry", article in *Commentary* (New York), October 1953.

62. Maurice Samuel, "The Sundering of Israel and American Jewry", article in *Commentary* (New York), September 1953.

63. Herbert Weiner, "The Liberal Religious Impulse in Israel": II, article in *Commentary* (New York), August 1955.

THE STATE OF ISRAEL AND
THE JEWISH RELIGIOUS CRISIS

(*Continued*)

IV. THE CAUSE OF THE RELIGIOUS CRISIS

    1. THE ELEMENT OF UNREALITY AND IRRELEVANCE

    2. THE INHERENT WEAKNESS OF LIBERAL JUDAISM

    3. THE COMMUNAL CHARACTER OF RELIGIOUS JUDAISM

    4. THE TALMUD AND THE RELIGIOUS CRISIS

    5. THE INTERIM OR TRANSIENT CHARACTER OF THE RELIGION OF TRADITIONAL JUDAISM

V. SUGGESTED SOLUTIONS

    1. A REVIVAL OF JEWISH RELIGIOUS OBSERVANCES

    2. REBUILDING JUDAISM ON THE FOUNDATION OF THE "JEWISH HERITAGE"

    3. PERSONAL RELIGION

    4. RELIGIOUS EDUCATION

    5. REINTERPRETATION OF THE RELIGIOUS CODE

    6. ENACTMENT OF NEW LAWS BASED ON THE PRINCIPLES OF TRADITIONAL LAW

    7. BY-PASSING THE EXISTING RELIGIOUS CODE OF TRADITIONAL JUDAISM

VI. THE PROPHETIC ASPECT OF THE JEWISH RELIGIOUS CRISIS

    1. THE RELIGIOUS CRISIS BEGAN IN THE YEAR A.D. 70

    2. JUDAISM PROVIDED AN "AS IF" SOLUTION

    3. FACTORS WHICH MADE THE "AS IF" SOLUTION OF A.D. 70 POSSIBLE

        a. Jewish faith in the Covenant remained unimpaired

        b. The ascendancy of Rabbinism

        c. The displacement of the Bible

        d. The hostility of the Gentile world

    4. THE COLLAPSE OF THE "AS IF" SOLUTION

    5. THE PROPHETIC SIGNIFICANCE OF THE RELIGIOUS CRISIS

        a. The prediction of Jewish religious neutrality

        b. The promise of a new revelation from God

        c. Not another Sinai revelation

        d. "And they shall teach no more . . ."

        e. "For I will forgive their iniquity . . ."

CHAPTER 4

THE STATE OF ISRAEL AND
THE JEWISH RELIGIOUS CRISIS

(Continued)

IV. THE CAUSE OF THE RELIGIOUS CRISIS

One of the lessons of Jewish history is that whenever the Jewish people had been abruptly thrust into contact with the nations of the world the Jewish religion was thereby profoundly affected. This was so in the era of the Babylonian exile in the sixth century B.C.; in the encounter with Hellenism in the second century B.C.; following the destruction of the Jewish Commonwealth in the year A.D. 70; on a smaller scale during the rise of Mohammedanism; and, lastly, in the wake of the Political Emancipation which began in Western Europe some 160 years ago and which has given birth to the present religious crisis.

Jewish investigators of the Jewish religious problem have been wont to regard the religious crisis of the Jews as part of a general decline in religious interest which began towards the end of the eighteenth century. This coincided with the advent of a new era when science and industrial progress were beginning to make rapid gains and life was becoming increasingly secularized. It was beginning to appear to many that man was going to be able to settle this world's problems and that religion was definitely on the way out. Then came World War One with its destruction and political upheavals, and the belief in man's self-sufficiency received a severe jolt. The events of the 1930's and, finally, World War Two brought complete disillusionment and loss of faith in man's ability to solve the basic problems of human life. "The real problem", says Professor Einstein, "is in the hearts and minds of men. It is not a problem of physics, but of ethics. It is easier to denature plutonium than to denature the evil spirit of man. What frightens us is not the explosive power of the atom bomb, but the equally explosive power of human personalities.

Man's skills have outstripped his morals. His engineering has leaped ahead of his wisdom. We cannot cancel or call back his scientific advance, but we can and must, if the world is to survive, help man to catch up. In God's name, if you still believe in God . . . we must somehow get control of what science has given the world, or else we shall likewise perish."[1]

As a result of the shattering and tragic events of the two World Wars there began a definite revival of religious interest in the Christian world. "In the past generation, Christian theology has made an impressive effort to rise to its proper task—which is to interpret life and history, man and the universe, in ultimate terms. Without rejecting the insights gained on other levels of analysis, it has striven to include and transcend them, to fuse them into a single *Weltanshauung* [world view] that can serve at once as the ultimate logic and dynamic of life.

"But what about Jewish theology? We have long prided ourselves on being universally recognised as the People of the Book. What have we done to make the Book relevant to the perplexities of our age? What has been our response in terms of creative religious thinking, theological interpretation, or prophetic witness? What word has Judaism had for mankind in agony? . . .

"The fact is that neither the world catastrophe nor the Jewish disaster, with which it is so inseparably linked, has evoked any creative response on the part of present-day Judaism."[2]

Over the years the present religious crisis has become something like a chronic disease: incurable but not threatening the patient's life. The Jews became reconciled and more or less indifferent to it. However, the destruction of a third of the nation in World War Two has greatly increased Jewish concern for Jewish survival. The important part which the Jewish religion had played in the past in assuring the survival of the Jews turned the attention of many Jews once more in the direction of the religious problem. But it was the sudden emergence of the State of Israel which has made many Jews, both in and outside of the State of Israel, painfully aware of the existence of a Jewish religious problem. Consequently, a more intensive search has begun for the cause of the trouble, and the investigation is now concentrated on the nature and essence of Judaism as the possible seat of the difficulty. A perusal of Jewish writings on the subject brings out the following factors as having an important bearing on the cause or causes of the Jewish religious crisis.

1. THE ELEMENT OF UNREALITY AND IRRELEVANCE IN
TRADITIONAL JUDAISM

In an article published in *Commentary* of January 1953 Dr. Hans Joachim Schoeps analyses the Jewish religious crisis and makes the following observations: "We Jews of the mid-twentieth century live today in what might be called a post-Jewish situation. That is to say, the reality of each day's living is such that it is no longer possible for most of us to experience our Jewishness simply and directly. This is true for both America and Europe—it may even apply to the secular State of Israel—and must be fully appreciated by anyone who hopes to say something about the present situation of Judaism that will be to the point.

"It is time for us to renounce all fictions of the 'as if' kind. We cannot act as if we were still living in the ghetto and as if it were possible artificially to keep alive the way of life that flourished there; we cannot act as if the laws of the Torah still signified for most of us the rules of conduct."

Speaking of the profound changes which religious Judaism experienced when the destruction of the Temple in A.D. 70 so suddenly deprived it of the sacrificial system of its worship, Dr. Schoeps declares that "the theocracy no longer existed, but its constitution remained in force as if it did. The Temple no longer existed, but the Jews the world over bowed in prayer in its direction as if it did. The High Priest no longer made his expiatory sacrifice on the Day of Atonement, but the ritual formula was learned and recited on that day as if he did. . . . This disregard of the actual facts, this abstracting of Judaism from every reality here and now, was a huge accomplishment. It did indeed 'save' Judaism—that is to say, by means of the 'as if', Judaism was adapted to exile and was removed to the plane of the timeless".

But all this suffered a change with the advent of the Emancipation. "It is therefore the Emancipation that is the most fateful breach in the continuity of Jewish history, for this time there was no bridge improvised to span the abyss. . . . Now the thread was really broken, and the great question that had lain hidden, all these years, in the heart of the year 70 first revealed itself for what it really was: the question of Judaism's destiny."[3]

Closely associated with the element of unreality is the element of irrelevance in traditional Judaism. The Talmudic Jew spends

years in studying subjects which for centuries have had no connection with Jewish life, as, for example, the laws concerning the
Temple services and the order of sacrifices; or many of the laws
of the Pentateuch involving situations which have been out of
existence for many, many centuries. Orthodox Judaism is described as out of touch with modern life. Much of Jewish religious
education consists of "letters and words, rather than ideas . . .
unrelated to the many present-day problems". The average Jew
attending Hebrew schools may be interested in obtaining information in matters of Synagogue, dietary laws and cemetary, but
not in spheres of wider human problems and needs.[4]

"The Jew who to any extent accepts the values and climate of
opinion of the twentieth century finds that much in his ancient
heritage is incomprehensible, irrelevant, or unacceptable."[5]

"More and more Halachah [Religious Code] seems to reveal
its inability to cope with the conditions and circumstances of contemporary Jewish life." "Life is surging past the walls of solidified
Halachah, which are crumbling under burdens of their unrelated-
ness to the needs of a living generation."[6]

2. THE INHERENT WEAKNESS OF LIBERAL JUDAISM

One of the factors contributing to the Jewish religious crisis is the
inherent weakness of Liberal Judaism. When traditional Judaism
began to break up towards the end of the eighteenth century the
Reform Synagogue sprang into existence in Western Europe and
stepped into the breach. But Liberal Judaism never achieved the
stature in Jewish life as Protestant Christianity did in Christendom.
According to Ernst Simon, Israeli educator and lecturer at the
Hebrew University, the failure of Reform Judaism may be
attributed to two fundamental causes: (1) Whereas Protestant
Christianity was a movement back to the Bible, Reform Judaism
by denying the Divine origin of the Bible "failed to provide a substitute for that unique Jewish content given to everyday life by
Orthodoxy"; (2) while Protestant Christianity had a theology to
fall back on, Reform Judaism was handicapped from the very beginning by the absence of a systematic theology. "Religious philosophy,
the philosophical interpretation and defence of Jewish religion, we
have had aplenty. But systematic theology—the interpretation of
God, the world, and man on the basis of the Jewish religion—that
is almost completely lacking in the older Hebrew literature."[7]

E

3. THE COMMUNAL CHARACTER OF RELIGIOUS JUDAISM

Judaism is a collective or national religion. For centuries prior to the Emancipation Jewish religious life had been organized on a communal basis. The disruption of the communal character of Jewish life in the wake of the Emancipation became one of the factors which precipitated the present religious crisis. "In the medieval state the Jew as an individual had no official existence; he was a cell of the Jewish community."[8] As a result of the Emancipation which followed in the wake of the French Revolution the Jew ceased to be a cell in the Jewish community and became a citizen of his native land. "With the disappearance of the ghetto, faith as a collective phenomenon and the all-inclusive regulation of life according to the Mosaic law ceased to exist."[9]

A fuller appreciation of the collective or national character of religious Judaism will help us to see the gulf which exists now between religious Judaism on one hand, and the Jewish individual, a member of a modern society, on the other hand. "There is no Jewish 'religion' at all, in the ordinary sense of the word, but only a 'national history' . . . Judaism does not—in the manner of religions—aim to gain acceptance by 'convincing' the individual but by giving him, as a member of a nation, historical self-consciousness. . . . It is not faith, then, which redeems the Jew, but historical self-consciousness: our decision to be members of a nation appointed by God, to accept His Law, to realize it in our state (and, after the loss of the state, to adhere to it all the more strongly) . . . presenting to humanity the example of a nation dedicated to the divine Law and thereby, in due course, together with all the nations, attaining to final redemption. Judaism, to be sure, teaches eternal truths; but, rather than preaching faith in them, it aims to implant them by a process of education; by a life according to the Law. This, then, is imposed upon the individual irrespective of his convictions . . . it binds him because it is the historic law of the nation."

"The Sinaitic revelation did not address itself to individuals as such; if it had, it could not have bound later ages. It was granted to the community, which gained its national unity by its readiness to accept it for its national law. Hence the eternal significance of the events at Mount Sinai: individuals come and go, but a nation lives forever . . .

"This is the true nature of Judaism, which has often been misunderstood. The bond between the divine Lawgiver and the horde of slaves whom He liberated from Egypt and elevated to a nation, does not depend upon the personal convictions of the individual, changing with time and circumstances: the individual does not abide by the law because he is convinced of it but because the transcending will of the nation binds him."[10]

A more recent exposition of the national character of Judaism is found in the following declaration: "It should be remembered, however, that Judaism, on the authentic level, does not know the Personal God whom the individual joins in a leap of faith. This type of God belief is Christian, and it was more than anything else responsible for the rejection of Jesus and his followers by the Synagogue. God, as Jews know Him, is the 'God of our Fathers'. His existence is proved not in the 'personal encounter' with the individual but in the declaration of His bond with His chosen people, Israel."[11]

4. THE TALMUD AND THE RELIGIOUS CRISIS

The Talmud is probably the greatest single factor involved in the Jewish religious crisis. The Karaites in the early Middle Ages repudiated the Talmud, denying its authority to regulate Jewish life, and attributing this authority exclusively to the Bible. The men and women representing the various movements and ideologies which have sprung up in Jewry since the beginning of the collapse of traditional Judaism, however much they differed among themselves in their approach to Jewish life, were united in their opposition to the Talmud. The Talmud is the body of Jewish religious literature, outside of the Bible. Judaism is a legalistic religion. The core of Judaism is the Mosaic Law as contained in the Pentateuch. The Talmud, among other things, is the interpretation of the meaning of the Mosaic Law and its application in the daily life of the Jew. Six hundred and thirteen commandments have been deduced from the Law of Moses covering every possible situation of Jewish life. Three hundred and sixty-five of these are negative commandments, i.e. things which a Jew must not do, two hundred and forty-eight are positive, i.e. things which a Jew must do.

Centuries of interpretations and reinterpretations have made the Talmud very complex and only remotely related to the

Mosaic Law. The observance of the Sabbath is a good illustration of what happened to the Law of Moses after passing through the mill of Talmudic legalism. To the Rabbinic mind the laws in the Pentateuch with reference to the Sabbath were too vague. The Rabbis were not satisfied with the general prohibitions of work on the Sabbath day as found in the Mosaic Law. Consequently, some thirty-nine kinds of work are listed in the Talmud from which a Jew must abstain on the Sabbath. These include handling, i.e. touching money, tearing paper, shining shoes, etc. A Jew may not carry "burdens" on the Sabbath. He would, therefore, wrap his handkerchief around his wrist and, when on his way to the Synagogue, deliver his prayer shawl and prayer book to his younger son who accompanied him and who, before he reached the age of thirteen, was free from many of the Rabbinic prohibitions.

As conditions changed and new situations arose Rabbinic laws had to be adapted to the new circumstances. To meet these new needs new laws had to be added to the old ones or the old ones reinterpreted. This procedure of reinterpreting old laws is sometimes referred to as legal fiction. By means of legal fiction the old laws, whether in the Pentateuch or Talmud, were kept intact but made to serve new purposes. Legal fiction made it possible to circumvent a commandment "if in so doing the community is better served. This is an expedient often resorted to. Its purpose is to preserve the meaning of the letter of the law while at the same time departing from its original intention".[12]

A classical example of how legal fiction operated is the following. The law of release as found in Deuteronomy chapter fifteen makes the cancellation of all debts in the seventh year compulsory. In an agricultural economy this law served to protect the farmer from losing his farm as a result of some misfortune. In a later era when the Palestine economy became more urban and commercial in character this law proved detrimental to free trade. It apparently discouraged people from lending money or granting credits for fear of losing them in the seventh year of release. One of the Mishnaic authorities, Rabbi Hillel the Elder (first century B.C.), devised a procedure which made it possible for the creditor to transfer the debt to the court with instructions to the court to collect the debt.[13] Thus on one hand the law is declared to be holy and unchangeable, while on the other hand, under the pretext of fulfilling it, it is actually annulled, broken, or made of

no effect. That the Talmudic Rabbis would consider this practice as doing God's will is most amazing. "That important segments of Rabbinic law have little basis in the Biblical text was
clearly recognized by the Mishnah, which speaks of many matters
as being 'mountains hanging by a hair'."[14]

In an illuminating article, "Halachah, Bastion or Pathway",
already referred to above, Elieser Berkovits states among other
things that "the commentators of the Talmud are not always
genuine interpreters; often, solving problems of interpretation,
they transform the Talmudic text into the starting point of hala-
chic concepts of which one may safely say that they were not
thought of by the original teachers of the Talmud themselves".[15]

That the modern Jew has definitely outgrown the moral, spiritual and intellectual atmosphere of the Talmud is realized by
many Jews. "Much as we admire the steadfastness and moral
dignity of the Jew produced by this authoritarian world-negating
thought structure, we must face a fundamental question with
respect to it: to what degree and on what level are we today really
interested in the main body of post-Biblical Jewish ideas, with its
unremitting moralizing, its image of man as a child doing good
and bad deeds and being rewarded and punished for them, its
over-emphasis on the rights and awesomeness of parents, its
teleology? . . . There is no doubt that the bulk of medieval literature generally is lacking in permanent meaning; and the state of
intellectual affairs among the Jews of those centuries was not such
as to lead them to outstrip the rest of Europe. Their own personality they had, one very fascinating when seen from certain
sides, but their ideas are not necessarily significant to us. . . . The
fact that they were Jews is in itself no reason why 'the reader
of today should enter into a living relationship with the men who
speak in these documents', nor is it a guarantee that with all the
good will in the world the modern reader can enter into such a
relationship with them."[16]

If the Jews have up to recently displayed very little interest
in the Bible, if the Jews in general have a meagre knowledge of
their own Bible and, proportionately speaking, fewer, by far, Jews
own and read the Bible than Christians; if it also be true, as the
"Perplexed Rabbi" maintains, that at the basis of the present
crisis of the Jewish religion lies the lack of faith on the part of
both Jewish clergy and laity in the Divine origin of the Bible,[17]
it is the Talmud which, having relegated the Hebrew Bible

to a relatively unimportant place in Jewish life, has contributed heavily to Jewish unbelief.

5. THE INTERIM OR TRANSIENT CHARACTER OF THE RELIGION OF TRADITIONAL JUDAISM

For centuries the Jew has been led to believe that only in Palestine is it possible to fulfil the Law and live a full religious life. "The land of Israel is the one place which is wholly suited for the Torah." It was in this belief that in the ages following the destruction of the Jewish Commonwealth by the Romans individual Jews emigrated to Palestine in order to spend there their declining years. This belief was dealt a severe and jarring blow by the sudden emergence of the State of Israel. Religious Judaism has to witness the unpleasant truth that it is actually less possible to practise the Jewish religion in Palestine than anywhere else in the world.

We should not wonder then to learn that the religious problem should have received the most intensive and thorough-going treatment in the State of Israel. One of the most illuminating articles on this subject, which has come to this writer's attention, under the caption "Religion and State", was written by Jeshaia Leibowitz, a religious Jew, a leader in the religious workers' group of the Jewish Labour Federation in Israel, and lecturer in organic chemistry at the Hebrew University. Leibowitz presents a searching analysis of the nature of the religious problem of the Jewish people, particularly as it affects the people in the State of Israel. In his introduction the writer states that "the restoration of Jewish national independence and the assumption of the functions and responsibilities of statehood by the Jewish people mean a supreme test for Jewish religion. In fact, this turning point in Jewish history presents Jewish religion with a problem which is not at all the political one of the inter-relationship of state and religion, but a purely and truly religious one within the frame of religious consciousness and religious practice itself. It is an intrinsic crisis of Judaism as embodied in Law and Commands—in the Halakha, and as fateful a crisis as that provoked 1,900 years ago by the destruction of the Temple. Just as the generation of Rabbi Yohanan ben Zakkai faced the momentous question: Can there be a legitimate continuation of Judaism in the Galut*

* Galut—Exile, Dispersion, or Diaspora; all countries of Jewish residence outside of Palestine.

and without the Temple?—so this generation of religious Jewry faces the question: Can there be a legitimate continuation of Judaism without Galut and without foreign domination."

The conclusion which the writer draws from his examination of the religious problem is that the national way of life, as it has come down over the centuries and whose beginnings go back to the days of the Second Temple, is based on the assumption "that the Jewish people in actual history lacks national independence and national functions and that, therefore, the Jew is not burdened by the duties and responsibilities of a citizen of a state". The religion of traditional Judaism "is a way of life for a man who does not include in the plans and prospects of his life the functions and duties of a responsible citizen of a state; it is a regime for a community which can dispense with problems of defence, of internal and external security, of foreign affairs and diplomatic relations, of the keeping of an army and a police and an administrative apparatus, of the decision on war and peace, of production for the supply of its own needs, even of a judiciary which functions not by voluntary consent of the parties but by compulsion".

"Religious Jewry", the writer continues, "is now faced by the momentous choice between two possible approaches to the religious crisis, and its choice may prove decisive for the future of Judaism." The two approaches to the religious crisis are—according to the writer—determined by the two different conceptions of the religion of traditional Judaism. According to one conception, the Jewish religion in its present form and contents can be practised only if the Jew lives in a Gentile environment and under Gentile domination. "In this case the traditional way of life prescribed by the existing Halakha may be considered as something absolute, independent of socio-political considerations. Hence, it is incumbent on the Jew as an individual and on the Jews as a community, in order to observe this Halakha, to exist within the framework of a foreign society and under a foreign domination responsible for maintaining this framework, until the ultimate and supra-natural Messianic redemption." If this view be accepted then "the establishment of the Jewish state in our times is a most grievous sin and a rebellion against the intention of the Torah".

According to the other concept, the Jewish religion does not exclude from its concern the socio-political area of life. The duties and responsibilities which the Jew assumes in relation to the State are no less part of his religious life than, for example, observance of the Sabbath, or the other practices presented by his religion. If this view is correct, and it represents the view of all religious Zionists, then it must be assumed "that the traditional religious way of life did not express the original intention of the Torah but presented merely the historically necessary—and, therefore, religiously legitimate—temporary adaptation of the Torah to circumstances in which the Jewish people had to dispense with the obligation of arranging its political and social existence according to the Law".[18]

V. SUGGESTED SOLUTIONS

The suggestions offered to cure the religious crisis fall into the following categories.

1. A REVIVAL OF JEWISH RELIGIOUS OBSERVANCES

This measure is offered, or has been offered, by Jews who are so-called survivalists. Many of these spokesmen are not religious Jews at all, but they recognize the great survival-value and strength which the Jewish traditional way of life displayed in the past. They, therefore, advocate a return to some of the religious observances of traditional Judaism in order to create a greater sense of group solidarity among the Jews. Since these proponents are interested primarily in the national survival of the Jews their solution is not actually designed to solve the religious problem. Furthermore, their approach to the problem is based on a misunderstanding of the real factors which lie at the basis of Jewish survival. The Jewish traditional way of life which played an important part in the survival of the Jews rested on strong religious convictions. These religious convictions of the past are no more today. Furthermore, as we have shown elsewhere, the traditional Jewish way is incompatible with modern Jewish life.

2. REBUILDING JUDAISM ON THE FOUNDATION OF THE "JEWISH HERITAGE"

By "Jewish heritage" is meant the Jewish way of life evolved by the Jewish people in its long history, its institutions, its literature, and its culture. Strictly speaking, the expression "Jewish heritage" takes in the period of Jewish history which followed the destruction of the Jewish Commonwealth by the Romans. This is the era of the Great Dispersion. The Bible, i.e. the Hebrew Bible, makes up only a very small and insignificant part of this "heritage". The bulk of this "heritage" is the Talmud and the literature which has grown up around it. In the eighteen centuries following the destruction of the Jewish Homeland nothing has moulded Jewish life as much as did Rabbinic literature embodied in the Talmud and related works.

There is a significant segment of Jewish opinion which cannot visualize the reconstruction of Judaism, or Jewish life, or Jewish belief, or Jewish nationalism, unless it be based on the foundation of this "Jewish heritage". Jews holding these ideas are mostly born and raised in a Jewish traditional environment and schooled in Jewish traditional learning. In an article entitled "Israel, Where Are You Going?", written by Prof. Joseph Klausner and published several years ago in *Haboker*, the writer makes the following statement: "Israel, where are you going? Will you build on the traditional foundations, the foundations established by our spiritual giants throughout more than three thousand years and which are still firm and fresh, a Jewish State which will faithfully guard the heritage of the past and synthesize it with the best of modern culture, thus placing Israel at the head of the nations of the Near East—or are you going to build a state which will be totally bereft, or nearly totally bereft, of the monotheistic belief, prophetic ethics, the messianic idea and Jewish idealism?"[19]

A more recent expression of the same attitude is given by Maurice Samuel. "Israel's greatest spiritual danger is that of a real break with the past while exhibiting a spurious re-established contact with it. There will be Hebrew, there will be great respect for the Bible as the national saga, there will be everlasting references to the associations of classical places and persons; but all this, I pointed out in the preceding article, will be remote legends and sentimentality if there is no middle ground of attachment and transmission, if the grandfathers are not included as well as the ancestors. If the immense and immensely significant two thousand years' continuity of Jewish life which—reading backwards—contains Sholem Aleichem, and Volozhin and Zhitomir, and the Hasidim, and Troyes and Worms, and Spanish Jewry, and Babylonian Jewry*—if this continuity ceases to exist for Israel, then

* Names of persons, movements, groups and places representing historical milestones in the development of this "Jewish heritage".

her self-identification with the Prophets will be as fictitious as the contemporary Greek's self-identification with Plato."[20]

This approach to the Jewish religious problem has serious limitations. In the first place the "Jewish heritage" is the product of a certain era in the history of the world. This "Jewish heritage" would have certainly assumed an entirely different character had there been no destruction of the Jewish Homeland in the year A.D. 70. The historical factors and influences which exerted a profound effect on the evolution of this "Jewish heritage" are gone. The Jewish Homeland has been recovered, and world conditions have radically changed. To what extent can present Jewish life, whether in the State of Israel or outside of it, become, under modern conditions, related to this "Jewish heritage" of the past?

3. PERSONAL RELIGION

There is a growing conviction, especially among the Jewish intellectuals, of the need of the kind of a religious belief which would satisfy the spiritual needs of the individual. "The decision regarding religious commitment should be made only on the basis of religious faith and belief as to what best ministers to the individual's deepest personal needs."[21] There is, however, one drawback in this attitude. With the Gentile, religion is an individual matter. His religion need have no relationship to his racial or national origin. The Jewish people are an exception to this general rule. With the Jews their religion and nationality are inseparable. A Jew cannot consciously affirm his Jewishness if his religious system fails to take a positive attitude to the destiny of the Jewish nation. There is some evidence to the effect that this concept is undergoing a change in the State of Israel where Jewishness is primarily a matter of nationality rather than religion. But it is doubtful whether this change is fundamental. Be that as it may, this relationship has not changed at all in the Diaspora, which still contains most of the Jewish population.

An attempt is being made to effect a compromise between Judaism as the collective religion of the Jewish people and Judaism as the personal religion of the individual Jew. The individual Jew—according to this view—becomes the recipient of God's Grace when he identifies himself with the redemptive and redeeming history of Israel. By this process of self-identification with

Israel's sacred history under the Covenant he becomes "a Jew-in-faith", "by re-enacting in his own life the redemptive career of Israel". The sacred history of Israel becomes his own spiritual history. Israel's exodus from Egypt—his own exodus. Israel's meeting with God at Sinai—his own encounter with God. Israel's wanderings in the wilderness under the guidance and protection of God—his own earthly pilgrimage in communion with God.[22]

There can be no quarrel with this spiritual interpretation of Israel's history. The question of vital concern to the spiritually-minded Jew is what significance is there in the ritual and cere-monial observances of Judaism? What should be his individual attitude to these observances?

The religious significance of the observances of Judaism, ex-plains Will Herberg—consists in the fact that they are "the acting-out of the Jew's affirmation of the election of Israel and its 'separation' as 'priest-people'".[23] The individual Jew, how-ever, must decide for himself what part of the ritual observances he should choose. It is incumbent upon each individual Jew to appropriate the Law as something his own. "Unless a mitzvah [commandment] is really made one's own, unless it can be and is performed with true inwardness, it has no effective power."[24]

Needless to say that the matter of the religious observances is the great weakness in this particular approach to the problem of personal religion for the individual Jew. Many Jews will continue to question the need of the ritual observances, and regard them as a hindrance rather than a help in their spiritual life. On the other hand, if the observances, such as those of the Sabbath, the great festivals, and the dietary laws are essential at all, they must be essential for all Jews or they are not essential for any Jew.

4. RELIGIOUS EDUCATION

One of the ways by which traditional Judaism perpetuated itself was the Jewish Religious School. Judaism laid great stress on the training of its young. The Jewish boys used to spend years studying the tenets of Rabbinic Judaism. The Jewish girls received their training from their mothers, private teachers, or in religious schools. Studying of the Torah was the highest reli-gious virtue. Even after they were married many Jews would set aside regular hours for study, either late at night, or in the early hours of the morning when the rest of the family was still asleep, or on the Sabbath day.

When the decline of traditional Judaism began in the era of Emancipation, the Jewish Religious School lost its place of importance in Jewish religious life. Many Jewish children exchanged the religious for the secular school.

The restoration of the Jewish Religious School to the place of prominence it held in the past is one of the most commonly suggested solutions for the Jewish religious crisis. A "maximum Jewish educational programme" is, we are told, "the only logical answer to the Jewish spiritual plight of our age".[25] But we are cautioned not to place too much hope on the Jewish Religious School. It is true that Jewish Day Schools spread Jewish education among Jews. "But again, it would be fatal to deceive ourselves by assuming that Jewish Day Schools can solve the problem. They can delay and postpone assimilation—they cannot prevent it."[26]

The whole subject of Jewish religious education in America as a means of resuscitating religious Judaism has received a thorough examination in an article by Rabbi Hertzberg entitled "Jewish Education Must Be Religious Education". The objectives of the Jewish Religious School—we are informed—are to fortify the child against antisemitism, to act as preventive psychotherapy, and to promote group solidarity. The Jewish educational system makes no provision to meet the religious needs of the individual American Jew. "Being human, he wonders about the ultimate meaning of life and seeks for some faith and purpose with which to face his death. Being contemporary, he is plagued by a sense of helplessness and futility. Being Jewish, he is confronted by the experiences of the last twenty years more sharply than ever with a sense of peculiar destiny. It is in all of these respects that the American Jew most seriously needs to come to terms with himself. To ignore the most personal—and hence most cosmic—feelings of the contemporary Jew means, when translated into educational theory and practice, to cut him off from just those sources of the Jewish heritage that might help him grapple with his loneliness, his demon, and his God."

The fond hope cherished in some Jewish circles that a strengthened religious school system might revive Jewish religious life is based on a misconception of the position which the Jewish religious school held in the past. In that bygone era the parents were religious Jews, the teachers devout men, and home, school and synagogue integral parts of a well-grounded religious way of life. This religious way of life has disappeared from both home and Synagogue, while the schools' teachers have no settled religious convictions, and no clear conception of the purpose of Jewish education. To expect the Jewish religious school, under these altered circumstances, to revise present-day trends, is to expect the impossible.

We agree with Rabbi Hertzberg who declares that, while many American Jews in search for religious values are willing to give up "even that most precious of democratic institutions, the public school", the parents are undecided as to the kind of religious education they want their children to have. "Can a valid and worthwhile school be created for children whose parents are muddled in their beliefs, to be run by educators who are rather certain of their doubts?"

Rabbi Hertzberg, therefore, states that "the present condition of the Jew clearly demands a new spiritual impulse", but that it is not "possible as yet to found the Jewish religious school on new and clear affirmations of faith. . . . There is no escape from dealing with our time as it really is. It is an age to which the Word has not yet been spoken, but which, in its deepest soul, is waiting for it.' . . . Under the circumstances, about the best we can do—it is also the least we ought to do—is to sit doggedly by the embers of Jewish teaching, by the opened Bible (in Hebrew!) above all, and prepare ourselves for the miraculous moment when the words enflame our spirit. Then we—adults and children alike—will know what we only can guess at now: what it means to be children of the Fathers and covenanted to God".[27]

The following three propositions designed to solve the religious problem have been put forward especially in connection with the religious crisis as it affects the people in the State of Israel. Since the religious problem in the State of Israel is of a much more urgent nature than the same problem in the Diaspora, the solutions offered there are more daring in their approach than anything yet suggested in the Diaspora.

5. REINTERPRETATION OF THE RELIGIOUS CODE

Soon after the re-establishment of the State of Israel, when it became evident that Jewish religious law is incompatible with the

normal functioning of a modern state, the question of reconsti-
tuting the Sanhedrin (the Supreme Jewish Religious Court) arose
in some Jewish circles. The purpose of reconvening the Sanhedrin, which for centuries had been out of existence, would be to
revise Rabbinic Law in order to adapt it to the needs of modern
life, especially to the needs of the State of Israel. However, it is
doubtful whether such a Rabbinic assembly would be representative of present-day Jewry, or even of the religious Jews of today.
There are some who argue that Jewry lacks authority to reconvene
such a Sanhedrin. We are told that an influential part of the
Rabbinate in the State of Israel is opposed to the whole idea. It
is felt in responsible Orthodox circles that only after Messiah
comes can such a Sanhedrin be reconstituted.

But there may be another reason behind the reluctance to reconvene the Sanhedrin. It is the recognition of the insurmountable difficulties in the way of revising Jewish religious law. In the
first place, no amount of reinterpretation of the law will succeed
in explaining away the true meaning of the law. The Law of
Moses forbids work on the Sabbath. True, the intent of the Law
was not that the Sabbath should become what it did become
under Rabbinic Judaism—a day of hardship instead of joy. But
there is no denying of the fact that under the Mosaic Law no
gainful or unnecessary work is permitted on the Sabbath. When
this Law was given to Israel the people lived under a pastoral
and an agricultural economy where complete cessation of work on
the Sabbath produced no hardships. In fact it must have proved
a great blessing. Even today we cannot picture to ourselves life
without the weekly rest-day. But under modern industrial conditions it is simply not possible to interrupt all manner of work
on any day. The same vexing problem is presented by many of
the other laws of the Religious Code.

The dilemma with which traditional Judaism is confronted at
the present, especially in the State of Israel, is this: Either it admits
that the observance of God's law given to Israel through Moses
is incompatible with modern conditions; or it undertakes to reinterpret, or interpret away, the law in such a manner as to give
the impression that it is keeping the law while actually it is breaking it. Rabbi Hillel of the first century B.C. chose the second step
in dealing with the law concerning annulment of debts in the
seventh year. The procedure which he introduced resulted in
the abrogation of that law under the pretence of observing it.

Traditional Judaism could not choose the first step without en-
tangling itself in a host of fatal contradictions, and it could not
adopt Rabbi Hillel's procedure without increasing the people's
disregard of and contempt for the traditional law.

6. ENACTMENT OF NEW LAWS BASED ON THE PRINCIPLES OF TRADITIONAL LAW

Recognizing the difficulty involved in adapting the Jewish
Religious Code to the needs of the State by means of revision or
re-interpretation, a suggestion was made by Moses Oona of the
State of Israel to formulate or enact a set of new laws based on
the principles of the traditional law. "The Torah doesn't even
have laws for many important areas of political life, and there has
so far been no effort to formulate a modern law based on the
principles of traditional law . . ."[28]

7. BY-PASSING THE EXISTING RELIGIOUS CODE OF TRADITIONAL JUDAISM

Meir Or, another Israeli Jew, commenting on Moses Oona's
suggestion to formulate new laws in accordance with the principles
of the traditional law, comes forward with the following proposals:
"It is our view that the establishment of the Jewish state marks a
decisive juncture in Israel's history and affects the very basis of
all Jewish life as we have hitherto known it. As the destruction of
the Second Temple [in its time] forced us to re-assess our religious
problems, so [now] the establishment of the state requires us to
make such a re-assessment. We must skip over the whole period
of the Galut and the Galut Halacha, going back to a time preceding the Halacha's canonization, so as to direct the Halacha's
development toward new horizons. This is a job we've got to do
even if it seems to go against the accepted and traditional . . ."[29]
According to this view the entire Rabbinic Religious Code,
which evolved in the centuries following the destruction of the
Jewish Homeland, should be set aside, and a new religious code
enacted. This is the most revolutionary approach yet made to the
Jewish religious problem.

While the last three solutions constitute a new milestone in the
Jewish attitude to the Jewish religion, they all share in common
serious limitations. There is a Rabbinic maxim which says: "Go

out and see what the people are doing." This principle is meant
to serve as a guide for the Rabbinic authorities concerned with the
abrogation of the existing laws or enactment of new ones. Before
undertaking to introduce any changes the Rabbis were first to
acquaint themselves with the people's attitude to the subject under
consideration. Present-day Rabbinic Judaism knows that one of
the most important factors in the Jewish religious problem is the
loss of faith in the Divine origin of the Law on the part of the vast
majority of the Jewish people. "Matters go deeper than that,"
declared the "Perplexed Rabbi". "What is really involved", he
continued, "is belief—belief in the Divine origin of the Torah. . . .
I have more than twenty years of experience in the practical
rabbinate and I have learned that what the average Jew wants is
not theorizing and philosophizing but—certainty. If I could really
convince my people that God appeared to Moses and gave him
the Torah for Israel, I would have no trouble at all turning my
congregation into *shomrey mitzvoth* [observers of the command-
ments]. But I can't convince them—in fact, I myself am not
convinced . . ." Recalling his experiences as a chaplain in World
War Two, he said: "My colleagues, the Protestant and the Catholic chaplains, had it easy. At before-zero-hour services they told
the men that Jesus would walk alongside them, protecting them
in battle or carrying them to Paradise should death strike them
down. The Christian boys went into battle utterly certain that if
evening would not find them back with their buddies, it would
mark their entry into Paradise. I could not speak to the Jewish
boys in this fashion. It would have been incompatible with my
Jewish philosophy cast into an intellectualist-rational pattern. . . .
I always dreaded that a dying soldier might ask me, 'What is
beyond the grave?' I knew I could not answer the question.
Luckily, I was never faced with this situation. But it may arise
tomorrow—what shall I say when one of my people will ask me,
'Rabbi, what lies beyond the grave?'" When asked whether he
did not think that the Psalms could "convey this consolation and
certainty" he replied: "You have to be in the practical ministry
to know the problems a spiritual leader faces. When a person is
dying, the poetic metaphors of the Psalms mean precious little
to him. He wants concrete, tangible help. He wants to cry to a
God who assures him, him personally, that He hears his cry. We
Jews have no such God to offer and this is why we are losing
out."[30] The problem facing religious Judaism is not how to make

the Jew conform to the existing Religious Code, or whether to revise the present Code, or to create a new religious code more suitable to changed conditions. The real problem is how to help the Jew find his way back to God.

VI. THE PROPHETIC ASPECT OF THE JEWISH RELIGIOUS CRISIS

1. THE RELIGIOUS CRISIS BEGAN IN THE YEAR A.D. 70

The Jerusalem Temple was ordained as the place where God of the Old Testament was wont to meet with His people. The Temple sacrifices defined and regulated Israel's relationship to God. The Temple priesthood acted as the mediating agency between Jehovah and Israel. The destruction of the Temple by the Romans in A.D. 70 confronted Judaism with a religious crisis of major proportions. The question which had to be answered was: can Judaism survive without the Temple?

2. JUDAISM PROVIDED AN "AS IF" SOLUTION

To the vexing question whether Judaism can survive without the Temple Judaism of A.D. 70 had no answer grounded in reality. This, because the Temple worship of Israel was based on the Law of Moses and the Law of Moses provided no definite alternative for a situation as created by the events of A.D. 70. The sages of Jamnia—the rallying point of religious Judaism in Palestine following the destruction of the Jewish Homeland—who took upon themselves to reconstruct Judaism on a new religious foundation evolved what Schoeps aptly calls the "as if" concept of Jewish history. "Theocracy no longer existed," Schoeps declares, "but its constitution remained in force as if it did. The Temple no longer existed, but Jews the world over bowed in prayer in its direction as if it did. The High Priest no longer made his expiatory sacrifice on the Day of Atonement, but the ritual formula was learned and recited on that day as if he did. Meanwhile, other things took the place of the actual sacrifice: study of Torah, good works, prayer—the fulfilling of these commandments counted as much as the animal sacrifice of ancient times." Thus Judaism was abstracted "from every reality of the here and now".[31]

That this "reconstruction" of Judaism was not regarded as a permanent solution may be seen from a perusal of the Prayer-Book which more than any other single source reflects the faith and hope of the Synagogue. In the first place, this changed religious status of the Jew was considered as a Divine punishment. The following confession is being recited on the great religious festivals of the year: "And because of our sins we have been exiled from our country and removed far from our soil, and we are unable to go up and to appear and to worship before Thee in the house of Thy choosing, in the great and holy house which was called by Thy Name, because of the hand which was stretched out [i.e. violence committed] against Thy Sanctuary."

That the Synagogue, representing the whole religious body of Israel, hoped for a restoration of the Temple system of worship is seen from the many petitions scattered through the pages of the Prayer-Book of which the following, recited on the great religious festivals of the year, is representative: "May it please Thee, Jehovah our God, and the God of our fathers, King of mercy, to have abundant compassion upon us and upon Thy Sanctuary, and rebuild it [i.e. Sanctuary] speedily, and increase its glory. Our Father and Our King, reveal the glory of Thy Kingdom unto us speedily and shine forth and be exalted over us in the sight of all living [flesh], and gather our dispersed ones from among the nations and assemble our scattered ones from the uttermost parts of the earth. And lead us to Zion, Thy city, with singing, and with an everlasting joy to Jerusalem, the place of Thy Sanctuary; and there we shall offer before Thee the sacrifices enjoined on us, the continual sacrifices according to their order, and the additional sacrifices according to their ordinance."

A similar prayer is recited on the weekly Sabbath day, and on the first day of the month. On the first day of the month, in addition to the above petition, we have the following plea: "Thou wilt prepare a new altar in Zion and we will offer upon it the burnt sacrifice appointed for the first day of the month, and we will willingly bring an offering of young he-goats and we shall all rejoice in the service of the Sanctuary . . ."

3. FACTORS WHICH MADE THE "AS IF" SOLUTION OF A.D. 70
   POSSIBLE

a. Jewish faith in the Covenant remained unimpaired

The destruction of the sacrificial system of Israel's worship did not destroy the Jewish people's faith in the Covenant. There is a saying that the Shechinah [God's presence] accompanied the Jews on their way into exile. They took with them into their dispersion the belief in the indestructibility of their Covenant relationship with God. And on the foundation of this abiding faith in the Divine origin and continued validity of the Covenant Rabbinic Judaism proceeded to rebuild the shattered religious life of the Jewish people.

b. The ascendancy of Rabbinism

As long as the Temple was in existence the priesthood held a dominating position in the life of the nation. Long before the catastrophe of A.D. 70 Rabbinism sought to eclipse the importance of the priesthood. It is doubtful whether it would have fully succeeded had the Temple not been swept away. The destruction of the Temple gave Rabbinism its long-sought opportunity. This Rabbinic antagonism to the priesthood is reflected in the following statement. "The Torah [i.e. Rabbinic Religious Law] is greater than the priesthood and the royalty."[32]

c. The displacement of the Bible

With the growth of Rabbinic tradition a gradual estrangement of the Jewish people from the Bible had set in. For all practical purposes study of the Old Testament was limited to the Law of Moses. Even the Law of Moses was in time overshadowed by Rabbinic law. "That important segments of Rabbinic law have little basis in the Biblical text was clearly recognised by the Mishnah, which speaks of many matters as being 'mountains hanging by a hair'."[33]

Rabbinic arrogance bordering almost on blasphemy is seen in the following derogatory remarks about the Scriptures: "The Post-Mishnaic Rabbis (middle of third century) have taught: The study of Scripture is a doubtful habit; that of the Mishnah is one for which a reward is received; but nothing is more commendable than the study of the Gemara."[34] "Give heed, my son, to the words of the scribes, rather than to the words of the Law [i.e. Law of Moses], for the words of the Law consist of positive and negative precepts (the transgression of which is not always a capital offence); but whosoever transgresses any of the words of the scribes is guilty of death."[35]

d. The hostility of the Gentile world

The development of traditional Judaism was greatly facilitated by the mounting outside pressure to which the Jewish people were subjected in the Middle Ages. While living in Gentile lands the Jew was almost completely shut out from the Gentile environment. The medieval Church and the Synagogue have done their best to build a fence around the Jew. In this terrible isolation from the outside world the Jew sought refuge and consolation in the religion of Rabbinism.

4. THE COLLAPSE OF THE "AS IF" SOLUTION

The advent of the French Revolution era swept away many of the elements which formed the basis of the "as if" solution applied to the Jewish religious crisis by the sages living towards the end of the first century A.D. The ghetto walls were broken down. The Jews in the emancipated countries were granted civic and political equality. Jewish isolation and exclusiveness came to an abrupt end.

The rationalism of the eighteenth century attacked the premises of all religion. In this general assault on all religious belief Judaism suffered the largest number of casualties, proportionately speaking. "Judaism emphasizes acts, rituals, habits, a way of life. Christianity, in contrast, places more emphasis on beliefs and doctrines." Judaism "taught a fairly rigid set of rituals to cover one's entire life. This rigidity permitted no defence in depth, so to speak. Once one had found . . . that it was more convenient to work on Saturday, or to shave, or to abandon traditional dress, one had no body of doctrine to fall back upon which could explain to one what remained really important in Judaism. . . . Under these circumstances, an entire way of life disintegrated."[36]

Another factor which served to deepen the religious crisis was the reawakened interest in the Bible. The lofty ideals of the Old Testament prophets, and the great linguistic value of the Hebrew

Bible for the renewed interest in the study of the Hebrew language, brought the Bible back from the obscurity with which traditional Rabbinism had surrounded it.

The emergence of the State of Israel is proving the greatest threat to the survival of traditional Judaism. There a Jew is a Jew, even if he denies the existence of God. The survival value which religious Judaism holds for the Jew in Gentile countries does not exist in the State of Israel where a Jew can be nothing but a Jew. The State of Israel is a living demonstration of the incompatibility of the Mosaic and Rabbinic Law with the functioning of a modern state. The conclusion which the Jew draws is that the Mosaic Law was not given by God. For God would not promulgate laws by which man cannot live.

5. THE PROPHETIC SIGNIFICANCE OF THE RELIGIOUS CRISIS

In probing into the nature of the Jewish religious problem the student of the Bible becomes greatly impressed with the light which the Old Testament sheds on it. We will devote the balance of this chapter to a discussion of certain prophetic aspects of the present Jewish religious crisis. This discussion will be based on Hosea 3: 4–5, and Jeremiah 31: 31–34 (31: 30–33 Heb.), as both of these passages seem to gather up into one single whole certain prophetic teachings relevant to the Jewish religious problem.

Hosea 3: 4–5: "For the children of Israel shall abide many days without king, and without prince, and without sacrifice, and without an image, and without ephod and teraphim: Afterward shall the children of Israel return, and seek Jehovah their God, and David their King, and shall come with fear to Jehovah and to his goodness in the latter days."

Jeremiah 31: 31–34 (31: 30–33 Heb.): "Behold, the days come, saith Jehovah, that I will make a new covenant with the house of Israel, and with the house of Judah. Not according to the covenant that I made with their fathers in the day that I took them by the hand to bring them out of the land of Egypt, which my covenant they brake, although I was a husband unto them, saith Jehovah. But this is the covenant that I will make with the house of Israel after those days, saith Jehovah: I will put my law in their inward parts, and in their heart will I write it; and I will be their God, and they shall be my people. And they shall teach no more every man his neighbour, and every man his brother, saying, Know Jehovah; for they shall all know me, from the least of them unto the greatest of them, saith Jehovah: for I will forgive their iniquity, and their sin will I remember no more."

a. The prediction of Jewish religious neutrality

Let us first of all establish the time element to which the Hosea prophecy refers. It does not apply to the time during which the First Commonwealth lay in ruins. This was a brief period of some seventy years, which is not the meaning usually conveyed by the Old Testament phrase "many days". Furthermore, the return from the Babylonian exile was not followed by a restoration of the Davidic monarchy. The prophecy cannot apply to the era of the Second Commonwealth for two reasons: (1) The Davidic monarchy was not re-established in the days of the Second Commonwealth; (2) the Temple sacrifices were restored. The substance of the Hosea prophecy requires, therefore, that the time interval be reckoned from the destruction of the Second Commonwealth in A.D. 70. The phrase "latter days", with which the passage in Hosea concludes, always refers in the Old Testament to the time of Israel's final and complete national restoration and spiritual redemption. The Hosea prophecy must, therefore, apply to the Great Dispersion era of Jewish history which began with the destruction of the Jewish National Homeland by the Romans. This era will end when the Davidic monarchy will be restored in the Land of Israel.

The description of the religious condition of the Jews during this period of "many days" is given in two couplets or contrasts: "Without a sacrifice and without an image", "Without an ephod and without teraphim". The sacrifices in the Old Testament were the divinely-instituted means by which the Jew approached God. In the days of the First Commonwealth the Jews often relapsed into idolatry, at which time they offered sacrifices not to Jehovah but to idols. This idolatrous condition is expressed by the word "image". Hosea tells us that during "many days" Israel will remain without true religion and without false religion. "Without an ephod and teraphim." The ephod formed part of the high priest's outfit in which the Urim and Thummim were set. Symbolically the ephod represented the means by which in the days of the First Temple the Israelites were enabled to learn the Will of God. As the "image" is the heathen counterpart of "sacrifice", so is "teraphim" the heathen opposite of "ephod".

The teraphim were a heathen kind of idol used for oracular res-
ponses. The Jewish commentator Iben Ezra says that Rachel
stole her father's teraphim in order to make it impossible for him
to discover by means of these oracles the direction in which Jacob
and his family fled.[37] In times of Israel's relapse into idolatry
teraphim were used by the Jews in the same manner as by the
surrounding pagan nations. Hosea predicts that during the long
period of the "many days" Israel will not seek to know the Will
of God either by lawful or forbidden means.

That the passage in Hosea describes the present religious state
of the Jewish people was the opinion of the great Jewish commentator of the Middle Ages, Rabbi David Kimchi. The following is
his exposition of the prophecy. "These are the days of this present
captivity, in which we are in the power of the Gentiles, and in the
power of their kings and princes, and we are 'without a sacrifice
and without an image', i.e. without a sacrifice to God, and without an image to false gods; and 'without an ephod, and without
teraphim', i.e. without an ephod to God, by means of which we
could foretell the future, as with the Urim and Thummim; and
without teraphim to false gods. And this is the present condition
of all the children of Israel in this present captivity."[38] If this
was true of the religious state of the Jews in the days of Rabbi
David Kimchi, some seven hundred years ago, it is infinitely more
true of the religious condition of the Jews of today. It is a state of
religious neutrality.

b. The promise of a new revelation from God

Elsewhere we have indicated that the basic weakness common
to the various proposals suggested as the solution for the religious
problem is the failure of their authors to realize that at the root
of the evil lies the Jewish people's loss of faith in the Divine origin,
therefore in the validity, of the Covenant. As long as the Jew
possessed this faith the gates of hell could not prevail against him.
He clung to his religious convictions with a determination and
tenacity which nothing but death could break. Having lost this
faith, no amount of revising or re-interpreting the old Religious
Code, or the promulgation of a new Code, will affect in the
slightest the Jewish attitude of indifference to the religious problem. We agree with Rabbi Hertzberg that "the present condition
of the Jew clearly demands a new spiritual impulse", and that
this "is an age to which the Word has not yet been spoken, but

which, in its deepest soul, is waiting for it".[39] If the Jew is ever going to be aroused and shaken out of his spiritual torpor, the Word must speak to him as truly as it did on the day when he stood at the foot of Sinai. Nothing short of a new confrontation of the Jew by God will win the Jew back to God. And it is of this new revelation from Heaven that Jeremiah speaks at the very outset of his prophetic utterance. "Behold, the days come, saith Jehovah, that I will make a new covenant with the house of Israel . . ."

c. Not another Sinai revelation

The Biblical revelation is a progressive revelation. "In many and various ways God spoke of old to our fathers by the prophets" (Letter to the Hebrews 1: 1, Revised Standard Version). When speaking to man God adapts his speech to man's spiritual and intellectual state and to his needs. "Not all at once, in sudden burst of glory, did God reveal Himself to human hearts. . . . Only as men are able to receive it will God reveal the riches of His grace."[40] Completely disregarding this truth legalistic Judaism has chained the Jew to the foot of Sinai. But the Jew has come a long way from Sinai intellectually and spiritually.

To Elijah of Old, the forerunner of Old Testament prophetism, who despaired of the disloyalty to the Sinai Covenant on the part of the Jews of his day, God granted a vision of the coming of a new Divine dispensation which was to supersede the dispensation of Sinai. "And, behold, Jehovah passed by, and a great and strong wind rent the mountains, and brake in pieces the rocks before Jehovah, but Jehovah was not in the wind; and after the wind an earthquake, but Jehovah was not in the earthquake. And after the earthquake a fire, but Jehovah was not in the fire; and after the fire a still small voice" (1 Kings 19: 11–12).

This truth is unfolded in great detail in the Jeremiah prophecy. The second Heavenly visitation with which God will confront Israel will not be a second Sinai. "Not according to the covenant that I made with their fathers . . ." Not a revision, or a re-interpretation of the Sinai covenant, but an entirely new covenant will God conclude with Israel.

What kind of new covenant will this be? "But this is the covenant that I will make with the house of Israel after those days. . . . I will put my law in their inward parts, and in their heart will I write it." Not another covenant of works, of do's and don't's, of positive and negative precepts, not a religion of the hands, but a religion of the heart. Under the Sinai covenant it is possible for the Jew to serve God with his hands and not know God in his heart. Under the new covenant the Jew will also serve God with his hands, not, however, in compliance with external commands, but because his heart will have been touched by God and transformed by God's Grace.

d. "And they shall teach no more . . ."

The Old Testament enjoins the Jews to pass the religious truths revealed to them on to their children. Religious education became the chief mainstay of Judaism. Unfortunately, in the hands of traditional Judaism religious education, like so many of the other precepts of the Pentateuch, became distorted and pulled out of their focus. It is important that we know that religious education in traditional Judaism means, for all practical purposes, study of the Talmudic commentaries. With the traditional Jew Bible study is limited to the weekly Sabbath portion read in the Synagogue, which is predominantly a portion from the five books of Moses. But the study of the Talmud is the main subject at school and at home, on weekdays and on holidays. The words of the Talmudic sages have become invested with a virtue which to the traditional Jew surpasses that of the words of Moses and those of the prophets.

One of the morning prayers lists ten good deeds which every Jew should endeavour to do. The tenth one refers to religious study. The prayer concludes with the statement that the inherent value of religious study equals that of the nine good deeds combined. "Excellence in scholarship", we are told, "is the kind of success traditional Jews worship and crave more fervently than all else, with the result that study and learning are idealized as the very meaning and purpose of the good life; the badge of nobility and honour. There is no greater bliss and satisfaction for a traditional Jew than to excel in Jewish scholarship . . . Study is so all-important to the Jew because the religious truths of his faith are not so much to be believed as to be comprehended." Maimonides—the great medieval Talmudic scholar—is said to have declared that "study unconditionally takes precedence over practice, for study leads to practice, but practice does not lead to study".[41] If practice without study is insufficient, then the statement by Maimonides implies that study is more important than practice. And this is one aspect of the principle "Torah Lishmah", study for the sake of study, apart from any practical value.

Even prayer—that spiritual exercise in which man communes with his Maker—is overshadowed by the all-important Talmudic study. Jews spending much time in prayer are said "to occupy themselves with transitory things". Anyone taking time out of his Talmudic studies to pray, his prayer becomes an abomination.[42]

This adoration of Talmudic lore did not necessarily generate a spirit of humility as seen from the haughty attitude of the Talmudic scholar to the Jew unversed in Talmudic scholarship. We are told that "there is no greater shame and degradation than to be an am Ha-Aretz".* "The ignoramus (in religious lore) cannot be pious", and Judaism's attitude "to the spurner of knowledge [i.e. of the Talmud] is almost cruel, for 'it is forbidden to pity him'".[43] Hassidism in the eighteenth, and Liberal Judaism in the nineteenth centuries, staged a revolt against this glorification of the Talmud. Many of the Jewish free-thinkers in the nineteenth and twentieth centuries came out of the Talmudic academies. And today Judaism is a religion of little study and of even less prayer.

If, with what we have said above in mind, we now turn to Jeremiah we will see at once the relevance of his message for the present-day religious situation. "And they shall teach no more every man his neighbour, and every man his brother, saying, Know Jehovah; for they shall all know me, from the least of them unto the greatest of them, saith Jehovah." In the new covenant which God will make with Israel there be will no need for religious study because all Israel will know God. And this experiential knowledge of God Israel will acquire not because of what the Jew will do for God, but because of what God will do for the Jew.

e. "For I will forgive their inquity . . ."

This last passage of the Jeremiah prophecy tells what God will do for the Jew which will enable the Jew to know God experientially: He will forgive his iniquities and remember his sins no more. Present-day Judaism seldom speaks of sin. "Judaism, today", declares Irving Kristol, "and especially liberal Judaism, despite the horrors of modern totalitarianism, seems unable to recognise sin when it sees it."[44] In the sixth chapter of Isaiah the prophet Isaiah relates a spiritual experience to which he traces his call to the prophetic office. One day he entered the Temple and saw a vision of the holiness of God. "Woe is me!" he cried out, "for I am undone; because I am a man of unclean

* am Ha-Aretz—an unlettered person.

lips, and I dwell in the midst of a people of unclean lips: for mine eyes have seen the King, Jehovah of hosts" (Isaiah 6: 5). Isaiah was stricken with a sense of his sinfulness when he was faced with the holiness of God. The Jews have lost the sense of sin because they have lost the sense of God's holiness. When God will once again pour out upon them the spirit of grace and supplication, when He will once more reveal Himself to them as the Holy One of Israel, they will turn to Him in sin-stricken repentance and say: "We are all become as one that is unclean, and all our righteousnesses are as a polluted garment" Isaiah 64: 6 (64: 5 Heb.).

NOTES TO CHAPTER 4

1. Quoted in *The Jews in the News* (Grand Rapids, Mich.), June 1953.
2. Will Herberg, "Has Judaism Still Power to Speak?", article in *Commentary* (New York), May 1949.
3. Hans Joachim Schoeps, "How to Live by Jewish Law Today", article in *Commentary* (New York), January 1953.
4. I. Jackobovits, "Judaism for the Twentieth Century", article in *The Jewish Spectator* (New York), December 1947.
5. Fritz A. Rothschild, "Conservative Judaism Faces the Need of Change", article in *Commentary* (New York), November 1953.
6. Elieser Berkovits, "Halachah, Bastion or Pathway?", article in *The Jewish Spectator* (New York), November 1953.
7. Ernst Simon, "Are We Israelis Still Jews?", article in *Commentary* (New York), April 1953.
8. Robert Gordis, "Creating an Organic Community", article in *Commentary* (New York), July 1950.
9. Hans Joachim Schoeps, idem.
10. Isaac Breuer, *The Problem of the Jew* (The Spero Foundation: New York, English Translation, 1947), pp. 58–9, 61–2.
11. T. W. Rosmarin, "The Art of Remembering", article in *The Jewish Spectator* (New York), April 1952.
12. Jakob Jocz, "Judaism and the State of Israel", article in the *Hebrew Christian* (quarterly organ of the International Hebrew Christian Alliance, London, England), Spring 1952.
13. Mishnah Shebiit 10: 3–4. See also Robert Gordis, "The Nature of Jewish Tradition", article in *Jewish Frontier* (New York), November 1947.
14. Mishnah Chagigah 1: 8; see Robert Gordis, ibid.
15. Elieser Berkovits, idem.
16. Harold Rosenberg. See his review of *In Time and Eternity: A Jewish Reader*; edited by Nahum N. Glatzer. The review is published in *Commentary* (New York), March 1947.
17. T. W. Rosmarin, "Perplexed Rabbis", article in *The Jewish Spectator* (New York), July–August 1949.

18. Jeshaia Leibowitz, "Religion and State", article in *The Jerusalem Post* (Jerusalem, Israel), September 19, 1952.
19. Joseph Klausner, "Israel, Where Are You Going?", article originally published in *Haboker*; quoted by T. W. Rosmarin, "A Bridge—To What Shore?", article in *The Jewish Spectator* (New York), December 1949.
20. Maurice Samuel, "Why Israel Misunderstands American Jewry", article in *Commentary* (New York), October 1953.
21. Milton R. Konvitz, "A Letter to David Daiches", article in *Commentary* (New York), May 1951.
22. Will Herberg, *Judaism and Modern Man* (The Jewish Publication Society of America: Philadelphia, 1951), pp. 288 ff. Copyright 1951 by Will Herberg. Used by permission of the publisher, Farrar, Straus and Cudahy, Inc.
23. Ibid., p. 298.
24. Ibid., p. 300.
25. T. W. Rosmarin, "The Jewish Day School Marches On", article in *The Jewish Spectator* (New York), April 1947.
26. J. Litvin, "The Galuth Must Be Liquidated", article in *The Jewish Spectator* (New York), October 1948.
27. Arthur Hertzberg, "Jewish Education Must Be Religious Education", article in *Commentary* (New York), May 1953.
28. Judd L. Teller, "Religious Modernism Stirs in Israel", article in *Commentary* (New York), June 1953.
29. Ibid.
30. Quoted by T. W. Rosmarin, "Perplexed Rabbis", article in *The Jewish Spectator* (New York), July–August 1949.
31. Hans Joachim Schoeps, idem.
32. *The Sayings of the Fathers* (Pirkey Aboth), 6: 6.
33. Robert Gordis, "The Nature of Jewish Tradition", article in *Jewish Frontier* (New York), November 1947.
34. Bava-Metzia, fol. 33, col. 1; quoted by Paul Isaac Hershon, *Genesis: With a Talmudical Commentary*, English Translation (Samuel Bagster and Sons: London 1883), p. 2.
35. Ibid., p. 3.
36. Nathan Glazer, "The Jewish Revival in America": II, article in *Commentary* (New York), January 1956.
37. See David Baron, *The Ancient Scriptures and the Modern Jew* (Morgan & Scott Ltd.: London, Sixth Edition), p. 28.
38. Quoted by David Baron, op. cit., p. 9.
39. Arthur Hertzberg, idem.
40. See *The Gospel According to St. John* in *The Speaker's Bible*, vol. 1 (The Speaker's Bible Office: Aberdeen, Scotland, 1931), p. 70.
41. See T. W. Rosmarin, "Mainstays of Jewish Survival", article in *The Jewish Spectator* (New York), March 1946.
42. Ibid.
43. Ibid.
44. Irving Kristol, "How Basic is 'Basic Judaism'?", article in *Commentary* (New York), January 1948.

CHAPTER 5

THE STATE OF ISRAEL AND WORLD JEWRY

I. Is There a Future for Diaspora Jewry?

    1. THE ISRAELI VIEW
    2. THE DIASPORA VIEW

II. Can the State of Israel become a Spiritual Centre for World Jewry?

THE STATE OF ISRAEL AND WORLD JEWRY

I. Is There a Future for Diaspora Jewry?

Prior to World War Two the most important Jewry—from the Jewish national point of view—outside of America, was the East European Diaspora. Living in a concentrated area, with a rich and intensely Jewish tradition, surrounded by a hostile Gentile environment, that Jewry was not threatened much by those disintegrating forces to which Western Jewry was chronically exposed. Streams of emigrants from Eastern European Jewry flowed intermittently, chiefly in two directions: one group went west reinforcing the Jewishly weak Jewries of the West, the other proceeded east, to Palestine, to swell the ranks of the rebuilders of the wastes of Zion.

In the period before World War Two, Western Jewries, constantly suffering from the ravages of inner dissolution, often referred to as assimilation, were kept Jewishly alive in two ways: (1) By intermittent human replenishments from East European Jewry; (2) by rallying around Jewish national goals and slogans, such as care for the oppressed Jewries abroad, and Zionism.

Two events have taken place in the wake of World War Two which have profoundly affected the position of the Jews in the world. One was the destruction of the bulk of European Jewry. The other, was the emergence of the State of Israel. The first of the two has wiped out the source from which the weak Western Jewries drew their human reinforcements. The second brought about the fulfilment of the aims of Zionism. The first dried up the source which kept reinjecting new blood into the chronically anaemic Western Jewries; while both events together deprived Western Jewries of the aims and ideals which helped keep them alive. With the destruction of East and Central European Jews relief and care for oppressed Jews were eliminated from the pro-Jewish activities of the Western Diaspora; while the reconstitution of the State of Israel has fulfilled its Zionist aspirations. The significance of these changes for the Diaspora, i.e. world Jewry outside the State of Israel, may be appreciated if it is realized that before World War One the bulk of Jews lived in countries where the Jewish nationality had great survival strength. Following World War Two the bulk of the Jews residing outside the State of Israel is concentrated in an environment strongly favouring the dissolution of the Jewish nationality.[1] The question confronting Diaspora Jewry at the present time is this: Can Diaspora Jewry survive when left to itself, will it be able to stand on its own feet now that it can expect no replenishment from the outside and without the inner cohesiveness which it derived from its major pro-Jewish activities of the past? The preoccupation of American Jews with the problem of Jewish survival in America proves its concern about the possibility of such a survival.[2] The experience of Jewish history of the distant and recent past makes the future of the Jewish position in America as a distinct national group highly uncertain.[3] The answer to this vital question comes from two different directions.

1. THE ISRAELI VIEW

This view to which most Israeli Jews subscribe is that the present Diaspora has no future. The Israeli Jews regard "Diaspora" as equivalent to "Exile". Prior to the reconstitution of the State of Israel the term "Diaspora" signified the dispersion of the Jewish people. As long as the Jews had no country of their own they were forced to live in the countries of their dispersion whether they were tolerated by their host country or not. In those countries where they were not tolerated "Diaspora" or "Dispersion" was equivalent to "Exile". It is different now. If a Jew is not tolerated in the country of his residence, and if he is free to leave, he can go to Israel. Under these circumstances "Diaspora" need not be "Exile".

To the Israeli Jews, at least to the great majority of them, every country of Jewish residence outside of the State of Israel is still "Exile". Galut (Exile)—one Israeli states—is not synonymous with persecution. It is a certain way the Jews feel about themselves all over the world outside of the State of Israel, and a certain way the non-Jews feel about the Jews. Even conditions in America have certain features which stamp America as part of the Exile. American Jews tend to concentrate in certain specific neighbourhoods, irrespective of their economic status. This is true not only of the immigrants, but also of the American-born Jews. Jews and Gentiles in America do not always frequent the same resorts, do not belong to the same clubs. Social contacts between Jews and non-Jews are not as frank and natural as between Gentiles themselves. [4]

The economic structure of the Jewish population in America also bears certain distinctive marks which tend to set the Jews apart. The Jews are gradually relinquishing certain manual occupations, such as tailoring, the furrier and clothing trades, which up to a generation ago have been largely in Jewish hands. Instead, Jews are heavily represented in the professions such as law, medicine, teaching, journalism, etc. Very few Jews enter the heavy industries, or the many new industries which have sprung up in the last generation.

One of the most incontrovertible proofs that Jewish life in America has definite Galut characteristics—this Israeli spokesman declares in a keen analysis of the Jewish position in the United States—is "the discrepancy—both overt and concealed—between economic advancement and lack of psychological security. . . . A well-known Jewish institution in New York carried out, in connection with its practical work, a statistical survey of the property and income of Jews in the U.S.A. The survey was duly completed, but it was never published. In America, as is well known, a man's income serves as evidence of his reputation and standing. No individual or group in America is ashamed of his or its economic achievements. Indeed, to an extent such achievements are regarded as testifying to their contribution to American civilization as a whole. But not so with the Jews. Here, apparently, the economic achievements of the community are regarded as liable to undermine its security". Whether the Jewish fear is based on objective reasons, or is merely imaginary does not matter. ". . . even if the feeling among the Jews is mainly subjective, it is a perfect expression of Galut [exile], as it was described in the dawn of our history: 'And thou shalt fear day and night . . . for the fear of thine heart wherewith thou shalt fear, and for the sight of thine eyes which thou shalt see.'" [5]

At a meeting of the American Jewish Conference in New York in 1943 Judge Proskauer, then president of the American Jewish Committee, made strenuous objection to a resolution favouring the creation of a Jewish State in Palestine. He contended that America is not "exile" and that the creation of a Jewish State might expose the Jews to the charge of dual loyalty, and that Jews are so attached to their country that "no reason could be devised for their forsaking it to settle in Palestine". One of the Rabbis visiting the U.S.A. and attending the conference put this question to Judge Proshauer: ". . . have you any assurance that your grand-children and great-grandchildren will remain Jews under present conditions in America? If you have no such assurance, can there be any doubt of the condition of exile in which we live here? However, in a completely Jewish state, we can be certain that Jews will remain Jews no matter what conditions prevail." [6] "The danger that threatens the Diaspora is not only persecution or discrimination. It is the 'kiss of death', the loosening of ties which for centuries kept fast the unity of Israel in exile." [7]

What is the solution for the problem of Jewish survival in the Diaspora? According to the Israeli leaders there is no complete and satisfactory solution except emigration to the State of Israel. Since it may be impossible for the time being for all Jews of the Diaspora to leave for Israel, the next best thing for Jewish sur-vival in the Diaspora is "a broadening and ever stronger bond with the State of Israel, and a Hebrew education at whose foundation lies the Bible". [8]

2. THE DIASPORA VIEW

The pessimistic Israeli view about the future of the Diaspora is shared by some Zionists living in the Diaspora. "The calami-tous situation of Jewry today is not fully grasped by many, even leading Jews, including scholars and prominent Zionists. But the Galuth is painfully drawing to its close. We Jews cannot remain in the Galuth—there is no choice for us—we must liquidate the Galuth or the Galuth will liquidate us. If we con-tinue for a long period to enjoy such emancipation as is today granted us in almost every country in the world, and remain a minority among other nations, we will inevitably disappear as a people." [9]

A small segment of Diaspora Jews is of the opinion that Diaspora Jewry can survive even if left to itself under present changed circumstances. By and large, however, the prevailing belief among the vast majority of spokesmen of present day

F

Diaspora is that Diaspora Jewry can survive only if it retains some spiritual bonds with the State of Israel Jewry.

If one studies the thinking of American Jews on the future of Diaspora Jewry—and American Jewry at present constitutes the bulk of Diaspora Jewry—one gains the conviction that American Jewry does not hold as nearly a pessimistic attitude on the future of Diaspora Jewry as the Israeli leaders do. There was a Diaspora centuries before the destruction of the Jewish Homeland in A.D. 70. When the Babylonian Exile came to an end only a small fraction of the Jews dwelling in the Babylonian Empire returned to Palestine. It is maintained by some that many Jews lived outside of Palestine even prior to the destruction of the First Commonwealth by the Babylonians.[10] According to one source half of the world's Jewish population in A.D. 70 lived outside of the borders of Palestine, while another source cites the number of Jews residing outside of Palestine in that era as three times the number of those living in Palestine. From this it is concluded that for some time prior to the destruction of the Second Jewish Commonwealth by Rome Palestine Jewry constituted only a fraction of world Jewry. If it is realized that the present world's Jewish population is much larger than in the first century A.D. one must conclude that, for the time being at least, the bulk of the Jews must remain outside of the borders of the present State of Israel. These considerations alone force a more positive approach to the whole question of the destiny of Diaspora Jewry.

Most spokesmen of American Jewry strenuously object to the Israeli identification of the present Diaspora with Exile. As far as the Western Diaspora is concerned—and most Jews outside of the State of Israel live at the present in countries of the Western Diaspora—it is definitely not Exile. Notwithstanding the existence of a certain amount of antisemitism in the lands of the Western Diaspora, the Jewish people living there consider these countries their home. They have a feeling of belonging there and have no desire to leave. The American Jew resents any application to America of the concept of "Exile". He knows only too well that America has for many years been a haven of refuge for millions of Jews. He is eternally grateful for the part which America has played in the survival of the Jews, and he is attached to this country with a deep and abiding love and with all the fibres of his being.

But if it is acknowledged that the present Diaspora is not identical with physical exile, it is at the same time conceded by many Diaspora Jews that not all is well with Judaism in the Diaspora. The Diaspora is not physical exile for the Jews but it is spiritual exile for their Judaism. Under the new conditions which are the outgrowth of World War Two the spiritual exile of Diaspora Jewry has become more real than ever. Diaspora Jewry is now more exposed to the forces threatening its inner unity than ever before. There is in this connection an increasing recognition of the growing importance of the State of Israel as the spiritual centre for World Jewry.[11] ". . . Israel," we are told, "must provide the substance about which Jewry in other lands will revolve".[12] "American Jews have it within their power to forge spiritual bonds with their brothers in Israel and to establish lines of communications which are far easier to fashion today than ever before in history." Co-operation between Israel and American Jewry "may well usher in a renaissance of the Jewish spirit . . . The people in Israel will always play a vital role in keeping the American Jews conscious of their Jewishness and loyal to Jewish values . . . American Jewry will help Israel to remain conscious of its humanity and of its relationship and responsibility to all the world."[13] It is suggested that a helpful interest in the welfare of the people of Israel on the part of the Jews in the Diaspora and the establishment of a spiritual interdependent relationship with Israel will help stem the drift of the Diaspora Jew away from Judaism, and promote Jewish solidarity.[14] It is stated that the "ingathering of the exiles", or the homecoming of the Jewish people, has a dual meaning. For those Jews who still live in oppression, this "ingathering of exiles" is physical. "They must be brought to safety in the land of Israel, integrated, rehabilitated and aided to become self-sustaining citizens of the State, able and willing to contribute to the physical and the economic resources of their country. Perhaps the Jews behind the Iron Curtain may yet be rescued for liberty. But for the Jews of the democratic world, among whom the Jewish community of the United States is pre-eminent, the process remains spiritual. They must be brought out of the exile of self-alienation to self-knowledge and self-fulfilment, so that they may live as members of a world people, centred in Israel, but at home wherever freedom truly lives."[15]

II. CAN THE STATE OF ISRAEL BECOME THE SPIRITUAL CENTRE FOR WORLD JEWRY?

". . . I believe that Israel must provide the substance about which Jewry in other lands will revolve."[16] What is the nature of this substance which world Jewry expects Israel to provide?

The Jews of the Diaspora expect the people of the State of Israel to produce a model State and evolve an ideal, as it were, way of life. This, not withstanding the fact that the citizens of the State of Israel are engaged in a bitter struggle for physical survival in a small, poor, and not fully developed country, and surrounded on three sides by deadly enemies. Consequently, they rejoice at every manifestation of the spirit of tolerance and magnanimity, and become despondent when they see Israel in her national self-interest resort on occasion to methods of expediency. "If to the Jews of the world, the country [of Israel] becomes an example of a novel life, they will be drawn to it; they will cherish it in their heart as a holy thing, and make sacrifices for its sake."[17] This noble way of life which the Diaspora Jews expect Israel to develop must, admittedly, be a Jewish way of life, a Jewish civilization.

But what sort of Jewish civilization is Israel to build which could extend its radiant influence to the far corners of Diaspora Jewry? One segment of Diaspora Jews maintains that this civilization must be a continuation of the millennial spiritual tradition of the Jewish people. The State of Israel can become a spiritual centre for world Jewry, "only if it encompasses 'everything Jewish'", if it does not reject the Galut spirit or the Galut tradition. "The Sabras' [nickname for native Israelis] attempts to shed the 'Galuth spirit' constitute a rebellion against the Jewish past—our strongest common bond. Jews cannot break this tie and hope to continue as Jews, even if they have as props Israeli citizenship and the air of Israel."[18]

The conditions under which Israel would qualify for spiritual leadership in relation to world Jewry were set forth in clear and forceful terms by one of the Diaspora's most brilliant essayists in an address delivered at the World Zionist Congress in Jerusalem in 1951. "Upon vast expanses of time," he declared, "and apparently out of nothing more than memories, strivings and aspirations, our people created such grand structures as the

Babylonian Talmud, the palaces of Kabbalah and Hassidism, the gardens of mediaeval philosophy and poetry, the self-discipline and inspirational ritualism of the Shulhan Arukh, the colour and aroma of Sabbaths and holidays. All these to a great extent are creations of the Galut, ex-territorial conquests, and however onerous was our isolation from the world we lived in, still it gave us a sense of aristocratic exclusiveness, of lineage, of superiority. We were without territory—yet possessed of clear and fixed boundaries that Jews devotedly guarded; without armies—and yet so much heroism; without a Temple—and yet so much sanctity; without a priesthood—and yet each Jew, in effect, a priest; without kingship—and yet with such unexcelled spiritual 'sovereignty'. Should we be ashamed of the Exile? I am proud of it, and if Galut was a calamity (Who can pretend it was not?) I am proud of what we were able to perform in that calamity."[19]

". . . The influence of present day Israel can be a fertilizing factor for Jewish cultural life in the Diaspora only on one condition: if the civilization of Israel should lean on certain, so to speak, extra-geographical elements in traditional Jewish culture, elements that have demonstrated their capacity to survive without the support and nourishment of a national soil." "When I hear so frequently the verse 'For from Zion shall go forth Torah' reverently quoted with reference to the Zion of our day, the present State in Zion, I too believe, as others do, that new and lofty cultural values will in time be created here [in the State of Israel]— values of universal scope and significance. But for the present I should rather rephrase it to say 'For from Zion went forth the Torah'; a Torah once came forth from this land, and in virtue of that Torah, later, generation upon generation, in one Exile after another, Jews created spiritual values which bear the stamp of creative effort and achievement. Those values and the psychic energies embodied in them must continue to be cultivated on the soil of the State of Israel, no doubt in new forms, with new stresses, and by different methods; they must be the foundations of that new civilization that is beginning . . . to emerge in the State of Israel."[20]

The "spiritual values" which the Jews have created in their long exile and which must become the foundation of the new civilization of the State of Israel are—according to the representatives of this group—those embodied in the Talmud, in the Jewish mystical teachings of the Kabbalah, in the Jewish medieval philosophy and poetry, especially of the Spanish era, in the religious code of the Shulchan Aruch of the seventeenth century, and the pietistic movement of Hassidism which came into existence in the eighteenth century—already referred to above. To this long list the Jewish writers add the ideals which emanated from the once-famous centres of Talmudic learning of Eastern Europe, now out of existence, and those set forth in the literary works of Jewish secular writers who lived in Eastern Europe in the nineteenth and beginning of the twentieth centuries, such as Mendel, Sholem Aleichem, Peretz and others.[21]

But what exactly are the ideals common to the various periods of the last 1,900 years of Jewish history which are supposedly capable of becoming the foundation of the new civilization in the State of Israel? Is it not true that in the last 150 years the Jewish people all over the world have increasingly become alienated from these ideals? Is it not a historical fact that the historical continuity of the last 1,900 years has been broken in the Era of Emancipation? Why should Jews want to transplant to the modern State of Israel a type of civilization or a way of life many of whose values have been dead and dying for the last 150 years? Why should Diaspora Jewry expect the State of Israel to build on a foundation which Diaspora Jewry has rejected as unsuitable for itself? The modern State of Israel can no more live by the concepts of traditional Judaism than modern England by the principles or ideals of Chaucer's England. For whether we like to admit it or not Talmudic Judaism was moulded and conditioned by certain historical forces, and therefore was a product of a certain particular historical era. With the passing away of that era, Talmudic Judaism began to disintegrate.

While the proponents of the ideas discussed above speak in general and vague terms of the need of building Jewish life in the State of Israel on the spiritual or cultural continuity of the last 1,900 years of Jewish history, the representatives of Orthodox Judaism are more specific in their approach to the problem. The attitude of this group has been well defined in an exchange of thoughts between one of its representatives and David Ben Gurion, Prime Minister of Israel. In his correspondence with the Prime Minister the Rabbi discusses the nature of the bond which might unite future generations of Diaspora—especially American—Jewry with those of Israeli Jewry. This bond, the Rabbi declares, must be religion. The State of Israel "must be the source of a

common religious fulfilment which transcends geographic boundaries, political allegiances, economic barriers, and social demar-
cations, and which can bind our grandchildren together. Torah
has related Jews from different lands together through the ages;
it must continue to do so in the future. And Israel must prove
itself to be the embodiment of Torah. Then, yes, then only, can
my grandchild be related to the Holy Land".[22]

But by "Torah" the Rabbi does not exactly mean the Old
Testament, certainly not the prophetic portion of it. To the
Prime Minister's suggestion that the Hebrew tongue and the
Bible in Hebrew can become the bridge between Diaspora and
Israel Jewry, the Rabbi states that Hebrew will never become
the vernacular of American Jews. As to the Old Testament
and the ideals of the Prophets on which the Prime Minister lays
so much emphasis, the Rabbi declares that the Old Testament
and particularly the Prophetic ideals are "no longer exclusively
Jewish."[23] According to the Rabbi the bridge between Israel
and American Jewry must be the Shulchan Aruch, the Old
Testament, and the Land of Israel. But there is no doubt that
of the three the Shulchan Aruch [Jewish Religious Code] is by
far the most important. "No book or land will spare them
[future generations of Jews]. Only life, distinctive, related Jewish
living in Israel and America can turn the tide of disaster . . .
We need a Shulchan Aruch that will work in daily practice (not
only in ideas), and that will carry the conviction for its adherents
that it is the right way for Jews because God so chose, or because
it just is. Such a code, steadily expanding yet founded on age-old
Jewish principles, can develop a united, vibrant Jewish people,
I hope, inside and outside Israel (as it did for our grandfathers)."[24]
To the Prime Minister's restatement of his conviction that the
Bible and the Land of Israel are capable of becoming the spiritual
link between Israel and the Diaspora the Rabbi makes this very
pertinent observation, that it was not the Bible and the Land of
Israel which preserved the Jew but the Jew's faith in God and
Divine guidance in history. By this faith the Jew preserved the
Land and the Bible, and by this faith the Bible and the Land pre-
served the Jews. "Without this firm faith, I cannot recognize
Israel's ability to survive, or to find strength in the Book of
Books, beyond that 'normal' survival strength which is found
in other peoples and which has always faltered and failed."[25]
But the Rabbi failed to explain how a certain religious code for

every-day life can become a bridge between the Jews of America and Israel when the vast majority of the Jews in either country refuse to live by it; or how the Jews without faith in the Divine origin of the religious code can be expected to live by it.

In concluding this discussion we shall make the following observations: The goal of modern Zionism was not the mere rebuilding of the wastes of Zion, but also the remaking of the Jewish personality. The Land of Israel was to become a haven for a revived Jewish spiritual life, a Merkaz Ruchani, i.e. a spiritual centre for world Jewry. The unprecedented revival of the Hebrew tongue, the extraordinary preoccupation with the study of the Bible, these two achievements of the State of Israel, show that the Land of Israel is moving in that direction. On the other hand, the present religious condition of the Israeli Jews as shown in our analysis in the preceding chapters, the spiritual vacuum, the searching and groping for religious certainty, all these prove that the State of Israel has not as yet fulfilled Zionist, hopes concerning a spiritual centre for world Jewry.

NOTES TO CHAPTER 5

1. Benno Weiser, "Ben Gurion's Dispute with American Zionists", article in *Commentary* (New York), August 1954.
2. Simon A. Dolgin, "Can We Stay Jews Outside 'The Land'?", an exchange of letters between David Ben Gurion and Simon A. Dolgin, published in *Commentary* (New York), September 1953.
3. T. W. Rosmarin, "America is not Babylonia", article in *The Jewish Spectator* (New York), March 1953.
4. Eliezer Livneh, "This is Galut", article in *The Jewish Spectator* (New York), February 1952.
5. Ibid.
6. Quoted by Aaron Pechenick, "American Jews and Israel", article in *The Jewish Spectator* (New York), April 1952.
7. David Ben Gurion, *Rebirth and Destiny of Israel* (Philosophical Library: New York, 1954), p. 430.
8. David Ben Gurion, "Can We Stay Jews Outside 'The Land'?", article in *Commentary* (New York), September 1953.
9. J. Litvin, "The Galuth must be Liquidated", article in *The Jewish Spectator* (New York), October 1948.
10. Robert Gordis, "Israel and the Diaspora in the Light of Tradition, History and Reality", article in *Judaism* (New York), Spring 1954.
11. Ibid.
12. Simon A. Dolgin, idem.
13. Robert Gordis, idem.

14. Benno Weiser, idem.
15. Robert Gordis, idem.
16. Simon A. Dolgin, idem.
17. I. Jefroykin, "Jewish State and Jewish Civilization", article in *Judaism* (New York), October 1952.
18. T. W. Rosmarin, "Israel and the Diaspora", article in *The Jewish Spectator* (New York), October 1949.
19. Hayim Greenberg, *The Inner Eye* (Jewish Frontier Publishing Association: New York, 1953), p. 78.
20. Ibid., pp. 77, 80.
21. Maurice Samuel, "Why Israel Misunderstands American Jewry", article in *Commentary* (New York), October 1953; also S. Rappaport, "Living in Two Civilizations", article in *The Jewish Spectator* (New York), June 1952.
22. Simon A. Dolgin, idem.
23. Ibid.
24. Ibid.
25. Ibid.

CHAPTER 6

THE STATE OF ISRAEL AND THE PROBLEM OF THE MESSIAHSHIP OF JESUS

I. GENERAL SURVEY OF THE SUBJECT

    1. THE PAST JEWISH ATTITUDE TO JESUS

    2. THE MODERN JEWISH ATTITUDE TO JESUS

        a. *The sources of information about Jesus*
        b. *The Jewishness of Jesus*
        c. *The dependence of Jesus on Jewish teachings*
        d. *The prophetic element in the teachings of Jesus*
        e. *The Messianic claims of Jesus*
        f. *The significance of Jesus for the world*
        g. *The significance of Jesus for the Jewish people*

II. SOME BASIC FACTORS IN THE JEWISH ATTITUDE TO JESUS

    1. THE JEWISH CONCEPT OF SIN AND MAN'S MORAL NATURE

    2. THE MODERN JEWISH CONCEPT OF HUMAN SIN IS INCONSISTENT WITH THE TEACHINGS OF THE OLD TESTAMENT

        a. *The Old Testament teaches that all men are sinners*
        b. *The Old Testament teaches that human nature is sinful*
        c. *The Old Testament doctrine of human sin is borne out by the lessons from Jewish history*
        d. *The Old Testament doctrine of human sin is borne out by the lessons from universal history*

    3. JUDAISM AND THE DOCTRINE OF MEDIATION

        a. *The modern Jewish view*
        b. *Mediation in the Old Testament*
        c. *Mediation in the Apocrypha and Pseudepigrapha*
        d. *Mediation in the Targums*
        e. *Mediation in Rabbinic literature*
        f. *Mediation in the Prayer Book*
        g. *Opposition to the doctrine of Mediation*
        h. *Conclusion*

    4. THE TORAH OF RABBINIC JUDAISM

        a. *The principles of the Torah of Rabbinic Judaism*
        b. *Modern Judaism and the Torah of Rabbinic Judaism*

THE STATE OF ISRAEL AND THE PROBLEM
OF THE MESSIAHSHIP OF JESUS

I. General Survey of the Subject

The relation of the Jewish people to Jesus of Nazareth is one of the strangest historical phenomena. Jesus was a Jew, His first followers were Jews, the Messianic movement he founded arose on Jewish soil, and the Messianic hope was a Jewish hope. Any Jewish movement which aimed at gaining adherents for its cause among the Gentiles was bound, if successful, to become a predominantly Gentile movement, as the Jews have always formed a very small part of the world's population. This was exactly the case with the Messianic movement of Jesus of Nazareth. Being cosmopolitan at heart, it soon spread outside the borders of the Land of Israel where it originated. In spite of the bloody and cruel persecutions which it experienced in the empire of pagan Rome, within two hundred years from its inception it became the faith of the major part of the population of the Roman empire.

Even after Christianity had become numerically a Gentile movement there never was a century without Jewish converts to Jesus. At times their numbers were reduced to a trickle, at other times they expanded to a broad stream. Official Judaism, however, and the vast majority of the Jewish people assumed, from the very beginning, a hostile attitude to the movement. This hostility was first aimed at Jesus Himself, but after His death it was transferred to His Jewish followers. Historically the Jewish attitude to Jesus and His movement may be divided into three parts: (1) From the birth of the movement, at the end of the first third of the first century A.D. until A.D. 70; (2) from A.D. 70 until the Political Emancipation of the Jews in Europe at the end of the eighteenth century; (3) from the beginning of the era of Emancipation until the present day.

I. THE PAST JEWISH ATTITUDE TO JESUS

We shall consider the first two historical periods together. The opposition which Jesus met during his short three years' ministry came from the various groups of the Jewish nation and for different reasons. He held many views in common with this or that particular group of Israel, but at the same time He differed sharply from all of them on other points. He maintained a positive attitude to the Temple which to Him was His Heavenly Father's House, the centre of Israel's worship. But He opposed the profit-minded and greedy high-priesthood. He did not preach rebellion against Rome, but He certainly did not favour the status quo attitude of the worldly Sadducees. He shared many of the views of the Pharisees, but He castigated their unspiritual legalism. And so it happened that the attitude to Him on the part of the various representative groups of Jewish life was shaped not by what He and they held in common, but by those things in which they differed. To the high-priesthood He became a Temple destroyer, to the Sadducees—a potential political rebel, and to the Pharisees—a threat to tradition, undermining the validity of the Law of Moses. The rank and file of the people were disillusioned when He failed to bring them political deliverance from the oppression of Rome. With the exception of a small group of His followers the whole nation was united in rejecting Him.

Following the Crucifixion the enmity to Jesus soon engulfed His followers. Several waves of persecution had taken place between A.D. 33 and A.D. 70. Nevertheless, the Jewish followers of Jesus managed to live among their people, attended the Temple and Synagogue services, and observed the Jewish religious practices. The political unrest experienced by the Land of Israel in that era, and Jewish preoccupation with the problem of political liberation from Roman power, have served to detract the people's attention from internal issues. In the meantime the young Christian movement gained adherents among the Jews and grew by leaps and bounds among the Gentiles outside of the Land of Israel.

The armed conflict with Rome which ended with the destruction of the Temple in A.D. 70 served to focus the attention of the Jewish people on the Jewish-Christian problem. The terrible defeat which the Jews suffered in this uprising provided the Jewish Christians with much propaganda fuel. The defeat was interpreted by them as God's judgment upon the nation for the rejection of Jesus the Messiah. The disillusionment which resulted from the defeat rendered many Jews susceptible to the arguments of the Jewish Christians. There is evidence to the effect that the cause of Jesus had gained many Jewish believers following the end of the Roman War.

The destruction of the Temple and the dispersion of the Jews throughout the then known Gentile world brought on an acute national and religious crisis within Jewry. The questions which demanded urgent solution were, first, how can Judaism, deprived of the sacrificial system of its worship, survive religiously; second, how can the Jewish people scattered in a hostile Gentile world survive nationally. The outcome of this crisis was the emergence of the Synagogue as the centre of Jewish religious life, and the substitution of prayers in place of the sacrifices. To be sure, the Synagogue had been in existence for a long time prior to the destruction of the Second Temple, but its position was of secondary importance as long as the Temple was in existence. With the disappearance of the Temple the priesthood and the Sadducees—the political allies of the priesthood—sank to a position of relative insignificance, while the Rabbis moved up to the forefront of Jewish life.

The leaders of Rabbinic Judaism soon gained the conviction that with the loss of the National Homeland the Jewish religion, centred in the Synagogue and the Rabbinic schools, could save the Jewish nation from national extinction. Accordingly, the religious system, whose beginning antedated the destruction of the Jewish Homeland, was now called upon to recast Jewish life. In this task of remoulding Jewish life, Rabbinic Judaism found its most formidable opposition among the Jewish followers of Jesus. Their cosmopolitan outlook, their belief that Jesus the Messiah by His vicarious Death and Resurrection has filled the Mosaic Law and instituted the era of Grace, their conviction that the rejection of Jesus brought upon the Jewish people their sorry plight, all of these factors brought the Synagogue and the Jewish followers of Jesus to a head-on collision. A series of measures were put in effect to counteract the influence of the Jewish Christians and, if possible, to separate them entirely from the Jewish community. In this struggle the Synagogue scored in due time a complete victory.

The various countermeasures which the Synagogue prepared against the Jewish Christians are discussed below under the following headings:

(1) *Social discrimination.* Selling and buying were forbidden, thus imposing a kind of economic boycott against Jewish Christians. No Jew was to accept medical treatment from a Jewish Christian physician. No help may be rendered to a Jewish Christian when in need or danger.[1]

(2) *Enactments against Christian writings.* Reading the Gospels or other Christian writings was forbidden. Even rescuing them from the fire was prohibited.[2]

(3) *Reciting of the Ten Commandments.* The Ten Commandments were recited daily in the Temple and also in the synagogues. Towards the end of the first century A.D. the reading of the Ten Commandments was discontinued in the synagogues. The reason given was "because of the misrepresentation of the Minim, that they might not say, These only were given to Moses on Sinai".[3] Apparently the Christians were teaching that of the Law of Moses only the Ten Commandments have permanent validity.

(4) *The "Birkath ha-minim".* One of the prayers in the Jewish Prayer-Book which forms a distinctive part of the three daily prayers is called Shemoneh Esreh, so called because, when originally composed, it consisted of eighteen benedictions. Around A.D. 100 another benediction was inserted which became the twelfth benediction and which to this day is known in the Prayer Book as the "Birkath ha-minim". It is generally agreed that the name was used to designate the Jewish Christians. In the present version this twelfth benediction reads as follows: "And for slanderers let there be no hope, and let all wickedness perish as in a moment; let all thine enemies be cut off speedily, and the dominion of arrogance do thou uproot and crush, cast down and humble speedily in our days. Blessed art thou, O Lord, who breakest the enemies and humblest the arrogant." The present version is not the original one. On account of censorship the original composition was altered. A number of older texts were located, among which is one which S. Schechter found among the Cairo Genizah papers, where in place of "slanderers" we have "apostates", "Nazarenes"

and "Christians".[4] The "Birkath ha-minim" is therefore a prayer which was inserted into the Prayer-Book around the end of the first century A.D. to be recited by every Jew three times daily and containing a curse pronounced upon the Jewish Christians. That Jewish and not Gentile Christians were meant is pretty certain, as the Synagogue was not much concerned with Gentile Christianity, and this curse was designed to eliminate the Jewish Christians from the body of the Jewish nation. With the introduction of this prayer the Jewish Christians who up till then attended the Synagogue services were forced to discontinue this practice, and separation between Jew and Jewish Christian became complete. In the course of time the very name of Jesus was all but forgotten among the Jews and many a Jew of the Ghetto hardly knew that He ever existed. This state of affairs prevailed for seventeen centuries.

2. THE MODERN JEWISH ATTITUDE TO JESUS

The modern Jewish attitude to Jesus is the outgrowth of the radical changes which have taken place in the position of the Jew since the beginning of the era of Political Emancipation in Europe at the end of the eighteenth century. When the Jew emerged from his Ghetto isolation and renewed his contacts with the Gentile world after a lapse of centuries, he began to learn many things about the Gentile world which were unknown to him before. He became convinced that not everything in the Ghetto was perfect, and not everything outside of the Ghetto was evil. His ideas with regards to Christianity underwent important changes. He discovered that many of the progressive ideas which agitated the minds and hearts of some of the best people in Europe had their foundation in the New Testament. All these factors aroused in the emancipated Jew a desire to get better acquainted with the Founder of Christianity. As a result of this, a vast Jewish literature grew up in the last hundred years dealing with the subject of Christianity. And there is much evidence that Jewish interest in Christianity is still on the increase.

In reviewing Jewish writings on the subject of Jesus we note, with very few exceptions, a remarkable consensus of opinion on important aspects of the problem. The reader is referred to the original works dealing with the subject.[5]

Here we will have to limit ourselves to mentioning the main points which reflect Jewish thinking on the subject of Jesus.

a. The sources of information about Jesus

There is general agreement among Jewish scholars that the Talmud supplies very little information about Jesus, and the few references we find there are historically untrustworthy. These references to Jesus in the Talmud, Klausner states, "partake rather of the nature of vituperation and polemic against the founder of a hated party, than of objective accounts of historical value".[6]

Most of the knowledge about Jesus the Jews of the Middle Ages derived from a blasphemous and historically worthless book or pamphlet named *Toldoth Yeshu*. It has been denounced and repudiated by many outstanding modern Jews. Its only value consists in that it reflects the Jewish state of mind with regards to Jesus which prevailed in the Middle Ages.[7]

The New Testament is considered by Jewish scholars to contain much about Jesus which is historically true. But even if one should exclude the New Testament and confine oneself to sources outside of it such as the Talmud, Josephus, the Greek and Latin writers of that era, and the Church Fathers, one is forced to conclude "that Jesus did indeed exist, that he had an exceptionally remarkable personality, and that he lived and died in Judaea during the Roman occupation".[8]

b. The Jewishness of Jesus

So estranged have the Jews become from Jesus in the seventeen centuries prior to the Emancipation era that Jewish writers have shown amazement upon discovering Jewish characteristics in Jesus. In part, at least, this Jewish tendency to stress the Jewishness of Jesus is a reaction against a tendency in some Christian circles to minimize the Jewish background of Christianity. "Jesus", we are told, "was a perfect Jew."[9] "Jesus of Nazareth, however, was a product of Palestine alone, a product of Judaism unaffected by any foreign admixture. There were many Gentiles in Galilee but Jesus was in no way influenced by them. . . . Without any exception he is wholly explainable by the scriptural and Pharisaic Judaism of his time." "Jesus was a Jew and a Jew he remained till his last breath. His one idea was to implant within his nation the idea of the coming of the

Messiah and, by repentance and good works, hasten the 'end'."
"In all this Jesus is the most Jewish of Jews, more Jewish than
Simeon ben Shetah, more Jewish even than Hillel."[10]*

c. The dependence of Jesus on Jewish teachings

Jewish writers have taken great pains to emphasize the Jewish
origin of the teachings of Jesus. Rabbinic literature has been
extensively searched for the source of many of the New Testament narratives. There is a group of Jewish writers which
refuse to see any originality in the teachings of Jesus. ". . . the
roots of the life and thought of Jesus lie entirely in Jewish
soil . . ."[11] "It is the Jewish view that Jesus added no important
original element to the religious and moral assets which had
been accumulated by the Jewish prophets and sages, and that
he has certainly been the more or less direct cause of lowering
the pure and lofty ideas about God and man current in
Judaism."[12] "The Beatitudes have undoubtedly a lofty tone,
but let us not forget that all that they teach can be found in
Isaiah and the Psalms. Israel finds nothing new here."[13]

The above declarations belong to an extreme segment of
the Orthodox group and are not necessarily representative of
Jewish thinking on the nature of the teachings of Jesus. Many
Jewish writers take a more objective attitude to this subject and
it is stated by them that the originality of Jesus lies not so much in
what He taught, as in how He taught, and in His new insights into
the meaning of Jewish teachings. "His doctrines were not perhaps
conspicuously original. He copied and elaborated the teachings
of contemporary Rabbis as he had heard them repeated from
earliest youth in the synagogue of his native place. He presented
them, however, in a new fashion untrammelled by the shackles
of ceremonial law, and enlivened by continuous parables of
haunting beauty."[14]

In the teaching of Jesus there is a "new expression of what
the religious leaders of Israel, and particularly the Prophets,
had sought to teach".[15] "He gave a fresh interpretation of
the laws governing the spiritual life, a fresh message concerning
the meaning and purpose of religion, a new illumination of the
sense and the object of the old law and of the old prophetic
utterances. Here lay his genius and originality."[16]

Montefiore endorses Wellhausen's view that "the originality

* Rabbinic authorities who lived in the Mishnaic period.

of Jesus lies in this, that he felt and picked out what was true and eternal amid the chaos and the rubbish, and that he enunciated and emphasized it with the greatest possible insistence and stress".[17] "Here [in the Gospels] we have religion and morality joined together at a white heat of intensity. The teaching often glows with light and fire. Nothing is to interfere with the pursuit of the highest moral and religious ideal; nothing is to come before it."[18]

d. The prophetic element in the teachings of Jesus

Many Jewish students of the subject of Jesus look upon Him as one of the prophets of Israel. "The inwardness of Jesus, the intense spirituality of his teaching . . . show his connection and kinship with the Prophets. He takes up and renews their messages."[19] "His teaching is a revival of prophetic Judaism and in some respects points forward to the Liberal Judaism of today."[20] To C. G. Montefiore Jesus is "one of the greatest and most original of our Jewish prophets and teachers".[21] "In the spirit of the ancient prophets of Israel, he inveighed against the exploitation of the poor by the rich, and the stranglehold which formalism seemed in his eyes to be establishing on religion."[22] Jesus "felt himself called to be another Isaiah, a deliverer from spiritual darkness to his people. He wished to give sight to the blind, to free the enslaved, to raise the poor and destitute."[23]

e. The Messianic claims of Jesus

Jewish students of the subject of Christianity agree that Jesus believed Himself to be Israel's Messiah. There are four Jewish conceptions of what the Messiahship of Jesus meant to Him. One of these is the political view. According to Robert Eisler Jesus was the head of a revolutionary movement of a religio-nationalist character aimed at the high-priesthood and its Roman overlords.[24]

The apocalyptic view of the Messiahship of Jesus is represented by E. R. Trattner. According to this view Jesus was convinced of the imminent coming of the Kingdom of God. He believed that God would intervene on behalf of Israel and the Kingdom of God would be established in a supernatural way. He felt that it was His task to prepare Israel for this event by calling upon them to repent.[25]

According to H. G. Enelow the Messianic mission of Jesus was of a spiritual character. "The Kingdom of God, he decided, was not political, it was not of this world: it was spiritual."[26] As to the question just what did the Messianic consciousness mean to Jesus, Enelow explains that it meant for Him that He was to realize inwardly, in Himself, the Kingdom of God, which was spiritual in nature. Enelow, together with most Jewish writers, is convinced that Jesus came not to overthrow the Law, or to found a new religion. Jesus came to fulfil the Law. To Enelow fulfilling the Law by Jesus meant not a mechanical fulfilment but "an absorption and application of its spirit, an inward apprehension of its content and the unfoldment of its purpose in actual life".[27] While such a spiritual conception of the Law was not new in Rabbinic teachings, there is with Jesus "a change of emphasis, and the change was toward the accentuation of the personal element, Jesus' own personal interfusion with his teaching". While the Rabbis "were interested in principles, in doctrines, in ideals",[28] Jesus was concerned in individuals. The Rabbis "taught impersonally . . . Jesus taught personally".[29]

Klausner brings out the fourth view of the nature of Jesus' Messiahship by combining some of the elements embodied in the political view of Eisler and apocalyptic views of Trattner. According to Klausner Jesus aimed to call upon His people to repent and practise righteousness in order to prepare them for the coming of the Kingdom of God which would be set up not by the sword, but through the agency of the Messiah endowed by God with supernatural powers.[30]

f. The significance of Jesus for the world

Maimonides, the great medieval Talmudic authority, who cannot be accused of harbouring any too friendly feelings for Christianity, saw in Jesus "a means for preparing the way for the King-Messiah"[31] to the Gentiles. But for many centuries Jews could see no significance at all about Jesus. It is only when Jew and Christian drew closer to each other that the Jew became aware of the tremendous influence which Jesus has exerted in the history of the world. ". . . it is estimated", says one Jewish writer, "that more than sixty thousand volumes have been written about him. Eight hundred languages and dialects tell his story . . . To me—because I am a Jew—this is an amazing thing, for nothing quite like it has ever happened on so large a scale in the annals of man."[32]

"No ethical system", states another Jewish authority, "or

religious catechism, however broad and pure, could equal the efficiency of this great personality, standing, unlike any other, midway between heaven and earth, equally near to God and to man . . . Jesus, the helper of the poor, the friend of the sinner, the brother of every fellow-sufferer, the comforter of every sorrow-laden, the healer of the sick, the up-lifter of the fallen, the lover of man, the redeemer of woman, won the heart of mankind by storm . . . Jesus, the meekest of men, the most despised of the despised race of the Jews, mounted the world's throne to be the earth's Great King."[33]

"No Jewish prophet before Jesus", we are told, "ever searched out the miserable, the sick, the weak, and the down-trodden in order to pour forth love and compassionate service. He went out of his way to redeem the lowly by a touch of human sympathy that is altogether unique in Jewish history!"[34]

"Had there been no Abraham, there would have been no Moses. Had there been no Moses, there would have been no Jesus. Had there been no Jesus, there would have been no Paul. Had there been no Paul, there would have been no Christianity. Had there been no Christianity, there would have been no Luther. Had there been no Luther, there would have been no Pilgrim fathers to land on these shores with the Jewish Bible under their arms. Had there been no Pilgrim fathers, there would have been no civil or religious liberty. Had there been no civil or religious liberty, tyranny and despotism would still rule the earth, and the human family would still live in mental, moral, and physical bondage.

"Without Jesus and without Paul, the God of Israel would still have been the God of a handful, the God of a petty, obscure, and insignificant tribe; the magnificent moral teachings of Moses would still have been confined to the thinly scattered believers in Judaism, and the great world of men and women would have been left so much the poorer because of their ignorance of these benign teachings.

"Let the Jew, despite the centuries of persecution and suffering, be thankful that there was a Jesus and a Paul. Let him more fully appreciate that, through the wonderful influence of these heroic characters, the mission of the Jew is being fulfilled, and his teachings are being spread to the remotest nooks and corners of the world by Christianity, 'a religion by which millions have been, and still are, quickened and inspired'. Let the Jews not forget that, through the influence of Jesus and Paul, the Ten Commandments of Moses, the sublime utterances of Isaiah, of Micah, of Jeremiah, the proverbs of Solomon, and the psalms of David, have brought, and are bringing, and will continue to bring, calm and comfort, joy and happiness, spiritual bliss and moral sunshine, into untold millions of homes."[35]

In his book entitled *Stormers of Heaven* Solomon B. Freehof has included a passage about the influence and significance of Jesus. " 'Jesus of Nazareth' is the most famous name in the world. The Galilean teacher looms as large today as he did centuries ago. His words are still on the tongues of men, and his parables are as fresh as when he first uttered them. Artists are as eager to paint him as they were in the Middle Ages. Scholars study him as much as ever. Prayers are addressed to him with unabated fervour . . . His career is known to every child in the western world. It is not necessary to retell the familiar story, from his birth in Bethlehem to his crucifixion on Golgotha. His sayings and parables are constantly quoted. They have become part of the daily speech of men . . . The secret of the influence of Jesus will perhaps always remain a mystery. After painstaking scholarship has explained all that is explicable, the secret of his power remains unsolved. Scores of men have believed themselves to be the Messiah and have convinced many of their contemporaries, but those who believed Jesus to be the Messiah have built a great church upon the rock of their belief. There were plenty of miracle workers in ancient times, but the miracles of Jesus have been retold to countless nations and are still remembered . . . That it is this personality which is the essence of his power should be evident to every objective student of Christian literature. It is not merely that legends have been woven around his name. Every great religious genius has been en-haloed with loving legend. The significant fact is that time has not faded the vividness of his image. Poetry still sings his praise. He is still the living comrade of countless lives. No Moslem ever sings, 'Mohammed, lover of my soul', nor does any Jew say of Moses, the Teacher, 'I need thee every hour.' "[36]

g. The significance of Jesus for the Jewish people

The significance of Jesus to the Jew stems from His significance to the world in general. The modern Jew takes pride in the fact that He who has exerted such a powerful influence on the destiny of mankind is flesh of their flesh and blood of their blood. But outside of this He is of no special importance to them as Jews. The Jewish preoccupation with the subject of Jesus is purely from the historical point of view. There is no room for Jesus in the religion of the Jews. Religiously, many a Jewish historic personage whose influence outside Judaism is nil is of far greater importance to the Jews than the name of Jesus. The Jewish people "whether modern or ancient, Reform or Orthodox, do not acknowledge the divinity of Jesus . . . Jews could not do that and still remain Jews". Jews are not even in a position to recognize Jesus simply as the Messiah, "for the reason that the ideas associated in the Jewish mind with the Messiah not only were left unrealized by Jesus, but have remained unfulfilled to this day".[37]

This is essentially also Klausner's position, and it reflects the general modern Jewish attitude to Jesus. "From the standpoint of general humanity he is, indeed, 'a light to the Gentiles'. His disciples have raised the lighted torch of the Law of Israel (even though that Law has been put forward in a mutilated and incomplete form) among the heathen of the four quarters of the world. No Jew can, therefore, overlook the value of Jesus and his teaching from the point of view of universal history. This was a fact which neither Maimonides nor Yehudah ha-Levi ignored . . . What is Jesus to the Jewish nation at the present day? To the Jewish nation he can be neither God nor the Son of God, in the sense conveyed by belief in the Trinity . . . Neither can he, to the Jewish nation, be the Messiah: the kingdom of heaven (the 'Days of the Messiah') is not yet come . . . But Jesus is, for the Jewish nation, a great teacher of morality and an artist in parable."[38]

II. SOME BASIC FACTORS IN THE JEWISH ATTITUDE TO JESUS

For those who believe that Jesus is Israel's Messiah and the Saviour of mankind the Jewish attitude to Jesus is a strange and painful mystery. When we consider the discipline and the training which Israel had, designed to prepare her for a worldwide mission, it is hard to realize that she failed when the decisive hour struck. But God was not surprised and His will was not frustrated. He moves in mysterious ways His wondrous works to perform.

Deep as the mystery of the rejection of Jesus by Israel is, it is nevertheless possible to analyse the various elements which underlie this rejection. We should state at the very outset that the un-Christian attitude of the medieval Church to the Jewish people is not the basic factor responsible for the Jewish attitude to Jesus. Jewish opposition to Jesus dates back to the days when Christianity was wholly a Jewish movement. It is deeply rooted in Jewish theological thinking—the seeds of which were deposited in the days following the return from Babylon. We shall now proceed with the discussion of these main theological issues which we think lie at the very basis of Israel's attitude to Jesus.

I. THE JEWISH CONCEPT OF SIN AND MAN'S MORAL NATURE

Generally speaking, the doctrine of Original Sin and the sinfulness of human nature were not held by the ancient Rabbis. The fall of Adam and its consequences for himself and his descendants are not denied in the Rabbinic writings. Adam's physical death was attributed to his sin. But that physical death of all men is also the consequence of Adam's fall is admitted by some Rabbinic authorities, while others attribute it to man's individual sin. [39]

As far as the moral consequences of the fall of Adam are concerned, no consistent view is to be found in the ancient Rabbinic writings. The Rabbis do teach that man is created with two inclinations or natures, the one to evil (Yetzer hara), and the other to good (Yetzer hatov). The evil inclination works in man from man's birth on, the good inclination makes its appearance later on, some say at the age of thirteen years. It is taught in the Talmud that God Himself has created the Evil Impulse in man. The existence of the Evil Impulse is taught to be absolutely necessary if the world is to continue. [40] There are passages in the Talmudic writings which indicate that man depends on God for victory over the Evil Impulse. [41]

When we consult the works of modern Jewish writers on this subject, we find that some of the ancient Rabbinic teachings are emphasized and carried to their logical conclusion, while others are minimized or glossed over. The effect on human nature of Adam's fall is generally denied or at best minimized, and great stress is laid on man's ability to attain righteousness without outside help. "Judaism", states Max Dienemann, "teaches that the soul of man from its very birth is pure and sinless, that man is by nature endowed with the faculty of doing what is good and of acting morally by his own strength . . . Christianity again teaches that man is from his very birth tainted by sin, that sin and guilt are the dominating power in human life . . . We enter", he continues, "into life with the full purity and originality of our God-derived nature, as if we had been the first human being that proceeded from the Creator's hand . . . The Christian is deeply convinced that man is under the domination of sin and that he is unfit of himself to do good. It is therefore clear to him that all piety must begin with the consciousness of man's sinfulness, and that his endeavour must be directed towards the one aim, how to get rid of his sins. All piety must, according to this view, begin with the recognition of the power of sin and with a deep longing after salvation. Quite different the Jew. His piety consists in the feeling that he is endowed with power to act morally, that he by his own actions is not only able but also enjoined to raise both himself and his posterity . . . In Judaism there is no room for salvation in the Christian sense, for according to it sin is something passing, and it does not recognize a realm of sin . . . The hope of salvation is to the Jew the hope of the breaking down of all tyranny and despotism and therefore at the same time the end of all the misery that is heaped upon him because he is and remains a Jew."

Realizing that his ideas on the subject of human sin may be in conflict with the teachings of the Old Testament, this writer states: "And yet in spite of all such sayings, Judaism has developed a doctrine standing in sharpest contrast to that sense which Christianity ascribes to this (Genesis 8: 21) and other passages. . . . Christianity, guided by this and similar passages in the Scriptures, has evolved its ruling doctrine, i.e. the doctrine of the fall and the sinfulness of man. But Judaism, with a constant perseverance lasting through all the generations, has passed over such passages in the Bible. When thoughts would begin to stir which came very near a recognition of the doctrine that guilt was a power ever operating in humanity, then they sank—almost unnoticed—into the canals which conducted their waters far away from the main current of Judaism."[42]

In a note on the Fall of Man as taught in the Book of Genesis, Chief Rabbi J. H. Hertz has this to say: "Judaism rejects these doctrines. Man was mortal from the first, and death did not enter the world through the transgression of Eve. Stray Rabbinic utterances to the contrary are merely homiletic, and possess no binding authority in Judaism. There is no loss of the God-likeness of man, nor of man's ability to do right in the eyes of God; and no such loss has been transmitted to his latest descendants. Although a few of the Rabbis occasionally lament Eve's share in the poisoning of the human race by the Serpent, even they declare that the antidote to such poison has been found at Sinai; rightly holding that the Law of God is the bulwark against .the devastation of animalism and godlessness. The Psalmist often speaks of sin and guilt; but never is there a reference to this·chapter or what Christian Theology calls 'The Fall'. One searches in vain the Prayer Book, or even the Days of Penitence, for the slightest echo of the doctrine of the Fall of man. 'My God, the soul which thou hast given me is pure' is the Jew's daily morning prayer . . . Instead of the Fall of man (in the sense of humanity as a whole), Judaism preaches the Rise of man; and instead of Original Sin, it stresses Original Virtue (Zchut Abbot), the beneficent hereditary influence of righteous ancestors upon their descendants."[43]

In the opinion of I. M. Wise: "To rise to self-conscious immortality and happiness is in man's power exclusively. Man is to all intents and purposes a free and independent being." "The Sinaitic revelation is the proof for the immortal and God-like nature of man." Sin in the opinion of Rabbi Wise is not a state but an action: "A sin according to Rabbinical definition, must be an action."[44]

Finally the, following statement by a recent writer: "Man's deeds, not his theological professions, bring him close to God or remove him from God . . . Nor, again, is sin something inherent in man's constitution, something transmitted through the generations from a mythical 'Fall'."[45]

We shall now attempt to show that this modern Jewish theological position on human sin is a departure from the teachings of the Old Testament and not borne out by the lessons from Jewish and universal history.

2. THE MODERN JEWISH CONCEPT OF HUMAN SIN IS INCONSISTENT WITH THE TEACHINGS OF THE OLD TESTAMENT

a. *The Old Testament teaches that all men are sinners*

Psalm 14: 2–3: "Jehovah looked down from heaven upon the children of men, to see if there were any that did understand, that seek after God. They are all gone aside; they are together become filthy; there is none that doeth good, no, not one."

Psalm 130: 3: "If thou, Jehovah, shouldest mark iniquities, O Lord, who could stand?"

Nahum 1: 6: "Who can stand before his indignation? and who can abide in the fierceness of his anger? . . ."

Malachi 3: 2: "But who can abide the day of his coming? and who shall stand when he appeareth? for he is like a refiner's fire, and like fullers' soap."

1 Kings 8: 46: ". . . For there is no man that sinneth not . . ."

Ecclesiastes 7: 20: "Surely there is not a righteous man upon earth, that doeth good, and sinneth not."

b. *The Old Testament teaches that human nature is sinful*

Sin is not an isolated phenomenon in human life. It is a state or condition common to all flesh and inherent in human nature.

"And Jehovah saw that the wickedness of man is great in the earth, and that every imagination of the thoughts of his heart was only evil continually", Genesis 6: 5.

"And Jehovah said in his heart, I will not again curse the ground any more for man's sake, for the imagination of man's heart is evil from his youth . . ." (i.e. "from the dawn of his knowledge of good and evil"—Chief Rabbi J. H. Hertz), Genesis 8: 21.

"Behold, I was brought forth in iniquity; and in sin did my mother conceive me", Psalm 51: 5 (51: 7 Heb.).

"Who can bring a clean thing out of an unclean? not one", Job 14: 4.

Lighthearted as is the modern Jewish attitude to sin, the Old Testament writers, especially the prophets, take a serious view of the problem of human sin. With Hosea, sin is no mere external act. Sinful Israel is likened by him to an adulterous wife in relation to her faithful and loving husband. "Contend with your mother, contend; for she is not my wife, neither am

I her husband; and let her put away her whoredoms from her face and her adulteries from between her breasts. I know Ephraim, and Israel is not hid from me; for now, O Ephraim, thou hast played the harlot, Israel is defiled", Hosea 2: 2 (2: 4 Heb.); 5: 3.

With Isaiah with whom God is the Holy One sin is rebellion against God. "I have nourished and brought up children, and they have rebelled against me," Isaiah 1: 2. Since rebellion against God is born of pride, sin is pride, and God's judgment is directed against this, the mother of all sin. "The lofty looks of men shall be brought low, and the haughtiness of men shall be bowed down, and Jehovah alone shall be exalted in that day. For there shall be a day of Jehovah of hosts upon all that is proud and haughty, and upon all that is lifted up; and it shall be brought low", Isaiah 2: 11–12.

With Jeremiah sin is a perversion of the human heart. "The heart is deceitful above all things, and it is exceedingly corrupt . . .", Jeremiah 17: 9.

"Behold, the days come, saith Jehovah, that I will punish all them that are circumcised in their uncircumcision. Egypt, and Judah, and Edom, and the children of Ammon, and Moab, and all that have the corners of their hair cut off, that dwell in the wilderness; for all the nations are uncircumcised, and all the house of Israel are uncircumcised in heart", Jeremiah 9: 25–26 (9: 24–25 Heb.).

"I, Jehovah, search the mind, I try the heart . . .", Jeremiah 17: 10.

"And I will give them a heart to know me . . .", Jeremiah 24: 7.

". . . I will put my law in their inward parts, and in their heart will I write it . . .", Jeremiah 31: 33 (31: 32 Heb.).

c. *The Old Testament doctrine of human sin is borne out by the lessons from Jewish history*

The story of mankind in the Bible is the story of the fall of man and God's plan to rescue him from the consequences of the fall. The fall of Adam recorded in the beginning of Genesis repeats itself in the experiences of the whole human race. In the days of Noah human corruption had reached such a degree that it became necessary to destroy the whole human race with the exception of one family. With Noah mankind was given a new chance to see what it could do. But in the course of time idolatry and human immorality became again widespread. Abraham was set apart and made to become the founder of a new nation through whom God was to accomplish the regeneration of mankind. In Abraham man was granted another opportunity to do better.

In time mankind became divided into two groups: the Israelites who were in possession of the Biblical revelation, and the Gentiles who lived outside of this revelation. It soon became evident, that when permitted to work out their own salvation, the Jews living under the Law of Moses, and the nations living outside of the Law, fared about the same. Shortly after they had received the Law of Sinai the Hebrews displayed such a rebellious spirit that they proved themselves unfit for entry into the Promised Land. Consequently, they were kept wandering in the wilderness for forty years until all those from twenty years up died out. The Hebrews who conquered the land of Canaan were for the most part a new generation, born and raised in the wilderness. About six hundred years later Israel was driven from the Land of Promise, and the First Commonwealth came to an end. When the Babylonian Exile was finished the Jews returned to the land of their fathers with a grim determination to do better. But some five hundred years later the Second Commonwealth was broken up. From the point of view of the secular historian the destruction of the First and Second Commonwealth of the Jews was just another instance of a weak nation being swallowed up by a strong nation. But from the Biblical or religious standpoint the destruction of the Jewish Commonwealth in Palestine was the result of Israel's moral failure. Repeatedly the warning had been made that the uninterrupted possession of the land by Israel depended on its compliance with the terms of the Sinai Covenant. With this agrees the teaching of the Synagogue as reflected in the Prayer-Book ("and because of our sins we have been exiled from our country . . .") and in the writings of traditional Judaism.

The post-Biblical history of the Jewish people following the destruction of the Second Commonwealth in A.D. 70 is, religiously speaking, essentially the same as prior to A.D. 70. After all the heroic attempts to comply with the Law of Moses in the great era between A.D. 70 and the end of the eighteenth century, the vast majority of the nation at last had to acknowledge the impossibility of living under the Law. Today, in or out of the

State of Israel, Jews for the most part live their lives as if the Law of Moses had never been given.

d. The Old Testament doctrine of human sin is borne out by the lessons from universal history

What religious history has taught the Jews, secular history is teaching the Gentiles, namely, that man has failed when left to work out his own salvation. The human race which came out of the Great Flood became in time divided into three great branches: the Hamites, the Semites, and the Japhethites. The Hamites were probably first in world leadership. Egypt, the empire of the Hittites, the empire of Nimrod, and the nations of Canaan, were Hamitic in origin. From the Hamites world dominion passed over to the Semites: Israel under David, Solomon and Uzziah, Assyria under Sennacherib, Babylon under Nebuchadnezzar, and the Arabs in the early part of the Middle Ages—all these have exercised world influence in their time. Then came the Japhethites, better known under the name of Aryans, who, with the defeat of Semitic Babylon by Japhethic Persia, have gradually moved up to the forefront of history, and to this day have remained the masters of the world. Thus the Hamites had their day and failed, the Semites had their day and failed, the Japhethites had theirs—and are failing.

According to Arnold Toynbee there have been twenty-one civilizations including our own. Most of the last twenty civilizations have disappeared. All of these civilizations, whether those which have disappeared entirely or the few on the way to extinction, displayed strikingly similar features in their development: "first, a phase of progressive advance punctuated by downs and ups; second, a phase of retrogressive decline, punctuated by ups and downs, and third, a final phase of utter collapse or partial integration in a new society".[46] The twentieth century exhibits many of the symptoms of the preceding civilizations. In a preface to a series of articles on "The Crisis of the Individual" published in *Commentary*, a Jewish monthly publication, we read the following statement. "In our time the individual human being has been more violently debased than in many centuries. Every aspect of the human personality—his civil rights, his individuality, his status, the dignity accorded him—all have been violated. Millions have been tortured and murdered . . . Yet the inviolability of the individual human being has been so much a part of Western civilization that it has been taken for granted. Whatever advances we hoped for in our culture were based on this ideal . . . It is not alone that this ideal has been crushed by tyrannical rulers, but it is feared that it is dying in the hearts of men. But this would mean an ominous lowering of the level of political and moral life."[47]

This universal pessimism is but a natural reaction to the disillusionment which men are experiencing as a result of the shattered dreams and unrealized hopes of the last generation. The unprecedented progress of technology in the second half of the nineteenth and the beginning of the twentieth century misled men into believing that soon all will be well with mankind. This, in spite of the clear and definite teachings of the Bible that man's salvation is dependent on God and human problems will never be solved without the moral and spiritual regeneration of the race, without a new birth from above. Thus the events since 1914 have combined to point up the utter groundlessness of modern Judaism's naïve faith in the moral strength of human nature when left to itself. The Bible and secular history have demonstrated that this belief has no foundation in reality.

3. JUDAISM AND THE DOCTRINE OF MEDIATION

Mediation is conceived as referring to the "method by which God and man are reconciled through the instrumentality of some intervening process, act or person". The idea of mediation stems from "a profound human instinct or need which finds expression in some form or other in most religions".[48] This need springs from a conviction in the human heart of the impassable gulf which separates God from man and the necessity of bridging this gap. In general, man's need of a Mediator is influenced by his concept of the holiness of God and his sense of sin. The more exalted one's concept of the holiness of God, the greater is the recognition of one's need of a Mediator between God and man.

a. The modern Jewish view

The modern Jewish view of a Mediator is strongly influenced by its approach to the problem of human sin. Briefly, Jewish thinking on this subject is that man is capable in his own strength to reach God and to fill the gap separating him from God;

therefore, the Jew has no need of a Mediator. Kaufmann Kohler states that Judaism does not recognize in principle any mediatorship between God and man.[49]

"We require no Mediator to save us from the effects of our guilt. Our own sincere repentance suffices to achieve for us Divine forgiveness."—Chief Rabbi Adler.[50]

Speaking on Atonement C. G. Montefiore has this to say: "On the one side is man, aspiring, struggling, sinning and repenting; on the other side is God, immutable, righteous, and alone. Between them and their dealings with each other there is neither intercessor nor barrier. God, the eternal giver, is ever ready to receive us . . . Judaism (whatever it may have been in the past) is now a religion without priests: no mystic rites or words intervene or mediate between man and God. When we are told that the Jewish God is distant, we smile with astonishment at the strange accusation. So near is He, that He needs no Son to bring Him nearer to us, no intercessor to reconcile Him with us, or us with Him. The child needs no one to bring him into the very presence of the Father."[51] "Judaism stands in need of no mediator and no mediation. It brings together in close relation man and God, and it declares that there is, and need be, and can be, no other being or thing to act as bridge or go-between or intercessor."[52] "No mediator is necessary . . . No intercessor is needed to bring man and God together."—O Lazarus.[53]

"God is ever near to His people, He works in the midst of their camp; the cloud of glory, the visible token of His Presence, rests upon the Sanctuary; He talks with men from Heaven. Such a Deity needs no mediator to bring Him into touch with humanity . . . Judaism repudiates the notion of a beneficent Being mediating between the Supreme and Man. No go-between can possibly be needed to bring the All-Father into communion with His own children."—Morris Joseph.[54]

We will now show that this modern Jewish attitude to the subject of Mediation is a definite departure from the teachings of the Old Testament and many of the post-Biblical Jewish religious writings.

b. Mediation in the Old Testament

In the Old Testament the principle of Mediation is clearly observable, although, except in Isaiah 53, it is not presented in as clear theological terms as in the New Testament.

(1) *Mediation by intercessory prayer.* Abraham's intercession for Sodom is one of the earliest examples of mediation by intercession of prayer. The important truth taught in this intercession is that the sinner may benefit from the merits of the righteous: God was willing to spare the wicked city if only ten righteous people had been found in Sodom.

Moses is the first Mediator in the Old Testament between God and Israel. He alone is allowed to come near to God. The people were ordered to stand from a distance (Exodus 19 and 20; Deuteronomy 5). After the sin of the Golden Calf Moses pleads with God to forgive Israel's sin, and was even willing to sacrifice his own life to avert God's wrath against the people. To the people of Israel Moses then said: "Ye have sinned a great sin; and now I will go up unto Jehovah; peradventure I shall make atonement for your sin", Exodus 32: 30. As it happened, God had His reason for not accepting Moses' offer of his own life, but we have here one of the first, if not the first, germ ideas of vicarious suffering for sin in the Old Testament.

Samuel pleads on behalf of Israel of his day (1 Samuel 7: 3–6). Jeremiah classes him with Moses as Israel's chief intercessory representatives in the past (Jeremiah 15: 1).

Elijah prays for the widow's sick son (1 Kings 17: 22) and for an end to the drought in Ahab's reign (1 Kings 18: 41–45).

(2) *The prophets.* The mediatorial character of the work of the prophets was in the direction from God towards man. They were God's messengers to the people. They proclaimed to the people God's Will and unfolded to them His purposes.

(3) *The priests.* The priestly function is primarily Godward, bringing man to God. The priest stands between a Holy God and sinful man. He brings to God the sinner's offerings. The representative and mediatory character of the priest's work finds its highest exemplification in the work of the High-priest on the Day of Atonement. With the names of the twelve tribes of Israel on his breast-plate, representing the whole nation, the High-priest enters the Holy of Holies to offer atonement for the nation's sins.

G

(4) *The angels*. In the Old Testament angels do not figure prominently as Mediators between God and man. The one indisputable example, however, is found in Daniel. "And at that time shall Michael stand up, the great prince who standeth for the children of thy people . . .", Daniel 12: 1; see also Daniel 10: 13, 21.

c. Mediation in the Apocrypha and Pseudepigrapha [55]

In this we include the writings which came into existence between the close of the Old Testament and the beginning of the New Testament era. They are known as the Apocrypha and Pseudepigrapha.

Two kinds of Mediators are met with in these writings. In the first group belong the spirits of the Old Testament heroes of faith, Adam, Abraham, and Moses. See, for example, The Life of Adam and Eve, par. 20; The Testament of Abraham, chap. 14. In the Ascension of Moses 12: 5, 6 we read: "All that was to happen on this earth did the Lord foresee, and behold it comes to pass . . . He hath appointed me for them, and because of their sins, that I might pray and supplicate for them."

In the second group the Mediators are angels. "I am Raphel, one of the seven holy angels, who bear the prayers of the saints upwards, and who have access to the glory of the Holy One", Tobit 12: 15. "And as you prayed, thou and thy daughter-in-law Sarah, I brought your sacrifice of prayers before the Holy One", Tobit 12: 12. The person speaking here is also an angel.

The angel Michael holds an important place in this literature as man's Mediator. In the Testament of Abraham, Abraham asks for Michael's intercession on his behalf. He also appears in the Life of Adam and Eve, par. 22. In Enoch 104: 1 we read: "I swear unto you, you righteous, that the angels in heaven remember you for good in the presence of the glory of the Great One." In the Testament of the Twelve Patriarchs, Levi 3: 5–6, we read of "the angels of the presence of the Lord, who serve Him, and make propitiation for all the sins of the righteous to the Lord. They offer to the Lord the reasonable sweet odour of incense and unbloody sacrifice". In 5: 7 of the same book we read again: "Hereupon I awoke and praised the Most High and the angel who intercedes for the race of Israel and all righteous men".

In conclusion, in these writings the concept of mediation

has advanced to a higher stage. In place of the mortal men of the Old Testament the Mediators between God and men are sinless beings, either angels, or the spirits of the Old Testament men of faith who in their earthly pilgrimage had experienced temptation and human frailties.

d. Mediation in the Targums [56]

The Targums are translations of Old Testament writings from Hebrew into Aramaic. But they are not translations in the strict sense of the word, rather a combination of translation and interpretation. There are four groups of these Targums: The Targum Onkelos to the Pentateuch, composed in the first century A.D.; the Targum Pseudo-Jonathan to the Pentateuch; the Targum of Jonathan to the Prophets—written in the first century A.D. by Jonathan ben Uzziel; the Targum to the Canticles.

There are two classes of Mediators in the Targums.

(1) *Human beings*. The miraculous crossing of the Red Sea by the Israelites has taken place through the merits of Abraham, the Patriarchs and other righteous (Targ. Cant. 1: 19; 6: 12; see also 7: 14). Israel was saved from God's wrath incurred by the sin of the Golden Calf because of Abraham's obedience to the Divine commandment to sacrifice Isaac (Cant. to 1: 13). In Targ. Cant. to 2: 17 we are again told that God was about to destroy the Israelites because of the sin of the Golden Calf when "He remembered the sacrifice which Abraham offered in Isaac, his son, on Mount Moriah".

Moses also holds a prominent position in the Targums as Mediator between God and Israel. "I stood between the Word of Jehovah and you", Targ. Onk. to Deut. 5: 5. ". . . When Moses, their Teacher, went up to Heaven, and brought about peace between them and their King", Targ. Cant. to 1: 5. "At that moment the anger of the Lord waxed against them and he was about to drown them in the waters of the sea, in the same manner as Pharaoh and his host were drowned, had it not been for Moses, the prophet, who spread forth his hands before the Lord, and removed the anger of the Lord from them", Targ. Cant. to 1: 9.

(2) *Superhuman beings*. Archangel Michael: "Then shall Michael, Israel's chief, say, If she be ready as a wall among the nations to give silver for the acquisition of the Unity of God's Name, then shall I and you be with their Teachers . . . And

even though she be destitute of precepts, we shall implore on her behalf mercy from heaven", Targ, Cant. to 8: 9.

The Metatron. This word is probably of Greek origin meaning one who occupies a rank next to the ruler. Metatron is sometimes identified with Enoch as in this passage. "Enoch ascended into Heaven through the Word of God, and He called Him Metatron, the Great Scribe", Targ. ps. Jon. to Gen. 5: 24. It is said that while Metatron appears in the role of an accuser of mankind in general, he acts as an intercessor for Israel.

The Memra. This is a personification of the Word of God. The Memra intercedes for Israel before God (Targ. Jon. to Jerem. 29: 14). "The Memra brings Israel nigh unto God, and sits on His throne receiving the prayers of Israel", Targ. ps. Jon. to Deut. 4: 7. "My Memra shall be unto you for a redeeming deity", Targ. Jon. to Isaiah 56: 13.

e. Mediation in Rabbinic Literature[57]

(1) *The merits of the Fathers.* Elijah's prayers on Mount Carmel were answered only when he invoked the memory of the Fathers (Shemoth R. c. 44). Abraham atones for the sins of Israel (Pesikta 154a). The world is preserved because of Abraham. The childless were blessed with children and the sick cured of their diseases through the merits of Abraham (Bereshith R. c. 39).

The people standing at the foot of Sinai were protected by the merits of Moses (Shir. R. to 4: 4).

(2) *The death of the righteous.* The death of the righteous has an atoning power (Pesikta 174b).

(3) *Angels.* The sacrifice of Isaac was averted through the intercession of angels. Angels are set over the prayers of men (Exodus R. 21). Every nation has its guardian angel who pleads before God the cause of that nation (Targ. ps. Jon. to Gen. 11: 7, 8).

"Michael is the heavenly high-priest whose altar, upon which he offers up sacrifice, stands in the fourth heaven". Michael is referred to as the "Advocate of the Jews".

(4) *Semi-divine beings.* The Metatron is the Mediator and Reconciler between God and Israel (Bemidbar R. c. 12).

The Ruach Hakodesh (Holy Spirit) is represented as Israel's defender (Vayikra R. c. 6).

f. Mediation in the Prayer-Book*

The Prayer-Book of the Synagogue holds a unique place in the religious life of the Jews. Until the end of the eighteenth century every Jew used the Prayer-Book three times daily. Many Jews even today are able to recite whole pages of the Prayer-Book from memory. It would, therefore, be of considerable interest to learn whether the Prayer-Book has anything to say about Mediation. For the Prayer-Book may be taken to reflect the settled belief of the Synagogue.

A review of the various prayers as contained in the Orthodox Prayer-Book—and until the end of the eighteenth century all Jews were Orthodox—shows three groups of Mediators or Intercessors.

(1) *The merits of the Fathers.* "Our Father, our King, for the sake of our fathers who trusted in Thee and whom Thou didst teach the statutes of life, so mayest thou be gracious unto us and teach us." (One of the morning service prayers beginning with the words: "With a great love thou didst love us. . . .")

"They pray in unison and, hastening to thy gates, repose upon the merit of her to whom thou didst promise visitation." (The merit mentioned here is that of Sarah, and this sentence is part of a prayer beginning with the words: "The terrible day of visitation has come.")

"Thou didst teach them to dwell upon the patriarchs' righteousness amid the utterance of prayer. . . ." (Morning Prayer on the First Day of New Year.)

"He will yet remember the love of the patriarch, our sire; yea, and for the sake of the son who was bound he will still our strife, and for the merit of the perfect one, the All-feared will bring forth our suit to the light of acquittal: for this is holy unto our Lord." (From Additional or Afternoon Service for New Year's Day, prayer beginning with the words: "For with thy holiness. . . .")

"For the sake of the only son who was proved as he lay bound on the altar, grant his offering redemption from the judgment-sentence." (Additional or Afternoon Service for New Year's Day, prayer beginning with the words: "Most high, if seated on thy judgment throne. . . .")

* Several of the prayers cited here are taken from Adler's Synagogue Service Prayer-Book.

"In thee do they trust, thou Shield of their fathers, upon whose merit they rely." (Morning prayer on the Day of Atonement beginning with the words: "Thou didst make the tenth day. . . .")

"Remember the binding of him and be gracious unto his posterity. O raise us near unto thee that we may live, yea, that we may live through our father's righteousness." (From the evening service for the Day of Atonement—from a prayer beginning with the words: "When the only child, beloved of his mother. . . .")

In the Additional Service for the Feast of the Tabernacles there is a prayer for rain beginning with the words: "Our God and the God of our fathers." In this prayer request is made for rain for the sake of the merits of Abraham, Isaac, Jacob, Moses, Aaron, and the Twelve Tribes of Israel.

In the Service for Hoshana Rabba there is a long prayer which begins with the sentence, "I beseech thee, O God, save! O Save, I beseech thee. Thou art our Father." In this prayer help is sought from God because of the merits of Noah, Abraham, Isaac, Jacob, and Moses.

(2) *The merits of the Martyrs.* "Our Father, our King, do it for the sake of those who were slain for thy holy Name."

"Our Father, our King, do it for the sake of those who went through fire and water for the sanctification of thy Name." (Morning service for New Year.)

(3) *The merits of the righteous dead.* ". . . May your merits, and your perfect life assist us in our needs and protect us in times of trouble. Increase you also your prayers to the Lord our God, that he, through His infinite mercy and His abundant lovingkindness and for the sake of our holy fathers, and for the sake of our pious ones who have fulfilled His will, may have compassion, pity and mercy upon us. . . ."[58] (A prayer recited upon visiting the graves.)

g. *Opposition to the doctrine of Mediation*

Here and there one finds in Rabbinic literature statements opposing the idea of Mediation. Only a few examples will be cited. In Berakhoth 9: 1 of the Jerusalem Talmud we read the following: "An appeal to a mortal patron for relief depends on his servant's willingness to permit the applicant to enter;

but appeals to the Almighty in times of trouble do not depend on the angel Michael or Gabriel; one needs only call upon God."[59]

And in the Prayer-Book we find the following item: "We depend not on a man, nor do we trust in a Son-God, but in the God of heaven, who is the true God."[60]

When the Egyptians pursued the Israelites near the Red Sea, Moses began to pray to God for deliverance. In commenting on this, Midrash R. states that God said to Moses: "Why prayest thou, my sons have already prayed to me and I have heard their prayer" (Shemoth Rabba ch. 21, par. 4, to Exod. 14: 15). The implication here is that Moses' prayer was no more effective than the prayer of the Israelites. This is in direct contradiction of what the same Midrash is teaching elsewhere about the mediatorial role of Moses.

In Sanh. 92b, we read that when Nebuchadnezzar remarked that one of those in the fiery furnace was like the Son of God, an angel is said to have rebuked him saying, "Has God a Son?"[61]

h. Conclusion

Mediation is a well-established principle in the Old Testament, in the Apocrypha and Pseudepigrapha, in the Targums in Rabbinic literature, and in the Prayer-Book. However, in the Rabbinic writings, there occur some utterances of a different kind whose obvious intention is to combat the idea of Mediation. The trend in modern religious Judaism is decidedly against the doctrine of Mediation. At the basis of this opposition are two factors: (1) Jewish opposition to Christianity at the core of which lies the Mediatorial work of Jesus Christ; (2) the absence of an exalted concept of the holiness of God, and of a deep sense of human sin, so characteristic of the religious content of modern Judaism.

4. THE TORAH OF RABBINIC JUDAISM

Jewish opposition to Christianity can never be fully understood without a proper realization of the place the Torah holds in the Jewish religion. The word "Torah" is often translated "Law", but to the Jew it means more than the "Law"; it denotes also teaching, and includes all of the Old Testament, and the Talmud and it "covers the whole sphere of Judaism, as it expresses itself both in doctrine and practice".[62] However, since the core of Judaism is the Religious Code, and the Jewish religion is unthinkable apart from its religious observances, "Torah" to the Jew is, for all practical purposes, synonymous with religious law.

Thus understood the Torah of Rabbinic Judaism consists of two large divisions: The written Law, by which is meant the Pentateuch, but specifically the Mosaic Law in the Pentateuch; and the Oral Law or the Talmud. The Oral Law is a large body of literature, outside of the Old Testament, whose object is the interpretation and reinterpretation of the Mosaic Law. But the term "Oral Law" is misleading, as the Mishnah and the Gemara, the two oldest component parts of the Oral Law, have been reduced to writing in the second and fifth centuries A.D., respectively. A better term is "Talmud" as it conveys the idea of learning. The Talmud is the sum total of Jewish religious learning in the process of which Rabbinism has striven to grasp the meaning of the Mosaic Law and to learn how to apply it in the daily life of the Jew.

Traditional Judaism believes that the Oral Law, as well as the Written Law, has originated with Moses, and both have the same validity. According to this view all that the Rabbis were to teach in the future had already been taught by Moses. "The doctrines of the Rabbis were the harvest from the seed which was sown at the time of the original Revelation."[63] This concept of the Talmud "provides Judaism with the possibility of growth and adaptability to circumstances".[64] Thus, the Talmud has only a beginning but actually no end, as the ever-changing circumstances in every generation have imposed upon Rabbinic Judaism the need to reinterpret the Law over and over again. This state of affairs·is the outgrowth of the very nature of Rabbinic Judaism, dealing as it does not so much in principles, as in case law, aiming to regulate every conceivable condition of Jewish life.

a. The principles of the Torah of Rabbinic Judaism

(1) *Obedience to its commandments.* The commandments of the Torah are considered to be the decrees of the King. The Jews as subjects of this King owe Him blind obedience. They need not know the reason, meaning or purpose of the commandments they are called upon to perform. R. Yochanan b. Zakkai was once asked by his disciples of the meaning of a certain law in the

Pentateuch. His answer was: "By your life, neither does the dead body make one unclean, nor does the water make clean; it is only a decree of the King of Kings. The Holy One, blessed be He, says: A command have I commanded, a decree have I decreed, and none may transgress against my decrees."[65]

Another example of the blind obedience expected of the Jews to the commandments of the Torah is the comment in connection with the injunction against killing a cow and her young on the same day (Leviticus 22: 28), and the robbing a nest of the mother bird and its young; the young bird may be taken, but the mother bird is to be set free (Deuteronomy 22: 6, 7). The Jewish people saw in this commandment an expression of God's compassion extended even to animals and birds, and in time of adversity they would pray: "Thou didst have pity and compassion upon the bird's nest, have pity and compassion also upon us. Thou didst have pity upon the animal and its young, have also pity and compassion upon us!" The Mishnah frowns upon this prayer, stating that "He who says, Even to the bird's nest thy compassion is extended, must be silenced, for he attributes the motives of God's action to compassion, while they are nothing but decrees", Berakhoth 33b.[66]

In the light of this conception of the commandments of the Torah as decrees of the King it becomes unnecessary that man should be sympathetically disposed to the Will of God as reflected in the Torah commandments (Sifra Qedoshim 93: 4).[67] It is not even needed that the Jew should have the intention to obey God and do His Will as long as he actually performs the commandments: "The Commandments require no special intention, or devotion", Rosh Hashanah 28b.[68]

One wonders whether this Rabbinic interpretation of the Law was not intended to silence the voice of scepticism with reference to the unreasonableness of some of the laws. Be that as it may, it certainly served to divorce man's actions from his motives. In fact, it invested this mechanical and automatic performance of the commandments with a special merit as seen from the statement that "the man who does what he is commanded is more acceptable with God than he who does things never commanded by God", Aboda Zara 3a.[69]

(2) *The doctrine of reward.* Modern Jewish scholars have been at great pains to gloss over, or put a different interpretation on, the problem of reward in religious Judaism. In all fairness we

must say that the better spirits among the ancient Rabbis deplored the prominent place which reward holds in the religion of the Jew. In the Sayings of the Fathers 1: 3 we read that "Antigonos of Socho was wont to say: Be not like servants who minister to their master with the view to receiving a reward, but be like servants who minister to their master without the view to receiving a reward, and let the fear of Heaven be upon you".

But that it was difficult even for the more noble spirits among the Rabbis to emancipate themselves entirely from the idea of reward may be seen from the following: Commenting on the words "Thou shalt love Jehovah thy God", Siphre 73a remarks as follows: "Act out of love. Scripture has made a distinction between him who acts out of love, and him who acts out of fear. (He who acts) out of love will receive a manifold reward, for it is said: Thou shalt fear the Lord thy God; him shalt thou serve, and to him shalt thou cleave (Deuteronomy 10: 20)."[70]

Notwithstanding the isolated voices of protest the doctrine of reward remained one of the great motives of Jewish piety, and the prevailing view of Rabbinic Judaism. "R. Chananya ben Akashya says, it has been the good will of the Holy One, blessed be He, to make Israel worthy of much reward, therefore he gave them a copious Torah and many commandments," (Sayings of the Fathers, last passage of chapter 5).

The above passage is intended to teach that by giving the Jews many commandments God granted them ample opportunities for acquiring much merit. According to R. Meir (second century A.D.), "there is no Jew who does not perform one hundred precepts every day . . . There is no man in Israel who is not surrounded by precepts: the phylacteries on his forehead and arm, the Mzuzah on his door, the four fringes on his garment," Jerus. Berakhoth, towards the end.[71] "Even the notorious sinners in Israel are as full of precepts as a pomegranate is of seeds", Chagigah, towards the end.[72]

The size of the reward is not known. "Be as particular about a light precept as about a grave one, for thou knowest not the grant of reward for each precept." Sayings of the Fathers 2: 1. "The reward will be measured in accordance with the labour and pain bestowed upon the precept", Sayings of the Fathers 5: 26.

The greatest of all merits which a Jew can gain comes from the study of the Torah. "Whosoever occupies himself with the

Torah for its own sake merits many things; and not only so, but the world is indebted to him, etc.", Sayings of the Fathers 6: 1. "If thou hast studied much Torah, much reward will be given to thee", Sayings of the Fathers 4: 12. Finally, this passage from the opening of the Mishnah Peah, which is also incorporated in the Daily Prayer-Book: "These are the things, the fruit of which man enjoys in this world, while its stock [principle] remains for him in the world to come: honouring father and mother, the practice of charity, timely attendance at the house of study morning and evening, hospitality to wayfarers, visiting the sick, dowering the bride, attending the dead to the grave, devotion to prayer, and making peace between man and his fellow; but the study of the Torah is equal to them all."

That great efficacy was attributed to the precepts may be seen from a passage in the Mishnah that a precept which a man does will appear as his advocate before God while his transgressions will be his accusers. "He who does one precept has gotten himself one advocate, and he who commits one transgression has gotten himself one accuser", Sayings of the Fathers 4: 13.

(3) *The Supremacy of the Torah.* The Jew looks upon the Torah as God's greatest gift to Israel. By studying it, by teaching it to others, and by fulfilling its commandments, the Jew takes upon himself "the yoke of the kingdom of Heaven", and merits "the world to come". This idea is well expressed in the following prayer recited at the daily evening service and recorded in the Daily Prayer-Book. "With everlasting love hast thou loved the house of Israel, thy people; a Law and commandments, statutes and judgments has thou taught us. Therefore, O Lord our God, when we lie down and when we rise up we will meditate on Thy statutes; yea, we will rejoice in the words of Thy Law, and in Thy commandments for ever; for they are our life and the length of our days, and we will meditate on them day and night. And mayest thou never take away thy love from us: Blessed art thou, O Lord, who lovest thy people Israel."

"The Torah is greater than the priesthood and the kingship", Sayings of the Fathers 6: 6. When Israel was ruled by her kings, and when the Temple stood in Jerusalem, the priesthood and the crown were the twin pillars of the nation's life. In the days of the Second Temple, when the crown passed into the hands of foreigners, the priesthood became the dominating element in the affairs of the nation. With the destruction of the Second

Temple, both the priesthood and the monarchy faded into insignificance, and the Torah became supreme and central in the life of the nation.

In due course of time, the Torah of Rabbinic Judaism became personified and vested with supernatural attributes. An analysis of these attributes of the Torah discloses how strikingly similar they are to the attributes of Christ in the New Testament. The New Testament teaches the pre-existence of Christ. Rabbinic Judaism teaches the pre-existence of the Torah (Sayings of the Fathers 6: 10). According to the New Testament God has created the world through Christ, the Rabbis teach that God has created the world through the Torah.[73] Christ is the only begotten Son of God; the Rabbis speak of the Torah as the daughter of God. We are told that at the giving of the Law God said to Israel: "You have taken my daughter, you must also take Me, for I cannot exist without her."[74] Christ is the supreme gift of God's love to men, as for example, John 3: 16; the Torah is the supreme gift of God's love to Israel. Christ is the Mediator between God and man, the Torah is Israel's advocate before God.[75]

There is no doubt but that this glorification of the Torah was Rabbinic Judaism's answer to the claims which the Jewish Christians were making on behalf of their Messiah. The Torah was to the Jew what Jesus Christ was to the Jewish Christian.

b. *Modern Judaism and the Torah of Rabbinic Judaism.*
  Orthodox Judaism

That this emphasis upon the Jew's blind adherence to the Law has remained to this day the prevailing attitude of Orthodox Judaism may be seen from the following utterances of modern Orthodox scholars: "The bond between the divine Lawgiver and the horde of slaves whom He liberated from Egypt and elevated to a nation, does not depend upon the personal convictions of the individual, changing with time and circumstances: the individual does not abide by the law because he is convinced of it but because the transcending will of the nation binds him. Abraham did not 'convince' his sons and his house but 'commanded' them to practice love and justice." "Judaism does not—in the manner of religions—aim to gain acceptance by 'convincing' the individual but by giving him, as the member of a nation, historical self-consciousness . . . It is not faith, then, which redeems the Jew, but historical self-consciousness . . .

Judaism, to be sure, teaches eternal truths; but, rather than preaching faith in them, it aims to implant them by a process of education; by a life according to the Law. This, then, is imposed upon the individual irrespective of his convictions . . . it binds him because it is the historic law of the nation."[76]

The following is a more recent pronouncement: "The basis of the Jewish religion since Ezra has been the Torah, the Law, or better still—Halachah, the 'way' of the Law in a man's life."[77]

c. Liberal Judaism

While Liberal Judaism does not believe in the Divine origin of the Talmud, or even the Pentateuch, it, nevertheless, holds the same position as Orthodox Judaism with reference to the principles underlying the Torah of Rabbinic Judaism as seen from the following statements: "All radiates out from the Law, and from it all depends."[78] "The second all-penetrating principle of the Synagogue is loyalty to the Torah."[79] Scheops holds that St. Paul's contention that man is unable of himself to observe the Law is contrary to the spirit of Judaism.[80]

Leo Baeck states that "only the right deed places man in the presence of God at all times and only it can be demanded of him at all times. Through it alone can man reach that deep inner unity with God, as well as that other unity with his fellow men . . . Judaism also has its Word, but it is only one word—'to do' . . . The deed becomes proof of conviction".[81]

NOTES TO CHAPTER 6

1. Strack and Billerbeck, *Commentar zum Neuen Testament aus Talmud und Midrasch* (München, 4 vols., 1922-8), pp. 332 f; quoted by Jakób Jocz, *The Jewish People and Jesus Christ* (S.P.C.K.: London, 1954), p. 45. Permission for use in the U.S.A. granted by Macmillan and Co., New York.

2. *Tosephta Shabbath, XIII,* 5; quoted by Bernard Pick, *Jesus in the Talmud* (The Open Court Publ. Co., Chicago, 1913), pp. 58-60.

3. *Talmud Berachoth* 12a or *Jerus. Berachoth* 3a; quoted by Bernard Pick, op. cit., p. 66.

4. Bernard Pick, op. cit., pp. 63-4. See also S. Schechter, "Genizah Specimens", *Jewish Quarterly Review,* x, p. 657; quoted by Jakób Jocz, op. cit., p. 53.

5. An extensive bibliography will be found in Jakób Jocz's work.

6. Joseph Klausner, *Jesus of Nazareth* (The Macmillan Co.: New York, 1925), pp. 18-19. By permission of the publishers.

7. Ibid., pp. 53-4.

8. Ibid., p. 70.

9. Kaufmann Kohler, *The Origins of the Synagogue and the Church* (The Macmillan Co.: New York, 1929), p. 218. Used by permission of the Alumni Association of Hebrew Union College, Cincinnati.

10. Joseph Klausner, op. cit., pp. 363, 368, 374.

11. Paul Goodman, *The Synagogue and the Church* (George Routledge & Sons, Ltd.: London, 1908), p. 230. By permission of Routledge & Kegan Paul, Ltd.

12. Ibid., p. 233.

13. Gerald Friedlander, *The Jewish Sources of the Sermons on the Mount* (George Routledge & Sons: London, 1911), p. 23; quoted by Jakób Jocz, op. cit., p. 115, by permission of Routledge & Kegan Paul, Ltd.

14. Cecil Roth, *A Short History of the Jewish People* (East and West Library: London, 1948), p. 142.

15. H. G. Enelow, *A Jewish View of Jesus* (Macmillan Co.: New York, 1920), p. 73. By permission of the publishers.

16. Ibid., p. 17.

17. Julius Wellhausen, *Israëlitische und jüdische Geschichte*, 5th ed., p. 390; quoted by C. G. Montefiore, "The Synoptic Gospels and the Jewish Consciousness", *The Hibbert Journal*, vol. 3 (1904–5), p. 659.

18. C. G. Montefiore, "The Synoptic Gospels and the Jewish Consciousness", *The Hibbert Journal*, vol. 3 (1904–5), p. 660.

19. C. G. Montefiore, *Some Elements of the Teachings of Jesus* (Macmillan & Co.: London, 1910), p. 20; quoted by Jakób Jocz, op. cit., p. 120.

20. C. G. Montefiore, *The Synoptic Gospels* (Macmillan & Co.: London, 1927), vol. 1, p. cxxxiv (Introduction). Used by permission of St. Martin's Press, New York.

21. C. G. Montefiore, "What a Jew Thinks about Jesus", *The Hibbert Journal*, vol. 33 (1934–5), p. 516.

22. Cecil Roth, op. cit., p. 142.

23. Moriz Friedländer, *Die religiösen Bewegungen innerhalb des Judentums im Zeitalter Jesu* (Berlin, 1905), p. 316; quoted by Jakób Jocz, op. cit., p. 135.

24. Robert Eisler, *The Messiah Jesus and John the Baptist etc.* (London, 1931). pp. 510ff.; quoted by Jakób Jocz, op. cit., p. 138.

25. Ernest R. Trattner, *As a Jew Sees Jesus* (Charles Scribner's Sons: New York, 1931), p. 64.

26. H. G. Enelow, op. cit., p. 130.

27. Ibid., pp. 66–8.

28. Ibid., p. 101.

29. Ibid.

30. Joseph Klausner, *From Jesus to Paul* (Macmillan Co.: New York, 1943), pp. 267–8, 437–8. By permission of the publisher.

31. Maimonides, Mishneh Torah, Melakhim XI, 4.

32. Ernest R. Trattner, op. cit., pp. ix, x (Foreword).

33. Kauffmann Kohler's address before the Congress of 1893; quoted by Jakób Jocz, op. cit., p. 126.

34. Ernest R. Trattner, op. cit., p. 40.

35. Harris Weinstock, *Jesus the Jew* (Funk & Wagnalls Co.: New York, 1902), pp. 28–9.

36. Solomon B. Freehof, *Stormers of Heaven* (Harper & Brothers: New York, 1931), pp. 205, 207, 208, 210.

37. H. G. Enelow, op. cit., pp. 171-2.

38. Joseph Klausner, *Jesus of Nazareth*, pp. 413-14.

39. Alfred Edersheim, *The Life and Times of Jesus the Messiah* (Longmans, Green & Co.: New York, 8th ed., 1899), vol. 1, pp. 165-6.

40. For original Jewish sources see references in Alfred Edersheim, op. cit., vol. 1, p. 167.

41. See Sukk. 52, Sukk. 62, Berachoth 17, Jerus. Berachoth chap. 4, p. 7; quoted by J. I. Landsman, "Judaism and Christianity", article in Yiddish in *Der Weg* (Warsaw, Dec. 1930).

42. Max Dienemann, *Judaism and Christianity*; quoted by J. I. Landsman, article entitled "Judaism and Christianity", published in *Our Jewish Neighbors*, June 1924, by the Board of National Missions of the Presbyterian Church, U.S.A., New York City.

43. Chief Rabbi J. H. Hertz. See his note on "Jewish View of the 'Fall Of Man'", in his edition of *The Pentateuch* (Soncino Press: London, 1938), p. 196.

44. I. M. Wise, *Judaism and Christianity* (Bloch & Co.: Cincinnati, 1883), pp. 95, 90, 66; quoted by Jacob Jocz, op. cit., p. 270.

45. Jakob J. Petuchowski, "The Jewish Mission to the Nations", article in *Commentary* (New York), October 1955.

46. D. R. Davies, *Divine Judgment in Human History* (The Sheldon Press: London, 1943), p. 22.

47. "The Crisis of the Individual," introduction to the second article in a series published in *Commentary* (New York), January 1946.

48. D. M. Edwards, *The International Standard Bible Encyclopaedia*, vol. 3, article "Mediation", p. 2018b. Used by permission of Wm. B. Eerdmans Publishing Co., Grand Rapids, Michigan, U.S.A.

49. Kaufmann Kohler, *Jewish Encyclopedia*, vol. 8, article "Mediator", p. 406b.

50. Chief Rabbi Adler, *Anglo-Jewish Memories*, sermon on "The Jewish Doctrine of Atonement" (Bloch Publishing Co.: New York, 1909); quoted by W. O. E. Oesterley, *The Jewish Doctrine of Mediation* (Skeffington & Son: London, 1910), pp. 156-7.

51. C. G. Montefiore, *Liberal Judaism* (Macmillan & Co.: London, 1903), pp. 45ff., 56; quoted by W. O. E. Oesterley, op. cit., pp. 165, 167.

52. C. G. Montefiore, *Outlines of Liberal Judaism* (Macmillan & Co.: London, 1912), p. 306. Used by permission of St. Martin's Press, New York.

53. O. Lazarus, *Liberal Judaism and its Standpoint* (Macmillan & Co.: London, 1937), p. 87. Used by permission of St. Martin's Press, New York.

54. Morris Joseph, *Judaism as Creed and Life* (Macmillan & Co.: London, 1903), pp. 78ff.; quoted by W. O. E. Oesterley, op. cit., pp. 175-7.

55. The source material for this section may be found in W. O. E. Oesterley, op. cit., pp. 30-49.

56. For references in this section see W. O. E. Oesterley, op. cit., pp. 50-61.

57. For references in this section see W. O. E. Oesterley, op. cit., pp. 79-88.

58. W. O. E. Oesterley, op. cit., p. 125.

59. Jerus. Berakhoth 9: 1; quoted by W. O. E. Oesterley, op. cit., p. 94.

60. See prayer beginning with Berik Shemeh in the morning Prayer-Book.

61. W. O. E. Oesterley, op. cit., p. 94.
62. Jakób Jocz, op. cit., p. 286. An unusually broad and comprehensive definition of the concept of Torah is found in an article by David S. Shapiro, "Whither, American Judaism?" in *The Jewish Spectator* (New York), January 1946.
63. A. Cohen, *Everyman's Talmud* (J. M. Dent & Sons: London, 1932), p. 157. Permission for use in the United States, its dependencies and the Philippine Islands granted by E. P. Dutton & Co. Inc., New York.
64. Jakób Jocz, op. cit., p. 290.
65. Pesiqta de Rab Kahana 40: 1; Pesiqta Rabbati 65: 1; Bemidbar Rabba, chap. 19; quoted by J. I. Landsman, "The Hopes and Ideals of Judaism", article in the *Hebrew Christian Alliance Quarterly* July 1924; published by the Hebrew Christian Alliance of America, Chicago, Ill.
66. Ibid.
67. Ibid.
68. Ibid.
69. Ibid.
70. Ibid.
71. Ibid.
72. Ibid.
73. Ibid.
74. Quoted by J. I. Landsman, "The Essence of Judaism", article in the *Hebrew Christian Alliance Quarterly*, January–March 1929.
75. Shemoth Rabba, c. 29.
76. Isaac Breuer, *The Problem of the Jew* (The Spero Foundation: New York, 1947), pp. 61–2; 58–9.
77. Jacob Taubes, "The Issue between Judaism and Christianity", article in *Commentary* (New York), December 1953.
78. C. G. Montefiore, "Rabbinic Judaism and St. Paul", *J.Q.R.*, January 1901, p. 173; quoted by Jakób Jocz, op. cit., p. 289.
79. Kaufmann Kohler, *The Origins of the Synagogue and the Church* (The Macmillan Co.: New York, 1929), p. 141.
80. H. J. Schoeps, *Jüdish-christliches Religionsgespräch* (Berlin, 1937), p. 53; quoted by Jakób Jocz, op. cit., p. 289.
81. Leo Baeck, *The Essence of Judaism* (Schocken Books: New York, Revised Edition, 1948), p. 56.

CHAPTER 7

THE STATE OF ISRAEL AND THE PROBLEM
OF THE MESSIAHSHIP OF JESUS

(continued)

THE STATE OF ISRAEL AND THE PROBLEM OF THE MESSIAHSHIP OF JESUS

(continued)

III. JEWISH INTERPRETATIONS OF THE MESSIANIC TEACHINGS OF THE OLD TESTAMENT

1. THE POSITION OF TRADITIONAL JUDAISM

Christian students of the Bible have often been accused by Jewish religious leaders of misinterpreting certain passages in the Old Testament in order to make them support the Messianic claims of the New Testament. However, a review of old Rabbinic sources will show that the vast majority of these portions of the Old Testament have been Messianically interpreted by Rabbinic authorities. At the end of the second volume of Edersheim's work on *The Life and Times of Jesus the Messiah* under Appendix IX we have a list of Old Testament passages applied Messianically in ancient Rabbinic writings. The author states that his list is not complete. Even so, it contains 456 passages of the Old Testament which Rabbinic Judaism applied to the Messiah or to Messianic times. Of these, 75 are from the Pentateuch, 243 from the Prophets and 138 from the third division of the Old Testament known as the Writings. It has over 558 separate quotations from Rabbinic writings which were used to support the Messianic meaning of the above 456 references from the Old Testament. The interested reader is referred to Edersheim's work for the complete list. We will cite a number of the more generally known passages.

Genesis 3: 15: "And I will put enmity between thee and the woman, and between thy seed and her seed; he shall bruise thy head, and thou shalt bruise his heel", referred to the Messiah in the Targum Pseudo-Jonathan, and the so-called Jerusalem Targum.

Genesis 49: 10: "The sceptre shall not depart from Judah, nor the ruler's staff from between his feet, until Shiloh come; and unto him shall the obedience of the peoples be", applied to the Messiah in Targum Onkelos, Targum Pseudo-Jonathan, the Midrash, Rashi and others.

Numbers 24: 17: " . . . there shall come forth a Star out of Jacob, and a Sceptre shall rise out of Israel . . ." applied to the Messiah in the Targum Onkelos, Targum Pseudo-Jonathan and others.

Psalm 2: 2, 6, 7, 8: "The kings of the earth set themselves, and the rulers take counsel together, against Jehovah and against his anointed, saying:

"Yet have I set my king upon my holy hill of Zion."

"I will tell of the decree: Jehovah said unto me, Thou art my Son, this day have I begotten thee."

"Ask of me, and I shall give thee the nations for thine inheritance and the uttermost parts of the earth for thy possession."

Verse 2 is applied to the Messiah in Aboda Zarah, the Midrash on Psalm 92: 11, etc.

Verse 6—applied to the Messiah in the Midrash on 1 Samuel 16: 1.

Verse 7—applied to the Messiah in Midrash on Psalm 2: 7; is one of the Messianic quotations in the Talmud (Sukk. 52a).

Verse 8 refers to the Messiah in Ber. R. 44 and in the Midrash on the passage.

Psalm 22: 7 (22: 8 Heb.): "All they that see me laugh me to scorn; they shoot out the lip, they shake the head, saying . . ." This is applied to the Messiah in Yalkut on Isaiah 40.

Psalm 22: 15 (22: 16 Heb.): "My strength is dried up like a potsherd, and my tongue cleaveth to my jaws, and thou hast brought me into the dust of death", referred to the Messiah in Yalkut.

Psalm 72. This whole psalm is viewed as Messianic in ancient Rabbinic literature.

Verse 1: "Give the king thy judgments, O God, and thy righteousness unto thy king's son." The first verse is thus rendered in the Targum: "Give the sentence of thy judgment to the King Messiah, and thy justice to the Son of David the King." See also the Midrash on the passage.

Psalm 110: 1: "Jehovah said unto my Lord, Sit thou at my right hand, until I make thine enemies thy footstool", applied

Messianically in the Midrash on Psalm 18: 36 (18: 35 in the English Version).

Isaiah 9: 6 (9: 5 Heb.): "For unto us a child is born, unto us a son is given; and the government shall be upon his shoulder; and his name shall be called Wonderful, Counsellor, Mighty God, Everlasting Father, Prince of Peace." This prophecy is applied to the Messiah in the Targum, in Bemidb. R. 11, and Debarim R. 1.

Isaiah 11: 1: "And there shall come forth a shoot out of the stock of Jesse, and a branch out of his roots shall bear fruit." This is Messianically applied in the Targum on verses 1 and 6; in the Talmud (Jer. Berach. 5a, and Sanh. 93b), and in several places in the Midrashim.

Isaiah 25: 8: "He hath swallowed up death forever; and the Lord Jehovah will wipe away tears from off all faces; and the reproach of his people will he take away from off all the earth; for Jehovah hath spoken it." Applied Messianically in Debar. R. 2; in the Talmud (Moed Q. 28b); in Yalkut, vol. 1, and vol. 2.

Isaiah 42: 1: "Behold, my servant, whom I uphold; my chosen, in whom my soul delighteth; I have put my Spirit upon him; he will bring forth justice to the nations." This is applied to the Messiah in the Targum, and in the Midrash on Psalm 2; also in Yalkut, vol. 2.

Isaiah 43: 10: "Ye are my witnesses, saith Jehovah, and my servant whom I have chosen. . . ." The Targum translates "My servant" into "My servant the Messiah".

Isaiah 49: 9a: "Saying to them that are bound, 'Go forth; to them that are in darkness, Show yourselves . . .'"; these words are quoted as the words of the Messiah in Yalkut, vol. 2.

Isaiah 52: 7: "How beautiful upon the mountains are the feet of him that bringeth good tidings, that publisheth peace, that bringeth good tidings of good, that publisheth salvation, that saith unto Zion, Thy God reigneth." In Yalkut, vol. 2, we read that three days before the coming of the Messiah Elijah will appear and stand upon the mountains of the Land of Israel; on the first day he will cry aloud: "Peace has come to the world, as it is said 'How beautiful upon the mountains, etc.'" On the second day, Elijah will again stand upon the mountains of the Land of Israel and shout: "'Good has come to the world, Good has come to the world,' as it is written, 'that brings good tidings of good'." On the third day, Elijah will stand on the mountains of Israel and shall say: "'Salvation has come to the world,' as it is written, 'That publisheth salvation'."

Isaiah 60: 1: "Arise, shine; for thy light is come, and the glory of Jehovah is risen upon thee." This is applied to Messianic times in the Targum; Ber. R. 1 with reference to Daniel 2: 2; in Ber. R. 2; Bemidb. R. 15 and 21. The pre-existence of the Messiah is taught in comments of the Yalkut on this chapter. We are told that "God looked forward to the age of the Messiah and His works before the creation of the world, and that he hid that light for the Messiah and His generation under His throne of glory". When Satan questions God for whom the light is reserved, he is told it is destined for Him who in the latter days will cover Satan's face with shame.

Isaiah 60: 2, 3, 4, 8—Messianically applied in the Midrashim. Verse 2 is Messianically applied in Sanh. 99a. Verse 7—Messianically applied in Aboda Zara 24a.

Jeremiah 23: 5, 6: "Behold, the days come, saith Jehovah, that I will raise unto David a righteous Branch, and he shall reign as king and deal wisely, and shall execute justice and righteousness in the land. In his days Judah shall be saved, and Israel shall dwell safely; and this is his name whereby he shall be called: Jehovah our righteousness." The Targum paraphrased this passage to read: "And I will raise up for David the Messiah the Just." This is one of the passages in the Bible from which according to the Rabbis one of the names of the Messiah is derived. See Baba Bathra 75b, and the Midrash on Psalms 21: 1, Proverbs 19: 21 and Lamentations 1: 16.

Jeremiah 31: 31–34 (31: 30–33 Heb.); "Behold the days come, saith Jehovah, that I will make a new covenant with the house of Israel and with the house of Judah. Not according to the covenant that I made with their fathers in the day that I took them by the hand to bring them out of the land of Egypt, which my covenant they brake although I was husband unto them saith Jehovah. But this is the covenant that I will make with the house of Israel after those days, saith Jehovah: I will put my law in their inward parts, and in their heart will I write it; and I will be their God, and they shall be my people. And they shall teach no more every man his neighbour, and every man his brother, saying, Know Jehovah; for they shall all know me, from the least of them unto the greatest of them, saith Jehovah, for I will forgive their iniquity, and their sin will I remember no more." This passage is referred to Messianic times in Yalkut, vol. 1 and vol. 2.

Ezekiel 11 : 19: "And I will give them one heart, and I will put a new spirit within you; and I will take the stony heart out of their flesh, and will give them a heart of flesh." Messianically applied to the days of the Messiah when the evil desire would be removed from the human heart; see Deb. R. 6 and other Midrashic passages.

Ezekiel 36: 25: "And I will sprinkle clean water upon you, and ye shall be clean: from all your filthiness, and from all your idols, will I cleanse you." Applied to Messianic times in the Targum, and in the Yalkut, vol. 1, and in the Talmud, Kidd. 72b.

Hosea 3 : 4–5: "For the children of Israel shall abide many days without king, and without prince, and without sacrifice, and without an image, and without ephod or teraphim. Afterward shall the children of Israel return, and seek Jehovah their God, and David their king, and shall come with fear unto Jehovah and to his goodness in the latter days." Verse 5 is applied to the Messiah in the Targum, and from it the Jerusalem Talmud (Ber. 5a) derives the name David as one of the names of the Messiah.

Micah 5 : 2 (5 : 1 Heb.): "But thou, Bethlehem Ephrathah, which art little to be among the thousands of Judah, out of thee shall one come forth unto me that is to be ruler in Israel; whose goings forth are from of old, from everlasting." This passage is Messianically interpreted in the Targum, in the Pirqé de R. Eliezer, C.3, and in later Rabbinic writings.

Haggai 2 : 6: "For thus saith Jehovah of hosts, yet once, it is a little while, and I will shake the heavens, and the earth, and the sea, and the dry land," Messianically applied in Debarim R. 1.

Zechariah 2 : 10 (2 : 14 Heb.): "Sing and rejoice, O daughter of Zion; for, lo, I come, and I will dwell in the midst of thee, saith Jehovah", Messianically applied in Midrash on Canticles 1 : 4.

Zechariah 3 : 8: "Hear now, O Joshua the high priest, thou and thy fellows that sit before thee; for they are men that are a sign; for, behold, I will bring forth my servant The Branch." The title "The Branch" is applied to King Messiah in the Targum.

Zechariah 6 : 12: "And speak unto him, saying, Thus speaketh Jehovah of hosts, saying, Behold the man whose name is The Branch. . . ." This passage is applied Messianically in the Targum, the Jerusalem Talmud (Ber. 5a), in the Pirqé de R. Eliezer, c. 48, and in the Midrashim.

Zechariah 9 : 9: "Rejoice greatly, O daughter of Zion; shout,

O daughter of Jerusalem; behold, thy King cometh unto thee; he is just and having salvation; lowly and riding upon an ass, and upon a colt the foal of an ass." This is Messianically applied in Sanh. 98a; in Pirqé de R. Eliezer, c. 31, and in several of the Midrashim.

Zechariah 12: 10: "And I will pour upon the house of David, and upon the inhabitants of Jerusalem, the spirit of grace and of supplication; and they shall look upon me whom they have pierced; and they shall mourn for him as one mourneth for his only son, and shall be in bitterness for him, as one that is in bitterness for his firstborn." This passage is applied to the Messiah the Son of Joseph in the Talmud (Sukk. 52a).

Zechariah 14: 2: "For I will gather all nations against Jerusalem to battle; and the city shall be taken, and the houses rifled, and the women ravished; and half of the city shall go forth into captivity, and the residue of the people shall not be cut off from the city." This is applied in many passages of the Midrashim to the wars in Messianic times.

Malachi 4: 5 (3: 23 Heb.): "Behold, I will send you Elijah the prophet before the great and terrible day of Jehovah cometh." This referred to the forerunner of the Messiah in Pirqé de R. Eliezer, c. 40, in Debarim R. 3, in the Midrash on Canticles 1: 1, in the Talmud, and in the Yalkut.

The rise and growth of the Christian movement has, in due course of time, brought about a definite change in the attitude of Rabbinic Judaism to the Messianic teachings of the Old Testament. The frequent use which Jewish Christians were making of the Old Testament in support of the Messianic character of the mission of Jesus forced the religious leaders of the Jews to re-examine the Messianic portions of the Old Testament. The national rejection of Jesus by the Jewish people induced the Rabbis to exercise greater caution in their interpretation of these Messianic teachings of the Old Testament. The manner in which Christian theologians applied to Jesus the Messianic predictions of the Old Testament often coloured Jewish understanding and interpretation of these portions of Scripture. This was especially true with reference to the mediatorial function and the vicarious sufferings of the Messiah. It is in the light of these considerations that one should read the Jewish expositions of Isaiah 53 and similar passages in the Old Testament dealing with the mediatorial work and vicarious atonement of the Messiah. And yet, it is remarkable how often in the past many Jewish expositors of the

Bible continued to interpret many of these prophecies as referring to the Messiah.

a. The mediatorial function and the vicarious sufferings of the Messiah

Isaiah 49: 8: "Thus saith Jehovah, In an acceptable time have I answered thee, and in the day of salvation have I helped thee; and I will preserve thee, and give thee for a covenant of the people, to raise up the land, to make them inherit the desolate heritages." There is a comment in the Yalkut on this passage to the effect that in every age the Messiah suffers for the sins of that generation (Yalkut, vol. 2).

Isaiah 52: 13: "Behold my servant will act wisely, he will be exalted, and lifted up, and shall be very high."

Verse 14: "Just as many were astonished at thee—so disfigured, his appearance was not human, and his form not like that of the children of men—"

Verse 15: "So shall he sprinkle many nations; kings shall shut their mouths at him, for they see what has not been told them, and that which they had not heard shall they understand."

Isaiah 53: 1: "Who has believed our report, and the arm of Jehovah over whom has it been revealed?"

Verse 2: "For he sprang up before him as a tender plant, and like a root-sprout out of dry ground: he had no form and no beauty; and we looked, and there was no look, such that we could have found pleasure in him."

Verse 3: "He was despised and forsaken by men; a man of griefs, and well acquainted with disease; and like one from whom men hide their face; despised, and we esteemed him not."

Verse 4: "Surely he has borne our diseases and our pains; he has laden them upon himself; but we regarded him as one stricken, smitten of God, and afflicted."

Verse 5: "Whereas he was pierced for our sins, bruised for our iniquities; the punishment for our peace was upon him, and through his stripes we were healed."

Verse 6: "All we like sheep went astray; we had turned every one to his own way; and Jehovah caused the iniquity of us all to fall on him."

Verse 7: "He was ill-treated; while he suffered willingly, and opened not his mouth, like the sheep that is led to the slaughter-bench, and like a lamb that is dumb before its shearers, he opened not his mouth."

Verse 8: "He was taken away from prison and from judgment; and of his generation who considered that he was cut off from the land of the living for the transgression of my people to whom the stroke was due?"

Verse 9: "And they assigned him his grave with sinners, but with a rich man in his death, because he had done no wrong, and there was no deceit in his mouth."

Verse 10: "Yet it pleased Jehovah to bruise him, to afflict him with disease; when his soul shall make an offering for sin, he shall see posterity, he shall prolong his days, and the purpose of Jehovah should prosper through his hand."

Verse 11: "As a result of the travail of his soul he shall see and be satisfied; through his knowledge will my righteous servant justify many, and their iniquities he will bear."

Verse 12: "Therefore I will give him a portion with the great, and with the strong ones will he divide spoil, because he has poured out his soul unto death, and he let himself be reckoned among transgressors, while he bore the sin of many, and made intercession for the transgressors."[1]

b. Ancient Jewish interpretations of the "Suffering Servant" in Isaiah

The Targum. Isaiah 52: 13: "Behold, my servant shall act wisely, etc.", is translated in the Targum of Jonathan which belongs to the first century A.D. as follows: "Behold my servant, the Messiah, shall prosper; he shall be high, and increase, and be exceedingly strong." The remainder of Isaiah's prophecy with reference to the Suffering Servant the Targum treats in a most unusual manner. The glories described in the chapter the Targum applies to the Messiah but the sufferings it assigns to Israel. However, Israel in this case suffers for her own sins, unlike the modern Jewish idea that Israel is suffering for the sins of the nations of the world. That the Targum's method of exposition is untenable is evident from the fact that the sufferings and glories in this chapter are plainly ascribed to one and the same person.[2]

The Talmud. In the Babylonian Talmud, Sanhedrin 98b, we read that the name of the Messiah is "The Leprous". This name is derived from Isaiah 53: 4: "Surely he has borne our diseases, etc., but we regarded him as one stricken, smitten of God, and afflicted." A better reading of this Talmudic passage is the following: "The Messiah—what is his name? The Rabbis say, 'The Leprous one is His name', those of the house of Rabbi say,

'The sick one is His name', etc." The word "Leprous" is derived from the Hebrew word "Nagua", which word the Rabbis take to mean stricken with leprosy. The house of Rabbi (i.e. R. Yehuda the Saint, ha-Nasi, the editor of the Mishna) base their name "The sick one" on the words, "he has borne our diseases etc.".[3]

The Midrashim. In Midrash R. Ruth 5, 6, which is a comment on Ruth 2: 14, the words of Boaz to Ruth "and dip thy morsel in the vinegar" are interpreted symbolically and mystically of the sufferings of the Messiah in accordance with Isaiah 53: 5: "He was pierced for our sins."

In the Midrash on 1 Samuel 16: 1 we are told of three measures of sufferings, one of which falls to the Messiah of whom it is written: "He was pierced for our sins."[4]

"Nowhere in Rabbinic literature", states David Baron, "are the sufferings of the Messiah so graphically described and so expressly stated that He is suffering for the sins of his people" as in the Midrash Pesikta Rabbati, chapters 33–38. In this Midrashic portion there is a story of a dialogue between God and the Messiah. God informs the Messiah that He will have to experience terrible sufferings for the sins of Israel. Messiah is asked whether He will be willing to undergo these sufferings. To this He replies: "Lord of all the worlds, with the gladness of My soul and the joy of my heart I take it upon Me, on condition that not one of Israel shall perish, and not only those alone should be saved who are in My days, but also those who are hid in the dust; and not only should the dead be saved who are in my days, but also those who have died from the days of the first Adam till now; and not only those, but also those who have been prematurely born. And not only those, but also those whom Thou hast intended to create, but who have not been created. Thus I agree, and thus I take all upon Me."

In the same Midrash there is also the following: "In the week when the Son of David comes, they bring beams of iron and put them (like a yoke) on His neck, until His stature is bent down. But He cries and weeps, and His voice ascends on high, and He says before Him: Lord of the World, what is My strength, the strength of My spirit, of my soul and of My members? Am I not flesh and blood? In view of that hour David wept, saying: 'My strength is dried up like a potsherd.' [Psalm 22: 15 (22: 16 Heb.)]. In that hour the Holy One—blessed be He!—says to Him: Ephraim, My righteous Messiah, Thou hast already taken this upon Thee from the six days of creation, now Thy anguish shall be like My anguish, for from the time that Nebuchadnezzar, the wicked one, has come and destroyed My house, and burned My sanctuary, and sent My children into exile among the nations of the world, by Thy life, and the life of My head, I have not sat down upon My throne. . . ."[5]

The Yalkut. In the Yalkut, vol. 2, par. 338, the person spoken of in Isaiah 52: 13 is said to be higher than Abraham, Moses and the ministering angels.[6] The Yalkut interprets of the Messiah Isaiah 53: 5: "Whereas he was pierced for our sins. . . ."

The Prayer-Book. In the Service for the Day of Atonement there is a hymn written by the hymn-writer Eleazar ben Qalir who, according to the Jewish historian Zunz, lived in the ninth century A.D.[7] We shall give only part of this remarkable hymn (beginning with the words: "Before the world was created").

"Our righteous Messiah has departed from us
　We are horror-stricken, and have none to justify us.
Our iniquities and the yoke of our transgressions
　He carries, and He is wounded because of our transgressions.
He bears on His shoulder the burden of our sins,
　To find pardon for all our iniquities.
By His stripes we shall be healed—
O, Eternal One, it is time that thou shouldst create Him anew!
O, bring Him up from the terrestrial sphere,
Raise Him up from the land of Seir*
To announce salvation to us from Mount Lebanon†
Once again through the hand of Yinnon."‡

Among the prayers of the Passover there is the following passage. "Flee my beloved, until the end of the vision shall speak; hasten, and the shadows shall take their flight hence: high and exalted and lofty shall be the despised one; he shall be prudent in judgment, and shall sprinkle many! Lay bare thine arm! Cry out, and say: 'The voice of my beloved; behold he comes.'" The last part of this prayer contains portions from Isaiah 52 and 53. David Levi, an English translator of the liturgy for the festival services, states that this prayer refers to the Messiah.[8]

　* Rome—where, as legend has it, the Messiah lives in humiliation and suffering.
　† Lebanon—stands here for the mount of the Temple from where the Messiah is supposed to proclaim to Israel the hour of redemption.
　‡ Yinnon—one of the names of the Messiah.

The Zohar. In vol. 2, 212a we have a legend of a report which the souls in the garden of Eden hand in to the Messiah about the condition of Israel in captivity. The Messiah weeps on listening to their report, and here the Zohar applies to Him the passage from Isaiah 53: 5. "He was pierced for our sins." In the same Zohar we have this touching story: "There is in the garden of Eden a palace called the palace of the sons of sickness: this palace the Messiah then enters, and summons every sickness, every pain, and every chastisement of Israel; they all come and rest upon Him. And were it not that He had thus lightened them off Israel and taken them upon Himself, there had been no man able to bear Israel's chastisements for transgression of the law: and this is that which is written, 'Surely our sicknesses He has carried'." [9]

c. The "Suffering Servant" idea in medieval Judaism

Rabbi Solomon ben Yitzchak—the great medieval Jewish commentator—applied Isaiah 53 to the sufferings of Israel at the hands of the Gentiles. It is thought by some that the terrible experiences of the Jewish people at the hands of the Crusaders influenced Rashi's interpretation of Isaiah 53. Rashi's opinions were adopted by Iben Ezra, Kimchi and others. However, he was opposed by Maimonides, who is probably the greatest Talmudic authority of the Middle Ages, by Alshech, and by many others. R. Moshe Cohen Ibn Crispin of Cordova, who lived in the fourteenth century, states that Rashi "distorts the passage from its natural meaning", for "it was given of God as a description of the Messiah, whereby, when any should claim to be the Messiah, to judge by the resemblance or non-resemblance to it whether he were the Messiah or no". R. Eliyya de Vidas, A.D. 1575, states: "The meaning of 'He was wounded for our transgressions . . . bruised for our iniquities' is that since the Messiah bears our iniquities, which produce the effect of His being bruised, it follows that whoso will not admit that the Messiah thus suffers for our iniquities must endure and suffer for them himself." [10]

Finally, the following is a statement by Arbabenel, who himself applied the "Suffering Servant" idea of Isaiah to Israel, while admitting that the majority of the ancient Jewish interpreters understood this prophecy to refer to the Messiah: "The first question is to ascertain to whom (this scripture) refers: for the learned among the Nazarenes expound it of the man who was crucified in Jerusalem at the end of the second Temple, and who according to them was the Son of God and took flesh in the virgin's womb, as it is stated in their writings. Jonathan ben Uzziel interprets it in the Targum of the future Messiah; and this is also the opinion of our learned men in the majority of their Midrashim."[11]

2. THE POSITION OF MODERN JUDAISM

a. *The Orthodox view*

"All the attributes of Messiah are those of a human being in his highest possible perfection. No superhuman qualities are ascribed to him; all his glory, all his success, is dependent on the Will of God. He is an ideal man, and an ideal king, but not more; if miracles are to be wrought, it is not Messiah who will perform them, but God, who will act wondrously for Messiah and Israel. The advent of Messiah is not expected to change the nature of man, much less the course of the world around us. The only change we expect is, that the Unity of God will be acknowledged universally, and that justice and righteousness will flourish over all the earth. Those who believe in the superhuman nature of Messiah are guilty of idolatry."[12]

b. *The Liberal view*

"The whole doctrine of the Messiah no longer concerns our religious life and aspirations. We do, indeed, believe in the conception of the Messianic age, or, at any rate, in the optimistic faith which underlies it. We believe that God rules the world and He means it to become not worse, but better. But we no longer believe in a personal Messiah who will lead back the Jews to Palestine, and exercise the sway and power of conqueror and King."[13]

"The future man will need no Messiah."[14] Liberal Judaism believes that the Kingdom of God will be brought about by the work of human progress. "It [the Kingdom of God] is the kingdom which cannot be attained merely because of birth or origin but only through the will of man; it is not given but achieved."[15] The Liberal Jew believes "that it is within man's power to bring God's kingdom upon earth".[16]

Thus we see that the Messianic views of Liberal Judaism constitute practically a complete abandonment of the Messianic teachings of the Old Testament.

3. CONCLUSION

Traditional Judaism of ancient and medieval times believed that: (1) The Messiah is a real, historical person and a descendant of David; (2) His chief mission is to bring national and political deliverance to Israel. "But first, the Jewish Messiah is above all a redeemer of his nation from subservience to foreign rulers."[17] (3) He will set up His kingdom in Israel which will become the spiritual centre of the whole world; (4) the Messianic age will be an era of material and spiritual happiness, death will be abolished, and the dead will rise; some of the Rabbis have taught that the Evil Impulse in human nature will disappear; (5) there are many scattered teachings to the effect that the Messiah's sufferings will atone for Israel's sins. That the sufferings of the Messiah will also atone for the sins of the Gentiles is something which is practically unknown in Jewish belief, notwithstanding the fact that in the Old Testament the universal character of Messiah's work is clearly set forth.

The Messianic views of traditional Judaism have been given up by modern Judaism with the possible exception of a small orthodox group. Modern Judaism does not believe that the Messiah is a historical personality. Instead, it believes in a Messianic Era brought about by human efforts and social progress. The outstanding feature of this Messianic Era is social and international justice. Liberal Judaism knows of no solution for the problem of evil in human nature, no answer to the perplexing question of death, and no satisfying explanation of the purpose and destiny of human life.

We may ask ourselves why has religious Judaism largely given up its belief in a personal Messiah? We shall attempt to set down a few of the more probable reasons.

Judaism's controversy with Christianity has been one of the earliest influential factors in the growing opposition to the belief in a personal Messiah. The frequent use which the Christians were making of the Old Testament in support of the Messiahship of Jesus proved quite embarrassing to Jewish theology. Rather than face the issue fairly and squarely Judaism chose to downgrade the whole doctrine of a personal Messiah.[18]

The collapse of traditional Judaism towards the end of the eighteenth century caused a further devaluation of this doctrine.

The belief in a Messianic Person suffered the same fate as many of the other tenets of traditional Judaism.

At the same time the advent of the Political Emancipation resulted in still greater depreciation of the doctrine of a personal Messiah. In Judaism the concept of a personal Messiah was always inextricably interwoven with the national restoration of the Jewish people. Centuries of bitter oppression at the hands of the Gentile world made the Jewish Messianic hope practically synonymous with the national restoration of the Jews and relegated the spiritual content of the Messianic hope to the background. Consequently, when the Jews were granted civil and political equality in Western Europe and began to feel themselves at home in the countries of their residence the doctrine of a personal Messiah who would lead them back to Palestine began to lose all interest for them. They eliminated from their Prayer-Book and from their theology any allusion to a personal Messiah. In the place of a personal Redeemer they substituted redemption, and they replaced the idea of a personal Messiah by the concept of a Messianic age which would come gradually as a result of progressive human effort.

There are signs of a strong trend back to the personal Messiah belief. The events of the last three decades are largely responsible for this change. The high hopes which the generation of the emancipation era held with reference to human betterment received their first blow in the second half of the nineteenth century with the rise of racial antisemitism. The two world wars, the destruction of European Jewry in the Nazi era, the recrudescence of human barbarism as practised by the Nazis and Communists, and the constant threat of atomic war have destroyed all hope that man, unaided by God, will ever bring in the Messianic age.

Significantly, the rebirth of the State of Israel has become an important stimulating factor in the direction of the revival of the personal Messiah idea among the Jewish people. The precarious international position of the State of Israel is strengthening the conviction that peace among the nations can never come apart from the Prince of Peace, and that Israel's—and the world's—salvation depends on God.

IV. THE JEWISH ATTITUDE TO JESUS: CONCLUDING REMARKS

The national rejection of Jesus and of His Messianic movement by the leadership of the Jewish people in the first century A.D.

was, humanly speaking, the end result of a historical process whose roots reach back to the very beginning of the Second Commonwealth. Wedged in between powerful states which were forever contending among themselves for world mastery, Israel in the course of time suffered the fate of many other small states which lay in the path of the great powers. The destruction of the northern part of the nation by the Assyrians and of the southern part by the Babylonians and the wholesale transfer of the native population to the home countries of the conquerors put a sudden end to the political isolation of the people of the First Commonwealth. For the first time in her national history since the exodus from Egypt Israel was thrown into intimate contact with the Gentile world. This world—she now discovered—was superior to her own, not only in the arts of war, but also in the arts of peace. Babylon's military might, her commerce, and the imposing architecture of the capital city, must have made an overpowering impression on the exiles from Judaea.

Unlike the other nations which the Babylonians had conquered the Judaean exiles refused to become absorbed by their conqueror. But a comparison of their lowly position with the power and greatness of the Gentile world could not but generate within their hearts an inferiority complex and a feeling of injured national pride, especially in view of their unique national history.

In conscious or subconscious search for a solution to this psychological conflict the Judaean exiles in Babylonia were thrown back on their spiritual heritage which they had so completely neglected in the days before the Exile. In this heritage they now discovered values which they seemed never to have seen before. It explained to them their past, it became their mainstay in their present plight, and their hope for the future. Synagogues sprang up in many places where the exiles assembled for prayer and the study of their sacred writings. Thus the Exile wrought a regenerating change in the hearts and minds of the Jews in Babylonia. And when at the end of seventy years they were permitted to return to the land of their ancestors, they renewed their covenant with God with great zeal, and submitted wholeheartedly to a life in conformity with the Law of Moses.

The permission granted to the exiles to return to Judaea was a concession made by Persia to their religious aspirations only. Politically, the status of Judaea had not changed at all. It became an appendage of Persia which had taken over the domains of defeated Babylon. From Persia Judaea passed under the dominion of Alexander the Great, and after the dismemberment of Alexander's empire Judaea became a province of Rome.

This position of political subjection of the Jewish community of the Second Commonwealth, as compared with the growing strength of the Gentile world, deepened Jewish antipathy for the Gentile world and enhanced its reverence for and loyalty to the sacred writings of the Old Testament. It was not, however, the whole of the Old Testament which won this place of prominence in the life of the people; certainly not the writings of the Prophets with their universal human overtones, but rather the Law of Moses, and especially the "Oral Law", which made its appearance in this era, and which in time eclipsed in importance even the Law of Moses.

This dominating position which the Law acquired was, in the first place, due to the growing conviction that the catastrophe which overtook the First Commonwealth was the result of the neglect of the Law by ancient Israel. But one wonders whether this preoccupation with the Law was not also motivated by a desire, conscious or subconscious, to overcome a feeling of national inferiority generated in the Jewish people by a world so completely dominated by the Gentiles.[19] Hence the notion of the dependence of the whole world on the Torah for its survival, and the lasting debt which the world owes to Israel for her willingness to take upon herself the yoke of the Torah. For when God decided to deliver His Torah to the children of men He offered it first to the various nations of the earth; but every one of them refused to accept it. At last God brought the Torah to Israel, and Israel did accept it. Moreover, had Israel not consented to accept the Torah God would have had to destroy the world.[20]

But the effect of Israel's decision to accept upon herself the yoke of the Torah would have been nullified had she not proven herself willing and capable to fulfil its precepts. Hence the centrality of the Torah in Jewish life, the prevailing belief that the Torah can be observed, and the multiplicity of rewards attached to the performance of its various precepts. Here, then, we have the beginning of the anthropocentric trend in Jewish religious thinking, the emphasis on what man can do for God, rather than on what God can do for man. Man need not appear before God altogether helpless, empty-handed and, as it were, completely obligated. He can achieve righteousness before God by his own

H

efforts. He can earn his salvation. That man may feel utterly helpless to comply with the demands of God's Law is unacceptable from the Jewish point of view. Such an admission would run counter to the whole trend of Jewish theology.

This then was the psychological state of mind and the spiritual condition of the Jewish people in the days when Jesus appeared in their midst. Under these circumstances the Messianic movement of Jesus among the Jewish people was foredoomed to failure from its very inception. His teachings, so akin in substance and spirit to the teachings of the Prophets, declared that men—all men, whether Jews or Gentiles—are sinners before God, unable to satisfy the demands of His Law, that, therefore, man can never attain righteousness before God by his own efforts; that all men —Jews as well as Gentiles—must begin life anew, must experience a new birth, a birth from above, before they can become members of the Kingdom of God.

With the destruction of the Jewish National Homeland in A.D. 70, and the world-wide dispersion which followed, Jewish anta- gonism to the teachings of the New Testament became further intensified. The cosmopolitan character of the Christian faith, which prior to A.D. 70 was of little significance from the point of view of Jewish nationalism, posed a serious threat to Jewish survival in the Dispersion. Any Jew accepting the Christian faith became a member of a predominantly Gentile movement and automatically cut himself off from his own people. In addition, the Jew now found it most difficult to conceive of Jesus as the promised Messiah of Israel, as long as the Jewish people were dispersed among the nations, without a country of their own, while Zion lay in ruins under the heels of foreign powers.

V. THE GROWING JEWISH APPRECIATION OF JESUS OF NAZARETH

There is much evidence that the problem of Jesus continues to disturb and agitate the pure in heart among the Jewish people. An increasing number of Jews are probing deep into their souls for an answer to the ever-haunting question: "Who is Jesus of Nazareth?" Here are some of their answers.

SHOLEM ASCH—AUTHOR

In an interview published in the *Christian Herald* Sholem Asch makes the following statement: "Ah, I couldn't help writing on Jesus. Since I first met Him, He has held my mind and heart. I grew up, you know, on the border of Poland and Russia, which wasn't exactly the finest place in the world for a Jew to sit down and write a life of Jesus Christ. Yet, even through those years, the hope of doing just that fascinated me. I floundered a bit at first; I was seeking that something for which so many of us search— that surety, that faith, that spiritual content in my living which would bring me peace and through which I might bring some peace to others. I found it in the Nazarene.

"For Jesus Christ, to me, is the outstanding personality of all time, of all history, both as Son of God and as Son of Man. Everything He ever said or did has value for us today, and that is something you can say of no other man, alive or dead. No other teacher—Jewish, Christian, Buddhist, Mohammedan—is still a teacher whose teaching is such a guidepost for the world we live in. Yes, it is true that Buddha influenced millions, but it is also true that only about—shall we say—five per cent of Buddha's teaching has basic value for the twentieth century. One or another of these teachers may have something basic for an Oriental, or an Arab, or an Occidental, depending upon where his teaching is best preserved; but every act and word of Jesus has value for all of us, wherever we are. He became the Light of the World. Why shouldn't I, a Jew, be proud of that?

"No other religious leader, either, has ever become so personal a part of people as The Nazarene. When you understand Jesus, you understand that he came to save you, to come into your personality. It isn't just a case of a misty, uncertain relationship between a worshipper and an unseen God; that is abstract: Jesus is personal!"[21]

MAX BROD—AUTHOR

"I am constantly amazed at the naïveté of our teachers and leaders who are surprised when I tell them that the best of our youth, our intellectuals, become Christians out of conviction. . . . Our 'leaders' do not believe it. To them a Jew never becomes a

Christian unless he wants to better his position. That Christianity has drawn to itself such noble souls as Pascal, Novalis, Kirkegaard, Amiel, Dostoyevsky, Claudel, etc., etc., and that it exercises a most overwhelming influence on the most earnest truth-seekers among us, of that our teachers know nothing."[22]

CONSTANTINE BRUNNER—PHILOSOPHER

"What is this? is it only the Jew who is unable to see and hear? Are the Jews stricken with blindness and deafness as regards Christ, so that to them only he has nothing to say? Is he to be of no importance to us Jews? Understand then what we shall do: We shall bring him back to us. Christ is not dead for us—for us he has not yet lived; and he will not slay us, he will make us live again. His profound and holy words, and all that is true and heart-appealing in the New Testament, must from now on be heard in our synagogues and taught to our children, in order that the wrong we had committed may be made good, the curse turned into a blessing, and that he at last may find us who has always been seeking after us."[23]

PROFESSOR ALBERT EINSTEIN

This is part of an interview published some time ago in the *Saturday Evening Post*.

"To what extent are you influenced by Christianity?"

"As a child I received instruction both in the Bible and in the Talmud. I am a Jew, but I am enthralled by the luminous figure of the Nazarene."

"Have you read Emil Ludwig's book on Jesus?"

"Emil Ludwig's Jesus is shallow. Jesus is too colossal for the pen of phrase-mongers, however artful. No man can dispose of Christianity with a *bon mot*."

"You accept the historical existence of Jesus?"

"Unquestionably! No one can read the Gospels without feeling the actual presence of Jesus. His personality pulsates in every word. No myth is filled with such life."[24]

WILL HERBERG—AUTHOR AND LECTURER

"And I must add that I am among those who see fundamental spiritual kinship rather than opposition between Judaism and at least the more Hebraic forms of Christianity. Indeed, I find that many of what I conceive to be crucial Jewish insights are illumined rather than obscured when viewed in the light of the development they have undergone in Christian doctrine. I therefore believe that whatever significant differences there may be between Judaism and Christianity considered as total systems, there is real and vital meaning in the idea of a Judeo-Christian religious tradition basically distinct from all other religions of the world."[25]

GUSTAV LAZLO—AUTHOR

When criticized by orthodox Jews for his un-Jewish attitude to Jesus in his novel *Spires, Bells and Dreams*, Gustav Lazlo, in a letter to the *Morning Post* of London, made the following statement: "The movement for the recognition of Christ by the Jews is not a phantasy arising from the brain of the author of *Spires, Bells and Dreams*. It is a fact. Not only in Hungary, where the movement has taken definite form, but in the hearts and minds of many men, ordinary men like myself, traders, men of affairs, the fact that Christ is the only leader who can take us anywhere worth going to is coming to new recognition."[26]

C. G. MONTEFIORE, LEADER OF LIBERAL JUDAISM IN ENGLAND

"We Jews do not mind saying that the greatest influence upon European and American history and civilization has been the Bible. But we too often forget that the Bible which has had this influence is not merely the Old Testament. It is the Old Testament and the New Testament combined. And of the two it is the New Testament which has undoubtedly had the greater influence and has been of the greater importance."[27]

FRANZ ROSENZWEIG—JEWISH RELIGIOUS WRITER

"Judaism and Christianity are to him [Rosenzweig] essentially of one piece, one religious reality: Judaism facing inward to the Jews, Christianity outward to the Gentiles. The two faiths are organically linked as complementary aspects of God's revealed truth. Yet they are not the same; they are distinct and different in their being and in their function. Judaism is the 'eternal fire', Christianity the 'eternal rays'; Judaism is the 'eternal life',

Christianity is the 'eternal way'. While Israel stays with God, Christianity goes out to conquer the unredeemed world for Him. And Christianity would not endure as a force for redemption did not Israel remain in its midst, in its very being serving as a witness to the Eternal. . . . Christianity is, in fact, 'Judaism for the Gentiles', through which the peoples of the world are brought to the God of Israel. Yet as close as are the two, so are they different, and the difference is not to be overcome by 'liberalism' or good will, since it is rooted in the different functions and vocations set for them by divine providence. Only when the goal is reached and the world redeemed, only at the 'end', will the final reconciliation and fusion take place; then all will indeed be one in the recognition of the unity of the Divine Name."[28]

HANS JOACHIM SCHOEPS—JEWISH THEOLOGIAN

"With Franz Rosenzweig, I would even go so far as to declare that perhaps no Gentile can come to God the Father otherwise than through Jesus Christ. In thus recognizing that the revelation of the church of Jesus Christ has its sphere of validity, from which only Israel is excepted by virtue of its direct election by the Father, I do not believe that I offend against Jewish tradition. For even if we go to great lengths in recognizing covenants of God with non-Israelitic mankind, the absolute validity of the revelation of the Torah to Israel remains unimpaired.

"According to Jewish tradition of the centuries, Israel was chosen, however undeserving, to be the bearer of God's covenant. The covenant concluded with the patriarch Abraham was sealed on Mount Sinai by the promulgation of the Torah, and confirmed through the mouths of the Prophets. This covenant, concluded with the seed of Abraham and extended to cover the ger tzedek (full proselytes) who joined with Israel, by no means excludes the possibility that outside Israel's sacred sphere God may have concluded other covenants beyond the scope of Jewish knowledge and judgment. In any event, the modern Jew need face no fundamental contradiction in regarding the 'new covenant' professed by the Christian church as in no way prejudicial to him and his own certitude of salvation. The Christian who, according to his belief, comes to the Father through Jesus Christ—or who, through the church in which Jesus Christ lives, participates by belief in the coming-to-the-Father of Jesus Christ—stands before the same God in whom we Jews believe, the God of Abraham, of Isaac, and of Jacob, the God of Moses our teacher, to whom Jesus also said 'Father'.

"This fundamental fact, which we can acknowledge at all times, guarantees Judaism's inner bond with Christianity and opens up the possibility of a Jewish-Christian rapprochement. The limit to such an understanding is that we cannot recognize Yeshuah ha-Nozri [Jesus of Nazareth] as the Christ, i.e. as the Messiah for Israel. We are, however, prepared to recognize that, in some way which we do not understand, a Messianic significance for non-Jewish mankind is attached to the figure of this man. . . .

"For the God who named himself to Moses as 'I will be who I will be' is in all the diversity of his revelations and covenants the eternally same God; he is absolute for the Jews as the God who is and will be, just as, by a different form of mediation, he has become God for the Christians. Hence Jews and Christians cannot and must not deviate from the absoluteness of their different testimonies of truth. And, consequently, they will go their separate ways through history according to the will of providence, up to that point in the future where the parallels intersect.

"The end of the two covenants will come to pass in the days of the Messiah, when 'old' and 'new' covenant become one covenant, when all mankind assembles under a single covenant to worship only God. The Messianism of Israel aims at that which is to come, the eschatology of the Gentile church at the return of him who has come. Both elective covenants confront the ebb and flow of the finite world in the shared expectation that the decisive event is still to come—the goal of the ways of God that he travels with mankind in Israel and in the Church.

"The church of Jesus Christ has preserved no portrait of its lord and saviour. If Jesus were to come again tomorrow, no Christian would know his face. But it might well be that he who is coming at the end of days, he who is awaited by the synagogue as by the church, is one, with one and the same face."[29]

VI. THE STATE OF ISRAEL AND THE PROBLEM OF THE MESSIAHSHIP OF JESUS

With the rebirth of the State of Israel the entire subject of the Jewish attitude to Christianity enters a new phase. The elements in the new situation are these:

I. THE POLITICO-NATIONAL ASPECT

The supra-national or cosmopolitan character of Christianity, which in the Diaspora constitutes a threat to the Jewish nationality, ceases to be this threat in the State of Israel. In the State of Israel, short of a war of extermination, the Jewish nationality has a better chance of survival than in any other country in the world. There a Jew is a Jew whatever his religious convictions may be.

2. JEWISH ISOLATIONISM

One of the chief goals of traditional Judaism was to isolate the Jew from the Gentile in general and from the Christian in particular. In the State of Israel this separation is impossible. In fact, the restoration of the State of Israel has placed Jew and Christian in a most unusual relationship to each other for the first time in nineteen centuries. As of November 1956 the population of the State of Israel numbered 45,000 Christians.[30] For the first time since the birth of Christianity Christians find themselves citizens of a Jewish State. In the State of Israel there are also a number of Christian Holy Places for whose safety the Government of Israel is directly responsible. Through the Ministry of Religious Affairs the Government maintains official contacts with the various Christian religious bodies in Israel. In Israel the Jew keeps stumbling into places intimately associated with the life and work of Jesus. In this connection the words of Sholem Asch are significant. Relating the circumstances which led to his decision to write *The Nazarene* he makes the following statement: "I suppose the final inspiration to write, the insistence that I write, came to me in Palestine. I saw that I could never write about Jesus until I went to his homeland. So I went, in 1907. Then the story really came alive. The whole landscape of the Holy Land held His footprints; every bush and tree and stone was afire with Christ."[31]

3. THE BREAK WITH THE PAST

An important factor in the Jewish-Christian relationship in the State of Israel is the trend among the young Israelis to repudiate the Galut era in Jewish history, already discussed on previous pages.

The deplorable part which the medieval Church has played in Jewish persecution has left an indelible mark on the mind and heart of the Jew in the Diaspora. These memories of the past form an important stumbling-block in Jewish-Christian reconciliation. In the State of Israel this psychological element is bound to lose its importance for a number of reasons. In the course of time the majority of Israeli Jews will consist of those born in Israel. These Israeli Jews will have never known "Christian" persecution. A large percentage of the Israeli Jews are the Oriental Jews who have known only one kind of Jewish persecutors—those of Moslem origin. From now on Jews emigrating to Israel from the West will be coming from countries where for many years the Christian Church has displayed a friendly attitude to the Jewish population. Since the Hitler era there has been among the Jews in the West a growing awareness of the significance of the Jewish-Christian spiritual heritage at this critical juncture of world history.

4. THE RENEWED INTEREST IN THE BIBLE

This subject has been dealt with in connection with the religious problem in Israel. We only wish to add that the State of Israel is becoming one of the great world centres of Bible research. One may state without the risk of contradiction that at no time in the history of the Jewish people has there been so much interest in the Bible, especially in its prophetic and historical portions, as there is today in the State of Israel. Even the New Testament is widely read. That this unprecedented development is destined to increase Jewish interest in the subject of Christianity goes without saying.

5. THE EMANCIPATION OF THE SPIRITUAL ELEMENT IN THE JEWISH MESSIANIC HOPE

To the Jew the redemption associated with the coming of the Messiah always meant the re-establishment of an independent national state in the Land of Israel. This hope runs through the whole of the Jewish Prayer Book. No Jewish prayer service is complete without a petition to God for the speedy national restoration of Israel. In 1948 this centuries-old Jewish dream became a reality with the declaration of independence of the State of

Israel. But the State of Israel was reconstituted without the Messiah. At the Chanukah (Feast of Dedication) festival celebration in 1950, observed in the State of Israel to commemorate the "ingathering of the exiles", a shofar (ram's horn) brought over from the Belsen concentration camp was blown to announce the end of the exile. "But Orthodox Jews took objection to the ceremony on the grounds that it behoved no one but the Messiah to blow the shofar on such an occasion. . . . Yet the shofar was sounded though not by Messiah."[32]

Does this mean that Israel's Messianic hope is being fulfilled without the Messiah? This conclusion may be acceptable to Liberal Judaism which has substituted the conception of a Messianic Age in place of a Messianic Person, but it will be unacceptable to traditional Judaism. And yet the whole centuries-old liturgy of the Synagogue will have to be revised. For this, being a Galut (Exile) liturgy, was composed for a people deprived of its national state, and made to express the nation's longings and hope for eventual national restoration. This hope having now been achieved, much of the Prayer Book of the Synagogue has been rendered anachronistic and obsolete. It certainly is true that "no religion can keep alive with its hopes fulfilled".[33] This extraordinary state of affairs must of necessity lead to an eventual separation of the spiritual from the national element in the Jewish Messianic hope in which they have been for ages so intimately entwined.

In bringing the discussion of the subject of the Jewish attitude to the Messiahship of Jesus to a close this writer wishes to state that the whole trend of Jewish history—Biblical as well as post-Biblical—compels him to believe that the Jewish people are eventually bound to acclaim Jesus as their God-promised Messiah; and that the reconstitution of the State of Israel is paving the way for the consummation of this event. This event will, however, not take place until the outworking of certain fundamental tendencies in Jewish and Gentile history will have reached its culminating point. The following chapters contain a discussion of these historical trends.

NOTES TO CHAPTER 7

1. The translation of Isaiah 52: 13–15; 53: 1–12 is based chiefly on the work by Franz Debitzsch; only in several instances was the American Standard Version followed.

2. David Baron, *The Servant of Jehovah* (Morgan & Scott: London, Second Edition, 1922), p. 11.

3. Ibid., pp. 146–7.

4. Alfred Edersheim, *The Life and Times of Jesus the Messiah* (Longmans, Green & Co.: New York, 8th Edition, 1899), vol. 2, Appendix IX.

5. See David Baron, op. cit., pp. 149–53.

6. Alfred Edersheim, op. cit., vol. 2, Appendix IX.

7. See David Baron, op. cit., p. 156.

8. Ibid, p. 15.

9. Ibid., pp. 157–8.

10. Ibid., p. 13.

11. Ibid., p. 12.

12. Michael Friedländer, *The Jewish Religion* (Shapiro, Vallentine & Co.: London, Seventh Edition, 1937), p. 160.

13. C. G. Montefiore, *Liberal Judaism* (1903), pp. 176 f.; quoted by W. O. E. Oesterley, *The Jewish Doctrine of Mediation* (Skeffington & Son: London, 1910), p. 170.

14. I. M. Wise, *Judaism and Christianity*, p. 102; quoted by Jakób Jocz, *The Jewish People and Jesus Christ* (S.P.C.K.: London, 1954; New York, Macmillan Company), p. 285.

15. Leo Baeck, *The Essence of Judaism* (Schocken Books: New York, Revised Edition, 1948), p. 125.

16. O. Lazarus, *Liberal Judaism and Its Standpoint* (Macmillan & Co.: London, 1937), p. 89.

17. Joseph Klausner, *From Jesus to Paul* (The Macmillan Co.: New York, 1943), p. 526.

18. Steven S. Schwarzschild, "The Personal Messiah—Towards the Restoration of a Discarded Doctrine", article in *Judaism* (New York), Spring 1956. For an exhaustive study of Jewish Messianism see Joseph Klausner's *The Messianic Idea of Israel* (The Macmillan Co.: New York, 1955).

19. "In Exile we saw the world with eyes of fear, strangeness of envy, disparagement or self-decrial, for we had no equal share or parity in it. Perhaps we could not understand other peoples, enveloped as we were either in gloomy feelings of inferiority or an unblushing sense of superiority."—David Ben Gurion, in "Israel—People and State", article in *The Jewish Spectator* (New York), May 1953.

20. *En Jacob* (Agada of the Babylonian Talmud, edited by Rabbi Jacob Ibn Chabib, English translation by Rabbi S. H. Glick: New York, 1921), vol. 5 (Aboda Zara), chap. 1, pp. 137–8.

21. Frank S. Mead, "An Interview with Sholem Asch", article in the *Christian Herald* (New York), January, 1944; quoted by D. B. Bravin in *The Dawn* (The Legum Memorial: Pittsburgh), March-April, 1944. Copyright by the *Christian Herald* and used by permission.

22. Quoted by D. B. Bravin, *The Dawn* (Pittsburgh, Pa.), January–February 1934.

23. Constantine Brunner, *Der Juden Hass und die Juden*; quoted by Jacob Gartenhaus, *The Jew and Jesus Christ* (The Sunday School Board of the Southern Baptist Convention: Nashville, Tenn., Second Edition, 1934), p. 20.

24. George Sylvester Viereck, "What Life Means to Einstein", article in the *Saturday Evening Post* (Philadelphia), October 26th, 1929; quoted by John S. Conning, *Will the Jews Ever Claim Jesus* (Board of National Missions of the Presbyterian Church: New York), p. 6.

25. Will Herberg, "From Marxism to Judaism", *Commentary* (New York), January 1947.

26. Gustav Lazlo in a letter to the *Morning Post* (London); quoted by John S. Conning, op. cit., p. 4.

27. Quoted by D. B. Bravin, *The Dawn* (Pittsburgh, Pa.), September–October 1932.

28. Will Herberg, "Rosenzweig's 'Judaism of Personal Existence'", *Commentary* (New York), December 1950.

29. H. J. Schoeps, "A Religious Bridge between Jew and Christian", *Commentary* (New York), February 1950.

30. *Facts About Israel*, March 1957, p. 45; published by the Israel Office of Information, New York City.

31. Quoted by Frank S. Mead, "An Interview with Sholem Asch", idem.

32. *Jewish Chronicle* (London), August 18, 1950; quoted by Jakób Jocz, "Judaism and the State of Israel", article in *The Hebrew-Christian*, Summer 1952; published by the International Hebrew-Christian Alliance, London, England.

33. Jakób Jocz, "Judaism and the State of Israel", idem.

PART THREE

THE REBIRTH OF THE STATE OF ISRAEL IN THE CONTEXT OF CURRENT WORLD HISTORY

CHAPTER I

THE DIVINE FORECAST OF GENTILE
WORLD HISTORY

THE DIVINE FORECAST OF GENTILE WORLD HISTORY

I. THE "TIMES OF THE GENTILES"

1. DEFINITION OF THE WORD "GENTILE"

The word "Gentile" is a translation of the Hebrew word "Goy". The plural, i.e. "Gentiles", is "Goyim" in Hebrew. The word occurs in the Bible for the first time in Genesis 10: 5 where we read of the "isles of the Gentiles". The original meaning of the Hebrew word Goy is nation, and "Goyim" = nations. Thus "Goy" meant any nation, and "Goyim" nations in general. Here and there in the Old Testament Israel is also referred to as "Goy", i.e. nation. "Seeing that Abraham shall surely become a great and mighty nation, and all the nations of the earth shall be blessed in him", Genesis 18: 18. "Nation" and "nations" in this sentence are rendered in the Hebrew "Goy" and "Goyim". "And I will make of thee a great nation," Genesis 12: 2. In this Divine statement to Abraham the word "nation" is "Goy" in the Hebrew. "And you shall be unto me a kingdom of priests, and a holy nation. . . .", Exodus 19: 6. Here again "Goy" is the Hebrew word referring distinctly to Israel. Speaking to Moses after the golden calf incident, God says: ". . . and I will make of thee a great nation". Again the word "Goy" occurs in the Hebrew text, Exodus 32: 10. Interceding for Israel Moses bases his plea for forgiveness partly on the ground that Israel is God's people. "And consider that this nation is thy people," Moses declares. The word "nation" as used here is "Goy" in the Hebrew, Exodus 33: 13. There are a number of other instances in the Old Testament where the word "Goy" meaning nation is applied to Israel.

In due course of time, however, Israel became the one nation in the whole world whose God was Jehovah, whereas all other nations served other gods. The word "Goyim", and its singular form "Goy", gradually assumed a religious connotation. It was the relationship to Jehovah which became the distinguishing mark and the dividing line. On one side were the people of Israel who belonged to Jehovah. On the other side were all other nations who were outside of Jehovah. If Israel forsakes Jehovah she becomes spiritually one of the nations. This is the meaning of the passage in Jeremiah 9: 25–26 (9: 24–25 Heb.) "Behold, the days come, saith Jehovah, that I will punish all them who are circumcised in their uncircumcision. Egypt and Judah, and Edom, and the children of Ammon, and Moab, and all that have the corners of their hair cut off, that dwell in the wilderness; for all the nations are uncircumcised, and all the house of Israel are uncircumcised in the heart."

With the arrival of Christianity a new group of people or peoples came into existence. The religious division of mankind into two groups, Israel and the nations or Gentiles, was henceforth changed into a threefold division: the Jews who are the Old Testament people of God, the Christians, composed of Jews and Gentiles, and who are the New Testament people of God, and the Gentiles who stand outside the Biblical revelation. "Give no occasion of stumbling," Paul declares, "either to Jews, or to Greeks, or to the church of God", 1 Corinthians 10: 32. The birth of Christianity and the subsequent world-wide dispersion of the Jews posed a serious threat to the Jewish nationality. In the incessant struggle of the Jewish people against the danger of national disintegration the word "Gentile" assumed the meaning of non-Jew.

2. WHAT ARE THE "TIMES OF THE GENTILES"?

This phrase occurs in the New Testament, in the Gospel of Luke, chapter 21, verse 24: "And Jerusalem shall be trodden down of the Gentiles, until the times of the Gentiles be fulfilled." To this writer's knowledge, the phrase "the times of the Gentiles" is not found anywhere else in the Bible, Old or New Testament. It forms part of the so-called Olivet Discourse which is recorded in Matthew chapter 24, Mark chapter 13, and Luke chapter 21. In answer to some questions of the apostles with reference to His prediction of the coming destruction of Jerusalem, Jesus made a lengthy declaration in which, among other things, He said that "Jerusalem shall be trodden down of the Gentiles until the times of the Gentiles be fulfilled".

THE REBIRTH OF THE STATE OF ISRAEL

The "times of the Gentiles" is the Biblical concept of Gentile history based on the two-fold relationship of the nations of the earth to God and to Israel. In its first aspect, i.e. in its relationship to God, it is more proper to refer to it as the "times of the Nations", and its distinguishing feature is the dominance of the human principle in world history. It is man's will as opposed to God's will which is the ruling principle in the affairs of the nations.

The beginning of the "times of the Nations" era of Gentile history coincides with the Tower of Babel episode as recorded in Genesis 11: 1–9. It is not the intention of the sacred writer to attribute to the Tower of Babel episode the origin of the nations. The splitting up of the human race into national groups was a natural development which came about in the process of the multiplication of the human race and man's gradual extension over the face of the earth. Following the Flood Noah's descendants were told by God to spread out and to repeople the earth laid waste by the ravaging waters of the Flood. Instead of doing this Noah's descendants, or a certain large number of them, decided to concentrate in the Babel area and there to centralize their activities. They began to build a city with an imposing tower which was to become the seat of a mighty empire and bring honour and glory to their name. In this collective undertaking they were motivated by the lust for power and fame, the consuming passion of men and nations ever since. As in the Garden of Eden man as an individual transgressed against the Will of God, in the Tower of Babel event mankind en masse sinned against God. It was the first concerted human rebellion against God. The Tower of Babel episode is therefore a fit beginning of the spiritual, or rather unspiritual, history of the nations of the earth, the "times of the Nations", whose guiding principle is the wilfulness of man.

But God has not abandoned the nations to their fate. He made sure in various ways that they know His Will. Through Israel in the Old Testament era and through Christianity in the New Testament era the nations of the world have come to know the Will of God concerning mankind's destiny. The decision whether to live in accordance with God's Law or to follow after one's own inclinations was left to man individually and to mankind collectively. In the era of human history referred to as the "times of the Nations" the nations of the world are permitted, if they choose, to follow their inclinations, and to shape their destinies apart from God. This does not mean that during this era God has abdicated as the Sovereign of this world. Far from it. The fate of Sodom and Gomorrah, of the nations of Canaan, of ancient Egypt, of Assyria, Babylon, Rome and others, amply prove that God has set certain moral bounds the overstepping of which has always spelled disaster. The prophetic significance of the Tower of Babel event lies also in this that as the first rebellion of the nations against God has met with defeat, so will the last rebellion of the earth's nations against God, at the end of the "times of the Nations", meet with a similar fate.

In its second aspect, in its relation to Israel, the "times of the Nations" phrase is more properly spoken of as the "times of the Gentiles", and this era began with the destruction of the First Jewish Commonwealth. This was the first interruption of Jewish national life in Palestine since it became organized under Joshua. The destruction of Jewish political life in Palestine by the Babylonians coincided with the rise of a succession of world powers. Babylon was the first of these world empires. World leadership, which after the Flood was first held by the Hamitic races, and from them passed on to the Semitic nations, was from now on to become concentrated in the hands of the Japhethic, or Aryan, peoples who were the last of the three divisions of post-diluvian mankind.

Prior to the Babylonian Invasion the First Jewish Commonwealth in Palestine was fully able to maintain itself as a sovereign state. Depending on the quality of its leadership its international position varied from one of relative strength to one of relative weakness. Under David, Solomon, and Uzziah the Jewish State occupied a commanding position in the Eastern Mediterranean. The destruction of the First Jewish Commonwealth by the Babylonians marked the beginning of a more permanent change in Israel's political situation in the world. While after the collapse of Babylon Persia, the first Aryan world power, granted the Jews permission to return to Palestine and reconstruct there their national life, Palestine remained a political appendage of one or another world power. Notwithstanding a brief period of relative political independence under the Maccabees Palestine of the Second Jewish Commonwealth remained in a position of political inferiority vis-à-vis the Gentile world. In this position Israel was to remain until the end of the "times of the Gentiles".

II. THE PROPHECY OF NOAH

"And Noah awoke from his wine, and knew what his youngest son had done unto him. And he said: 'Cursed be Canaan, a servant of servants shall he be unto his brethren. And he said: Blessed be Jehovah, the God of Shem, and let Canaan be his servant. God enlarge Japheth, and let him dwell in the tents of Shem, and let Canaan be his servant',", Genesis 9: 24-27.

I. THE MATERIAL SUPREMACY OF THE ARYAN RACE

It is quite possible that this prophetic declaration was made by Noah as he was approaching the end of his earthly pilgrimage. If this be true, then Noah knew of the Tower of Babel incident at the time he uttered this prophecy. Thus Noah had ample opportunity to observe the various traits of character and the distinctive mental and moral qualities of his descendants.

This is one of the most amazing prophetic utterances in the whole Bible. This writer believes that it originated with Noah. But its wonder is not diminished one particle even if one assumes that Noah could not have possibly been its author, that this is the observation made by some one many centuries after Noah. If we examine its contents we shall see that the major elements of this prophetic message did not even begin to be fulfilled till some time after the close of the Old Testament era. No man, unaided by the spirit of God, could have possibly foretold, prior to the close of the Old Testament era, the shape of events as forecast in this passage. We have here a prophetic outline of the history of the descendants of the three sons of Noah who gave rise to the three main divisions of the human race. The Hamitic branch was to become subservient to the other two branches; the Semitic race was to provide spiritual leadership; while Japheth was to achieve material and political supremacy in the world.

And yet for many centuries following Noah's pronouncement the actual state of the world seemed to contradict the contents of this prophecy. "All the greatest empires of the earliest antiquity were Hamitic: the mighty and long-continued kingdom of Egypt; the great empire of Nimrod, of whose gigantic and magnificent cities and temples we have ocular evidence in our own day; all the seven nations of Canaan; and above all, this mighty, warlike, extensive, and long-lasting empire of the Hittites—all were Hamitic. Wherever the eye turned, the posterity of the youngest son of Noah would in those early ages have been observed to be in the ascendant."[1]

"Egypt and Babylon, Mizraim and Nimrod—both descendants of Ham—led the way and acted as the pioneers of mankind in the various untrodden fields of art, literature, and science. Alphabetic writing, astronomy, history, chronology, architecture, plastic art, sculpture, navigation, agriculture, textile industry, seem all of them to have had their origin in one or other of these two countries."[2]

But as the centuries rolled on the fortunes of the Hamitic races underwent a gradual change. "These sons of Ham had ample time and a wide sphere allowed them in which to show forth what was in them, in which to display the character that was subsequently to bring down upon them the degradation predicted. God never inflicts undeserved judgements; He waits until men fill up the measure of their iniquity . . . Egypt and Babylon, the Canaanites and the Hittites, one and all fell into the lowest depths of idolatry, and into the vilest forms of sensualism, cruelty, and sin; they perished in their own corruption, and were the victims of their own iniquities."[3] One by one they were in due course of time overcome, first by the Semitic, and later by the Japhethic races.

Next in point of time to attain world prominence were the Semites. They subjugated one Hamitic nation after another, and some of them founded great empires, as in the case of Assyria and Babylon. The Assyrian empire lasted about six and a half centuries and held in subjection a vast territory from Suza, in Persia, to lower Egypt. After the collapse of Assyria, Babylon slowly moved into its place, and under Nebuchadnezzar it became a world empire. But its life was shorter than that of its predecessor Assyria, and it was finally overthrown by the Persians. In the seventh century A.D. the Semitic Arabs broke out of their desert places and within one century they extended their rule over a large territory stretching from India, in Asia, to North Africa, and to Spain in Europe. But they were soon rolled back by the Europeans in the West, and the Tartars in the East.

The Japhethites, or Aryans, were the last of the three great divisions of mankind to move up to the forefront of world affairs. The destruction of the Semitic Babylonian empire in 538 B.C. by Cyrus the Persian was the beginning of Japhethic world rule. A few years later, in 525 B.C., Hamitic Egypt was conquered by

Cambyses, the successor of Cyrus. From the Aryan Persians world leadership slipped into the hands of Alexander the Great, also an Aryan. After the break up of Alexander's empire there was for a while no single dominating power. But there were definite signs that Rome was pressing forward for the place of world mastery. Rome's ambitions in that direction were challenged by the powerful and rich city-state of Carthage in North Africa. The Carthaginians were Hamitic by race and Semitic by language, religion and culture. Their gifted and able general Hannibal invaded Italy and defeated the Roman armies in several battles. In the last minute, however, the army of Hannibal, which had almost reached the gates of Rome, was rolled back, and in the decisive battle at Zama, south of Carthage, in 202 B.C., completely defeated, and Carthage destroyed. Had Rome lost that war there might have never been a Roman empire, and the march of the Aryan races to world leadership might have come to a premature end. With the elimination of Carthage the last serious obstacle in the path of Aryan world supremacy was swept away.

In later centuries Aryan supremacy was again challenged on several occasions: by the Huns in the fourth and fifth centuries, the Arabs in the eighth century, the Mongols in the thirteenth century, and the Turks from the middle of the fifteenth to almost the end of the seventeenth century. One by one, all these invasions were repelled, and beginning with the sixteenth century the European Aryans embarked on a programme of world conquest. In a short time they have spread out over the whole face of the earth. At the present they are in full possession of three out of five continents; they control Africa even though they constitute a small fraction of the population of that continent; and even in Asia, in spite of the rising nationalism of the Asian peoples, the Aryans as represented by India, Russia and America still exercise a decisive influence. In world politics, in economics, in culture, science and the arts, the Aryan races, the descendants of Japheth, have been leading the world for the last 2,500 years. "God enlarge Japheth"—and He did.

2. THE SPIRITUAL LEADERSHIP OF THE SEMITIC RACE

"And he said: Blessed be Jehovah, the God of Shem. . . . God enlarge Japheth, and let him dwell in the tents of Shem . . .", Genesis 9: 26, 27.

No material advantages were held out to Shem. Spiritual supremacy was to become his peculiar treasure. The Aryan or Japhethic races were to be attracted to the God of Shem in a special way. Indirectly this passage hints at the close association of Shem's descendants with the descendants of Japheth. In what a marvellous manner this portion of Noah's prophecy had been fulfilled! When Babylon surrendered to Persia, this first Aryan nation to gain the status of a world power found in the ageing saint and prophet Daniel a dependable and trustworthy statesman. It is quite possible that Daniel's association with the new government had something to do with the permission granted to the Jewish exiles to return to Palestine and reconstitute their national life there. Thus from the very beginning of Aryan world supremacy the Aryan nations came under the influence of the faith of Israel, and Israel's spiritual heritage was made available to them. The best elements in Western Civilization cannot be understood apart from Christianity. "God has been the Lord God of Shem in an altogether peculiar and distinctive sense. The Saviour of the world descended from this son of Noah. Revealed religion has flowed through Semitic channels . . . Every psalm of David, and every Christian hymn and sacred song of later days, every authentic narrative of the earliest ages of humanity, the sublime law of Sinai, and the beatitudes and parables of Christ, the visions of prophecy, the teachings of apostles, the testimony of the martyrs, the missions of modern Christianity—all that has lifted our world from ruin and misery and darkness and death, all that has purified and ennobled it and opened to it a door of hope for the future—all has come to it through Shem."[4]

III. Gentile World History according to the Prophetic Writings of Daniel: the Great Image of Nebuchadnezzar's Dream

The writings of Daniel do not stand alone. They are related to the other prophetic writings of the Bible; especially to those of Jeremiah who laboured in the tragic years preceding the destruction of the kingdom of Judah; to Ezekiel who, like Daniel, lived and laboured in the Babylonian exile; to Zechariah, a post-exilic prophet, who was looking to a more complete, and final restoration of Israel in the future; to the writings of the New Testament, especially the Olivet Discourse recorded in the Gospels, and the book of Revelation. The several prophetic messages in Daniel are interlocked with one another. Together they present to us a Divine forecast of Gentile history. Separately they deal with the various aspects of Gentile history. In this part of the chapter we will confine ourselves to the first of Daniel's prophecies based on the image of Nebuchadnezzar's dream.

"The king answered and said to Daniel, whose name was Belteshazzar, Art thou able to make known unto me the dream which I have seen, and the interpretation thereof?

"Daniel answered before the king, and said, The secret which the king hath demanded can neither wise men, enchanters, magicians, nor soothsayers show unto the king. But there is a God in heaven that revealeth secrets, and He hath made known to the king Nebuchadnezzar what shall be in the latter days. Thy dream, and the visions of thy head upon thy bed, are these. As for thee, O king, thy thoughts came into thy mind upon thy bed, what should come to pass hereafter; and He that revealeth secrets hath made known to thee what shall come to pass. But as for me, this secret is not revealed to me for any wisdom that I have more than any living, but to the intent that the interpretation may be made known to the king, and that thou mayest know the thoughts of thy heart. Thou, O king, sawest, and, behold, a great image. This image which was mighty, and whose brightness was excellent, stood before thee; and the aspect thereof was terrible. As for this image, its head was of fine gold, its breast and its arms of silver, its belly and its thighs of brass. Its legs of iron, its feet part of iron, and part of clay. Thou sawest till that a stone was cut out without hands, which smote the image upon its feet that were of iron and clay, and broke them in pieces.

"Then was the iron, the clay, the brass, the silver, and the gold, broken in pieces together, and became like the chaff of the summer threshing-floors; and the wind carried them away, that no place was found for them; and the stone that smote the image became a great mountain, and filled the whole earth. This is the dream and we will tell the interpretation thereof before the king.

"Thou, O king, art a king of kings, unto whom the God of heaven hath given the kingdom, the power, and the strength, and the glory. And wheresoever the children of men dwell, the beasts of the field and the birds of the heavens hath He given into thy hand, and hath made thee to rule over them all: thou art the head of gold. And after thee shall arise another kingdom inferior to thee; and another third kingdom of brass, which shall bear rule over all the earth. And the fourth kingdom shall be strong as iron, forasmuch as iron breaketh in pieces and subdueth all things; and as iron that crusheth all these, shall it break in pieces and crush. And whereas thou sawest the feet and toes, part of potter's clay, and part of iron, it shall be a divided kingdom; but there shall be in it of the strength of the iron, forasmuch as thou sawest the iron mixed with miry clay. And as the toes of the feet were part of iron, and part of clay, so the kingdom shall be partly strong, and partly broken [i.e. brittle]. And whereas thou sawest the iron mixed with miry clay, they shall mingle themselves with the seed of men; but they shall not cleave one to another, even as iron doth not mingle with clay.

"And in the days of those kings shall the God of heaven set up a kingdom which shall never be destroyed; nor shall the sovereignty thereof be left to another people; but it shall break in pieces and consume all these kingdoms, and it shall stand forever. Forasmuch as thou sawest that a stone was cut out of the mountain without hands, and that it broke in pieces the iron, the brass, the clay, the silver, and the gold, the great God hath made known to the king what shall come to pass hereafter, and the dream is certain, and the interpretation thereof sure", Daniel 2: 26-45.

This vision of the image which Nebuchadnezzar saw in a dream probably came to him in response to his concern about the destiny of the great empire which his father and he acquired after many years of intense warfare and bitter struggle. As in the case of the other great revelations in the Bible those in Daniel were made at a critical stage in the world's history. The political map of the civilized world of that day was undergoing radical changes. One nation after another was struck down by the mighty onrush of Nebuchadnezzar's armies, and the world became unified politically under the leadership of Nebuchadnezzar with Babylon the world's capital city. In the process of this political rearrangement of the ancient world the kingdom of Judah not only was conquered, but its capital city and the centre of its religious life were destroyed, and the people carried off to Babylon. To the people of the Judaean kingdom, who until now were more or less isolated from the main currents of Gentile life, this destruction of their homeland and their transplantation to Babylon were indeed the beginning of the "times of the Gentiles". From now on until the end of the "times of the Gentiles" they were to remain in a politically inferior position with relation to the Gentile world. The object of Daniel's revelations was, therefore, first, to convey a message of comfort to the Judaean captives, and, second, to sound a warning to the Gentile world not to behave as if they were the true and permanent masters of the earth.

The message of the image of Nebuchadnezzar's dream is a sweeping, general, Divine preview of a certain aspect of Gentile world history. It is a condensed outline of the course and destiny of Gentile civilization and Gentile world power. Four empires come and go. Babylon, beginning with Nebuchadnezzar, Persia, Greece under Alexander the Great, and Rome. Babylon heads the list for three reasons; first, because of the association of ancient Babel with mankind's first collective rebellion against God in the Tower of Babel incident; second, because Babylon continued to be the world centre of the two succeeding world empires, and also because of some indications in the Bible that the city of Babylon is destined to re-emerge as a focal point of the last Gentile world power which will come into existence in the final phase of the "times of the Gentiles".

Persia which attained to world leadership following the collapse of Babylon is the second of the four empires in the image of Nebuchadnezzar's dream. Persia's importance in this Divine view of history is derived from the fact that it is the world power which God had used to accomplish Israel's partial national restoration.

Greece under Alexander the Great is the third empire in the image and its significance consists in that it has brought the whole ancient civilized world under the influence of the Greek language and Greek culture. Even the Jews in Palestine could not escape the all-pervading influence of Hellenism. Many Jews adopted Greek names and Greek customs. The Old Testament was translated into Greek, the first translation of the Bible into a non-Semitic language. The whole Maccabean conflict was the Jewish reaction to the denationalizing effect of Hellenist culture.

Rome, the fourth empire in the image, is that Gentile world power which has accomplished the second destruction of the Jewish Homeland and brought about the world-wide dispersion of the Jews. Rome also caused the shifting of the centre of world events from Asia to Europe.

The feet and the toes represent the last Gentile world power which will exercise world rule at the end of the Gentile Era. The time interval separating the fourth from the final Gentile world power is disregarded in this prophetic revelation, even as is the interval between the third and the fourth empires. The reason for listing the toes and feet together with the legs, or the last Gentile world power with the Roman Empire, is because the centre of the activities of the last Gentile world power and its final destruction by God's intervention will take place in the Mediterranean area, which was the heart of the territory of the Roman empire.

The next aspect of the prophetic message of Nebuchadnezzar's image is the symbolism of the metals by which the various world empires are represented in the image: gold, silver, brass, iron, iron plus clay. The best possible explanation of the symbolism of the metals is that they signify the various stages of development through which Gentile civilization passes from its beginning to its end. This development displays a downward trend, from the precious metal gold to the common metal iron. In his interpretation of the dream Daniel declares to Nebuchadnezzar that the second empire represented in the image by silver will be inferior to the first which is represented by gold. If this downward trend of Gentile history is taken to apply to the moral or spiritual sphere then the metallic sub-divisions of Nebuchadnezzar's image indicate the gradual moral deterioration of Gentile civilization. This conception would be in accord with the other prophetic passages in Daniel where the various Gentile empires are represented by beasts. It would also harmonize with many teachings in the Bible with respect to the growing and cumulative effect of human wickedness in the history of the world. According to this view Gentile history will come to an end when the cup of its wickedness has been filled to the brim. Thus Gentile civilization collectively would suffer the same fate at the end of its history as have the cities of Sodom and Gomorrah, the cities of Canaan, and many peoples of antiquity.

As the weight of the upright image of Nebuchadnezzar's dream pointed to its feet, so is the burden of the message centred on the last Gentile world system represented by the feet and toes. Notice that Daniel's interpretation of the image revelation speaks practically nothing about the intervening Gentile world empires, beyond mentioning their rise and fall. But it dwells at length on the first and on the last of these world systems. On the first, because of the importance of Babylon as was shown above. It is, however, on the last phase of Gentile civilization, the feet and the toes, on which our full attention is focused. It is the end of the "times of the Gentiles" which is the heart of this revelation. "But there is a God in heaven that revealeth secrets, and He hath made known to the king Nebuchadnezzar what shall be in the latter days . . .", Daniel 2: 28. This expression of "latter days" or "end of the days" is a familiar phrase in the Old Testament, and it points to the time of, or events related to, Israel's final and complete restoration. It occurs for the first time in Genesis 49: 1 in connection with Jacob's prophetic utterance before his death. "And Jacob called unto his sons and said: Gather yourselves together that I may tell you that which shall befall you in the latter days." And in the tenth verse he gives the well-known Messianic passage: "The sceptre shall not depart from Judah, nor the ruler's staff from between his feet, until Shiloh come, and unto him shall the obedience of the peoples be." The phrase is met with again in the Balaam prophecy as recorded in the book of Numbers 24: 14; in Deuteronomy 31: 29; in Isaiah 2: 2 we read: "And it shall come to pass in the latter days, that the mountain of Jehovah's house shall be established on the top of the mountains, and shall be exalted above the hills; and all nations shall flow unto it"; also in Jeremiah 23: 20; 30: 24; 48: 47; 49: 39; Ezekiel 38: 16; Hosea 3: 5; Micah 4: 1. In the book of Daniel the phrase is found [in Daniel 10: 14]—"Now I am come to make thee understand what shall befall thy people in the latter days; for the vision is yet for many days."

Now to return to the feet and toes sub-division of the image. As we have pointed out above, the burden of the whole prophetic message of the image is directed to the last phase of Gentile civilization as represented by the feet and toes. "And whereas thou sawest the feet and toes, part of potter's clay, and part of iron, it shall be a divided kingdom; but there shall be in it of the strength of the iron, forasmuch as thou sawest the iron mixed with miry clay. And as the toes of the feet were part of iron, and part of clay, so the kingdom shall be partly strong, and partly broken [brittle]. And whereas thou sawest the iron mixed with miry clay, they shall mingle themselves with the seed of men, but they shall not cleave one to another, even as iron doth not mingle with clay", Daniel 2: 41–43. This refers to the iron-clay period. The head of the image is represented by gold, the feet and toes—by iron and clay. If the various metallic sub-divisions of the image are also understood as representing the various stages in the development of Gentile systems of government, then the head of gold symbolizes the nobility form of government, while the feet and toes of iron-clay designate the government of the common man. The French and Industrial Revolutions brought to the fore a new force in the social and political life of Western civilization. The common man who was called upon to turn the wheels of the newly born industries, the mass of labourers who were herded together to operate the newly sprung up factories, were slowly becoming transformed into a new element of increasing importance in the political, economic and social scene of Western civilization. This submerged bottom layer of human society—the feet and the toes of the body politic—this mass of iron and clay, was in the last century catapulted into world prominence, and brought to the forefront of national and international relations.

In Daniel's description of the iron-clay stage of Gentile civilization there is so much which bears strong resemblance to the present era of the world's history that one cannot help believing that we are now in the iron-clay period of prophecy. The prophet is impressed with the strength and power which this last Gentile world system shall wield, "but there shall be in it of the strength of the iron". But in spite of this enormous strength this last Gentile world empire will lack inner coherence and real unity. "It shall be", we are told, "a divided kingdom", and "the kingdom shall be partly strong, and partly brittle", "they shall mingle themselves with the seed of men, but they shall not cleave one to another, even as iron doth not mingle with clay."

And now we come to the very climax of the prophetic message of the second chapter of Daniel. World history throughout the era of the "times of the Gentiles" is characterized by the rise and fall of great world empires. One empire after another made its appearance on the stage of human history, arrived at the top of power and prominence, then began to decline, and in the end was struck down by another up-and-coming power, and the historical cycle commenced once more. But the last Gentile world system is according to the prophecies of Daniel—with which all other prophetic writings concur—to be destroyed by the direct intervention of God. "And in the days of those kings shall the God of heaven set up a kingdom which shall never be destroyed; nor shall the sovereignty thereof be left to another people; but it shall break in pieces and consume all these kingdoms, and it shall stand forever", Daniel 2: 44.

NOTES TO CHAPTER 1

1. H. Grattan Guinness, *The Divine Programme of the World's History* (Hodder and Stoughton: London, 1889), p. 105.
2. *Rawlinson's Ancient Monarchies*, vol. i., p. 60; quoted by H. Grattan Guinness, op. cit., pp. 106-7.
3. H. Grattan Guinness, op. cit., p. 107.
4. Ibid., p. 109.

THE PRESENT-DAY WORLD CRISIS
OF GENTILE CIVILIZATION

I. THE MAIN FEATURES OF THE CURRENT WORLD CRISIS

    1. THERE IS A GENERAL AWARENESS OF THE EXISTENCE OF A GRAVE WORLD CRISIS

    2. THERE IS A GENERAL FEAR OF THE EFFECTS OF AN ATOMIC WAR

    3. THE WORLD-WIDE SCOPE OF THE CURRENT CRISIS

    4. THE TREND TO POLITICAL UNIFICATION OF THE WORLD

II. THE CAUSES OF THE CURRENT WORLD CRISIS

    1. THE ECONOMIC CONCEPT

    2. THE MORAL CONCEPT

III. THE HISTORICAL BACKGROUND OF THE CURRENT WORLD CRISIS

    1. SOROKIN'S VIEW OF THE THREE GUIDING PRINCIPLES OF HUMAN HISTORY

        a. The ideational principle

        b. The idealistic principle

        c. The sensate principle

    2. THE SENSATE PRINCIPLE OF WESTERN CIVILIZATION

        a. It has perverted the idea of truth

        b. It has debased the human personality

        c. It has distorted and degraded the concept of history

    3. THE GENERAL BREAK-DOWN OF THE SENSATE PHASE OF PRESENT-DAY WESTERN CIVILIZATION

        a. The loss of the sense of certainty

        b. The loss of faith in science

        c. The loss of faith in the redemptive processes of history

        d. Man's loss of faith in himself

THE PRESENT-DAY WORLD CRISIS
OF GENTILE CIVILIZATION

I. THE MAIN FEATURES OF THE CURRENT WORLD CRISIS

1. THERE IS A GENERAL AWARENESS OF THE EXISTENCE OF A GRAVE WORLD CRISIS

Since World War One there has been a growing awareness of the existence of a serious world crisis. There have been some keen observers of modern life who even before the outbreak of the First World War expressed misgivings about the destiny of Western civilization. On the other hand, there were many optimists who even after the First World War were convinced that the war was a mere temporary interruption of man's onward march. The world-wide economic crisis in the decade preceding the outbreak of World War Two, the rise of totalitarian movements in the world, the failure of the League of Nations, and, finally, the tragedies of World War Two, and the ushering in of the era of the atomic bomb, these happenings have removed all doubts that a grave crisis is confronting the whole world. One of the earliest students of history to sense the approaching danger was Oswald Spengler whose work entitled *The Decline of the West* appeared in German in 1918, although the manuscript had been completed in 1917. "Spengler's viewpoint was that civilizations go through a life cycle just as do individuals. A civilization is born, which is followed by a childhood and a youth period, a period of full maturity, and then old age, senility, and ultimately death. It was his conviction that the process of death for Western civilization had already set in."[1]

Spengler's ideas made a deep impression on contemporary thinking. A multitude of books have been published in subsequent years dealing with the same subject. In the last twenty years, but especially since the end of World War Two hostilities, discussion of the present state of the world has shown increasing evidence of a general alarm and sense of futility and hopelessness. The following is a representative body of contemporary thought concerning the basic issues and problems of the world of today.

"Contemporary history is being wound up, an unknown era is upon us, and it must be given a name."—Nicolas Berdyaev.[2]

"It has become a banality to say that we live in a time of historical crisis, that a whole epoch is ending, and a new one, as yet without a name, is beginning. Some are glad for this, others sorry, but all agree upon the fact. In reality what is happening is something even deeper. We are witnessing a judgment upon not one epoch in history, but upon history itself."—Nicolas Berdyaev.[3]

"Western civilization, after doing so much to disintegrate and reorganize Eastern civilization, is now beginning to fall apart, through its own internal inconsistencies . . . All existing human cultures are 'reaching for the stars' in wistful dissatisfaction with their present divided and distracted condition. There has been no such unstable equilibrium of religions and cultures in world history since the time of Christ."—Walter M. Horton.[4]

". . . every important aspect of the life, organization, and the culture of Western society is in the extraordinary crisis . . . Its body and mind are sick and there is hardly a spot on its body which is not sore, nor any nervous fibre which functions soundly."—Pitirim A. Sorokin.[5]

"Contrary to the optimistic diagnosis, the present crisis is not ordinary but extraordinary. It is not merely an economic or political maladjustment, but involves simultaneously almost the whole of Western culture and society, in all their main sectors. It is a crisis in their art and science, philosophy and religion, law and morals, manners and mores; in the forms of social, political, and economic organization, including the nature of the family and marriage—in brief, it is a crisis involving almost the whole way of life, thought, and conduct of Western society. More precisely, it consists in a disintegration of a fundamental form of Western culture and society dominant for the last four centuries."—Pitirim A. Sorokin.[6]

"We live amidst one of the greatest crises in human history. Not only war, famine, pestilence and revolution, but a legion of other calamities are rampant over the whole world. All values are unsettled; all norms are broken. Mental, moral, aesthetic, and social anarchy reigns supreme . . . Humanity has become a distorted image of its own noble self. The crisis is omnipresent and involves almost the whole of culture and society from top to bottom. It is manifest in the fine arts and science, in philosophy and religion, in ethics and law. It permeates the forms of social, economic, and political organization and the entire way of living and thinking."—Pitirim A. Sorokin. [7]

"The mingled hope and doubt with which so many people view the postwar world and the feeling of futility that so many experience today as they try to adjust themselves to circumstances are sufficient indications of a cultural dislocation. Certain basic elements no longer serve to help people come to grips with their problems."—Charles D. Kean. [8]

"Many months ago the British Broadcasting Co. put a number of experts 'on the air' in a series of national broadcasts concerning the atomic discoveries. 'Never since the beginning of recorded history', said one of the speakers (Earl Russell), 'has mankind been faced by so terrible a problem. Either we must consent to an entirely novel form of political and military organization, or, if we fail in this, we must expect a world-wide disaster surpassing in its horror all that past misfortunes enable us to imagine'."—John S. Hayland. [9]

"We are living in an age of transition from laissez-faire to a planned society. The planned society that will come may take one of two shapes: it will be ruled either by a minority in terms of a dictatorship or by a new form of government which, in spite of its increased power, will still be democratically controlled."—Karl Mannheim. [10]

"Everyone really knows, or senses, the change; and this general awareness accounts for the feverishness of the social atmosphere. Many respond with a crude hedonism, aiming to get what they can—money, pleasure, women, liquor—in what time is left. Some turn to religion, often of a mystical type. The generals respond by trying to hold their armies together, and by herding scientists and technicians into the martial laboratories. The statesmen frantically test one political combination after another . . . It is hardly possible to exaggerate the profundity of the present world political crisis. The trouble with many of the policies which are proposed, or even followed, in the attempt to meet the crisis, is that even their most triumphant achievement would not at all lessen the crisis."—James Burnham. [11]

"For us there stands the question: to what extent and who and why did this in every respect remarkable century [nineteenth century] bring to birth the catastrophe that now covers the whole world? What were the forces that compelled it in that direction? If it really did comprise the transition that was to change the earth into a new star, why did this transition come to an end, or how was it possible for it to end in the most hideous contest and the most frightful devastation the earth has ever seen."—Alfred Weber.[12]

"All my thinking is permeated through and through with the conviction that a whole epoch of history is coming to an end, that an entire civilization is on the point of perishing, and that we are on the eve of witnessing the emergence of a new world the outlines of which are still not clearly defined."—Nicolas Berdyaev.[13]

"Never before since human beings first existed have they been faced with so great a danger as that which they have brought upon themselves by a combination of unrivalled skill and unrivalled folly."—Bertrand Russell.[14]*

2. THERE IS A GENERAL FEAR OF THE CONSEQUENCES OF AN ATOMIC WAR

"Lecturing within a few months of the atomic bomb explosion of 1945, a leading member of the British section of the atomic team, which had succeeded in reaching this immense achievement, proclaimed that if ever Great Britain goes to war again with an adequately equipped enemy, her cities and the population in them will last fifteen minutes."—John S. Hayland.[15]

"The uniqueness of atomic weapons is to be found first of all in this: that they create a definite material possibility of the total annihilation of human life . . . If we wish to know the historical meaning of nuclear technology, as it might be called, we must begin, then, by recognising its most distinctive consequence: that it makes possible, not at all probable, but quite definitely possible, the early total annihilation of human life . . . The more heavily industrialized a nation, the more concentrated its industrial areas, the more intertwined its communication and transport, the more vulnerable it is . . . It may very well turn out, then, that Western civilization, by releasing nuclear energies, has committed suicide.

"If a workable solution for the problem of atomic weapons is not found within a relatively few years, Western civilization will

* Since the completion of this section the Russian and American sputniks have both been launched into space, causing a marked increase in the general awareness of a global crisis.

cease to be the dominant civilization of the world (if it does not disappear altogether), and it will be replaced probably by one of the other existing civilizations.

"Nothing that we can do will guarantee permanent peace. Nothing will make it certain that atomic weapons will not some day wipe out civilization and mankind."—James Burnham.[16]

To a question asked of Albert Einstein whether it is "an exaggeration to say that the fate of the world is hanging in the balance", he replied: "No exaggeration. The fate of humanity is always in the balance . . . but more truly now than at any known time."—Albert Einstein.[17]

"But let no one think that the expenditure of vast sums for weapons and systems of defence can guarantee absolute safety for the cities and citizens of any nation. The awful arithmetic of the atomic bomb does not permit of such an easy solution."—President Dwight D. Eisenhower.[18]

"Now that we know that the Soviets have achieved a thermo-nuclear explosion, the defence of our homes, our cities, and our lives is given a new and awful urgency . . . One hundred atomic bombs dropped on selected targets in North America could kill or injure not just hundreds or thousands but millions of people. A grim calculation by informed experts can forecast the number of millions of casualties. This calculation leads to the conclusion that America might not survive this kind of attack even though we were able in the meantime to destroy our enemy."—James R. Killian, Jr. and A. G. Hill.[19]

"Although the future seldom turns out quite as one expects, I think it is safe to say at the outset that our world for some time to come will be on a walk through a 'valley of the shadow of death'. The first business of this generation is to see to the survival of science and philosophy, yes, even of all of civilization. Unless we clearly recognize this colossal fact, the Road Ahead, by every human reckoning, will be a very short dead end. Had you been with me last fallout in the Pacific at Eniwetok, you would have no doubt that mankind now has within the range of its grasp means to exterminate the human race. As each atomic test unfolds new and more terrifying secrets, the significance of this statement becomes clearer and clearer. I am certain we are not on this road to survival yet . . . Let me remind you that the Road Ahead is a toll road."—Thomas E. Murray.[20]

"Our superiority in weapons and our short head start over

Russia places in our hands a deterrent to Russian attack, but it has long been clear that with the passage of but a few years this lead could be nullified and the effectiveness of our deterring stockpile diminished. Russia has the capability today to hurt us badly, and we are faced with the ugly fact that within two years she will have the capability to virtually destroy us if she moves first. Since we have consistently underestimated the Russians, let's call it one year—not two. Time is therefore running out."—Gordon Dean.[21]

"The development of atomic and hydrogen bombs makes it appear likely that groups of men could, if they wished, or were driven to it, annihilate the greater portion of humanity."—Harrison Brown.[22]

"We are in mortal peril. The Soviet government is constructing hydrogen bombs and inter-continental bombers as fast as it can in order to inflict on us a nation-wide hydrogen-bomb Pearl Harbour. It will not stop. It can only be stopped. Our skies will be filled with death unless we either destroy the productive centres of the Soviet Union before they produce enough bombs and bombers to annihilate us, or swing the world balance of power strongly against the Soviet Union, so that when it possesses those weapons of annihilation, it will not dare to use them."—William C. Bullitt.[23]

3. THE WORLD-WIDE SCOPE OF THE CURRENT CRISIS

The world-wide character of the present-day crisis stems from the fact that Western civilization has for many years been and still is the world's dominant civilization. World communication, transport and commerce have brought the remotest parts of the world close together. A discussion of this aspect of the present crisis follows in the passages below:

"The expansion of Europe since 1492 has reduced the seven cultural areas which then existed to one all-inclusive cultural area ... Cultural contacts between West and East have so multiplied in recent times that we now live, for the first time in human history, in one 'planetary' world, where every cultural area is engaged in a lively process of give and take with every other cultural area. In such a world, the problem of Western civilization is not capable of a purely Western solution, nor is the problem of Eastern civilization capable of a purely Eastern solution. The problem of civilization has become one planetary problem, which demands a planetary solution."—Walter M. Horton.[24]

Even the spirit of rebellion against Western colonial imperialism which has been building up in the East has failed to stem the tide of Westernization. One, at least, reason for this may be the conviction of the Eastern peoples that they can best resist the West with Western methods. Be that as it may, Westernization of the East has proceeded, in some parts at least, at a rapid pace. Some Easterners believe that they can adopt Western technology, but shun the spiritual ideas of the West. However, this process of Westernization of the Orient has gradually undermined the spiritual basis of Oriental civilization.

"The whole world today, in a sense, is reaching for the stars. Traditional sanctions and time-honoured creeds have broken down everywhere, both East and West. The fact that so many suppose it possible to adopt the externals of Western culture without its spiritual basis, or vice versa, proves that the two have become deeply alienated from each other. The same disharmony between the spirit and body of civilization, between the ends for which and the means by which men live, exists in all the Eastern cultures. No culture can be a satisfactory home for human beings so long as it remains in this state of dissociation and disharmony. No existing culture is a satisfactory home for the present inhabitants of our planet."—Walter M. Horton.[25]

"Machines and mass production, rapid transportation and communication, world-wide economic interdependence through the world-wide division of labour and resource, the spread of science and its applications, all these have so linked all parts of the world together, so reduced the time and space dimensions applicable to human society, that the world is today as intimate a community as a county was a thousand years ago."—James Burnham.[26]

"From the beginning, mankind has been partitioned; in our day we have at last become united. The Western handiwork that has made this union possible has not been carried out with open eyes, like David's unselfish labours for the benefit of Solomon; it has been performed in heedless ignorance of its purpose, like the labours of the animalculæ that build a coral reef up from the bottom of the sea till at length an atoll rises above the waves. But our Western-built scaffolding is made of less durable materials than that. The most obvious ingredient in it is technology, and man cannot live by technology alone."—Arnold J. Toynbee.[27]

In his discussion of the various factors responsible for the restlessness and stirrings in the backward regions of the world, Frank Laubach makes the following statement: "What caused this tremendous change from sullen hopelessness to grim resolve? A great many factors. The first were the teachings of Jesus, especially the gospel of Luke and the companion Book of Acts. Here was 'good news for the poor, release to the captives, liberty to those who are oppressed, sight to the blind' . . . 'blessed are you poor, blessed are you that hunger now, for you shall be satisfied; blessed are you that weep now, for you shall laugh. Woe to you that are rich, woe to you that are full now, for you shall hunger' (Luke 6: 20–25) . . . The words, compassionate deeds of Christ, and His death made Him the friend of the poor, of sinners, of outcasts. It is very likely that the millions who zealously distributed the Bible never realized what new hope and what strong new determination the poor and oppressed derived from Jesus . . . The Bible is dynamite, and it is the most widely sold book of all time.

"But the thing which has really broken the masses loose from their moorings in the retarded areas is the vast new network of the communications. The Portuguese, Italian, Dutch, French, and English explorers of the fifteenth to the eighteenth centuries started it. Then came steamships, railways, automobiles . . . then aeroplanes, motion pictures and telephones, businessmen in swank homes, countless business enterprises . . . then World War One, with our soldiers going everywhere, well fed, generous with their money; then tourists sweeping by—all these factors together produced in the hungry masses a great envy and a great longing to be like these 'millionaires', a great longing to better the condition of their children, to rise out of their wretched hovels to the new level that they saw in these foreigners. This turn took a sudden rise in 1920 and it has been rising ever since, with ever-greater momentum."[28]

That the current world crisis has not by-passed the Islamic countries may be seen from the following passage: "Yet the dangers to which Islam, as a religion, is exposed today are perhaps greater than any that it has faced in the past. The most patent come from those forces which have undermined, or threaten to undermine, all theistic religion. The extreme pressure of secularism, whether in the seductive form of nationalism, or in the doctrines of scientific materialism and the economic interpretation of history, has already left its mark on several sections of

Muslim society. But even this, however insidious its influence, is probably less dangerous in the long run than the relaxation of the religious conscience and the weakening of the catholic tradition of Islam."—H. A. R. Gibb.[29]

The gravity of the nature of the world crisis as affecting Asia, especially the countries of the Far East, has been ably analysed in a recent article in Foreign Affairs. We shall quote a few passages from it: "Perhaps more alarming than the magnitude and complexity of the socio-economic problems of the region is the spiritual and cultural condition of the Asian intelligentsia. Often the inheritor of an ancient and noble cultural and spiritual tradition, the Asian intellectual is left, as a result of many centuries of erosion and stagnation, with a legacy which is largely fatalism, passivity and the acceptance of authority."—M. R. Masani.[30]

"Asia is living in thirty centuries at one and the same time. The stone-age runs parallel to the machine-age, feudalism and mysticism of the middle ages mix with democracy and rationalism of the new era, and communalism is to be found side by side with the economic plan of today. It is the dualism of this situation which has made the position of the Asian intellectual so difficult . . . If in addition we realize that the Asian intellectual is fully aware of the fact that the modern world is itself facing a crisis, that its values are menaced by a tide of secularism, scepticism and relativism, we know why he is vacillating between the two crises: the crisis of the Asian community and culture as a consequence of the impact of the West which has not yet ended, either in his surroundings or in his own soul; and the other greater crisis, the crisis of the modern people, embracing the whole of mankind."—Takdir Alisjahbana.[31]

"To my mind, the first component of the malaise from which the Indian intellectual suffers is utter uncertainty and instability. Political independence has been achieved in an age when the forces of communism and democracy are drawn up against each other in preparation for a mighty war of extermination and, in between the two, there are any number of warring groups owing allegiance to an infinite variety of shades of pink faith . . . What makes our burden appear so heavy is that we are not spiritually equipped to bear it. There is no faith and no object of faith. Along with the breaking up of the social and economic fabric, old values are also losing their hold and new ones have not replaced them. Religion has become a mummery and old traditions, taking the memory back through a thousand years of the nation's history, embodying its hopes and aspirations, its ideals and experiences, are being brushed aside with a contemptuous shrug. Spiritual vacuity has become almost a badge of intellectual superiority."—Dr. Sampurnanand.[32]

4. THE TREND TO POLITICAL UNIFICATION OF THE WORLD

Even before World War Two there have been advocates for political unification of the world as the cure for many of the world's ills. This movement has received great impetus with the introduction of the atomic era. There is a growing belief that only a world government can save mankind from annihilation by nuclear weapons. Among the proponents of the creation of a world government are many responsible citizens who are convinced that in these days the world is not safe as long as the various nation-states have the right and power to wage war; that war, at least atomic war, can be prevented if all nuclear weapons, or any other world destructive weapons, were to be placed in the hands of a world government. It is felt in many quarters that if such a world government is not brought into being voluntarily, it will be imposed upon the world by force by the victor in the next war.

"The discovery of atomic weapons has brought about a situation in which Western Civilization, and perhaps human society in general, can continue to exist only if an absolute monopoly in the control of atomic weapons is created. This monopoly can be gained and exercised only through a World Empire, for which the historical stage had already been set prior to and independently of the discovery of atomic weapons. The attempt at World Empire will be made, and is, in fact, the objective of the Third World War, which in its preliminary stages has already begun. It should not require argument to state that the present candidates for leadership in the World Empire are only two: the Soviet Union and the United States . . . only a monopoly of atomic weapons, which could be exercised only by what would be in effect a World Empire, could save Western Civilization, and perhaps all organized human society from destruction. Only a World Empire could, in that sense, 'solve' the problem of atomic weapons . . .

"The determining facts are merely these: Western Civilization has reached the stage in its development that calls for the creation of its Universal Empire. The technological and institutional character of Western Civilization is such that a Universal Empire of Western Civilization would necessarily at the same time be a World Empire. In the world there are only two power centres adequate to make a serious attempt to meet this challenge. The simultaneous existence of these two centres and only these two, introduces into world political relationships an intolerable disequilibrium. The whole problem is made incomparably sharper and more immediate by the discovery of atomic weapons, and by the race between the two power centres for atomic supremacy, which, independently of all other historical considerations, could likewise be secured only through World Empire."—James Burnham.[33]

"Do I fear the tyranny of a world government? Of course I do. But I fear still more the coming of another war or wars. Any government is certain to be evil to some extent. But a world government is preferable to the far greater evil of wars, particularly with their intensified destructiveness. If such a world government is not established by a process of agreement, I believe it will come anyway, and in a much more dangerous form. For war or wars will end in one power being supreme and dominating the rest of the world by its overwhelming military strength . . .

"But I also believe that world government is certain to come in time and that the question is how much it is to be permitted to cost. It will come, I believe, even if there is another world war, though after such a war, if it is won, it would be world government established by the victor, resting on the victor's military power, and thus to be maintained permanently only through the permanent militarization of the human race.

"Mankind can only gain protection against the danger of unimaginable destruction and wanton annihilation if a supranational organization has alone the authority to produce these weapons . . .

"A tremendous effort is indispensable. If it fails now, the supranational organization will be built on the ruins of a large part of the now existing world. Let us hope that the abolition of the existing world international anarchy will not need to, be bought by a self-inflicted world catastrophe the dimensions of which none of us can possibly imagine. The time is terribly short. We must act now if we are to act at all."—Albert Einstein.[34]

"In a longer view, we have to consider not only the possibility of a third world war, but also the further future. I suppose that

if war broke out tomorrow, there would still be human beings when it ended. But if they had no more wisdom than we have, they would soon be preparing for a fourth world war; and, apart from statesmanship, there is no reason to expect this process to stop until the human race is extinct. If, therefore, we think the survival of man worth while, we must have as our goal the total prevention of large-scale wars. The only way to secure this is to have in the world only one armed force possessed of a monopoly of the major weapons of war. Unless such a single force is created in the next fifty years, it seems hardly likely that man will survive."
—Bertrand Russell.[35]

"I believe it is a foregone conclusion that the world is in any event going to be unified politically in the near future . . . I think the big and really formidable political issue today is, not whether the world is soon going to be unified politically, but in which of two alternative possible ways this rapid unification is going to come about."—A. J. Toynbee.[36]

In an article in *The Nation* (June 5, 1945) Dr. George A. Bernstein informs us that "since 1941, sixteen state legislatures have passed a resolution along the lines suggested in 1940 by Robert Lee Humber of the United World Federalists. In nineteen other states the resolution has been adopted by at least one house of the legislature. In February, Virginia took an even stronger stand by calling for a general conference of the United Nations for the purpose of forming a federated world government. On election day in 1946, in the State of Massachusetts, 638,000 people, seventy-two per cent of those voting on the question, said that the Senator in the General Court of that district should be instructed to vote to request the President and Congress of the United States to direct our delegation to the United Nations to propose amendments to the Charter which would create a world federation for preventing war."[37]

II. THE CAUSES OF THE CURRENT WORLD CRISIS

1. THE ECONOMIC CONCEPT

This school of thought ascribes the world's ills to the laissez-faire, i.e. non-regulated, non-controlled, variety of capitalist industrialism. The proponents of this theory point to the many evils and abuses which this type of industrialism has made possible.

It has produced the machine man, and the mechanization of society. "The essence of personality is freedom, self-determination, spontaneity. The essence of the machine is necessity, predetermination and repetition. The entire action of the machine is foreordained, confined to a given path of movement, like the piston, for instance . . . As mechanization extends, the sphere in which man can act as personality (i.e. freely and spontaneously) contracts. He, too, tends to become a machine, which means that he is being dehumanized. He is passively submitting to an external condition, which is the utter antithesis of active response to inner impulse and will. This process of mechanization has now invaded the sphere of mind, the result of which is the emergence of Mass-Man. That is to say, vast numbers of men and women in present-day industrialized society display the same passivity in their mental processes as they do in their physical . . . Labour is not raw material, but living men and women, immortal souls, who, by being degraded into raw material, suffer violence and dehumanization."[38]

That present-day industrialism has eliminated many of the abuses with which it is charged in the above passage is a well-known fact. In the United States and in the other countries of the West the attitude to labour has in recent years undergone a complete change. The labouring man is not looked upon any more as a "medium of exchange" as a source from which to extract profit, but as a partner in an undertaking in which both management and labour work together, not only for the good of both parties, but for the welfare of the whole community. Present-day industry has rid itself of the old short-sightedness and selfishness, and displays a sense of responsibility and concern for the welfare of its employees. Working conditions have improved immeasurably, and pensions and insurance systems have been introduced to protect the employee against accident, sickness and old age.

Another, and possibly more serious criticism levelled against capitalist industrialism is that it is beset with inner contradictions, and contains within it the seeds of its own destruction. Thus we are told that modern big capitalist industrialism is constantly in search for new sources of supply and new world markets for its products. At the basis of all international wars and conflicts between nations—we are also told—is this unceasing struggle and scramble for the world's sources of supply and markets. In the beginning of the industrial era England was the chief producing country. She had no problem of finding raw materials for her expanding factories and selling her industrial products to foreign countries. In time, however, the trend to industrialization has spread to practically every country in the world. This has resulted in the drying up of the sources of supply and the shrinking of the world's markets. The economic decline of Great Britain is attributed to this very fact that she finds an ever-decreasing demand for her industrial products. We are told also that in a world in which every nation is seeking to sell to others more and more and buy from others less and less, capitalist industrialism cannot survive, let alone prosper. To offset the loss of foreign markets industrialized countries are striving to increase a greater demand for the products of industry on the part of their own people. This is done by encouraging more home consumption. This policy, however, produces a vicious cycle in the end. Furthermore, in any country with a well-developed industry, the home market, however large, is incapable of absorbing all of its own products. The way out of this dilemma—we are informed—is some kind of planned economy, or state capitalism or state socialism.

That a planned economy is not the whole answer to this problem is evident from that fact that the peoples of the highly industrialized West are by and large economically better off than in those parts of the world which have adopted a planned economy. After some forty years under a system of a planned economy the people of communist Russia still live under a dictatorship, while their standard of living is much lower than that of the peoples of the West.

2. THE MORAL CONCEPT

There is a growing conviction that the causes of the present world crisis are too complex to be accounted for by economic factors alone. The more serious students of human history trace the difficulties besetting the world today to the materialism of our age, to the displacement of God from the centre of life to its periphery, and to man's preoccupation with himself and with the material things of life.

"To attribute the ills of our time to stupidity is a false diagnosis. The trouble is much deeper down. It lies in the abysmal heart and will of self-centred man ... Modern man is the product of a fervid obsession with material and social progress, with a gospel of more and more things. His life consists in the accumulation of wants and of the means to satisfy them ...

"Thus in our highly technical and completely secular civilization, the human status of man—man as spirit, as personality, as moral agent—has declined as never before. It is more anti-human, in my judgment, than the degradation and the violence of the workers in the early years of the Industrial Revolution. Their drunkenness and violence and brutishness were, in their way, the protest of beings who were still personal against the injustice they suffered. But man today, mass-man, is passively submitting to the new slavery gradually creeping upon him."— D. R. Davies.[39]

"In America we have created a new race, with healthy physiques, sometimes beautiful bodies, but empty minds: people who have accepted life as an alternation of meaningless routine with insignificant sensation ... At their best, these passive barbarians live on an innocent animal level: they sun-tan their bodies, sometimes at vast public bathing beaches, sometimes under a lamp. They dance, whirl, sway, in mild orgies of vacant sexuality, or they engage in more intimate felicities without a feeling, a sentiment, or an ultimate intention that a copulating cat would not equally share ... Shopgirls and clerks, millionaires and mechanics, share the same underlying beliefs, engage in the same practices ... Half dead in their work; half alive outside their work. This is their destiny. Every big city counts such people by the million; even the smaller provincial centres ... produce their full share of people equally empty of human standards and aims."— Lewis Mumford.[40]

"The whole situation sums up to what may be called a new apocalyptic. We live in an age of decision, of choice between right and wrong, between good and evil, between life and death, such as has never occurred before. If we choose wrongly, we may be the last generation of mankind. It is hard to consider these things except under the ægis of religion. The atomic scientists today are like the ancient Hebrew prophets warning mankind of the instant urgency of Divine judgment. 'God or Mammon'—and Mammon means godless power! We cannot serve two masters; and if we choose Mammon we choose death, by universal suicide. The Prophets, and Jesus Christ, proclaimed that there is one remedy and one only. Men must recognize in time the one supreme sovereignty of God."—John S. Hayland.[41]

"It is of the utmost importance that each of us understands the true nature of the struggle now taking place in the world. It is not a struggle merely of economic theories, or of forms of government or of military power. At issue is the true nature of man. Either man is the creature whom the psalmist described as 'a little lower than the angels' . . . or man is a soulless, animated machine . . ."—President Dwight D. Eisenhower. [42]

"Bewildered by the awful problems of this prolonged crisis of a civilization, uncertain and afraid, disillusioned with the ideals of liberal democracy in action, sceptical or half-hearted in genuine religious belief, men grasp at the communist myth so that their spirits may not altogether drown."—James Burnham. [43]

"The fact that many modern definitions of religion do not even include God indicates what has happened: religion has been transformed from a total integration of life through relation to a supernatural God into total integration through self-realization. The convictions leading to this transformation are again the same: all meaning that the individual can find in his life is inherent in his own nature; and any meaning that he cannot find in himself is both unattainable and practically irrelevant, therefore properly to be ignored."—Emil L. Fackenheim. [44]

III. The Historical Background of the Current World Crisis

I. SOROKIN'S VIEW OF THE THREE GUIDING PRINCIPLES OF HUMAN HISTORY

Whatever may be the view of world history to which one subscribes, a knowledge of the past is indispensable if one is to understand the present. Is the present world situation an isolated phenomenon, or does it stand in some relationship to past history? There are many excellent works on this aspect of our problem. One of the best in this writer's view is a study entitled *The Crisis of Our Age* by Pitirim A. Sorokin, professor of sociology at Harvard University, who has written voluminously on this subject and to whom reference has already been made above. Sorokin states that many of the great cultures or civilizations in the world's history rest on a certain fundamental principle or basic value which forms the integrating centre of this particular civilization, and "serves as its major premise and foundation". Such a culture "represents a unity or individuality whose parts are permeated by the same fundamental principle and articulate the same basic value. The dominant part of the fine arts and science of such a unified culture, of its philosophy and religion, of its ethics and law, of its main forms of social, economic, and political organisation, of most of its mores and manners, of its ways of life and mentality, all articulate, each in its own way, this basic principle and value."[45]

According to Sorokin the great civilizations or cultures of the past have exhibited three types of basic value or major principle, which he calls the ideational, idealistic, and sensate. A culture based on the ideational principle is one whose integrating centre is a supersensory and superrational God. Such a culture "is predominantly otherworldly and religious, oriented toward the supersensory reality of God and permeated by this value".[46] The sensate principle is based on the premise "that the true reality and value is sensory. Only what we see, hear, smell, touch, and otherwise perceive through our sense organs is real and has value. Beyond such a sensory reality, either there is nothing, or, if there is something, we cannot sense it; therefore it is equivalent to the non-real and the non-existent. As such it may be neglected".[47] We see from this description that the sensate principle is the exact opposite of the ideational. It is a this-worldly value or reality; God, or the spiritual reality of life, is displaced from the centre to the periphery of life. The idealistic type of culture is a synthesis or blending of elements of the ideational and the sensate principles.

All three major principles have been exemplified in the Egyptian, Babylonian, Greco-Roman, Hindu, Chinese, and many of the other great civilizations. "The sensate truth of the Creto-Mycenaean culture gave way to ideational truth in the Greece of the eighth to the sixth century B.C., and this to the idealistic truth of the fifth century B.C. This was displaced, in turn, by the sensate truth of the period from the third century B.C. to the fourth century A.D. which was followed by the ideational truth of Christianity during the period from the sixth century to the end of the twelfth. In the thirteenth century idealistic truth once more became paramount, to be succeeded by a third phase of sensate truth, which has maintained its sway from the sixteenth century up to the present time. Accordingly, instead of the alleged progressive linear trend of sensate truth throughout the course of history, we witness a series of oscillations from one dominant system to another. The reason for such oscillations is readily comprehensible. No single system comprises the whole of truth; nor is it, on the other hand, entirely false."[48]

a. The ideational principle

In order to gain a better understanding of the nature and causes of our present world crisis it is imperative that we have at least a general knowledge of the three great basic principles or values which dominated human history from time immemorial to this day. The ideational principle is based on Divine truth as embodied in revealed religion. It is chiefly concerned with glorifying God in man's life and all human relations. The goal of human life is the realization of the Divine Will. To know God and His Will becomes the object of human learning. All other types of human knowledge not directly concerned with religion are of secondary importance. This principle may be called the principle of faith. "The mentality dominated by the truth of faith is dedicated to the eternal verities, in contradistinction to the temporal truth of the senses."[49]

b. The idealistic principle

The idealistic principle is a truth which is arrived at by the blending of the ideational and the sensate principles. It is a combination "into one organic whole of the truth of the senses, the truth of faith, and the truth of reason".[50]

c. The sensate principle

The sensate principle is the variety of truth which is derived from or arrived at by means of our senses. In this system of truth, also called empiricism, man's sense organs become his chief source of knowledge of sensory reality. This sensory knowledge becomes man's chief judge of what is true or false, of what is valid or irrelevant. "Any system of sensate truth and reality implies a denial of, or an utterly indifferent attitude toward, any supersensory reality or value. By definition, supersensory reality either is non-existent, or, if it exists, is unknowable to us and therefore equivalent to the nonexistent."[51]

From the very nature of things the sensate system favours man's preoccupation with the study of his physical environment. Consequently, the transition from a civilization based on the religious principle as the dominating element to one based on the sensate principle is marked by a revival of the natural sciences. In the above-mentioned work by Sorokin we have a diagrammatic sketch representing the growth of the number of inventions and scientific discoveries from the eighth century B.C. till A.D. 1900. These facts and figures show that "during the ideational centuries of Greco-Roman culture (from the eighth to the sixth century B.C.) the number of discoveries and inventions is low. With the second half of the sixth century B.C. the number greatly increases, remaining on a high level up to the fourth century A.D.—a period dominated (as we have seen) by a sensate art and (as we shall see) by the truth of the senses. Beginning with the fifth century A.D., it sharply declines, remaining very low until the thirteenth century—a period dominated by an ideational art and by ideational truth. Starting with the thirteenth century, it begins to rise more and more rapidly, until in the eighteenth and nineteenth centuries it reaches an unprecedented high level, the nineteenth century alone yielding more discoveries and inventions than all the preceding centuries together".[52]

These, in short, are the three varieties of truth, which have shaped and moulded the three types of human culture or civilization. The ideational or religious culture is motivated by some variety of revealed religious truth; the sensate type of civilization is moved by the truth arrived at through man's senses; while in an idealistic culture man is guided by an organic combination of elements of the ideational and sensate principles achieved by human reason.

When either the ideational or sensate systems of truth arrives at a position when it regards itself as possessing the full truth and as being the truth itself while everything in the other system is false, then there is an irreconcilable conflict between the two. The negative attitude which the emerging Christian movement assumed to the sensate Greco-Roman civilization of the first centuries of the Christian era may have been occasioned by the bitter and violent hostility which it had encountered in the world. The clash between the two lasted until Christianity attained complete victory over the sensate Greco-Roman culture around the sixth century. The sensate principle was submerged and remained submerged until the twelfth century. In its conflicts with the sensate system of thought the Medieval Church developed an undesirable approach to many of life's problems. This is especially true of its negative attitude to those branches of human endeavour not directly related to religion.

2. THE SENSATE PRINCIPLE OF WESTERN CIVILIZATION

The situation described above prevailed until the twelfth century when medievalism began to decline and the sensate concept of life which lay buried, but never completely dead, for six centuries, made its reappearance. This re-emergence of the sensate principle of life ushered in the Renaissance era, and almost from the very beginning it displayed the same hostility to the ideational truth of Christianity as at their first encounter in the first few centuries of our era. The Protestant Reformation which came to birth in the sixteenth century was engaged in the struggle on two fronts from the very beginning of its existence. On one hand, it was striving to recall the Medieval Church to the purity of Biblical Christianity; on the other hand, it declared war on the unspiritual trend of the Renaissance movement. The intellectual history of the West of the last four centuries is the story of the clash and conflict between these two concepts of life: the spiritual, God-centred, world and life view of Biblical Christianity, and all the secular, man-centred, philosophies which have grown out of the humanism of the Renaissance movement.

To appreciate the nature of the intellectual impasse which Western Civilization has reached it is necessary for us to see what concepts the Western mind has evolved about such weighty problems as truth, the human personality, and human history.

a. It has perverted the idea of truth

"Scientific propositions are mere 'conventions' and . . . of several conventions, the one which under the circumstances is most convenient, 'economical', expedient, useful, or 'operational' for a given individual is most true."[53] Truth is therefore relative. There is one truth for labour, another truth for capital; one truth for communists, another for fascists; one for liberals, another for conservatives; one for atheists, another for believers, etc. This conception of truth transforms truth into an ideology which varies with the particular group which upholds it under certain given circumstances.[54] Truth changes with time. What was true yesterday may be false today, and what is true today may prove false tomorrow.[55]

b. It has debased the human personality

A very important feature of secularist, atheistic humanism is its materialistic approach to the human personality. Thus man is conceived by some of our leading physicists as an "electron-proton complex"; "a combination of physico-chemical elements"; by some of our biologists as "an animal closely related to the ape or monkey"; by our psychologists as "a reflex mechanism", "a variety of stimulus-response relationship"; and by the sociologist, as a tool and instrument manufacturer. "Some, indeed, go so far as to deprive man even of mind, or thought, of consciousness, of conscience, and of volition, reducing him to a purely behaviour-istic mechanism of unconditioned and conditioned reflexes."[56]

Thus man, who according to the Bible, Old and New Testament, is a child of God, created in God's image, invested with all the potential dignity and sacredness of God's ambassador, has been utterly degraded by Western science and philosophy. And it is this kind of scientific and philosophic thinking of the West which has provided fascism, nazism and communism with the moral and intellectual justification for the concentration camp tortures, brain-washings, slave labour camps, death marches, and all other barbarisms which they have been perpetrating upon human beings.

c. It has distorted and degraded the concept of history

This debasement of the conception of truth and the degradation of the human personality have been extended to the sphere of human history. While the Bible and the believer view the whole of human history as a grand Divine scheme designed to redeem mankind and restore man to perfect fellowship with God, secular historians look upon human history as "nothing but an incessant interplay of cosmic rays, sunspots, climatic and geographic changes, and biological forces (drives; instincts; conditioned, unconditioned, and prepotent reflexes; physio-economic com-plexes and 'residues')—forces in whose hands man is as but clay, and which stage all the historical events, and create all the cultural values".[57]

3. THE GENERAL BREAKDOWN OF THE SENSATE PHASE OF PRESENT-DAY WESTERN CIVILIZATION

We have already mentioned a few of the deplorable effects of the humanist way of life which has re-emerged in the Renaissance period. We will conclude our discussion of this subject by citing several other devastating consequences of this secular philosophy.

a. The loss of a sense of certainty

"Our ideals seem to have gone dead; we no longer believe in them; and we don't disbelieve in them either. That is our dilemma. We neither believe nor disbelieve. We are neither hot, nor cold; and it paralyses our capacity to decide and to act."[58] Having given up faith in God, and rejected the Bible as God's revealed truth, man's life became filled with contradictions and uncertainties. We sail an uncharted sea, and without compass. We neither know where we come from or whither we are going.

b. The loss of faith in science

There was a time when man, quite naïvely, expected science to solve all human problems. Various pronouncements made by men of science were accepted as the ultimate truth. Representatives of science were filled with pride and regarded themselves as possessing all wisdom while considering religious truth of no consequence and relevance to modern man. The experiences of the last twenty years have disillusioned many in the ability of science to cure the world's ills. In the great economic crisis of the 'thirties science stood idly by with nothing to offer; while in the last decade we have become acutely aware of the threat to mankind's survival inherent in many of the scientific inventions.

c. The loss of faith in the redemptive processes of history

The nineteenth century especially had a firm belief in the "inevitability of progress through science and the perfectibility of man through education".[59] Man was believed to be essentially good. He was expected to derive from science all the power he needs, all the knowledge he needs—from education, and all the freedom he wants—through democracy. The millennium was to be established by human efforts alone. Slowly but surely the events since World War One have combined to shatter the fondest hopes of the nineteenth century. "Since 1914 one tragic experience has followed another, as if history had been designed to refute the vain delusions of modern man."[60] The Biblical doctrine of the natural depravity of human nature, so offensive to modern man, has given fresh evidence of its truth in the terrible reality of the events of the last twenty-five years.

d. Man's loss of faith in himself

There is a growing conviction that present-day world problems are beyond human power and ability to solve. Intellectual confusion, chaos and frustration, and an ever-deepening sense of human inadequacy and helplessness is the heritage left to us by a man-centred, humanist, and secular civilization which has increasingly dominated the history of the world in the last four hundred years.

NOTES TO CHAPTER 2

1. T. B. Maston, *A World in Travail* (Broadman Press: Nashville, Tenn., 1954), p. 19. By permission of the Sunday School Board of the Southern Baptist Convention, Nashville, Tenn.

2. N. Berdyaev, *The End of Our Time* (Sheed and Ward: New York, 1933), p. 11.

3. N. Berdyaev, *The Fate of Man in the Modern World* (Morehouse Publishing Co.: New York, 1935), pp. 1–2.

4. Walter M. Horton, *Can Christianity Save Civilization?* (Harper and Brothers, Publishers: New York, 1940), p. 105.

5. Pitirim A. Sorokin, *The Crisis of Our Age* (E. P. Dutton & Co., Inc.: New York, 1942 edition), p. 13.

6. Ibid., pp. 16–17.

7. Pitirim A. Sorokin, *Man and Society in Calamity* (E. P. Dutton & Co., Inc.: New York, 1942), p. 308.

8. Charles D. Kean, *Christianity and the Cultural Crisis* (Association Press: New York, 1945), p. 7.

9. John S. Hayland, "The New Apocalyptic", published in *The Hibbert Journal*, July 1948.

10. Karl Mannheim, *Diagnosis of Our Time* (Kegan Paul, Trench, Trubner and Co.: London, 1947), p. 1. By permission of Routledge & Kegan Paul.

11. James Burnham, *The Struggle for the World* (The John Day Co., Inc.: New York, 1947), pp. 32–3, 198. Copyright 1947, James Burnham.

12. Alfred Weber, *Farewell to European History* (Yale University Press: New Haven, 1948), p. 64.

13. N. Berdyaev, *Towards a New Epoch* (Geoffrey Bles: London, 1949), p. v.

14. Bertrand Russell, "The Danger to Mankind", article in the *Bulletin of the Atomic Scientists*, University of Chicago Press, January 1954.

15. John S. Hayland, idem.

16. James Burnham, op. cit., pp. 28, 29–30, 31, 33, 140.

17. Albert Einstein, *Ideas and Opinions* (Crown Publishers, Inc.: New York, 1954), p. 161.

18. President Dwight D. Eisenhower, from an address before the United Nations, December 8, 1953, published in the *Bulletin of the Atomic Scientists*, Chicago University Press, January 1954.

19. James R. Killian Jr. and A. G. Hill, "For a Continental Defense", article in the *Bulletin of Atomic Scientists*, January 1954.

20. Thomas E. Murray, from a speech delivered at the seventy-fifty anniversary celebration of Duquesne University in Pittsburgh, published in a release from the United States Atomic Energy Commission of November 11, 1953; quoted by Wilbur M. Smith in the *Moody Monthly*, Chicago, Ill., February 1954.

21. Gordon Dean, "Tasks for Statesmen", article in the *Bulletin of the Atomic Scientists*, January 1954.

22. Harrison Brown, *Must Destruction Be Our Destiny?* (Simon and Schuster, Inc.: New York, 1946), pp. 64–5; quoted by Wilbur M. Smith in the *Moody Monthly* (Chicago), September 1954.

23. William C. Bullitt, "Should We Support An Attack on Red China?", article in *Look* (New York), August 24th, 1954; quoted by Wilbur M. Smith in the *Moody Monthly* (Chicago), November 1954.

24. Walter M. Horton, op. cit., pp. 103, 106.

25. Ibid., pp. 156–7.

26. James Burnham, op. cit., p. 17.

27. Arnold J. Toynbee, *Civilization On Trial* (Oxford University Press: New York, 1948), p. 91.

28. Frank Laubach, *Wake Up or Blow Up* (Fleming H. Revell Co.: Westwood, N.J., 1951), pp. 30–2.

29. H. A. R. Gibb, *Mohammedanism, an Historical Survey* (Oxford University Press: New York, 1954), pp. 188–9.

30. M. R. Masani, "The Mind of Asia", article in *Foreign Affairs* (New York), July 1955.

31. Takdir Alisjahbana; quoted by M. R. Masani in "The Mind of Asia", *Foreign Affairs* (New York), July 1955.

32. Quoted by M. R. Masani in "The Mind of Asia", *Foreign Affairs* (New York), July 1955.

33. James Burnham, op. cit., pp. 55, 122–3, 134.

34. Albert Einstein, op. cit., pp. 120, 131; 150–1. The first two passages are reprinted from the *Atlantic Monthly* (Boston) and used by permission of the Estate of Albert Einstein and Mr. Raymond Swing.

35. Bertrand Russell, idem.

36. Arnold J. Toynbee, op. cit., p. 127.

37. George A. Bernstein, from an article in the *Nation*, June 5, 1948; quoted by Wilbur M. Smith in the *Sunday School Times*, Philadelphia Pa., Nov. 27, 1948.

38. D. R. Davies, *The Sin of Our Age* (Macmillan Co.: New York, 1947), pp. 105–6, 111. By permission of the publishers.

39. Ibid., pp. 6, 59, 107.

40. Lewis Mumford, *Faith for Living* (Harcourt, Brace and Co.: New York, 1940), pp. 38–9.
41. John S. Hayland, idem.
42. President Dwight D. Eisenhower, from his State-of-the-Union message in January 1955; quoted by the *Baltimore Sun*, January 11, 1955.
43. James Burnham, op. cit., p. 120.
44. Emil L. Fackenheim, "Self-realization and the Search for God", article in *Judaism* (New York), October 1952.
45. Pitirim A. Sorokin, *The Crisis of Our Age*, p. 17.
46. Ibid., p. 21.
47. Ibid., p. 19–20.
48. Ibid., p. 104.
49. Ibid., p. 102.
50. Ibid., p. 82.
51. Ibid., p. 86.
52. Ibid., p. 87.
53. Ibid., p. 117.
54. Ibid., pp. 117, 119.
55. Ibid., p. 120.
56. Ibid., p. 121.
57. Ibid., p. 122.
58. John McMurray, *Freedom in the Modern World* (Faber & Faber, Ltd.: London, 1935), p. 28; quoted by T. B. Maston, op. cit., p. 105.
59. Gregg Singer, "The Collapse of Western Culture", article in the *Westminster Theological Journal* (The Westminster Theological Seminary, Philadelphia), May 1953.
60. Reinhold Niebuhr, *Faith and History* (Charles Scribner's Sons: New York, 1949), pp. 6–7.

CHAPTER 3

THE CURRENT WORLD CRISIS IN THE LIGHT OF THE TEACHINGS OF THE BIBLE

In order that we may grasp the full significance of what the Bible has to say with reference to the closing days of man's rule on earth it is necessary to see how the various elements of current world history correspond to the teachings of the Bible on this subject.

I. THE BIBLE PREDICTS A TIME OF UNPRECEDENTED DISTRESS

Joel 3: 1, 15–16: "For, behold, in those days, and in that time, when I shall bring back the captivity of Judah and Jerusalem. The sun and the moon shall be darkened, and the stars shall withdraw their shining. And Jehovah shall roar from Zion, and utter his voice from Jerusalem, and the heavens and the earth shall shake: but Jehovah shall be a refuge unto his people, and a stronghold to the children of Israel." Notice that this world distress coincides with the return of the Jews to Palestine.

Isaiah 26: 20–21: "Come, my people, enter thou into thy chambers, and shut thy doors about thee: hide thyself for a little moment, until the indignation be overpast. For, behold, Jehovah cometh forth out of his place to punish the inhabitants of the earth for their iniquity; the earth also shall disclose her blood, and shall no more cover her slain."

Isaiah 34: 1–2: "Come near, you nations, to hear; and hearken, you peoples; let the earth hear, and the fulness thereof; the world and all things that come forth from it. For Jehovah hath indignation against all the nations, and wrath against all their host; he hath utterly destroyed them, he hath delivered them to the slaughter."

Zephaniah 3: 8: "Therefore wait you for me, saith Jehovah, until the day that I rise up to the prey; for my determination is to gather the nations, that I may assemble the kingdoms, to pour upon them mine indignations, even all my fierce anger; for all the earth shall be devoured with the fire of my jealousy."

Jeremiah 30: 23-24: "Behold, the tempest of Jehovah, even his wrath is gone forth, a sweeping tempest; it shall burst upon the head of the wicked. The fierce anger of Jehovah shall not return, until he have executed, and till he have performed the intents of his heart; in the latter days you shall consider it."

These are but a few of a large body of similar passages in the Old Testament. Some of the others are listed in the chart in the second chapter of Part One under the heading "Universal Judgment of the Nations". With some exceptions the Old Testament writers are primarily concerned with the world crisis in its final stage, when the world shall reel under the weight of God's judgment at the time of his direct and decisive intervention on the side of the Land of Israel. In the New Testament, however, the last world crisis covers a longer period of time.

Luke 21: 9, 11, 25-26: "And when you shall hear of wars and tumults, be not terrified, for these things must needs come to pass first; but the end is not immediately. And there shall be great earthquakes, and in divers places famines and pestilences; and there shall be terrors and great signs from heaven. And there shall be signs in the sun and moon and stars; and upon the earth distress of nations, in perplexity for the roaring of the sea and the billows. Men fainting for fear, and for expectation of the things which are coming on the world: for the powers of heaven shall be shaken."

Similar statements are recorded in Matthew 24 and Mark 13, and they constitute part of the Olivet prophecy of Jesus.

2 Timothy 3: 1: "But know this, that in the last days grievous times shall come."

2 Peter 3: 12: "Looking for and earnestly desiring the coming of the day of God, by reason of which the heavens being on fire shall be dissolved, and the elements shall melt with fervent heat."

II. The Biblical Teachings Concerning Wars at the End of the Age

From a study of the magnitude of wars from the standpoint of the number of casualties per million of population and the size of the armies involved during the long period from 500 B.C. to A.D. 1925, Sorokin found an almost steady increase of the war index in the last four hundred years. The first quarter of the twentieth century shows the highest war index. From this he concludes that "the twentieth century will unquestionably prove to be the bloodiest and most belligerent of all the twenty-five centuries under consideration".[1]

If we now turn to the Bible we find that the horrors of war will be a major element in the world's distress in the closing phase of this Age. Here are a few of these Biblical passages:

Joel 2: 1–3, 10: "Blow you the trumpet in Zion, and sound an alarm in my holy mountain; let all the inhabitants of the land tremble; for the day of Jehovah cometh, for it is near at hand. A day of darkness and gloominess, a day of clouds and thick darkness, as the dawn spread upon the mountains; a great people and a strong; there hath not been ever the like, neither shall be any more after them even to the years of many generations. A fire devoureth before them, and behind them a flame burneth; the land is as the garden of Eden before them, and behind them a desolate wilderness; yea, and none hath escaped them. The earth quaketh before them; the heavens tremble; the sun and the moon are darkened, and the stars withdraw their shining."

Jeremiah 25: 15–33. This is one of the bloodiest world war descriptions in the whole Bible. We will cite only a few passages:

"For thus saith Jehovah, the God of Israel, unto me: Take this cup of the wine of wrath at my hand, and cause all the nations to whom I send thee, to drink it (verse 15). And they shall drink, and reel to and fro, and be mad, because of the sword that I will send among them" (verse 16). Then follows a detailed record of the truly world-wide character of this last conflict:

"Thus saith Jehovah of hosts, Behold evil shall go forth from nation to nation, and a great tempest shall be raised up from the uttermost parts of the earth. And the slain of Jehovah shall be at that day from one end of the earth even unto the other end of the earth; they shall not be lamented, neither gathered, nor buried; they shall be dung upon the ground" (verses 32–3).

Matthew 24: 6, 21–22: "And you shall hear of wars, and rumours of wars . . . For then shall be great tribulation, such as hath not been from the beginning of the world to this time, no, nor ever shall be. And except those days had been shortened, no flesh would have been saved . . ."

III. The Moral Decline of Man at the End of the Age

The Bible has much to say about dehumanization at the end of the "times of the Gentiles". A word of caution is in place here. Many of the evils besetting mankind in these days are as old as the human race. The philosopher George Santayana said "that the elements in this crisis have been working in the body politic for ages . . . For the virulent cause of this long fever is subjectivism, egotism, conceit of mind".[2] What we have now is a new eruption of human depravity which—according to teachings of the Bible—will reach its full climactic and demonic development as we near the end of the Age. It is the culmination, the full fruition, and climactic development of the effects of human wilfulness, which is to characterize the end of the Age. The following is a description of man's moral condition in the final phase of the Age.

1. DECEPTION

Matthew 24: 11: "And many false prophets shall rise, and shall lead many astray."

2 Thessalonians 2: 11 (Paul's Second Letter to the Thessalonians): "And for this cause God sendeth them a working of error that they should believe a lie."

1 Timothy 4: 1 (Paul's First Letter to Timothy): "But the Spirit saith expressly, that in later times some shall fall away from the faith, giving heed to seducing spirits and doctrines of demons."

2 Timothy 3: 13 (Paul's Second Letter to Timothy): "But evil men and impostors shall wax worse and worse, deceiving and being deceived."

One of the most disquieting phenomena in these days is the tendency to lie and deceive, increasingly evident in the individual, social, commercial and political areas of life. While this is true of the so-called free world, lying and deceiving is one of the well-developed techniques constantly used by totalitarian governments and their followers to gain their objectives. The whole fabric of communism is a Satanic deception. These are the words from the Communist Manifesto published in 1847: "There are besides eternal truths, such as freedom and justice, that are common to all states of society. Communism abolishes eternal truths; it abolishes all religion, and all morality, instead of constituting them on a new basis; it therefore acts in contradiction to all past historical experience." [3]

2. SELF-LOVE

The blackest picture of human character to be displayed in the closing days of our Age is to be found in Paul's Second Letter to Timothy.

2 Timothy 3: 1–4: "But know this, that in the last days grievous times shall come. For men shall be lovers of self, lovers of money, boastful, arrogant, abusive, disobedient to parents, ungrateful, unholy, inhuman, implacable, slanderers, without self-control, fierce, haters of good, traitors, reckless, swollen with conceit, lovers of pleasure rather than lovers of God."

Is it not significant that Paul's list of human traits in the last days should be headed by self-love? "For men will be lovers of self." What a commentary on the display of selfishness and self-interest in so many spheres of life at the present time! "This concentration of man at the end of the age upon the gratification of his own desires, upon obtaining what he wants, by whatever false or brutal way it can be obtained, has become, as many of our philosophers and theologians recognize, the predominating undertone of Western Civilization in the last century. As this century dawned, Mr. Harold Begbie, for instance, in his little-known book, *The Weakest Link*, well said: "Look where you will, it is the spirit of I Myself which is paramount. Life exists for Me: all the dim eons behind have toiled to produce Me. This brief moment in the eternal duration of time is only an opportunity for My pleasure and My ease: I care not a jot for the ages ahead and the sons of men who shall inhabit the earth when I am dust beneath their feet. Give Me My rights. Stand clear of My way. I want and I will have." [4]

3. BOASTFULNESS

"Proud", "Arrogant", "Abusive"—in the Revised Standard Version; "Boastful", "Haughty", "Railers"—in the Standard Version. While these traits of human character are deep-seated vices of human nature in general, we have been witnessing a fresh outburst of it in current history. In his autobiography Mussolini makes the following boastful statement about himself: "I am superman, incarnate, even as Napoleon, of whom I secretly believe I am the incarnation, was the heaven-sent messenger; I, because like Napoleon, am lawgiver as well as war lord. I am the State."[5]

4. THE WEAKENING OF FAMILY TIES

"Disobedient to parents." The growing rate of divorces, the large percentage of children born out of wedlock and increasing juvenile crime give a timely meaning to this first-century prophetic forecast. Nowhere, however, has there been such a deliberate attempt to destroy family life as in totalitarian countries. "Nowhere is its [Nazism's] destructiveness more impressive than in family life. It is loud in the praise of prolific procreation, but its whole system is destructive of family life . . . The sowing of dissension within the family, the alienation of the young from the old, the breaking up of family life through excessive claims on the young, 'in the service of an idea', is surrendering the youth of the nation to elements which on a continually growing scale are trampling on the last vestiges of traditional moral training." These are the words of one of Hitler's former associates who in due time began to see the full depravity of the Nazi system.[6]

Conditions in the communist countries are just as bad if not worse. A frightful picture of sexual licence in communist countries is painted in an article by Leland Stowe, and printed in the *Reader's Digest* of March 1955. We will quote a few passages from this article: "Unrestrained sexual licence is the principal means by which the Communist regimes today seduce their young people and chain them to Moscow's objectives. The use of Party-promoted 'free love' as an instrument of Soviet conquest throughout the Kremlin's captive nations has caused a rampant scourge of promiscuity, affecting a majority among some twenty-five million satellite youths. Under the new 'Bolshevik morality', young boys and girls have been seduced into rejecting such 'outmoded bourgeois prejudices' as premarital chastity and wedded fidelity . . . Unbridled free love has evolved into a perfected programme, ready to demoralize youth wherever Communism attains power.

"The resulting scourge of promiscuity is yielding a tragic harvest of illegitimate children, venereal disease on an epidemic scale, and widespread prostitution, some of it State-operated . . . In Czechoslovakia, statistics for 1953 show a 28 per cent increase in illegitimacy compared with 1938. In Poland, unmarried mothers helped boost the 1953 birthrate to an all-time high—500,000 in a population of some 26,000,000. In all satellites, maternity wards cannot accommodate the rising flood of unmarried expectant mothers. At overcrowded public clinics girls of fifteen and sixteen desperately seek pre-natal care."

About 65 per cent of the population in Ostrava (Czechoslovakia) is infected with venereal disease—relates a recent Czechoslovak refugee. Among the 3,000,000 people living in the uranium district in East Prussia there are 200,000 cases of venereal disease—a refugee physician informed U.S. officials. "A medical checkup of some 3,000 women workers at Stalinvaros, Hungary, revealed that two-thirds were suffering from venereal disease . . .

"The Communists create opportunities for promiscuity under every pretext. Teenagers are driven into Red youth-organizations by threat of social ostracism. They are won over by ceaseless rounds of sports contests, night rallies, Party-sponsored dances, youth camps and 'homes'. Such activities leave the doors open for sexual adventures . . .

"Under Communist sex policy no pretext of protection is provided for women and girls. The more attractive ones are fair game for the Red bosses . . . A former book-keeper reports that the numerous women's barracks at Stalinvaros are 'open house' to male workers at night. Local secret police units, he says, treat female workers as brothel inmates and seldom tolerate a refusal. Those who resist are raped . . .

"'Especially with the younger women you notice this terrible degeneration,' says a Polish sailor. 'Nice girls, educated and well-mannered, will sleep with practically anyone who gives them a good meal or a Western lipstick. Dance halls are crowded with willing pickups.'"

Prostitution in the service of the State is a unique communist institution. It was developed in Soviet Russia to spy upon and trap possible foes of the regime. Now it has been expanded in the puppet nations. Great numbers of women have been forced into what amounts to State-operated white slavery. Women are led into prostitution for spying purposes. "Every satellite hotel has its bevy of police-directed seducers. Well groomed and multilingual, they are on the lookout for foreign tourists, businessmen, journalists. What they collect in payment is their own; the information obtained in the process goes to the police."[7]

5. RECRUDESCENCE OF HUMAN SAVAGERY

Reference to this in Paul's prophetic passage is expressed by the word "fierce" in 2 Timothy 3: 3. The original Greek word means "untamed", "uncivilized", "wild", "savage", "fierce". The world in the last forty years has experienced, and still does, this fresh resurgence of human savagery. Nazi Germany and Japan during World War Two, and communist Russia and her satellites to this very day, have been the principal perpetrators of human crimes which in their brutality have exceeded anything which man has been guilty of in the past. Many of the Nazi leaders who were brought to trial at Nuremberg at the end of World War Two were university graduates and some had doctorate degrees from the finest European institutions of higher learning. Here is an excerpt from the official indictment of Nazi atrocities.

"The murders and ill-treatment were carried out by divers means, including shooting, hanging, gasing, starvation, gross overcrowding, systematic undernutrition . . . kickings, beatings, brutality and torture of all kinds, including the use of hot irons and pulling out of finger nails and the performance of experiments by means of operations and otherwise on living human subjects.

"In a little more than two years, over 22,000 died of exhaustion alone at Buchenwald. In Malthausen 700 priests alone died of exhaustion. In Maidanek 1,500,000 persons were exterminated. In Auschwitz 4,000,000 persons were exterminated, including citizens of the United States, Great Britain, and France. In the Lwow region the Germans exterminated 700,000 Soviet people, and in the Jewish Ghetto alone 133,000 were tortured and shot. In Czechoslovakia as a result of torture, beating and hanging in two Gestapo prisons, 200,000 persons were killed, and many other thousands subjected to criminal treatment."[8]

How can we account for the behaviour of the German people under the Nazi regime? How are we to explain that so many German citizens from all walks of life, including university professors, have lent their support to, and actively and premeditatively participated in, the most abominable crimes? The following explanation comes from the pen of a German observer: "It was the outbreak of forces certainly collective in origin, certainly stimulable by psychology and capable of being roused under certain conditions, but forces coming from greater depths than psychology ever plumbed. It was a sudden darkening of mind that then set in, an occultation in which one felt the uncanny wing-beat of those powers whose effects one had read in history-books as the unaccountable appearance of psychic mass-epidemics, but which one had never appreciated as real, let alone actually possible within the body of one's own people. The wing-beat of the dark daemonic forces: there is no other term for their supra-personal and at once transcendent power."[9]

In spite of the strict censorship and tight restrictions imposed on the movements of foreigners in the communist countries enough is known to prove that communism does not fall behind Nazism in human cruelty. In 1944 it was estimated by well-informed persons that the Russian slave-labour camps numbered around twenty million people.[10] When whole families are sent to slave-labour camps, the father is sent to one camp, the mother and children to another camp. "It was the practice to send men to lumber and mining camps in northern Siberia, while women and children did better in the brick-yards and co-operative farms in southern Kagakstan . . . no deliberate cruelty is intended in breaking up families. After all, it is absurd to argue that it is cruel to peel a potato. Cruelty is something which one can inflict only on human beings or animals. Once you reach the point of reducing men and women and children to the status of instruments, the concept of cruelty vanishes."[11] The cruelties perpetrated on the inmates of the slave-labour camps as related by the few who were fortunate enough to escape are simply incredible. "Soviet Russia has made the term Communism and, to a degree slightly less, the term Socialism utterly putrid. Marxism stinks in the nostrils of history. From its materialist assumptions about history and man, it has rotted and festered into a bloody tyranny, into a cynical a-moralism, into the corruption of conscience."[12]

IV. World Unification at the End of the Age

In the preceding chapter we have presented the generally-held conviction that only a world government can save this world from destruction, and that, whether we like it or not, world uni-fication is bound to come. There is nothing radically new about this trend to a world government. Whether motivated by the yearning for power on the part of men or by a desire to eliminate international conflicts, men have for centuries dreamed of and tried to bring about world unification. This was true of ancient and medieval history, and of the history of the last four centuries. The League of Nations after World War One, and the United Nations after World War Two, were brought into existence to assure world peace. But all these attempts to unify the world, or a large part of it, whether by force or otherwise, have so far failed. According to the Bible men will at the end of the Age make a last mighty effort to bring about world unification and at this time succeed, but only for a short while. This brief period of world unification will be the most tragic period of human history. The head of this world government is referred to as the beast in Daniel in the Old Testament, and in Revelation in the New Testament. This will be a time when Satan will reign and rule supreme in the world. "And they worshipped the dragon [i.e. Satan] because he gave his authority unto the beast; and they worshipped the beast saying, Who is like unto the beast? And who is able to make war with him? And there was given unto him a mouth, speaking great things and blasphemies; and there was given to him authority to continue forty and two months. And he opened his mouth for blasphemies against God, to blaspheme his name, and his tabernacle, even them that dwell in the heaven. And it was given unto him to make war with the saints, and to overcome them: and there was given to him authority over every tribe, and people and tongue and nation," Revelation 13: 4-7.

Here we have a world government holding in its mighty grip all nations of the earth, presided over by a blasphemous beastly tyrant, under the guidance and inspiration of Satan himself. But his reign will last only three and a half years (forty-two months). After this short period of time world human government will be destroyed by God's direct intervention, and the world will become unified indeed under Divine rule. And "the kingdom of the world is become the kingdom of our Lord . . .", Revelation 11: 15.

V. The Political Re-emergence of the Lands of the Bible

A most significant feature in the Biblical passages depicting the historical era belonging to the "Time of the End" is the political re-emergence of certain nations which for centuries were politically out of existence. Israel, Egypt, Assyria, Edom, Ammon, Moab, and others are participating in the "Time of the End" events as politically independent nations.

Some of the prophetic writings of the Old Testament devote whole chapters to a discussion of the destiny of the nations of what we would now call the Middle East. According to Isaiah's writings Babylon (Isaiah 13 and 14), Egypt and Assyria (Isaiah 19), and Edom (Isaiah 63: 1–6) shall be kept until the "Time of the End". Jeremiah speaks of the preservation of Egypt (Jeremiah 46: 25–26), Moab (Jeremiah 48: 46–47), Ammon (Jeremiah 49: 5–6), Elam (Jeremiah 49: 34–39).

Some of these nations are to be preserved until the "Time of the End" era when they are judged and destroyed in the "Time of the End" upheavals. Others, like Egypt and Assyria, are converted to Jehovah, they survive the "Time of the End" distress, and become a blessing to the world. "In that day shall Israel be the third with Egypt and with Assyria, a blessing in the midst of the earth; for that Jehovah of hosts hath blessed them, saying, Blessed be Egypt my people, and Assyria the work of my hands, and Israel mine inheritance", Isaiah 19: 24–25.

The amazing thing is that these nations which for more than two thousand years have had no independent political life have regained political independence only since the end of the First World War, and some of them, as Syria, Lebanon and Jordan, only since World War Two. Some of these restored nations do not bear the same name as in Biblical times, but their geographical location is approximately the same. Present-day Iraq occupies ancient Mesopotamia or Assyria; Jordan takes the place of Ammon and Moab. Syria is ancient Damascus. Egypt and Israel have retained their old names. Now, all these nations lost their independent political status over two thousand years ago, and all of them have regained political life at about the same time. In Israel's case political restoration involved the ingathering of remnants of a people scattered all over the world, and the physical rehabilitation of a country which for centuries lay buried in ruins. Are all these events a coincidence?

VI. "The Dwarfing of Europe"

One of the most astonishing historical developments of our time is the eclipse of Europe or "The Dwarfing of Europe" as Toynbee calls it in his book *Civilization on Trial*. In 1914 Europe was the master of the world by reason of the fact that out of the world's eight great powers then in existence five were centred in Europe, while Russia, the sixth, though partly in Europe and partly in Asia, was definitely oriented towards Europe. In less than one generation Europe has lost its world-dominating position. To appreciate the nature of this change one needs to call to mind the position which Europe held in the world prior to 1914. Ever since the sixteenth century Europe has been extending its influence to the rest of the globe. It has conquered two new continents and peopled them with Europeans. It has extended its control to a third continent, Africa, and established a European State in the southern tip of that continent. It has gained possessions in Asia and exercised there a controlling voice for some time. European technology and ideas were adopted all over the world. Up to the very outbreak of the First World War European man-power, money and technical know-how flowed in a steady stream to America to help in the development of this fast-growing continent.

The following are some of the underlying causes for the change in Europe's position since the First World War. These are not listed in any particular order of importance:

(1) The universal trend to industrialization in many parts of the world outside of Europe resulting in the progressive shrinkage of Europe's foreign markets.

(2) The rise of a number of large and powerful states outside of Europe.

(3) The two World Wars had a devastating effect on the economy of Europe. Up to World War One Europe was the largest creditor continent. Europeans invested heavily in industries and public services of the United States which at that time was a large debtor country. After the First World War the situation reversed itself. Europe destroyed its own resources and had to liquidate many of its investments abroad.

(4) The development of atomic weapons. The densely populated and highly industrialized states of Europe and their proximity to Soviet Russia make Europe highly vulnerable in any future conflict in which atomic weapons will be used.

(5) Russia's post-war aggressiveness. The creation by Russia of satellite nations towards the end of World War Two has reduced Europe politically to little more than Western Europe.

VII. The Jewish Exodus from Europe: Its Relation to the Eclipse of Europe

This is another historical development which has been consummated before our very eyes, and which is fraught with great prophetic significance. From the New Testament and other sources we know that even before A.D. 70 there were Jewish communities in many regions of the European part of the Roman empire. The great Dispersion which began after A.D. 70, and especially following the end of the Bar-Kochba war against Rome in A.D. 132–135, brought more Jews to the European continent. At that time European civilization was confined to Italy, Greece and the coastlands of the Mediterranean. The rest of Europe was in a barbaric or semi-barbaric state. As Roman civilization continued to spread to the European continent, more Jews established themselves there. Jewish residence in Europe dates back to the very beginning of European civilization, when, with the exception of Italy, and Greece, none of the present-day European nations were in existence, and it was in Europe that the bulk of the Jews lived until World War Two.

It is against these facts that we must weigh the significance of the liquidation of the larger part of European Jewry. Most of this liquidation has taken place in World War Two as a result of the extermination of some six million Jews by the Nazis. Of great significance is the Jewish reaction to their position in Europe following World War Two. Jewish communities were wiped out in Europe many times in the past. But when the storm subsided the Jews usually reconstructed their shattered homes and started life all over again. If they were forced to leave one part of Europe, they moved to another part, and after some lapse of time they usually gained permission to return to their former settlements.

Following World War Two a significant change has taken place in the Jewish attitude to Europe. By and large, Jews who have survived the tragedies of the Second World War refused to make a new beginning in Europe. They began to feel that the European phase of Jewish history, which, incidentally, forms the largest chapter of the history of the Jewish people, has definitely come to an end. Consequently, they have voluntarily completed the process of liquidation of Jewish corporate existence in Europe, and they left in a mass exodus for the Land of Israel. This did not include the Jews in Russia of whom not much is known at the present except that the Russian Government would not permit them to leave; and it did not include the Jews of Great Britain and countries like Sweden, where the Jews have been spared the experiences of their brethren in Nazi-occupied Europe. It is, however, generally admitted in Jewish quarters that with the elimination of the large Jewish populations in Central and Eastern Europe the days of the remaining smaller Jewish communities in Western Europe are numbered. Thus within a few years the bulk of European Jewry, which constituted the largest concentration of Jews for 1,900 years, has ceased to exist.

Since the Jews have been living in Europe from the very beginning of its recorded history they have for centuries been intimately associated with Europe's economic and cultural life. In the Middle Ages, in the era of Renaissance, and during the rise of European industrialism and modern commerce in the eighteenth century, the Jews played a vital role in the economic, scientific and intellectual life of Europe. The German antisemites undertook an impossible task when they attempted to prove to the world the superiority of the German nationality, knowing, as they did, how heavily the German Jews have contributed to German science, industry, commerce, literature and the arts. The programme of Jewish extermination on which the Nazis had embarked and so successfully carried through must have been a desperate move on their part designed to rid Germany of a national inferiority complex, and to convince themselves that the German Jews had nothing to do with Germany's high position in the world.

What the Nazi adventure has achieved for Germany we all know. Germany has suffered the most crushing defeat in her history. The eastern part of the country, the seat of Prussian militarism, and always a hotbed of antisemitism, has been detached from the remainder of the country, and from all appearances it may remain separated from Germany for a long time to come. We can depend on the Russians and the Poles to do in the meantime a good job of de-Germanization of this part of Germany, and one is safe to assume that the Germany of the future, with the German Jews gone, will never regain the high position in the world which she had enjoyed prior to the Nazi era.

Generally speaking, the Jews living in Christendom fall into two large groups: The "Ashkenazim" are the German- and Yiddish-speaking Jews who were concentrated in Eastern and Central Europe and their descendants who have emigrated to America. The "Sephardim" are the Spanish- and Portuguese-speaking Jews and their descendants who resided in Southeastern Europe and in the East. The German chapter of modern European Jewish history bears strong resemblance to the Spanish chapter of Medieval European Jewish history. To the Spanish Jews Spain was the country of their birth to which they were deeply attached and which they loved passionately. The greatness of Spain of the fifteenth century was in a large measure due to the energy and resourcefulness of her Jewish inhabitants. Lecky's eloquent tribute to the part which the Jews have played in the development of European civilization applies especially to the Spanish era: "While those around them", he stated, "were grovelling in the darkness of besotted ignorance; while juggling miracles and lying relics were the themes on which almost all Europe was expatiating; while the intellect of Christendom, enthralled by countless superstitions, had sunk into a deadly torpor, in which all love of inquiry and all search for truth were abandoned, the Jews were still pursuing the path of knowledge, amassing learning and stimulating progress with the same unflinching constancy that they manifested in their faith. They were the most skilful physicians, the ablest financiers, and among the most profound philosophers; while they were only second to the Moors in the cultivation of natural science. They were also the chief interpreters to Western Europe of Arabian learning."[13]

As in other parts of Europe Jewish life in Spain had its trials as well as triumphs. But for many years they lived happily in their native land, participating in all phases of the life of the country, and contributing much to the welfare, prosperity and greatness of Spain. But in due course of time, under the influence of the infamous Spanish Inquisition, a plan was prepared to displace the Jews from Spanish life in which they have been so deeply rooted. Discriminations, abuses, indignities and massacres were heaped upon them in ever-increasing measure in an effort to induce them to accept Catholicism or leave the country. When none of these persuasive methods proved sufficiently successful the Spanish Jews were ordered to leave. "A word, and they might have remained in full possession of peace, honour and wealth, but astonishingly few spoke that word. It had been their country for centuries, the country to which their forefathers had added dazzling splendour and to which they themselves were attached with all the fibres of their being. The exiles saw nothing before them but the dark hostility that would greet them everywhere, the utter degradation to which their brethren had been reduced in other lands. Nevertheless, all this was braved for the sake of the Lord God of Israel, for the sake also of the freedom of the human conscience to which civilized men of all opinions now pay sincere homage."[14]

In the same year of 1492 in which the Spanish Jews were driven out of Spain Columbus discovered America. God was thus preparing a place of refuge not only for persecuted Jews but for oppressed people everywhere. This year was also the beginning of the end of Spain as a world power. In less than a century since the expulsion of the Jews the Spanish Armada sailed out to reconquer England for Catholicism, and met with an overwhelming defeat, and Spain, which up to then was "mistress of the world and queen of the seas", entered an era of decline and decay from which she has not recovered to this very day.

Jewish experiences with Spain and Germany display a general principle which operates in the relations between the Jewish people and the nations of the world. The Divine promise given to Abraham, "I will bless them that bless thee, and him that curses thee I will curse" has never been revoked. God has had a controversy with His people Israel. The Synagogue has never denied that Israel's exile from her Land was in consequence of her sins. "Because of our sins have we been exiled from our country" is the Synagogue's public confession as recorded in the Prayer-Book. But "I am very sore displeased with the nations that are at ease; for I was but a little displeased and they helped forward the affliction" God declares in Zechariah 1: 15. God is greatly angry with the nations, for they have used this controversy between Him and Israel as a pretext to vent their hatred on Israel. We therefore feel strongly that there is a real relationship between the departure of the Jewish people from Europe and the "dwarfing of Europe." The exodus of the Jews from Europe, with whose destiny they have been intimately bound up from the very beginning of Europe's civilization, is an historical event of the first magnitude, an ominous sign of Europe's eclipse. The return of the Jews to Palestine coincides with a shift of the centre of gravity of world events from Europe to the Middle East.[15]

VIII. THE OLIVET PROPHECY

"And Jerusalem shall be trodden down of the Gentiles until the times of the Gentiles shall be fulfilled", Luke 21: 24b.

The Olivet Prophecy was uttered by the Lord Jesus about three or four days before His death on the Cross. To the very end of His earthly ministry the apostles had been waiting for Jesus Christ to overthrow Roman rule in Palestine and to usher in the glorious Messianic kingdom. When, therefore, instead of fulfilling their hopes the Lord Jesus began to speak of His approaching death and the coming destruction of Jerusalem the apostles became deeply distressed. Having left the Temple where He had been teaching daily in the last week of His earthly ministry the Lord Jesus and His small apostolic band arrived at the foot of the Mount of Olives. While there four of the apostles asked Him two questions: (1) When will the predicted destruction of Jerusalem take place? (2) What will be the sign of the end of the Age and of His return to earth? "Tell us," they said, "when shall these things be, and what shall be the sign of Thy coming, and the end of the Age?" Matthew 24: 3; Mark 13: 4; Luke 21: 7. The substance of His reply to these two questions constitutes the Olivet Prophecy which, together with the parables which follow, present to us the most comprehensive prophetic pronouncement in the New Testament, outside of the book of Revelation, dealing with the subject of the end of the Age. See Matthew, chapters 24 and 25; Mark, chapter 13; Luke, chapter 21.

There was a danger that the destruction of Jerusalem some thirty years after the Crucifixion of Jesus Christ would be misinterpreted by His followers as the "birth pangs" of the Messianic Era, to be followed immediately by the consummation of the Age and the reappearance of Christ. The "birth pangs" of the Messiah refer to a belief among the Jews according to which the coming of the Messiah will be preceded by a time of distress and sufferings for both Israel and the world.[16] The Lord Jesus did not find any fault with the basic idea of this belief. But in the Olivet

Prophecy He declared that the coming destruction of Jerusalem by the Romans would be the mere beginning of the "birth pangs" of the Messiah. "And when you shall hear of wars and rumours of wars, be you not troubled; these things must needs come to pass; but the end is not yet. For nation shall rise against nation, and kingdom against kingdom; there shall be earthquakes in divers places; there shall be famines: these things are the beginnings of the birth pangs", Mark 13: 7–8.[17] In other words, the entire course of history, between the destruction of the Jewish State by the Romans thirty-seven years after the Crucifixion and the return of Jesus Christ, will be the "birth pangs" of the Messiah and marked by wars and rumours of wars, uprisings, persecution, famines, and pestilences. That this period of years, between the destruction of the Jewish State by the Romans and the return of Jesus Christ, would be quite long the Lord Jesus clearly indicated when He compared His departure to a man going on a trip to a far country and returning home after a long absence. See Matthew 25: 14, 19 King James Version.

But it is not God's intent to leave His children in the dark. In order that subsequent generations may interpret events correctly the Lord Jesus gave three signs which would help them to recognize the end of the Age when it comes. These signs are as follows:

1. *The proclamation of the Gospel to the whole world.* "And this Gospel of the Kingdom shall be preached in the whole world for a testimony unto all the nations; and then shall the end come", Matthew 24: 14. This is one of the three signs. Every nation and every country is to have the opportunity to know what the message of Jesus Christ is. That the task of making the message of Jesus Christ known to the whole world is rapidly approaching its completion may be seen from the following information received from the American Bible Society: By the end of 1956 at least some part of the Bible had been published in 1,109 languages and dialects. While there are still many semi-civilized or primitive peoples that do not have any part of the Bible translated in their tongue—some of these peoples do not even have a written language—the Bible, in whole or in part, "has been translated, published and introduced at least in the official language of every country in the world".[18] "And this Gospel of the Kingdom shall be preached in the whole world for a testimony unto all the nations; and then shall the end come."

2. *A time of world-wide distress*. This is the second sign. While the whole era of human history between the destruction of the Jewish State by the Romans and the return of Jesus Christ was to be—in accordance with the predictions of the Lord Jesus—a time of wars, rumours of wars, uprisings, disturbances of all kinds, famine and pestilence, the end of this era will experience a great intensification and multiplication of these evils. The same evils which were to afflict the human race in that entire period were to reach a terrible climax towards the end of this period, and bring on a world crisis such as never was before and never will be. "For then shall be the great tribulation, such as hath not been from the beginning of the world until now, no, nor ever shall be. And except those days had been shortened, no flesh would have been saved: but for the elect's sake those days shall be shortened", Matthew 24: 21–22.

3. *The restoration of Israel*. "And Jerusalem shall be trodden down of the Gentiles until the times of the Gentiles be fulfilled", Luke 21: 24b. This is the last of the three historical events whose fulfilment was to be associated with the return of Jesus Christ. "Jerusalem" in this instance is used of the nation of Israel in its politico-national connotation in the same sense in which Paris stands for France, London for the British Empire, or Washington for the United States of America.

About one hundred years ago Bishop Ryle made the following comment on the passage in Luke as cited above: "While the nations of Europe are absorbed in political conflicts and worldly business, the sands in their hour-glass are ebbing away. While governments are disputing about secular things, and parliaments can hardly condescend to find a place for religion in their discussions, their days are numbered in the sight of God. Yet a few years and the 'times of the Gentiles will be fulfilled'. Their day of visitation will be past and gone. Their misused privileges will be taken away. The judgments of God shall fall on them. They shall be cast aside as vessels in which God has no pleasure. Their dominion shall crumble away, and their vaunted institutions shall fall to pieces. The Jews shall be restored. The Lord Jesus shall come again in power and great glory. The kingdoms of this world shall become the kingdoms of our God and of His Christ, and the 'times of the Gentiles' shall come to an end."[19] In 1917, the year in which Europe was approaching the end of its first war of self-destruction, Oswald Spengler completed his work entitled

The Decline of the West (the word "West" stands here for the dominant Gentile civilization). In the self-same year the British Government issued the Balfour Declaration in which it solemnly promised to help the Jewish people to re-establish themselves in Palestine. At the end of World War Two, in which war Europe's decline became further advanced, the world witnessed the re-emergence of the State of Israel. Thus, much of Bishop Ryle's prediction one hundred years ago is fulfilled today. The re-appearance of the State of Israel thus coincides in time with the decline of Gentile civilization. And this is essentially the meaning of the passage in Luke 21: 24b.

In concluding the Olivet Prophecy about events associated with His return the Lord Jesus made the following statement: "But when these things begin to come to pass, look up, and lift up your heads; because your redemption draweth nigh. And He spoke to them a parable: Behold the fig tree, and all the trees. When they now shoot forth, ye see it and know of your own selves that the summer is now nigh. Even so ye also, when ye see these things coming to pass, know ye that the kingdom of God is nigh", Luke 21: 28–31. In Matthew the same statement has this significant variation: "Even so ye also, when ye see all these things, know ye that He is nigh, even at the doors", Matthew 24: 33. We live in a period of world history when for the first time we are witnessing the beginning of the simultaneous fulfilment of all three world events which Jesus Christ listed as those which would herald His return: (1) The completion of the task of the propagation of the Gospel throughout the world; (2) a time of world-wide distress; (3) and the restoration of Israel.

NOTES TO CHAPTER 3

1. Pitirim A. Sorokin, *The Crisis of Our Age* (E. P. Dutton & Co., Inc.: New York, 1942 edition), pp. 213–16.
2. George Santayana, "Epilogue on My Host, the World", article in the *Atlantic Monthly*, January 1949; quoted by Wilbur M. Smith in the *Sunday School Times* (Philadelphia), January 29, 1949.
3. Quoted by Wilbur M. Smith, *World Crisis and the Prophetic Scriptures* (Moody Press: Chicago, 1952), p. 314.
4. Quoted by Wilbur M. Smith in an article entitled "Characteristics of Men in the Last Days", published in the *Sunday School Times* (Philadelphia), January 29, 1949.

5. Benito Mussolini, *My Autobiography* (Hurst & Blackett Ltd., London, 1936); quoted by Wilbur M. Smith in the *Sunday School Times* (Philadelphia), January 29, 1949.

6. Hermann Rauschning, *The Revolution of Nihilism* (The Alliance Book Corporation; New York, 1939); quoted by Wilbur M. Smith in the *Sunday School Times* (Philadelphia), January 29, 1949.

7. Leland Stowe, "Sexual Licence: Key Soviet Strategy", published in the *Reader's Digest* (The Reader's Digest Assn., Inc., Pleasantville, N.Y.), March 1955.

8. *The Case Against Nazi War Criminals*, pp. 138-9; quoted by Wilbur M. Smith, *Sunday School Times* (Philadelphia), February 5, 1949.

9. Alfred Weber, *Farewell to European History* (Yale University Press: New Haven, 1948), p. 160.

10. D. R. Davies, *The Sin of Our Age* (The Macmillan Co.: New York, 1947), pp. 118-19.

11. Ibid., p. 121.

12. Ibid., p. 122.

13. W. E. H. Lecky, *History of Rationalism*, I, p. 282; quoted by Paul Goodman, *A History of the Jews* (London, 1909 or 1911), p. 66.

14. Paul Goodman, *A History of the Jews* (The Temple Primers, 1909), p. 96.

15. Arnold J. Toynbee, *Civilization On Trial* (Oxford University Press: New York, 1948), p. 93. Toynbee predicts that this shift of the weight of world events will take place to the vicinity of ancient Babylon, i.e. in the country of Iraq.

16. Alfred Edersheim, *The Life and Times of Jesus the Messiah*, vol. 2, eighth edition, revised (Longmans, Green & Co.: New York, 1899), p. 433.

17. American Standard Version. See also marginal note in the King James Version.

18. Personal written communication from the librarian of the American Bible Society dated April 25, 1957.

19. Rev. J. C. Ryle, B.A., *Expository Thoughts on the Gospels: St. Luke*, vol. 2, p. 371 (Wertheim, Macintox and Hunt: London, 1859).

PART FOUR

THE REBIRTH OF THE STATE OF ISRAEL: THE LAST STAGE IN ISRAEL'S TRAINING FOR HER MISSION

ISRAEL'S DESTINY OF SUFFERING

ANTISEMITISM: ITS ESSENCE AND MEANING

1. THE EXTRA-BIBLICAL VIEW OF ANTISEMITISM

    a. Religious prejudice
    b. Xenophobia
    c. The economic factor
    d. The scapegoat element

2. THE BIBLICAL VIEW OF ANTISEMITISM

    a. Foretold in the Bible
    b. Hatred of Israel is hatred of the God of Israel
    c. The penal aspect
    d. The disciplinary aspect

CHAPTER I

ISRAEL'S DESTINY OF SUFFERING

In the following chapters of this subdivision we will trace the main features of the human principle in Jewish history, its repeated failures to bring salvation to the Jewish people, its complete breakdown in the "time of the end" era, and Israel's final submission to the Will of God.

ANTISEMITISM: ITS ESSENCE AND MEANING

Next to the survival of the Jew the most baffling historical phenomenon is the hatred which he has repeatedly encountered among the nations of the earth. This hostility to the Jews, which goes under the name of antisemitism, is as old as Jewish existence. It is endemic, i.e. like many contagious diseases it is always with us to some degree. But under certain circumstances it assumes epidemic proportions and characteristics. It is prevalent wherever Jews reside in sufficiently large numbers to make their neighbours aware of their presence. "The growth of antisemitism", Chaim Weizmann declares, "is proportionate to the number of Jews per square kilometre. We carry the germs of antisemitism in our knapsack on our backs."[1]

I. THE EXTRA-BIBLICAL VIEW OF ANTISEMITISM

Those who have studied the problem of antisemitism from the secular point of view attribute it to the following causative factors.

a. Religious prejudice

From the earliest times the religion of the Jew has set him apart from the rest of mankind. Notwithstanding his hatred of the Jews the Roman antisemite Tacitus had this to say with reference to their religion: "The Jews acknowledge one God only, and him they see in the mind's eye, and him they adore in contemplation, condemning as impious idolators all who, with perishable material wrought into human form, attempt to represent the Deity. The God of the Jews is the great governing mind that directs and guides the whole frame of nature, eternal, infinite and neither capable of change nor subject to decay."[2]

Unlike many of the ancient peoples, especially the educated among the Greeks and Romans, the Jew lived his religion in his daily life. It was Jewish religious practice which generated much of the animosity to the Jews. Jewish aversion to any material representation of the Deity made them appear in the eyes of the Gentiles as irreligious, as having no belief in God. Their refusal to participate in the national festivities of the State bearing a pagan religious character and to pay religious homage to the State drew the charge of civic disloyalty against them. The Jewish dietary laws preventing the Jews from sharing with the Gentiles in the pleasures of the table, and Jewish opposition to intermarriage, unless the Gentile party accepted Judaism, were a constant source of irritation and made the Jews appear as anti-social beings. Even the Jewish Sabbath, one of the greatest gifts bestowed upon the world by the Jewish people, made them appear ridiculous to many Gentiles who charged them with laziness and wasting away a seventh part of their lives.

One of the earliest instances of anti-Jewish incidents in which religion played an important part is the one recorded in the book of Daniel. The earliest recorded accusation levelled against the whole Jewish nation is found in the book of Esther. Haman, the highest official in the Persian Empire next to the king, was offended when Mordecai the Jew refused, for religious reasons, to bow to him in recognition of his official rank. Realizing that Mordecai's conduct reflected the attitude of the entire Jewish community in the Persian Empire, Haman conceived of a devilish plan to exterminate all the Jewish people in the empire. The following is his accusation against the Jews addressed to the Persian king: "There is a certain people scattered abroad and dispersed among the peoples in all the provinces of thy kingdom; and their laws are diverse from those of every people; neither keep they the king's laws: therefore it is not for the king's profit to suffer them. If it please the king let it be written that they be destroyed . . .", Esther 3: 8–9.

Outside of Palestine the largest concentration of Jews in the ancient world was in Alexandria, Egypt. Attracted there because of its proximity to Palestine and by the special privileges granted to them by the successors of Alexander the Great, the Jews made Alexandria the centre of the Diaspora. It soon became also the centre of antisemitism. In fact, from the third century B.C. Egypt is said to have become a hotbed of antisemitism much as Germany under the Nazis.[3] The foremost Egyptian antisemite was an Alexandrian by name of Apion who unleashed a flood of distortions and malicious slander against the Jews. His fabricated lies became the source material for later Greek and Roman antisemites. In one of his stories this Apion declares that in compliance with a secret Jewish law the Jews slaughter a Greek man once a year and eat his flesh. This Apion appears, therefore, to have originated the ritual murder lies about the Jews which were exploited by various Jew-haters in later times.[4]

Many of the Roman writers harboured feelings of ill-will to the Jews both on account of the Jewish religion, whose essence they never fully understood, and because of Jewish exclusiveness. Among these are such familiar names of antiquity as Horace, Cicero, Tacitus and Seneca. The latter called the Jews the "most wicked nation", ridiculed their Sabbath observance and complained that "the way of life of this most wicked nation has already won so much influence that it is already being accepted all over the world. The vanquished have imposed their laws on the victors".[5]

In the Middle Ages the Jews encountered religious antisemitism in the countries of Islam as well as of Christendom. The Church has for centuries been engaged in anti-Jewish activities and was chiefly responsible for the political, civic, and economic disabilities of the Jews. The basic factors which made this attitude possible, in spite of the fact that both the Founder of the Christian faith and all its early followers were Jews, were these: (1) Jewish hostility to Christianity; (2) the Christian movement became in time a purely Gentile movement; (3) the appalling ignorance in the medieval Church of the teachings of both the Old and the New Testament concerning the position of Israel in the Divine programme of world redemption.

b. Xenophobia

Another element which is believed to be at the basis of antisemitism goes under the name of xenophobia. By this is meant the feeling of distrust and antipathy held towards those belonging to an alien group. In spite of living among the Gentiles for centuries the Jews have retained such distinct national characteristics as to make them appear an alien group in Gentile eyes. While in normal times this antagonism to aliens remains dormant in human hearts, it assumes explosive proportions in times of adversity. On such occasions the stranger is looked upon as an enemy in disguise.

c. The economic factor

The vast majority of the people in medieval Europe were farmers. The Jews were forbidden to own land, and even many trades were closed to them. They were, therefore, forced into the money-changing and commercial branches of economic life. Thus there was little or no competition in the economic field between Jew and Gentile in medieval Europe. Economic factors, therefore, did not play any significant part in the anti-Jewish attitude of medieval Europe.

This situation changed radically with the end of medievalism. The aversion to trades, professions and commerce, dominant in medieval Europe, gradually gave way, and many Gentiles took their place in the changed economic structure of their countries. At the same time large numbers of young Jews, having attained civil and political rights in many countries, took advantage of the educational facilities and the various economic opportunities previously denied to them. Jew and Gentile thus met as competitors in the various economic fields and this gave rise to economic antisemitism. The Gentile middle class in many countries, especially in Germany, became the chief exponent and supporter of this new antisemitism, sometimes called racial antisemitism. This new form of antisemitism, while sometimes more refined, is no less virulent than the religious antisemitism of the Middle Ages. And to this day, wherever Jews and Gentiles are competing in the same economic area, economic antisemitism is a potent factor.

d. The scapegoat element

In times of national or international distress anti-Jewish prejudice has often been exploited by governments and vested interests in order to divert from themselves the dissatisfaction of the masses. This scapegoat element was often used by the Russian Tzarist regime in its desire to befog the issues and turn the minds of the people away from the real nature of the country's troubles.

It has been suggested that this scapegoat factor was the chief stuff of German antisemitism, especially in the years between the two world wars. The defeat suffered by Germany in World War One was an intolerable blow to German pride and its concept of Teutonic supremacy. In their desire to rationalize the Germans began to explain away the real cause of events. Germany, they argued, did not really lose the war, in fact they were on the verge of winning it. But a stab in the back by German Jewry with the help of world Jewry turned the tide of the war and sealed Germany's doom. That this was a palpable lie was known to all sane people. German Jewry loved its country passionately and participated, out of proportion to its numbers, in the conflict on the side of its country. But a defeated and broken Germany was experiencing an emotional conflict which it could not easily resolve. To admit its limitations, its mistakes or guilt is no less unpleasant to a nation than it is to an individual. A psychologically more tolerable way out had to be found, and the Jew, on whom the Germans never wasted too much love, was found peculiarly suitable to play the part of Germany's scapegoat.

2. THE BIBLICAL VIEW OF ANTISEMITISM

a. Foretold in the Bible

Even before Israel came into being as a nation her destiny of suffering had already been predicted. To Abraham God had made the following declaration: "Know of a surety that thy seed shall be sojourners in a land that is not theirs, and shall serve them; and they shall afflict them four hundred years; and also that nation, whom they shall serve, will I judge . . .", Genesis 15: 13–14.

The burning bush which Moses saw in the wilderness, the bush which burned but was not consumed, is certainly symbolic of Israel's Destiny of Suffering, of Israel's indestructibility, but also of the fires of affliction through which she must pass until she has been purged of all her dross and made into God's fit vessel.

In the twenty-eighth chapter of Deuteronomy we have a

description of the painful road which Israel was destined to travel. One needs to read through the whole chapter and compare it with the tragic experiences during the siege of Jerusalem by the Romans and the long centuries of exile which followed the destruction of the Jewish Homeland by Rome to realize with what terrible literalness the predictions of Deuteronomy 28 have been fulfilled.

In the prophetic books of the Old Testament we also find many predictions concerning the sorrows and sufferings which were to be the lot of the Jewish people.

How does the Bible account for Israel's destiny of suffering?

b. Hatred of Israel is hatred of the God of Israel

Psalm 44: 22 (44: 23 Heb.): "Yes, for thy sake are we killed all the day long; we are accounted as sheep for the slaughter."

The above passage is representative of a Biblical concept which runs through the entire Bible—Old and New Testament— to the effect that hostility to Israel is a disguised form of hostility to the God of Israel. This applies to the antisemitism in the pre-Christian as well as the Christian era. Many Jews have been wont to attribute the antisemitism of the Christian era to certain teachings of the New Testament. If the New Testament is antisemitic because it points out certain Jewish shortcomings then the Old Testament should also be considered antisemitic. If the New Testament is the source of Christian antisemitism then how are we to account for the much friendlier attitude to the Jews in the countries of Evangelical Christianity where the teachings of the New Testament are better known and their influence on human behaviour is fairly strong? "If a man say, I love God, and hateth his brother, he is a liar: for he that loveth not his brother whom he hath seen, can not love God whom he hath not seen," 1 John 4: 20. This writer has personally known Christians whose love for the Jews has touched him deeply. No Gentile who accepts the New Testament concept of sin and salvation can help feeling grateful to the Jewish people for the part which they played in making this salvation possible.

In recent years Jewish thinking concerning "Christian" antisemitism has undergone a significant change. "Antisemitism," Will Herberg declares, "is the other side of the election and vocation of Israel. However it may express itself on the social, economic, cultural and political levels, whatever may be its involvement with other factors in the ongoing life of society, antisemitism is, at bottom, the revolt of the pagan against the God of Israel and his absolute demand. This was obvious in pre-Christian antisemitism, but it is equally true of antisemitism in the Christian world. . . ."[6] Houston Stewart Chamberlain, who may be considered the forerunner of the neo-pagan antisemitism of modern times, is reported to have made this revealing observation: "The Jew came into our gay world and spoiled everything with his ominous concept of sin, with his Law and his cross."[7]

"And we shall never," states Morris Samuel, "underrate the maniacal, world-wide seizure of antisemitism unless we transpose the terms. It is of Christ that the Nazi-Fascists are afraid; it is in his omnipotence that they believe; it is him that they are determined madly to obliterate. But the names of Christ and Christianity are too overwhelming, and the habit of submission to them is too deeply ingrained after centuries and centuries of teaching. Therefore they must, I repeat, make their assault on those who were responsible for the birth and spread of Christianity. They must spit on the Jews as 'the Christ-killers' because they long to spit on the Jews as the Christ-givers."[8]

Referring to "Christian" antisemites Sigmund Freud says: "Under the thin veneer of Christianity they have remained what their ancestors were, barbarically polytheistic. They have not yet overcome their grudge against the new religion which was forced on them, and they have projected it on to the source from which Christianity came to them. . . . The hatred for Judaism is at bottom hatred for Christianity. . . ."[9]

The antisemitism of Russian communism is basically of the same nature: hatred for Israel is a disguised form of hatred for the God of Israel. For some forty years the Russian Government has been trying to exterminate religion in Russia—and so far has failed. The religion of the vast majority of the Russian people is the religion of the Bible. Communism is well aware that the peoples who oppose communism—whether in the West or in the East—are influenced by the Bible whose concept of man and the world is the very antithesis of the beliefs and practices of communism. To the rulers of Communist Russia the Jew in their midst is a constant and pointed reminder of the Bible.

c. The penal aspect

Many of the evils which have been visited upon the Jewish people in the course of history are attributed in the Bible to Israel's disobedience to the Will of God. The long and painful account of things to come, as contained in Deuteronomy 28, is prefaced with the following passage: "But it shall come to pass, if thou wilt not hearken unto the voice of Jehovah thy God, to observe to do all his commandments and his statutes which I command thee this day, that all these curses shall come upon thee, and overtake thee," Deuteronomy 28: 15.

d. The disciplinary aspect

The training of Israel and her preparation for her Divine Mission appears to be the chief purpose of Israel's destiny of suffering. In Israel's history we witness a conflict between two principles: the Divine versus the human. To be sure, the same is also true of Gentile history. But it is especially true of Jewish history which has experienced such a large measure of Divine Revelation. Upon the outcome of this struggle between the Divine and the human in the history of Israel depended the success or failure of Israel's Divine calling. But God has not called Israel to fail. The very fact of Israel's Divine calling carries with it the assurance that God will accomplish through Israel all he purposed to do. Israel's destiny of suffering is a historical process unfolding the painful encounter between the Divine and the human. In this spiritual warfare now the one, now the other principle gains the upper hand. But there is no question as to which of the two shall have the final victory. When this historical process will have reached its climactic end God will have attained full and complete victory over Israel, as he did in the long ago over Israel's ancestor Jacob in the darkness of that tragic night beside the waters of Jabbok, Genesis 32: 9–31 (32: 10–32 Heb.).

In the Old Testament this antagonism between the Divine and the human in Israel's history is well expressed in Isaiah 55: 8–9: "For my thoughts are not your thoughts, neither are your ways my ways, saith Jehovah. For as the heavens are higher than the earth, so are my ways higher than your ways, and my thoughts than your thoughts." In the New Testament the same idea is stated in a passage in Paul's Letter to the Romans. The ninth, tenth and eleventh chapters of this letter are the Israel chapters. In them Paul analyses the nature of Israel's calling. He begins his great theme with the following words: "I say the truth in Christ, I lie not, my conscience bearing witness with me in the Holy Spirit, that I have great sorrow and unceasing pain in my heart. For I could wish that I myself were accursed from Christ for my brethren's sake, my kinsmen according to the flesh: who are the Israelites; whose is the adoption, and the glory, and the covenants, and the giving of the law, and the service of God, and the promises; whose are the fathers and of whom is Christ as concerning the flesh, who is over all, God blessed for ever, Amen," Romans 9: 1–5. Then in the next chapter he makes the following statement: "For being ignorant of God's righteousness, and seeking to establish their own, they did not subject themselves to the righteousness of God," Romans 10: 3.

The conflict between the Divine and human in Jewish history is especially evident in two areas of Jewish life. The first of these is the sphere of Jewish separateness. There is a remarkable passage in the Bible which sheds much light on this subject. "Lo, it is a people that dwelleth alone, and shall not be reckoned among the nations," Numbers 23: 9. This is one of those amazing statements in the Bible which bear the unmistakable mark of Divine inspiration. For however late a date one should assign to the recording of this passage, it surely was written centuries before the Jews had acquired the characteristics described in it. Israel was to stand alone, it was not to be reckoned among the nations. The ordinary attributes which define any other nation can not define Israel. The usual norms by which we judge any other people are not applicable to the Jews. They are in this world but in a sense not of this world. "It is a people that dwelleth alone, it shall not be reckoned among the nations."

If we accept the proposition that God has chosen Israel to be His messenger to the nations, we shall agree that He must see to it that Israel shall preserve her national identity, or He would be in need of another messenger. The separation of Israel from the other nations was especially essential in the beginning of her national history, as Israel was not planted on some inaccessible, uninhabited island, but in a geographical region many of whose peoples were related to Israel by race and language. Even religiously the Israelites of the First Commonwealth, i.e. prior to the Babylonian Exile, differed little from their neighbours.

For not until the Second Commonwealth did the Jewish people really become the people of Jehovah.

Now, this policy of national separateness never met with the wholehearted approval of the entire nation of Israel. In fact the very opposite policy was pursued by the people in the days of the First Commonwealth. When political changes made it desirable to establish a more stable form of government than that provided by the so-called "Judges", the people of Israel requested Samuel, the last of these "Judges", to set up a monarchy. Samuel was shocked by their request. But we read that God comforted Samuel, saying, that it is not Samuel that the people of Israel rejected, they rejected God himself. Now, we feel sure that it is not the mere decision of the people to set up a monarchy that meant the rejection of God. Changed circumstances required a firm, stable and uninterrupted form of government. Rather it was the people's attitude that was objectionable to God. In the same breath in which they made known to Samuel their desire to establish a monarchical form of government they also told him that they want to be like all the nations, 1 Samuel 8: 19. It was this which was contrary to God's will. For it was God who determined that they shall not be like other nations.

It was not until the Remnant had returned to Palestine from the Babylonian Exile that the people of Israel began to develop a national consciousness and an awareness of being the chosen people of God. But even in the days of the Second Commonwealth the tendency to be like other nations was not dead. It was suppressed but not eradicated. In the era of Alexander the Great and his successors it burst forth in great strength. Judaism was seriously threatened by Greek civilization, as thousands of Jews adopted the Hellenistic way of life. The Maccabee Uprising stemmed the tide of Hellenism, but the later rulers of the Maccabee dynasty yielded to its influences. Following the world-wide dispersion of the Jews after the destruction of the Second Commonwealth by the Romans, the strength of assimilationism—which is the modern name for the tendency to be like all the nations—varied from generation to generation and from country to country in proportion to the degree of tolerance which they received in the various countries of their residence. In fact, had the Gentile world not practised discrimination against the Jews living in its midst, the Jews—humanly speaking—would have ceased to exist as a distinct national group.

The modern assimilationist movement among the Jews began in Germany at the end of the eighteenth and beginning of the nineteenth century. It was the direct result of the political emancipation of the Jews in Central and Western Europe which came in the wake of the French Revolution. From Germany assimilationism spread to many other countries, but it proved most successful in the West. As a result, the numerical strength of the Jewish communities in the West showed a steady decline. It is said that if not for the intermittent reinforcements by Jewish immigrants from Eastern Europe the Jewish communities in the emancipated countries of Europe would have died a natural death even had Hitlerism never come to Germany.

The advent of Nazism in Germany put an abrupt halt to the entire movement of assimilationism. As a result of Nazi activities many distinguished German families, prominent in the scientific, industrial and cultural life of Germany, have suddenly been made aware of their Jewish ancestry. The position of these people who thought of themselves as nothing but Germans is beyond comprehension to any outsider. Nazism has laid bare the complete bankruptcy of the philosophy of assimilationism as a solution to the Jewish problem.

The second area of Jewish history in which the Divine and the human have been at war with each other is the sphere of religion. For this the reader is referred to previous chapters. At the risk of repetition we wish to emphasize or re-emphasize certain characteristic features which religious Judaism has acquired by way of historical development. In the days of the First Commonwealth, which lasted from the entry into the Land of Promise until the Babylonian Exile, the people of Israel were for all practical purposes idol worshippers. This was certainly true of the Northern Kingdom, and to a large extent it was also true of the Southern Kingdom of Judah. The Northern Kingdom was wiped out by the Assyrians and it disappeared without a trace. Some 150 years later the Southern Kingdom was destroyed by Babylon, but a remnant of its people returned some seventy years later and reconstituted the Second Jewish Commonwealth.

The catastrophe which had overtaken the First Commonwealth and the experiences of the Babylonian Exile purged the Jewish Remnant of all traces of paganism. Convinced that unfaithfulness to Jehovah on the part of their fathers was responsible for the destruction of their country, the Remnant that returned at the end of the Babylonian Exile was determined that this should happen no more. This will account for the stern monotheism which the people of the Second Commonwealth developed, and also their firm resolve to live by the letter of the Law of Moses. Their devotion to, their reverence for and pre-occupation with the Mosaic Code were so great that they neglected the prophetic writings of the Old Testament. They thus deprived themselves of the opportunity to learn from the prophetic writings the true place which the Mosaic Code holds in Biblical Revelation.

In their eagerness to fulfil the Law of Moses, the Jews have developed a body of religious literature designed to interpret the meaning and application of the Law of Moses. In time this body of literature has assumed large proportions and came to be known as the Talmud. The Talmud, which is the interpretation, elaboration and amplification of the Mosaic Code, has been the basis of religious Judaism for some 1,900 years.

Now, the Prophets of the Old Testament taught again and again the importance of the religion of the heart and looked forward to the day when the Mosaic Law—the religion of the hand—would give way, and the religion of the heart would take its place (see Jeremiah 31: 31–34). But the religious Judaism of the Second Commonwealth and in the centuries following the destruction of the Second Commonwealth clung doggedly to the religion of the hand. However much the various religious groups and parties in Jewry may differ from one another, the one thing which is common to them all is their conception of religious Judaism as a religion of works. Man can never sink so low as not to be able of his own will and by his own power to make a come-back. If man's relationship to God is broken, man can re-establish it by his own strength. This emphasis on man's ability to save himself by his own moral act puts man in a position of independence in relation to God. "It ultimately implies that man is able to stand before God on his own merits."[10] It also implies that man need not appear before God empty-handed, and therefore he owes God nothing. Needless to say that such a doctrine makes for self-righteousness and generates in man's heart not humility before God but pride, that mother of all sin. It is this spirit of boastfulness, unthinkable in any Biblical saint, which breathes from the following statement attributed to one of the greatest Rabbinic authorities, Rabbi Simeon ben Yochai, and so characteristic of religious Judaism: "I have seen the children of the world to come, and they are few. If there are three, I and my son are of their number; if they are two, I and my son are they."[11]

Traditional religious Judaism has failed no less than assimilationism. It is now the religion of a small group of the Jewish people. The vast majority of the Jews stand outside of it.

Prior to the Second World War Polish Jewry numbering some three and a half million Jews was the home of traditional religious Judaism; Germany was the home of Jewish assimilationism. The destruction by the Nazis of the Polish and German Jewries has wiped out simultaneously the centre of traditional Judaism and that of Jewish assimilationism, both of which represented the two-fold Jewish approach to the problem of Jewish destiny. Is it perhaps permissible to assume that the disaster which has befallen Polish and German Jewries, apart from its human and moral aspect, bears the stamp of a Divine judgment upon two ways of life, which God has "numbered, weighed, and found wanting"?

NOTES TO CHAPTER 1

1. Quoted by Bartley C. Crum, *Behind The Silken Curtain* (Simon and Schuster: New York, 1947), p. 169.
2. Quoted by M. Jupiter, "Jews, Greeks and Romans", article in the *Contemporary Jewish Record* (New York), August 1942.
3. Hugo Valentin, *Antisemitism* (The Viking Press: New York, 1936), pp. 21-2.
4. Ibid., p. 23.
5. M. Jupiter, idem.
6. Will Herberg, *Judaism and Modern Man* (The Jewish Publication Society of America: Philadelphia, 1951), p. 273.
7. Quoted by Will Herberg, op. cit., p. 274.
8. Maurice Samuel, *The Great Hatred* (Alfred A. Knopf: New York, 1940), pp. 127-8.
9. Sigmund Freud, *Moses and Monotheism* (Alfred A. Knopf: New York, 1939), p. 145.
10. Jakób Jocz, *The Jewish People and Jesus Christ* (S.P.C.K.: London, 1954; New York, Macmillan Company), p. 289.
11. Alfred Edersheim, *The Life and Times of Jesus the Messiah* (Longmans, Green, and Co.: London, 1899), vol. i, p. 540.

THE CLIMACTIC END OF ISRAEL'S DESTINY OF SUFFERING: A. IN THE LIGHT OF THE TEACHINGS OF THE BIBLE

THE CLIMACTIC END OF ISRAEL'S DESTINY OF SUFFERING: A. IN THE LIGHT OF THE TEACHINGS OF THE BIBLE

There is a body of teachings scattered through the pages of the Bible and dealing with the "Time of the End". By the "End" is not meant the end of the world, but the end of the Age, or the end of the human phase, as it were, of world history during which man is allowed to work out his own salvation. In the Third Part of this work our attention was focused on the Gentile aspect of the Time of the End. In this and the next chapter we will dwell primarily on the Jewish phase of the same stage of world history.

Of the passages in the Bible concerned with this problem we shall cite only a few of the more generally known. But a word of caution is in place at this juncture. It is of the utmost importance to know the prophetic point of view in order to grasp the full meaning of the propetic writings of the Bible. The prophet is not primarily a historian. He does not write history. He interprets it. While the prophet may be dealing with local and contemporary issues, by and large he approaches the problems and needs of his generation from the long range and theological point of view. To the prophet the defeat of the Assyrian or Babylonian armies, while a contemporary incident, loses its purely local and contemporary aspect and assumes a transcendent significance. The hostility of these enemies of ancient Israel becomes to the prophetic seer a symbol of the bitter and abiding enmity of the ungodly world to the people of God; while in the defeat of their forces he sees a preview of the final and complete overthrow of all of Israel's enemies.

The highlights of the Biblical teachings with reference to the Jewish aspect of the "Time of the End" are as follows: Israel's Destiny of Suffering reaches its climactic end at a time of a frightful world conflict. In this World War the Land of Israel is invaded and the Jewish National Homeland is on the verge of total destruction. It is at this most critical point of Israel's history that God intervenes on behalf of Israel. He delivers a crushing blow to the invading host and accomplishes Israel's complete and permanent national restoration and its spiritual redemption.

We shall now proceed with a discussion of some of the distinguishing features of this great world conflict as it will affect the destiny of Israel at the "Time of the End".

I. IT IS THE "TIME OF JACOB'S TROUBLE"

This phrase is from a description of these future events as recorded in Jeremiah: "For thus saith Jehovah: We have heard a voice of trembling, of fear, and not of peace. Ask ye now, and see whether a man doth travail with child; wherefore do I see every man with his hands on his loins, as a woman in travail, and all faces are turned into paleness? Alas! for that day is great, so that none is like it: it is even the time of Jacob's trouble; but he shall be saved out of it," Jeremiah 30: 5–7. If one reads the whole of chapter 30 and several of the following chapters one will realize that while the immediate reference may be to the Babylonian invasion of the Land of Israel, the events described in these chapters actually embrace a much larger era of Israel's history. "For that day is great, so that none is like it," we are told. The catastrophe which befell Israel's Land in A.D. 70 and A.D. 132–135 was definitely worse than that of the Babylonian invasion. The events sketched in these chapters do not constitute a true and factual record either of the sufferings brought on by the Babylonian invasion, or the partial restoration which came at the end of the Babylonian exile. But to the prophet the Babylonian invasion of the Land of Israel became the foreshadowing of another invasion—the last and worst—to take place at the "Time of the End".

In the book of Daniel 12: 1 we have reference to the same event as recorded in Jeremiah 30: 5–7. Even the expression "a time of trouble" used in Daniel is strikingly similar to the "time of Jacob's trouble" which occurs in Jeremiah. ". . . And there shall be a time of trouble such as never was since there was a nation even to that same time: and at that time thy people shall be delivered, every one that shall be found written in the book", Daniel 12: 1.

In the New Testament we find a similar description of the same critical stage in Israel's history. "For then shall be great tribulation, such as hath not been from the beginning of the world until now, no, nor ever shall be", Matthew 24: 21.

In Revelation, the last book in the New Testament, the events described in chapters 6 to 16 appear to deal with happenings in the Land of Israel at the Time of the End. In chapter 7, verse 14 this period is called "the great tribulation".

The First World War was probably the bloodiest conflict as compared with any other war which had preceded it. The Second World War exceeded the First in its cruelty, frightfulness, and power to wreak widespread destruction. Every successive bloody conflict of world-wide scope seems to outdo those which preceded it. This, however, is not what the Biblical writers have in mind when speaking of the era of "Jacob's trouble". They see it as part of a most frightful and most destructive conflict ever to be experienced by the human race. Notice that in Matthew 24: 21 we are told that it will be a time "such as has not been from the beginning of the world until now, no, nor ever shall be", and in the next verse Jesus declares that "except those days had been shortened, no flesh would have been saved: but for the elect's sake those days shall be shortened", Matthew 24: 22.

II. THE COMING INVASION OF THE LAND OF ISRAEL

Daniel, Ezekiel and Zechariah, all three, speak of an invasion of the Land of Israel. If we carefully study these passages, in and not out of their context, we shall find that the invasion spoken of in these three prophetic books is none other than the last one which is to take place at the "Time of the End".

The passages in Daniel concerning the destiny of Israel in the "Time of the End" era are recorded in the second, seventh, eighth, ninth, tenth, eleventh and twelfth chapters. The unbiased and well-informed student of the Bible will easily convince himself that apart from the occasional allusion to contemporary events the facts related in the above-mentioned chapters actually deal with the "Time of the End". The Holy Land is invaded (see Daniel 8: 9; 11: 16, 41), and war is waged against the people of Israel. The only similarity between Antiochus Epiphanes and the head of the invading army of the future is the blasphemous character of both. But even this is only a superficial resemblance as may be seen from a close study of the character and the doings of these two personalities. Antiochus Epiphanes merely tried to force the Jews to accept the religion and way of life of the Greek world. The head of the invading army of the future is a Satanic person who will pose as a god and demand homage which men pay to God only.

In the thirty-eighth and thirty-ninth chapters of Ezekiel we have a detailed description of this invasion of the Land of Israel by a powerful army made up of many national groups. Since Ezekiel was one of the exiles in Babylon he could not possibly have referred to the Babylonian invasion which at that time had been a thing of the past, nor does the outcome of the invasion of Ezekiel thirty-eight and thirty-nine bear the slightest resemblance either to the invasion of Antiochus Epiphanes in the second century B.C. or to the experiences under the Roman regime in the first century B.C. and first century A.D. The invasion which Ezekiel is speaking of is one by an international force from the north. Rosh, Meshech, Tubal, Persia, Cush, Put, Gomer and Togarmah —these are neither Syrian nor Roman names. Then, also, the description of the restored Jewish community in the Land of Israel at the time of this invasion bears a striking similarity to the people of the present State of Israel. This may be seen from the following passage in Ezekiel. ". . . In the latter years thou shalt come into the land that is brought back from the sword, that is gathered out of many peoples, upon the mountains of Israel, which have been a continual waste; but it is brought forth out of the peoples, and they shall dwell securely, all of them. And thou shalt ascend, thou shalt come like a storm, thou shalt be like a cloud to cover the land, thou, and all thy hordes, and many peoples with thee . . . To take the spoil and to take the prey; to turn thy hand against the waste places that are now inhabited, and against the people that are gathered out of the nations, that have gotten cattle and goods, that dwell in the middle of the earth", Ezekiel 38: 8–9, 12.

Finally in Zechariah chapters twelve, thirteen and fourteen we have another description of this last invasion of Palestine. Again we are told that this is an invasion by many nations, Zechariah 12: 2, 3, 9 and 14: 2. Let us cite one of these passages: "For I will gather all nations against Jerusalem to battle; and the city shall be taken, and the houses rifled, and the women ravished; and half of the city shall go forth into captivity, and [or but] the residue of the people shall not be cut off from the city", Zechariah 14: 2.

A deeper insight into the meaning of the phrase the "time of Jacob's trouble" may be gained if we recall that particular experience in Jacob's life which Jeremiah undoubtedly had in mind. Jacob is the father of the twelve tribes of Israel. He spent a large part of his life in exile away from his native land. After some twenty years he gathered up his family and his material possessions and started out on his way back to the land of Canaan. When he crossed the border into the land of Canaan he began to lay plans of appeasing his brother Esau with whom he has had a long-standing feud. It was this enmity which Esau bore towards him that caused Jacob to flee his country and seek temporary refuge in his mother's native land and among her relatives. Has Jacob during these many years of exile learned—what God unquestionably intended him to learn—that the means which he had used back at home to secure the Abrahamic Covenant were dishonourable and unworthy of that Covenant? No sooner did Jacob re-enter his native land than word reached him that Esau was marching against him at the head of a large band of armed men. Upon hearing this report we are told: "Then Jacob was greatly afraid and was distressed . . ." Genesis 32: 7 (32: 8 Heb.). The word "distressed" used here is the same Hebrew word which is translated "trouble" in Jeremiah 30: 7 "Alas! for that day is great, so that none is like it: it is even the time of Jacob's trouble."

After dividing up his family into two groups so that if Esau attacked one the other could escape; after doing what he could to avert, or at least to soften, the blow which might be in store for him, Jacob decided to spend some time in prayer. He remained in seclusion on one side of the brook of Jabbok where he unburdened himself before God. Did Jacob in the loneliness of that dark night, when confronted by God, do some heart and soul searching? Did he come to feel that God might have a purpose in his present plight? Certainly God could not permit that Esau should with one stroke destroy him and his family. What would in that case become of God's Covenant with Abraham and Isaac. But if God was to use him to accomplish His purposes, the purposes of the Abrahamic Covenant, he, Jacob, will have to rid himself of much which is objectionable in his old nature and experience a spiritual rebirth. This is what has actually taken place when that dark night of intense spiritual conflict was over. Jacob came out of it physically crippled, but not destroyed. Spiritually, however, he was a new creature, Jacob became Israel.

In his discussion of Israel's future destiny as outlined in chapter thirty and those which follow it, Jeremiah might have wished to emphasize the similarity in the course of events in the life of Jacob upon his return to the land of Canaan, and in the history of Israel at the time of her future restoration. Upon returning to the land of her forefathers Israel, like Jacob of old, will encounter old enemies. Before her redemption has become full and complete she will become involved in a life-and-death struggle for her survival. This will be Israel's supreme national crisis, the "time of Jacob's trouble", a time of unprecedented distress. But she will not become submerged. A remnant will be saved, the nation will experience a spiritual rebirth and achieve a full and permanent national restoration.

III. Analysis of the "Time of Jacob's Trouble"

1. POLITICAL UPHEAVALS IN THE MEDITERRANEAN AREA

These political disturbances in the Mediterranean area are described in the book of Daniel. "Daniel spake and said, I saw in my vision by night, and, behold, the four winds of heaven brake forth upon the great sea", Daniel 7: 2. "The great sea" in the Old Testament refers to the Mediterranean. In the book of Numbers 34: 6–7 we read: "and for the western border [of the Promised Land] ye shall have a great sea for the border thereof: this shall be your west border. And this shall be your north border: from the great sea ye shall mark out for you mount Hor." Mount Hor is located right against the Mediterranean. In Joshua 1: 4 the western border of the Promised Land is again said to be the great sea. ". . . and unto the great sea, toward the going down of the sun, shall be your border". See also the following passages in which the "great sea" can refer only to the Mediterranean: Joshua 9: 1; 15: 12; 15: 47; 23: 4. Ezekiel 47: 10, 15, 19, 20; 48: 28.

In the course of these political disturbances four successive political powers will arise in the Mediterranean area. These political powers are portrayed under the symbolic representation of certain beasts perhaps to indicate their character and conduct, (Daniel 7: 3–8, 17.) Whether all four powers or only the fourth power shall arise in the "Time of the End" era is not certain. Daniel's interest is focussed on the fourth power, as this political unit becomes the principal actor in the drama of the last phase of the "Times of the Gentiles". This political organization emerges as a league or confederacy of ten Mediterranean states. "After this I saw in the night visions, and, behold, a fourth beast, terrible and powerful, and strong exceedingly . . . and it had ten horns", Daniel 7: 7. These ten horns mean ten states as explained further on in the same chapter: "And as for the ten horns, out of this kingdom shall ten kings arise . . .", Daniel 7: 24.

According to the account in Daniel, chapter eleven, Israel, Egypt, and Assyria (present-day Iraq) will at first not be members of this Mediterranean confederacy. Assyria (present-day Iraq), however, will in due time be conquered, and added to the Mediterranean Confederacy. In the course of time the Mediterranean Confederacy will come under the leadership of one designated in Daniel as the "Little Horn" referring to his lowly descent. This "Little Horn" originates in one of the four areas into which the empire of Alexander the Great had been divided (see Daniel 8: 3-9). It appears that the purpose of the passage in Daniel 8: 3-9 is to indicate the geographical area, not the time factor, where the "Little Horn" of the "Time of the End" era will originate. He will arise in one of the four territories into which the empire of Alexander the Great had been divided after his death. As he is considered to be the same person who in Ezekiel thirty-eight and thirty-nine invades Palestine under the name of Gog, it is thought that the place of origin of the "Little Horn" of Daniel is the region between the Black and Caspian Seas in Asia Minor.[1]

This "Little Horn", who begins his career as an insignificant ruler of a small people, ("contemptible person", "with a small people", Daniel 11: 21, 23), takes advantage of unsettled conditions in the Middle East and establishes himself as the ruler of Assyria (Iraq) (Daniel 11: 21). In time he attacks and subdues three member states of the Mediterranean Confederacy and gains the leadership of this Mediterranean Confederacy which from now on is ruled by him from Assyria (Iraq) as the centre of his newly acquired empire. This will bring to fulfilment the prediction that the city of Babylon shall be rebuilt and become once again the capital of a world empire. Babylon was the centre of the nations' first rebellion against God as recorded in the Tower of Babel episode in Genesis. The "Times of the Gentiles" era in relation to Israel began when Babylon, centuries after the Tower of Babel episode, had become the capital of Nebuchadnezzar's world empire. Babylon continued as the capital of the Persian world empire after the fall of the Chaldean empire. It remained the capital of the world empire of Alexander the Great after he had conquered Persia, and Babylon is to become once again, and for the last time, the capital of the powerful world empire of the Mediterranean-Asia Minor Confederacy, which is the most Gentile world power of Nebuchadnezzar's dream as recorded in Daniel, chapter two.

It is when the "Little Horn" becomes the leader of this new world power centred in Assyria (Iraq) that he is referred to in Daniel as the "king of the north" (i.e. second king of the north) (Daniel 11: 40). He is at the head of the "northern army" mentioned in the book of Joel 2: 20. He is the "Assyrian" in Isaiah 10: 5. Not only is Assyria north with reference to Palestine but to invade Palestine from Assyria the invading army would take the northerly route to avoid the more direct westerly route leading through impassable desert country.

Should the reader object to our exposition of these Biblical writings on the ground that in the Bible they record contemporary events we would ask him to study carefully the context of these passages and see for himself whether the passages in question concern contemporary events. Take, for example, the passage in Isaiah 10: 5 to 12: 6 where the "Assyrian" episode is alluded to. Have all the events mentioned in this section ever become fulfilled in Israel's history? We have here a description not only of the invasion of the Land of Israel by the "Assyrian" but what this invasion is supposed to do for the people of Israel. Its purpose is stated in 10: 12, 22–23. "Wherefore it shall come to pass, that, when the Lord hath performed his whole work upon mount Zion and on Jerusalem, I will punish the fruit of the stout heart of the king of Assyria, and the glory of his high looks. For though thy people, Israel, be as the sand of the sea, only a remnant of them shall return: a destruction is determined, overflowing with righteousness. For a full end, and that determined, will the Lord, Jehovah of hosts, make in the midst of the whole land." If God has accomplished the full measure of disciplining Israel by means of the Assyrian and Babylonian invasions in the days of the First Commonwealth why has Israel not been restored fully and permanently after the Babylonian Exile?

If we return to the book of Daniel we again read of events which have never as yet taken place. Take, for example, the human image of Nebuchadnezzar's dream. In Daniel's interpretation of this dream we read the following: "And in the days of those kings shall the God of heaven set up a kingdom which shall never be destroyed, nor shall the sovereignty thereof be left to another people, but it shall break in pieces and consume all these kingdoms, and it shall stand forever", Daniel 2: 44. Have these things ever taken place in the history of the world? And so it is with the remaining messages in Daniel and the other books in the Bible whose subject is the "Time of the End". The total picture in every instance just do not fit into contemporary history.

That there may be no confusion in the minds of men many Biblical writers are careful to emphasise that the message is for the "end of the days". This subject has been discussed in Part Three of this book. The same emphasis is particularly prominent in Daniel. Since Daniel, like many other contemporary Jews, were led to believe that the end of the Babylonian Exile will bring total and permanent restoration of the Israelitish kingdom, and since some of the visions vouchsafed to Daniel touch on contemporary events, it was extremely important to impress on Daniel the real time factor of the prophetic messages. And so in chapter two, when interpreting Nebuchadnezzar's dream of the four world empires, Daniel makes this remark at the very conclusion of the message. "The great God hath made known to the king what shall come to pass hereafter", Daniel 2: 45*

In the vision of the ram and the he-goat of chapter eight there was a danger that Daniel would think it concerned relations between Persia and the rising power of Greece or Macedonia. To set Daniel straight on this the following statement is made by the interpreter of the vision. ". . . But he said unto me, Understand, O son of man; for the vision belongeth to the time of the end." "And he said, Behold, I will make thee know what shall be in the latter time of the indignation; for it belongeth to the appointed time of the end." "And the vision of the evenings and mornings which hath been told is true: but shut thou up the vision; for it belongeth to many days to come", Daniel 8: 17, 19, 26.

In order to prepare Daniel's mind for the last group of prophetic revelations as recorded in chapters eleven and twelve the angelic messenger declares to him: "Now I am come to make thee understand what shall befall thy people in the latter days; for the vision is yet for many days", Daniel 10: 14. And, finally, in the last

* See also Daniel 2: 28 and discussion of the meaning of the term "Latter days" on page 252.

chapter of the book of Daniel, at the conclusion of the whole series of prophetic utterances, we have the following deeply significant words: "But thou, O Daniel, shut up the words, and seal the book, even to the time of the end: many shall run to and fro, and knowledge shall be increased"; Daniel 12: 4. "And I heard, but I understood not: then said I, O my lord, what shall be the issue [the latter end] of these things? And he said, "Go thy way, Daniel; for the words are shut up and sealed till the time of the end", Daniel 12: 8-9.

The words in Daniel 12: 4, 8-9 are crucial for the proper understanding of Daniel and, for that matter, of many of the other prophetic writings. "Shut up the words, and seal the book, even to the time of the end." Here we have an indication that for a long time the contents of Daniel will be sealed, i.e. their meaning will be imperfectly understood. It is only as we will approach the "Time of the End" era that men will gain a deeper insight into the meaning of these revelations. This is what many believe to be the meaning of the statement "Many shall run to and fro and knowledge shall be increased." When we come nearer the stage of world history designated as the "Time of the End", contemporary events will gradually illumine and unfold the full significance of these prophetic revelations.

We shall now resume the account of the doings of the "Little Horn". He has become the leader of a powerful world empire. He engages in war activities and his realm expands towards the south, east and in the direction of the Holy Land, Daniel 8: 9. His expansion to the east brings Persia [Iran] into his sphere of influence. This accounts for the presence of Persians in the armed forces invading the Land of Israel as recorded in Ezekiel 38: 5. His expansion southward adds Egypt, Ethiopia and Libya to his realm, Daniel 11: 43. Some of Israel's neighbouring peoples escape his destructive blows, probably by surrendering to him in good time, Daniel 11: 41.

As to Israel, it will be offered an alliance of some sort. It has grown prosperous in the years since her partial restoration (see Ezekiel 38: 10-13), but what chance of escape does a small people have in a world of power politics? In Daniel this pact between Israel and the world power of the "Little Horn" is mentioned first in chapter 9: 27. "And he shall make a firm covenant with many for one week" [a period of seven, i.e. seven years]. It is described in more detail in Daniel chapter eleven. Apparently there will be a sharp division of opinion in Israel about the wisdom of such an alliance. The godly group will be opposed to it. The ungodly part of the nation will strongly favour the proposition. The "Little Horn" will take full advantage of this situation by making his offer especially attractive to the ungodly group. The timing of this offer of a pact with Israel may be occasioned by some temporary military reverses which the "Little Horn" will suffer, (Daniel 11: 30–35). The opposition of the godly minority party in Israel will not prevail, and the alliance will be concluded.

After three and a half years the treaty with Israel is abrogated. It is possible that the "Little Horn" is led to take this step by the growing restlessness among the subdued nations of his empire (Daniel 11: 44). The uncertain international situation and, possibly, also the growing strength of the underground resistance movement in Israel make it necessary for him to take a more direct hand in Israel's affairs. Be that as it may, the breaking of this treaty begins a regime of terror. This is the beginning of the "time of Jacob's trouble", the "Tribulation" era, lasting three and a half years (see Daniel 7: 25; 9: 27; 12: 7; Revelation 12: 14).

By this time the "Little Horn" is virtual master of the world, history's most cruel, most profane and most blasphemous person. The centuries-old rebellion of the nations against God, and human sin and depravity—all find their culmination in the person of the "Little Horn". In him wicked man makes a last and desperate attempt to dethrone God. The most complete description of his character and doings, and the world-wide distress of this three-and-a-half-year period is to be found in the book of Revelation.

In the New Testament the "Little Horn" is known under several names. The Apostle Paul speaks of him as "the man of sin" and "the son of perdition" in 2 Thessalonians 2: 3; in Revelation he is referred to as the beast; the Apostle John calls him the Anti-Christ in 1 John 2: 18. It has been suggested that the significance for Israel of this three-and-a-half-year period of "Jacob's trouble" is derived from the fact that this is exactly the time of the earthly ministry of Jesus the Messiah. As Israel has rejected Him, who for three and a half years had been in their midst, going about and doing good, she is destined to spend the same time interval in the clutches of the Anti-Christ, the false Messiah.

2. ISRAEL'S MIRACULOUS DELIVERY

The big invasion of Israel by the forces of many nations under the leadership of the "Little Horn" mentioned in Daniel is described in detail in Ezekiel thirty-eight and thirty-nine, and in Zechariah twelve, thirteen and fourteen. The courage and determination of the godly remnant in Israel, its open defiance of the policies of the "Little Horn" and his Jewish collaborators, has encouraged many in Israel to follow their example. In the book of Revelation the number of this movement is given as 144,000. Whether this is an actual or symbolic number does not matter. Their influence will spread far and wide beyond the borders of Israel and a large number of Gentiles in the whole world will be encouraged to take an open stand on the side of God and against the blasphemous tyrant (see Revelation 7: 4–14). It is possible that it is this state of affairs which will prompt the "Little Horn" tyrant to strike at Israel with all his fury and to exterminate this centre of resistance which by now will have become world-wide in scope.

It is this invasion of Israel, whose obvious purpose is to wipe Israel off the face of the earth, which brings about God's direct intervention. It is described in detail in many of the prophetic books of the Bible, especially in Ezekiel and Zechariah. Here are a few passages from these two prophetic books.

Ezekiel 38: 18–22: "And it shall come to pass in that day, when Gog shall come against the land of Israel, saith the Lord Jehovah, that my wrath shall come up into my nostrils. For in my jealousy and in the fire of my wrath have I spoken. Surely in that day there shall be a great shaking in the land of Israel; so that the fishes of the sea, and the birds of the heavens, and the beasts of the field, and all creeping things that creep upon the earth, and all the men that are upon the face of the earth, shall shake at my presence, and the mountains shall be thrown down, and the steep places shall fall, and every wall shall fall to the ground. And I will call for a sword against him unto all my mountains, saith the Lord Jehovah: every man's sword shall be against his brother. And with pestilence and with blood will I enter into judgment with him; and I will rain upon him, and upon his hordes, and upon the many peoples that are with him, an overflowing shower, and great hailstones, fire, and brimstone."

Zechariah 12: 2-4: "Behold, I will make Jerusalem a cup of reeling unto all the peoples round about, and upon Judah also shall it be [and against Judah also shall it fall to be] in the siege against Jerusalem. And it shall come to pass in that day, that I will make Jerusalem a burdensome stone for all the peoples; all that burden themselves with it shall be sore wounded; and all the nations of the earth shall be gathered together against it. In that day, saith Jehovah, I will smite every horse with terror, and his rider with madness; and I will open mine eyes upon the house of Judah, and will smite every horse of the peoples with blindness."

Zechariah 14: 2-4, 12-13: "For I will gather all nations against Jerusalem to battle; and the city shall be taken, and the houses rifled, and the women ravished; and half of the city shall go forth into captivity, and [but] the residue of the people shall not be cut off from the city. Then shall Jehovah go forth, and fight against those nations, as when he fought in the day of battle. And his feet shall stand in that day upon the mount of Olives, which is before Jerusalem on the east ... And this shall be the plague wherewith Jehovah will smite all the peoples that have warred against Jerusalem: their flesh shall consume away while they stand upon their feet, and their eyes shall consume away in their sockets, and their tongue shall consume away in their mouth. And it shall come to pass in that day, that a great tumult from Jehovah shall be among them; and they shall lay hold everyone on the hand of his neighbour, and his hand shall rise up against the hand of his neighbour."

Zechariah 13: 8-9: "And it shall come to pass, that in all the land, saith Jehovah, two parts therein shall be cut off and die; but the third shall be left therein. And I will bring the third part into the fire, and will refine them as silver is refined, and will try them as gold is tried. They shall call on my name, and I will hear them: I will say, It is my people; and they shall say, Jehovah is my God."

3. ISRAEL'S SPIRITUAL REBIRTH

In the vision of the valley of the dry bones as recorded in Ezekiel thirty-seven the prophet describes Israel's national restoration followed by her spiritual regeneration (Ezekiel 37: 10). The true time sequence of these events is shown in Zechariah. The passage in Zechariah 13: 8-9 cited above relates the fiery trials which Israel shall experience in her land in the period of "Jacob's trouble". God will make use of world events to bring about Israel's spiritual regeneration. Israel's changed attitude to God is well described in Isaiah sixty-four from which we shall quote a few passages:

"O that thou wouldest rend the heavens, that thou wouldest come down, that the mountains might quake at thy presence ... When thou didst terrible things which we looked not for, thou camest down, the mountains quaked at thy presence ... For we are all become as one that is unclean, and all our righteousnesses are as a polluted garment: and we all do fade as a leaf; and our iniquities, like the wind, take us away. And there is none that calleth upon thy name, that stirreth up himself to take hold of thee; for thou hast hid thy face from us, and hast consumed us by means of our iniquities", Isaiah 64: 1, 3, 6–7 (63: 19; 64: 2, 5–6 Heb.).

In this remarkable passage we have a complete and radical change in Israel's attitude to God. She confesses her utter sinfulness. She acknowledges that her self-righteousness is filthy rags. She declares that the whole nation has become estranged from God. She hints that her godlessness is in some way related to God's turning away His face from Israel. She, therefore, pleads for a new revelation from heaven. Thus Israel's history arrives at the same stage of development as Gentile history does, as we have shown in the Third Part of this book. Both Jews and Gentiles will confess man's complete failure, when left to himself, to work out his own salvation.

The answer to Israel's confession and prayer is recorded in Zechariah. A new revelation from God comes simultaneously with God's visible and direct intervention in the hour of Israel's greatest peril. "And it shall come to pass in that day, that I will seek to destroy all the nations that come against Jerusalem. And I will pour upon the house of David, and upon the inhabitants of Jerusalem, the spirit of grace and of supplication; and they shall look unto me whom they have pierced; and they shall mourn for him, as one mourneth for his only son, and shall be in bitterness for him, as one that is in bitterness for his first born. In that day shall there be a great mourning in Jerusalem, as the mourning in Hadadrimmon [on the occasion of the death of young King Josiah slain by Pharaoh Necho as recorded in 2 Kings 23: 29–30] in the valley of Megiddon. And the land shall mourn, every family apart. ... In that day there shall be a fountain opened to the house of David and to the inhabitants of Jerusalem, for sin and for uncleanness", Zechariah 12: 9–12; 13: 1.

Israel's spiritual rebirth will not be the work of man, it will not be brought about by human means or effort. It will be the work of God. God will pour out upon them His spirit of grace and supplication. The Jew of today cannot pray. Even if he does pray he merely recites words. It is only when God shall grant them the spirit of grace and supplication will the Jews be able to pray. This new spirit in them will remove their spiritual blindness. "And they shall look unto me whom they have pierced." Many Rabbinic authorities have interpreted this passage as applying to Messiah the son of Joseph. Not being able to reconcile the prophetic descriptions of a suffering and conquering Messiah as belonging to one and the same person, Rabbinic imagination has created a second Messianic person, Messiah, the son of Joseph, who was to suffer and die, while the Biblical Messiah, the son of David, would be victorious over Israel's enemies. Thus Rabbi Abraham ben Ezra of the twelfth century interprets the above passage in Zechariah 12: 10 in this fashion: "All the heathen shall look to me to see what I shall do to those who pierced Messiah, the son of Joseph."[2] Abarbanel (Rabbi Dan Isaac ben Jehudah who lived in the fifteenth century) states: "It is more correct to interpret the passage of Messiah, the son of Joseph, as our Rabbis, of blessed memory, have interpreted it in the treatise Sukkah, for he shall be a mighty man of valour of the tribe of Joseph, and shall at first be captain of the Lord's host in that war (namely, against Gog and Magog), but in that war he shall die."[3]

Finally this passage from Moses Alshech, another Rabbinic authority, who lived in Safed, Palestine, in the second half of the sixteenth century: "I will do yet a third thing, and that is, that 'they shall look unto Me', for they shall lift up their eyes únto me in perfect repentance, when they see Him whom they pierced, that is Messiah, the Son of Joseph; for our Rabbis, of blessed memory, have said that He will take upon Himself all the guilt of Israel, and shall then be slain in the war to make an atonement in such manner that it shall be accounted as if Israel had pierced Him, for on account of their sin He has died; and, therefore, in order that it may be reckoned to them as a perfect atonement, they will repent and look to the blessed One, saying, that there is none beside Him to forgive those that mourn on account of Him who died for their sin: this is the meaning of 'They shall look upon Me'".[4]

From the above we may see how difficult it is for well-meaning Jews to get away from the fact that this "simple, unadorned", yet profoundly significant, statement in Zechariah 12 : 10 must mean what it says, that Israel's spiritual rebirth will be accomplished by the sudden reappearance of her Messiah who had died for her sins. History knows only of one such Person who died for the atonement of Israel's sins and for the sins of all mankind. This Person is Jesus of Nazareth, the Son of David.

NOTES TO CHAPTER 2

1. G. H. Lang, *The Histories and Prophecies of Daniel* (The Paternoster Press London, 1950), Chapters VII, VIII, XI, and Appendix C.
2. David Baron, *The Visions and Prophecies of Zechariah* (Morgan & Scott: London, 1919), p. 440.
3. Ibid., pp. 440-1.
4. Ibid., pp. 441-2.

THE CLIMACTIC END OF ISRAEL'S DESTINY OF SUFFERING: B. IN THE LIGHT OF CURRENT WORLD EVENTS

THE CLIMACTIC END OF ISRAEL'S DESTINY OF SUFFERING: B. IN THE LIGHT OF CURRENT WORLD EVENTS

I. THE REAWAKENING OF THE MIDDLE EAST

Prior to the First World War the passages in the Bible which speak of a final restoration of Israel must have imposed a severe strain on the faith of many a Bible student. For centuries Palestine had been a ruined, desolate, deserted, insignificant province of the backward and disintegrating Turkish empire. How could the Jews ever be restored to a country which had remained wrecked for ages?

Moreover, the same restoration passages in the Bible speak also of an unusual amount of activity on the part of the nations surrounding Palestine. But these nations had for many centuries been out of existence. When Israel became subjugated over 2,500 years ago, first by Assyria, and finally by Babylon, her neighbours on her northern, eastern and southern borders had met with a similar fate. But whereas the Jews refused to become absorbed by the Babylonians, and after seventy years gained permission to return to Palestine and rebuild their national life, the peoples of Palestine's border countries did not fare quite the same. In the first place, they did not manifest the same national survival strength as the Jews did. They mixed, mingled and intermarried freely with the invaders, and thought nothing of adopting the invaders' religion, language and culture. They had been conquered successively by Assyria, Babylon, Persia, Alexander the Great and his successors, and Rome. With the rise of Mohammedanism these countries were overrun by the Arabs and subsequently they were taken over by Turkey. So for some 2,500 years the border nations of Palestine had not known political independence and during this long era had changed hands many times. Economically, they fared even worse. Once densely populated, with a thriving agriculture, a flourishing industry and commerce, these regions, under the Arabs and Turks, became impoverished and depopulated, presenting to the outside visitor a sorry spectacle of abject misery, apathy, filth and disease. Humanly speaking, the nations which had inhabited these countries 2,500 years ago were dead and buried long, long ago. How could their countries possibly play an active part in the era of Israel's restoration as maintained in the Bible?

What has happened in the Near and Middle East, and in the rest of Asia, since the First, and especially since the Second World War, is current history and common knowledge. The picture in that part of the world has radically changed almost overnight. Simultaneously with the Jewish colonization programme in Palestine there began a reawakening movement among the nations of the East, with the result that political conditions prevailing in and around Palestine today resemble very closely those in existence in Biblical times: Israel is back in Palestine, her neighbours on her northern border are Syria and Lebanon, on her southern border Egypt, while Jordan is her eastern neighbour. Iraq, the successor to ancient Babylonia, is in the north-east of this area. So we have now the same political line-up of nations in and around Palestine as in ancient times with some minor changes in the names or the territorial holdings of some of these nations.

II. ARAB HOSTILITY TO ISRAEL

The Arab nations are the peoples of Egypt, the Arab Peninsula, Jordan, Iraq, Syria and Lebanon. Racially, the peoples of the Arab Peninsula are probably the pure Arabs. The other nations listed above are primarily Arab by language and, in part at least, in their world outlook and way of life. The combined size of the territories of their countries amounts to over 1,600,000 square miles with a population of over 40,000,000. The State of Israel occupies an area of 8,048 square miles with a population of less than 2,000,000. Relations between the State of Israel and the Arab states present the strangest phenomenon in international affairs. While the war between them officially ended with the conclusion of the 1949 armistice there are no dealings between them. Why should nations numbering some 40,000,000 people, occupying a combined territory of over 1,600,000 square miles, and having vast underpopulated spaces, nurture such an intense hatred for a people less than 2,000,000, crowded into a small area of 8,048 square miles? What is the meaning of this? Whatever explanation one may offer will be unsatisfactory unless one takes into consideration the prophetic element. This was beautifully stated by Charles Malik, the Lebanese statesman who is an Arab Christian: "The rise of Israel is certainly a great historic event whose total consequences it is impossible now to foretell. But it is safe to affirm that as a result the Near East has now entered upon a new critical stage of development. The fate of the Near East is now intertwined with that of Israel . . . The Old Testament theological challenge has to deal with the great mystery of Ishmael and Isaac. Whoever broods with a pure and loving heart upon this mystery and contemplates in its light the present spiritual situation between Jews and Arabs in the Near East must experience a profound emotion of wonder. What we behold is something not purely immanent, not something just human or historical or economic or political: there is a significance splashing irresistibly and mysteriously upon us from the beyond . . . To dismiss the present conflict between the children of Isaac and the children of Ishmael, who are all children of Abraham, as just another ordinary politico-economic struggle, is to have no sense whatever for the awful and holy and ultimate in history. When history shall finally reveal its secret (of which we here and now already catch a real glimpse), the present confrontation between Isaac and Ishmael may turn out to be . . . one of the major keys unlocking that secret."[1]

That the attitude of the Arab nations to the State of Israel is a revival of the enmity which prevailed between ancient Israel and its neighbouring nations may be seen from the following statement as recorded in Psalm 83: 1–8 (83: 2–9 Heb.):

"O God, keep not thou silence: hold not thy peace, and be not still, O God.

For, lo, thine enemies make a tumult; And they that hate thee have lifted up the head.

They take crafty counsel against thy people, And consult together against thy hidden ones.

They have said, Come, and let us cut them off from being a nation; that the name of Israel may be no more in remembrance. For they have consulted together with one consent; against thee do they make a covenant:

The tents of Edom and the Ishmaelites; Moab and the Hagarenes;

Gebal, and Ammon, and Amalek; Philistia with the inhabitants of Tyre:

Assyria also is joined with them. . . ."

Some of the nations named above have disappeared or lost their national distinctive identity by intermarriage and fusion with other nations. There is no question that present-day Arab nations, with the possible exception of Egypt, are descendants of some, if not all, of those listed above. In any case, present-day Arab peoples inhabit the same border countries of the present State of Israel as those mentioned in the Psalm. Whether the above Psalm alludes to an alliance of Israel's neighbours aimed against Israel in the time of Jehoshaphat as recorded in 2 Chronicles 20, or in the time of the Maccabees as found in 1 Maccabees 5, does not matter. We have in these days an identical situation: a league of the same bordering nations with the avowed purpose of wiping Israel off the map. In this Psalm Israel states that her surrounding countries have formed an alliance whose aim is to destroy Israel. "Come, and let us cut them off from being a nation; that the name of Israel be no more in remembrance." The following is an excerpt of a recent statement by one of the Arab rulers as reported in the press: "Israel to the Arab world is like a cancer to the human body and the only way of remedy is to uproot it just like a cancer . . ." Then he went on to say that the Arab states should be prepared to sacrifice up to 10,000,000 of their people in order to wipe out Israel.[2]

III. THE PROBLEM OF THE MIDDLE EAST

This problem consists in the great strategic value and the huge oil wealth of this region on one hand, and the marked weakness and instability of this area's political, economic and social structure. Edgar A. Mowrer once said that "nothing is more likely to cause trouble than great wealth in feeble hands. It is an invitation to aggression. Except for the American-backed Turks and the Palestine Jews, there is nothing in the Middle East that could resist a Soviet cavalry raid, still less a tank column".[3]

The Mediterranean area, especially its eastern part, has been the hub of civilization for some five thousand years. When this portion of the Mediterranean region became part of the Muslim world and was subsequently cut off from Europe it gradually slipped into a state of economic and cultural stagnation. With the disintegration of the Turkish empire European influence began to reassert itself in this region and the Middle East roused itself to a new life.

The size of the Middle East is about that of Europe. Its population is slightly over 100,000,000. Less than half of this number are Arabic speaking.[4] The geographic location of the Middle East is most unique. It is the meeting point of three continents: Europe, Asia and North Africa. It lies between the two largest population masses in the world: that of South-east Asia and Europe. Its political importance may be seen from a glance at the map. To the north-east from this area lie Russia and China with a combined population of some 700,000,000 under communist rule; while south-east from here lie India and Pakistan with a population of over 400,000,000. Some of the Middle East nations have a common border with Russia. The Middle East possesses one of the most important international waterways, the Suez Canal, cut through in the second half of the nineteenth century, and affording a vital communication link between Europe and the Far East.

The most important single asset of the Middle East is oil. The bulk of the world's oil supplies are concentrated in two areas: in the western hemisphere it is centred on the Caribbean Sea, in the eastern hemisphere it is centred south of the Caucasus. The Near East alone has the largest oil reserves in the world. These account for over 40 per cent of the total known oil deposits in the whole world, and more oil reserves continue to be located there. The factories of Europe, its ships and planes, depend on the Middle East oil for their source of power. It is noteworthy that the oil fields in the Near East are concentrated in the Persian Gulf area. It is in this region, it will be recalled, that the last Gentile World power will, according to the Bible, have its centre.

As long as the Middle East was a self-contained unit, shut off from Western influence, there was no Middle East problem in the sense in which it is today. The present crisis of the Middle East dates back to its encounter with the West. The Middle East suffers from both the good and the ill effects of Westernization. The bad effects are primarily those of secularism which lies at the root of the crisis in the rest of the world. The good effects are those of Western technology, Western ideas of individual and religious liberty, and the Western concept of democracy and the nation-state. It is the clash between the dynamic civilization of the West and the static and stagnant civilization of the Middle East which has precipitated a conflict in almost every area of life in this region. This conflict is greatly intensified by this region's geographic position between two spheres of influence representing the two opposing camps of the world, and by the presence in its midst of the all-important oil reserves mentioned above. It is the failure on the part of the Middle East peoples to resolve this crisis which makes this area so highly unstable and a source of grave anxiety to the free world, and of deep satisfaction to the forces of communism.

We shall now review in a general way the principal elements which enter into the making of the Middle East crisis. Whether we shall use the term "Near East" or "Middle East" our discussion of this subject will be limited to the Arab-speaking nations living in this region.

I. THE WEAKNESS OF THE ECONOMY OF THE MIDDLE EAST

Agriculture in the Arab countries is still predominantly semi-feudal. We have there a small class of landlords owning most of the land, but living mostly in the cities, and a large landless peasantry, working the land as share-tenants or landless agricultural workers. In Egypt 65 per cent of the land is owned by 6 per cent of the land-owners, while the remaining 35 per cent of the land is owned by the 94 per cent of small-holders. This proportion may have been changed some by the recent agrarian laws passed by the military government. [5] About half of the land in Syria is owned by large landowners. In Iraq the proportion of large landowners is even higher. [6] In Syria large tracts of land are owned by influential politicians, money-lenders, tribal chiefs and old families. The tenant's contract is usually for a year, at the end of which it may be cancelled. He receives no compensation for any improvements which he may have made. The landlord, who in most cases is an absentee, only visits the farm to collect rent. In Iraq the peasant may receive as little as one-twenty-first of the harvest, the remainder goes to the landlord for rent. This system provides the tenant no incentive to make any improvements on the land and is a big factor in the land's deterioration. The plight of the peasantry is made still worse by the constant burden of the peasants' indebtedness, usually contracted at high interest rates, the landowner often being the money lender.

Besides Egypt other Arab countries have made legislative attempts to break up the large landholdings and redistribute them among the landless peasantry. But big landowners who constitute the governing class in most Middle East countries resist all attempts to pass satisfactory land reform laws. "As the peasants learn from the newspapers and radio about agrarian revolutions in other countries they are not likely to remain for an indefinite period content with their present state of landlessness, nor will they be duped by promises of political independence . . . Here lies one of the most explosive elements in the present Middle East situation."[7] "Unless there is a substantial improvement in the condition of the peasant masses, the Middle East will be ripe for an agrarian revolution. It is a land-hungry area, and the situation resembles in a dangerous way conditions in Russia prior to the Revolution of 1917."[8]

The source of income of the vast majority of the people in the Middle East countries is from agriculture. Outside of Israel modern industry hardly exists in the Middle East countries, except, of course, for the industry concerned with the extraction, refining and marketing of oil. It is said that outside of oil the Middle East is generally poor in mineral resources. But the mineral resources of the Middle East area have not yet been fully explored. There are substantial supplies of iron, copper, chrome, phosphates, and manganese in the area, and an abundance of various minerals in the Dead Sea. Israel has demonstrated what can be done if there is the right spirit and determination. Well-developed industrial enterprises could go a long way toward solving many of the region's problems. But there are serious obstacles which stand in the way of industrial development of the Middle East countries, Israel excepted. These limiting factors are four-fold:

(1) The semi-feudal land tenure system is probably the greatest offender. This system is responsible for the low agricultural productivity. The undernourished and underpaid peasant has neither the incentive nor the means wherewith to buy the necessary equipment to raise the productivity of the soil. Since no country can expect to develop a national industry unless there is a demand for its products among its own people there can be no hope of industrial

development in the Middle East until the purchasing power of its peasantry is raised. And this means a complete overhaul of the entire land-holding system in the Middle East.

(2) The serious shortage of technical skill is another factor limiting the prospect of industrial development in the Middle East. There is a lack of skilled workmen, or trained and competent industrial managers and supervisors. Arab young men who have studied engineering abroad, when they return to their home countries prefer "white collar" jobs to getting their hands dirty; among the educated classes there is still great prejudice to manual work. The Point Four Programme is doing a great deal to overcome this deficiency. "However, the introduction of new technology into agriculture, industry, public health and government administration is very difficult and complex. It cannot simply be imported from the West but requires much cultural readjustment and assimilation."[9]

(3) The shortage of capital is another serious obstacle in the industrial development of the Middle East. Most investors in the Middle East are primarily interested in large profits and quick returns. They prefer to invest their money in land rather than in industry. According to United Nations estimates the countries in the Middle East are saving on average 6 per cent of their national income. In order to raise the per capita income annually by 2 per cent the Middle East people would have to invest in industry and agriculture 15 per cent of their national income. It is maintained that with increased revenues from oil and greater mobilization of internal capital these countries could raise the rate of their national savings to 10 per cent. This means that there would still be a need of importing foreign capital amounting to at least 5 per cent of the national income.[10] But the political tensions, instability, the constant threat of nationalization of industries, and the many discriminatory laws against foreign capital impede the flow of money from abroad.

(4) Last, but not least, another limiting factor retarding the industrial development of the Middle East is the system of low wages and the absence of an enlightened policy to the question of organized labour. Fear of communist infiltration dominates the attitudes of Middle East governments to the problem of the trade union movement. Thus the various labour laws in the Middle East countries, especially Arab countries, are designed to discourage the development of the trade movement. "... a truly progressive policy

is hardly to be expected so long as political power remains in the hands of a small group of landowners and industrialists."[11]

2. THE SOCIAL BACKWARDNESS OF THE MIDDLE EAST

Social services are hopelessly inadequate in the Middle East. The majority of the population is still illiterate. Illiteracy, disease and squalor, along with abject poverty, are the things which strike the visitor to these parts. Preventive medicine and sanitary measures are woefully inadequate. Bilharzia and ankylostomiasis are widespread in Egypt. Malaria and trachoma, with its high toll of blindness—in other Middle East countries. A serious obstacle in the eradication of these evils is the general attitude of the Muslim population. "All disease, they believe, comes from Allah, and if He, in His inscrutable wisdom, decrees restoration to health, scientific treatment in a hospital will make no difference."[12] "A child born crippled limps through life; a child made blind by trachoma is a victim of Allah's will, not man's. And who was to say that Allah chose wrongly in singling out this child? In this gateway [i.e. Cairo] to the Middle East, I realized I had plunged back through the centuries to an almost unbelievable way of life. . . . It was truly pointed out to us that as far as the Middle East was concerned, the French and American Revolutions might never have taken place. The doctrine of human rights and personal liberty—the concept that man had dignity as a human being and the latent power to lift himself from the mire of animal existence—had not penetrated the citadels of Islamic authoritarianism."[13]

3. THE POLITICAL INSTABILITY OF THE MIDDLE EAST

The non-representative form of government under which the peoples of the Middle East live vary all the way from an absolute autocratic monarchical system as exists on the Arabian peninsula, to a constitutional monarchy as prevails in Iraq and Iran, to the republican form of government of Syria,* Lebanon, and Turkey. Egypt at the present time is neither a monarchy nor a republic, but ruled by a military dictatorship.

There is scarcely any part of the world today in which the domestic political scene is as unstable as in the Arab countries of

* At this writing Syria and Egypt are united under one military dictatorship.

the Middle East. They have accepted from the West such Western concepts of government as parliamentarianism, democracy, elections, political parties, freedom of religion, of assembly, of press, etc., but they have retained the form, not the substance, of these ideas. "Parliamentary elections are usually rigged, or conducted in an atmosphere of violence . . . Political parties centre around personalities rather than principles. Indeed, most political leaders are drawn from one group only—that of the land-owners, industrialists, tribal sheikhs and professional men, and only occasionally from prosperous members of the middle classes . . . Standards of political morality are disappointingly low."[14] These are the words of one intimately acquainted with Middle East conditions.

Here are the remarks of another Middle East observer: "Standards of administration are still low; the margin of public security is narrow; the gap between Government and governed is wide. There is neither public trust in the intentions of the rulers, nor a popular opinion strong enough to impose itself upon them. Moreover, Arab Governments on the whole represent the possessing classes: the land-owners and merchants, with the educated elements associated with them."[15]

The following observations are by one to whose findings we have already referred before: "It was my impression, after speaking with Tewfik [an Egyptian nationalist] and the young intellectuals he represented, that they were unsure of themselves. During the war, they did not know whether to be pro-Nazi or pro-Ally. Democracy, as a term, confused them. In a land in which 85 per cent of the population is illiterate, in which a tiny group representing perhaps 5 per cent possesses nearly 95 per cent of the country's riches and rules with complete cynicism so far as responsibility to the people is concerned, democracy, with its emphasis upon power in the hands of the masses, is a frightening concept."[16] "If the Arab leaders were truly concerned with the poverty and disease which condemns their people to constant misery, would not their first concern be to feed their populations, to eradicate illiteracy, and to raise the standard of living by developing the great latent resources of their lands? Syria and Iraq were half empty. Iraq had only a fraction of its cultivable land worked. It seemed to me it would be the mark of wisdom for the Arab leaders to devote themselves to such causes—which would give them genuine power—and at the same time welcome the Jews for the economic good they would bring and the 'know-how' they would furnish."[17]

"They [i.e. the Arab States of Iraq, Saudi-Arabia, Syria, Lebanon and Yemen] represent one of the last leftovers of medieval feudalism. Ruled by little cliques of Pashas and Clergy, in complete disregard of the most elementary interests of the masses of the population, the Arab lands, if left to themselves, hold out no promise either for the advancement of their peoples or for positive participation in world civilization. Some of these Arab states . . . have enjoyed independence for many decades . . . What have they done with their independence? Have they in any way elevated the masses of the people, spread literacy and culture, introduced proper medical care, or maternity hospitals, improved sanitary conditions, built proper dwellings for the working man, fought infant mortality, improved social conditions, and in general promoted progress in their respective countries? Unfortunately, one must admit that the opposite is true. In none of the Arab lands has any progressive movement in the political field, in economics, or in social conditions, materialized. Independence was made an instrument for more shameless exploitation of the masses of the people, for further enrichment of the few and for further degradation of the poor. . . . In the Middle East the rich are actually free from taxes. They are the government, free of any control by the masses of the people, and they manipulate matters in such a manner as to have the peasant carry the whole burden of the State budget. Corruption is rampant, freedom non-existent, except for the freedom of the rulers to exercise their absolute power over their peoples and States."[18]

In addition to the professional politicians referred to above there are four other groups which contend for mastery on the political scene in the Middle East countries:

(1) One consists of those who received their education abroad and became imbued with the ideals of Western democracy. They maintain that genuine democracy has never had a real chance in the Middle East and it should be given a trial.

(2) In the second group are those who believe that all the evils from which the Middle East is suffering now is due to the weakening of Islam. Only a return of the people to the laws, precepts and usages of primitive Islam will solve all the vexing problems besetting this region. The members of this group are prompted as

much by political as by religious motives. Their expressed or un-expressed desire is to destroy Western ideas and influence. A number of these groups have sprung up in the last three decades the most powerful of which is the reactionary Muslim Brother-hood. "It is a body which would capitalize religious zeal for political ends, and which is prepared to seize power by every means at its disposal, be it intimidation, intrigue, or ruthless force."[19]

(3) The followers of communism comprise the third group. We will discuss the subject of communism in the Middle East in another section.

(4) The fourth group is the army. The army has on various occasions seized power in Iraq, Syria and Egypt. When the army takes over the reins of government it usually disbands all political parties it finds in existence. In Iraq every government between 1936 and 1941 was formed under army influence.

There is a constant struggle for power going on between these groups. At times two or more factions may unite to gain a common objective, but this union is of a transient nature. The political instability of the Middle East countries, especially the Arab states, may be seen from the following long list of political acts of violence committed in the various Arab countries in recent years:

"Egyptian Prime Minister Achmed Maher Pasha, assassinated February 1945;

"Egyptian Prime Minister Mustapha Nokrashi Pasha, assassi-nated by Moslem Brotherhood, December 1948;

"Egyptian Moslem Brotherhood leader Sheikh Hassan el Banna, assassinated February 1949;

"Syrian President Kuwatli with Parliament and Government deposed by Colonel Husni Za'im in military coup, March 1949;

"Colonel Za'im and Prime Minister M. Barazi assassinated by Colonel Sami Hinawi in military coup, August 1949;

"Colonel Hinawi deposed by Colonel Shishekly in military coup, December 1949;

"Syrian President H. Atassi with Parliament and Government deposed by Colonel Shishekly, November 1950;

"Syrian ex-dictator S. Hinawi assassinated October 1950;

"Lebanese Prime Minister Riad e-Solh assassinated June 1951;

"King Abdullah of Jordan assassinated July 1951;

"King Farouk ousted by coup d'etat, July 1952;

"King Talal of Jordan, deposed August 1952;

"Lebanese President S'shara el Khoury deposed September 1952;

"Iraqui Premier Mustapha el Omari deposed by military coup, November 1952;

"Egyptian Dictator Naguib deposed and reinstated February 1954;

"Syrian Dictator Shishekly deposed by coup, February 1954."[20]

4. COMMUNISM IN THE MIDDLE EAST

Communist propaganda in the Middle East derives its strength from the failings of the existing political, economic and social order. Communist appeal is said to be strong among university students, underpaid workers and dissatisfied civil service employees. In fact, it finds a ready hearing among all disgruntled elements. The trade-unions, El Azhar University, the army, the police and the Muslim Brotherhood are said to be infiltrated with communist elements. "Their [Arab] undemocratic societies are seedbeds wherein skilfully propagated communism can be made to flourish like poison ivy."[21] "If Communism has not already spread far in the Middle East, that is mainly because Russia has not yet shown her hand there. When she gives her main attention to the Arab countries, she will find all the conditions for the spread of her doctrines and influence. Therefore, it is not enough for the Western Powers to make military agreements with Arab Governments and then confine themselves to a correct, neutral and passive diplomatic attitude. Whatever agreement is made, the situation will still be dominated by those factors, positive and negative, which incline men's spirits away from the West and towards Russia."[22]

No discussion of communist penetration in the Middle East is complete without taking into consideration the influence, positive or negative, of Islam. Islam, as we know, is the way of life of the vast majority of the people in the Middle East. However incompatible Islam and communism may appear to be, competent observers maintain that there is much which these two ideologies share in common.[23] Some of the outstanding features which are common to both communism and Islam are as follows: ". . . their totalitarian doctrine, their fanaticism and collectivism, their division of the world into two sectors . . ., their concept of a community of believers which is always in the right, and finally their dependence on the state to control economic life. . . . Arab intellectuals may readily accept Marxism as both an explanation of present trends and a guide for future action. Communism makes a powerful appeal by its intense anti-western sentiment and its opposition to colonialism, and to race and colour prejudice." [24]

The methods which both groups use to attain their goals are quite identical. "Political assassination and the secret activity of fanatical sects are a specialty of the political life of the Moslem Orient, due, doubtless, both to the existence and diversity of the ethnic and religious groups and to their concealed existence." [25]

The spiritual crisis which Islam has been experiencing is another important factor tending to deepen Arab interest in communism. The vast majority of the Arab intellectuals are convinced that Orthodox Islam, which is a totalitarian and legalistic religious system still seeking "to regulate the whole life, social and individual, by the Sharia Law", [26] is out of date and out of step with conditions and problems of modern life. There is a growing estrangement from and indifference to the precepts and practices of Islam on the part of large segments of Arab society. All efforts of various Islamic groups to restore the authority of Islam in the life of the people have so far proven ineffective. The same may be said of the various attempts to reinterpret Islam to make it more adaptable to the needs of this present era. It has been said that there is "no inner power in the Muslim countries themselves which produces sufficient moral directive and determination to effect this transformation". [27] "Indeed the fundamental problem of the Arab world, political no less than individual, is that of nihilism which is the more dangerous because of its combination with nationalist feeling and the techniques of modern war. It is a danger which can only be countered if the Arab mind can find and appropriate a system of beliefs which satisfies its deepest cravings. Here too we must not ignore the possibility of a cataclysm: a turning of the Arab mind towards the Communist belief, which does at least provide a systematic and coherent doctrine not only of society but of man and the universe." [28]

5. ISLAM'S ATTITUDE TO CHRISTIANITY IN THE MIDDLE EAST

The intolerant attitude of Islam to Christianity throws much light on the prophetic teaching concerning the position of the Middle East in the "Time of the End" era. Islam, though it drew heavily from both Judaism and Christianity, was from the beginning of its existence hostile to both its predecessors. Of the two, Christianity has from the beginning been the more serious opponent on account of its being the religion of West, and also by virtue of its universal and missionary character. "The legal status of a convert [to Christianity] and his family is, in most cases, undetermined. The convert's life is in danger, and Muslim law requires that he be disinherited. He often loses his employment and his wife and children are usually separated from him. A woman convert is subject to the Muslim law of guardianship, which, if applied, means that she is placed under the control of her nearest Muslim male relative until she has passed the age of marriage. Pressure is often put on her to marry a Muslim. In the eyes of the Muslim public the apostate is a traitor both to his religion and to his community, and deserves all that comes to him. . . . One other form of religious disability is the series of administrative restrictions imposed on non-Muslims before permission is granted for the erection of a place of worship."[29] "Christians are debarred (e.g. in Egypt) from some of the higher ranks of the Civil Service, and the number of appointments allowed them is, in some countries, limited to their proportion of the total population. The law in Egypt about the employment of nationals in commercial firms is interpreted in such a way as to identify an Egyptian with a Muslim."[30]

Opposition to Christianity in the modern world is not confined to Muslim countries. In communist China the Government has done its best to discredit the Christian Church in the eyes of the Chinese people. In Russia the communist regime has pursued an anti-Christian policy since it has seized power. But the Chinese people will not so easily forget the benefits bestowed upon them by the Christian missionaries: the educational institutions which they have opened in their country, the hospitals which the Christians have established, the sacrificial spirit of the many young men and women who had left their homes in the West and had gone to China to help improve the lot of the common people. In Russia, on the other hand, Christianity, chastened and purged of its pre-revolutionary sins, has survived as a spiritual force among the people in spite of all the repressive measures devised against it by the Russian regime.

It is different, however, in the Muslim Middle East, especially in the Arab countries. Hostility to Christianity in the Arab countries is probably more deep-seated than anywhere else in the world. "Nothing excites the fanaticism of the Muslim masses more than the word 'tabsheer' (that is, the preaching of the Gospel) or rumours that a Muslim has been baptised."[31] This intense hostility to Christianity in the Arab Middle East becomes deeply significant if we recall to mind the prophetic teaching, discussed on previous pages, to the effect that the beast-like ruler of the last world empire, who in the New Testament is called the Anti-Christ, is destined to arise in the Middle East at the "Time of the End" era.

From the above survey of conditions of the Middle East— economic, social, political and religious—we can see the existence of certain basic factors whose development is preparing the Middle East for the events of the final phase of the "Times of the Gentiles". And this is what we should expect if the Land of Israel is to be caught in the vortex of the final struggle of the Gentile world against God and His Anointed. We will conclude our discussion of this subject with the following words by one well acquainted with the Arab Middle East: "The Arab East may yet become the cradle of a new civilization, but in the event of a global conflict, it may become one of the major battle grounds and graveyards of the clashing modern civilizations."[32]

NOTES TO CHAPTER 3

1. Charles Malik, "The Near East: The Search for Truth", article in *Foreign Affairs* (New York), January 1952. Copyrighted by the Council on Foreign Relations, New York.
2. *The Sunday Sun* (Baltimore, Maryland), January 10, 1954.
3. Edgar A. Mowrer, *Problems of the Middle East* (Proceedings of a Conference held at the School of Education, New York University, June 5th–6th, 1947), p. 106.
4. Charles P. Issawi, *The Near East and the Great Powers* (Harvard University Press: Cambridge, Massachusetts, 1951, edited by Richard N. Frye), p. 57. Copyright 1951 by the President and Fellows of Harvard College. Used by permission of the publishers.
5. S. A. Morrison, *Middle East Survey* (S.C.M. Press: London, 1954), pp. 79–80. Permission for use in U.S.A. granted by Harper & Brothers, New York.
6. Charles Malik, idem.
7. S. A. Morrison, op. cit., p. 83.
8. Ibid., p. 85.

9. Charles Malik, idem.
10. Ibid.
11. S. A. Morrison, op. cit., p. 91.
12. Ibid., p. 94.
13. Bartley C. Crum, *Behind the Silken Curtain* (Simon and Schuster: New York, 1947), p. 153.
14. S. A. Morrison, op. cit., p. 103.
15. Albert Hourani, "The Decline of the West in the Middle East"—II, article in *International Affairs* (Royal Institute Of International Affairs, New York), April 1953.
16. Bartley C. Crum, op. cit., pp. 149-50.
17. Ibid., pp. 152-3.
18. Eliahu Ben-Horin, *Problems of the Middle East* (Proceedings of a Conference held at the School of Education, New York University, June 5th-6th, 1947), p. 95.
19. S. A. Morrison, op. cit., p. 105.
20. *The Jews in the News* (Grand Rapids, Michigan), September 1954. Since this article was published more political upheavals have taken place in Arab countries.
21. Edgar A. Mowrer, op. cit., p. 107.
22. Albert Hourani, idem.
23. Ibid.
24. S. A. Morrison, op. cit., p. 106.
25. Robert Montague, "Modern Nations and Islam", article in *Foreign Affairs* (New York), July 1952.
26. S. A. Morrison, op. cit., p. 127.
27. Ibid.
28. Albert Hourani, idem.
29. S. A. Morrison, op. cit., p. 112.
30. Ibid., p. 115.
31. Ibid., p. 111.
32. Jamil M. Baroody, *Problems of the Middle East* (Proceedings of a Conference held at the School of Education, New York University, June 5th-6th, 1947), p. 2.

ISRAEL'S MISSION TO THE NATIONS

I. THE SURVIVAL OF THE JEWISH PEOPLE

1. A UNIQUE PHENOMENON

The survival of the Jews is the world's most unique and baffling historical phenomenon. The Jews are one of the oldest racial or national groups in the world. If the beginning of their national history is counted from the time when they settled in Egypt under Joseph then their history extends over a period of some 3,500 years. The long national history is not, however, the outstanding feature of the Jewish people. There are other races today with as long a history as the Jews. The uniqueness of the Jewish people is their survival in spite of the fact that their Homeland had been destroyed twice and the people dispersed from their country. As a rule, when people leave their home country and emigrate to a foreign land they become thoroughly assimilated with the people of the host country after one generation, if not sooner. The Jews as a group are a notable exception to this rule. In spite of having been scattered all over the world for many centuries they have retained their national identity and their national characteristics, and this, notwithstanding all the efforts of the various host countries to obliterate their separate identity by force or other means.

2. HOW TO ACCOUNT FOR IT?

a. *The natural view*

According to this view the survival of the Jews can be explained on the basis of the interaction of two factors: (1) Outside pressure; (2) inner loyalty. The greater the pressure from a hostile world from without, the stronger the group loyalty from within. That this principle was operating in the various countries of Jewish dispersion, and in certain periods of history, is obvious to every student of Jewish history. If the various Gentile countries having Jews in their midst had been willing to treat their Jewish subjects the same as their non-Jewish subjects, the Jews—humanly speaking—would have become extinct as a separate national group. In support of this supposition one can point to the steadily declining numbers of Jews in the countries of Western Europe where for many years they have enjoyed equal civil right. What this theory does not explain is why the Gentile countries have not universally and consistently pursued a policy of toleration, since it proved so effective in obliterating Jewish distinctiveness; nor does this view account for the periodic outbreaks of anti-semitism in the various parts of the world—as if directed by some higher force—which served to increase Jewish group solidarity and check the process of Jewish national disintegration.

We are told that the German philosopher Hegel who attempted to explain various historical phenomena found it impossible to account for the problem of Jewish survival. "It is a dark, troublesome enigma to me," he is reported to have said. "I am not able to understand it. It does not fit any of our categories. It is a riddle."[1]

b. The supranatural view

"I remember", declares the Russian philosopher Nicolas Berdyaev, "how the materialist interpretation of history, when I attempted in my youth to verify it by applying it to the destinies of peoples, broke down in the case of the Jews, where destiny seemed absolutely inexplicable from the materialistic stand-point. And, indeed, according to the materialistic and positivist criterion, this people ought long ago to have perished. Its survival is a mysterious and wonderful phenomenon demonstrating that the life of this people is governed by a special pre-determination, transcending the process of adaptation expounded by the materialistic interpretation of history. The survival of the Jews, their resistance to destruction, their endurance under absolutely peculiar conditions and the fateful role played by them in history; all these point to the particular and mysterious foundations of their destiny."[2] There is only one sound and logical view by which to account for the indestructibility of the Jews. This view is set forth in the Bible where the survival of the Jews is attributed to the unchangeable Will of God, and where

M

the preservation of the Jews is part and parcel of their national destiny as a people chosen of God to fulfil a certain mission in the world. The following are a few portions from the Bible bearing on this subject.

Leviticus 26: 44–45: "And yet for all that, when they are in the land of their enemies, I will not reject them, neither will I abhor them, to destroy them utterly, and to break my covenant with them; for I am Jehovah their God. But I will for their sakes remember the covenant of their ancestors, whom I brought forth out of the land of Egypt in the sight of the nations, that I might be their God: I am Jehovah."

Isaiah 54: 9–10: "For this is as the waters of Noah unto me; for as I have sworn that the waters of Noah shall no more go over the earth, so have I sworn that I will not be wroth with thee, nor rebuke thee. For the mountains may depart, and the hills be removed; but my lovingkindness shall not depart from thee, neither shall my covenant of peace be removed, saith Jehovah that hath mercy on thee."

Jeremiah 31: 35–36 (31: 34–35 Heb.): "Thus saith Jehovah, who giveth the sun for a light by day, and the ordinances of the moon and of the stars for a light by night, who stirreth up the sea, so that the waves thereof roar; Jehovah of hosts is his name: If these ordinances depart from before me, saith Jehovah, then the seed of Israel also shall cease from being a nation before me forever."

Jeremiah 33: 25–26: "Thus saith Jehovah: If my covenant of day and night stand not, if I have not appointed the ordinances of heaven and earth; Then will I also cast away the seed of Jacob, and of David my servant, so that I will not take of his seed to be rulers over the seed of Abraham, Isaac, and Jacob. . . ."

These are only a few of a large body of teachings concerning the survival of the Jews. The same truth is implied in the various passages dealing with the national restoration of the Jewish people some of which are listed in the chart in chapter one.

II. The Meaning of Israel's Mission

1. PRELIMINARY OBSERVATIONS

Israel's Mission stems from Israel's chosenness, i.e. from the Divine call extended to Israel to fulfil a certain historical task.

There are many misconceptions, on the Jewish as well as the non-Jewish side, as to the true meaning of Israel's chosenness, due chiefly to an incomplete knowledge of the teachings of the Bible on this subject. The election of Israel began with Abraham. Before he had any offspring God had made to Abraham a solemn and irrevocable promise that through his descendants all the families of the earth shall be blessed. To emphasize this truth Abram's name was changed to that of Abraham, to indicate that he will become the father, i.e. the spiritual father, of many nations (Genesis 17: 1–8). "The change of name emphasizes the mission of Abraham, which is 'To bring all the peoples under the wings of the Shechina'."[3] These promises were in due time confirmed to Isaac (Genesis 26: 2–5), and to Jacob (Genesis 28: 13–15).

It was this Abrahamic Covenant which constitutes the basis of the covenant which God had made at Sinai with the people of Israel. "And because he loved thy fathers, therefore he chose their seed after them, and brought thee out with his presence, with his great power, out of Egypt", Deuteronomy 4: 37.

The election of Israel leaves, therefore, no room for national pride and boastfulness. Had God selected one of the existing nations such a choice might have implied a certain superiority over other nations. But in choosing Israel God had not singled out one nation in preference to all other nations; He brought a non-existing nation into being for a certain definite mission. Thus He made national boastfulness and pride impossible. This idea is implied in the above-cited passage in Deuteronomy 4: 37: "And because he loved thy fathers, therefore he chose their seed after them . . ." And also in the following statement: "Jehovah did not set his love upon you, nor choose you, because ye were more in number than any people; for ye were the fewest of all peoples. But because Jehovah loved you, and because he would keep the oath which he swore unto your fathers, hath Jehovah brought you out with a mighty hand, and redeemed you out of the house of bondage, from the hand of Pharaoh king of Egypt", Deuteronomy 7: 7–8.

Nor does the Election of Israel mean that in revealing Himself to Israel God had left the rest of the world in the dark, as it were. The Bible records God's communication with men in the ages before Abraham; and even after He has concluded His covenant with Abraham God did not confine His self-manifestation to Abraham's descendants. This is seen in the case of Melchizedek and Balaam. The same God who revealed Himself to Israel in some ways made Himself known to the heathen nations in other ways. The Apostle Paul declares in the epistle to the Romans that the heathen nations did possess a knowledge of God. "For what can be known about God is plain to them, because God has shown it to them. Ever since the creation of the world his invisible nature, namely, his eternal power and deity, has been clearly perceived in the things that have been made . . .", Romans 1: 19-20, Revised Standard Version.

The Election of Israel does not intend to minimize the importance of the contribution to human welfare which the other nations have made and are making. Philosophy, science and art have never attained in Israel the same degree of excellence as among the other nations of the world. However, by virtue of her Election Israel was granted a fuller measure of Divine Revelation. To Israel, as to no other people, God made known His purposes concerning the destiny of mankind. "Did ever a people hear the voice of God speaking out of the midst of the fire, as thou hast heard, and live?", Deuteronomy 4: 33. "Keep therefore [the commandments] and do them; for this is your wisdom and your understanding in the sight of the peoples, that shall hear all these statutes, and say, Surely this great nation is a wise and understanding people", Deuteronomy 4: 6.

2. THE JEWISH VIEW

a. *Israel's Election*

Though a purely spiritual concept in the Bible, the problem of Israel's Election has been viewed by traditional Judaism in racial terms. In Pirkey Abbot (Sayings of the Fathers) 1: 1 we read: "All Israel shall have a part in the world to come." However, in the eleventh chapter of the tractate Sanhedrin this statement is qualified by denying a portion in the future life to those Israelites guilty of certain transgressions. But that traditional Judaism laid great stress on the religious value of Jewish birth must be admitted by the unbiased student of the Jewish religion. For centuries every Israelite recited in his daily morning prayers the following: "Blessed art thou, Jehovah our God, King of the universe, that thou hast not created me a heathen." And the Prayer-Book in this, as in many other instances, reflects the faith of the Synagogue.

It is this misplaced confidence in Jewish racial origin which has moulded the undesirable features in traditional Judaism's attitude to the Gentile convert to Judaism. Moore states that "to the old classification, Priests, Levites, (lay) Israelites, a fourth category was added, Proselytes; and sometimes a subdivision puts them far down in the table of precedence . . . only above (heathen) slaves who had been circumcised and emancipated by their masters".[4] "Speaking generally," Moore says, "the tone of the utterances about Proselytes is friendly, though not unduly enthusiastic."[5] Even Bamberger—who writes more from the Jewish standpoint—lists five different areas in which the Gentile convert to Judaism was placed in a position inferior to that of the born Jew.[6] For a Gentile to become a follower of the God of Israel meant, according to traditional Judaism, to break completely with his past, to cut himself off from his people, parents, wife, and children, and to join himself to the Jewish people. This politico-national element of traditional Judaism functioned as a barrier, instead of a bridge, between the Gentile world and the God of Israel.

A perusal of the literature dealing with this subject will prove that modern Judaism has retained the basic concept of traditional Judaism on the importance of Jewish birth as a means of salvation. Thus Kaufmann Kohler, though a liberal Jew, holds that "in Judaism the community of race to that extent forms the basis of the community of faith that even the disbelieving Jew still remains a member of Jewry".[7] "Neither doctrine nor ideology, neither works of morality nor works of lovingkindness, important as they are, make up the Jewish Mission for mankind. The mere existence of the Jewish people stands out before everything and above everything we might consciously apprehend as our mission for mankind. The Jewish people must exist; it is the Jew who makes the Jewish mission possible."[8] "The nations of the world", declares Franz Rosenzweig, "cannot rely entirely on blood-relationship; they drive their roots into the night of the dead, yet life-spending soil . . . We alone trust to blood"[9] (meaning Jewish birth).

That this is an unspiritual and un-Biblical concept of Israel's Election is clear. If Jewish birth is the foundation of the Election of Israel, how could Terah, though the father of Abraham, be left out of the Abrahamic Covenant? Why was Ishmael, though a son of Abraham, not counted a son of the Covenant? Why did Esau, though a son of Isaac, remain outside of the Covenant? Why were all Israelites, from twenty years up, forbidden to enter the Land of Promise, and left to die in the Wilderness? To Jeremiah the circumcised, but unspiritual Jew, has the same standing before God as the heathen (Jeremiah 9: 25-26; 9: 24-25 Heb.). To Isaiah Jewish history is a continuous sifting process by means of which God separates the wheat from the chaff until the holy seed alone is left. Out of this seed, likened to the stem of a felled tree, a new Israel will evolve which will fill the whole earth with fruit (Isaiah 6: 9-13; 27: 6).

b. Israel's Mission

In the last part of the Second Commonwealth Judaism was a missionary religion. Evidence for this is found in the New Testament as well as in secular history. Matthew 23: 15 tells us of the great zeal with which the missionary activity was pursued ("for ye compass sea and land to make one proselyte"). In his missionary travels the apostle Paul frequently found Gentile proselytes and sympathizers attached to the various synagogues.

Even though Judaism had given up missionary activities some time after the destruction of the Jewish Homeland in A.D. 70, the hope for the conversion of the Gentiles remained much alive, as seen from the many fervent prayers in the liturgy. The following are excerpts from the Daily Prayer-Book: "Give thanks unto Jehovah, call upon His Name, make known His deeds among the people." "Therefore we hope in Thee, Jehovah our God, that we may speedily behold the glory of Thy might, when Thou wilt remove abominations from the earth and when the idols shall be utterly cut off; when the world shall be established under the sovereignty of the Almighty; and when all flesh shall call upon Thy Name; when all the wicked ones of the earth will be turned unto Thee. All the inhabitants of the world shall know and acknowledge that unto Thee every knee must bend, and every tongue must confess. Before Thee, Jehovah our God, they shall bow and fall down, and give honour unto Thy precious Name; and they shall all accept the yoke of Thy Kingdom; and Thou shalt speedily reign over them for ever and ever; for the kingdom is Thine, and Thou wilt reign in glory forever; as it is written in Thy Law, Jehovah shall reign forever. And it is said, And Jehovah shall be King over the whole earth; in that day Jehovah shall be One and His Name One."

Present-day spokesmen of religious Judaism maintain that the mission of Judaism is to be itself, to live according to its precepts. "True, the prophets spoke of the end of days and of messages to all mankind"—an American Rabbi states in his letter to David Ben Gurion, Israel's Prime Minister. "These, as I view them, were not goals for conscious striving, but natural results promised by the Deity for living His way. In other words, Israel was bid to live in God's way. The mission to be attained was God's. Hence I must rebel against any missionary inspiration or justification for Jewry. . . ."[10] This is the Orthodox view.

Liberal Judaism believes in the need of a missionary programme for Judaism. In fact, the early representatives of Reform Judaism conceived of the world-wide dispersion of the Jews as being missionary by God's design. The basic reason, however, for the non-missionary character of modern religious Judaism is its painful awareness that it lacks a vital message even for the Jew, let alone for the Gentile.

3. THE LESSON FROM ISRAEL'S FAILURE

"You only have I known of all the families of the earth; therefore I will visit upon you all your iniquities", Amos 3: 2. God's Revelation to Israel was a privilege. The greater the privilege, the heavier the responsibility which goes with it. "And to whomsoever much is given, of him shall much be required; and to whom they commit much, of him will they ask the more", Luke 12: 48. The destruction of the Jewish Homeland in A.D. 70 is, from the standpoint of the Bible, evidence of Israel's failure. Exile from the Land of Israel is for Israel exile from God ("And because of our sins have we been exiled from our country").

The failure of Israel contains a solemn warning to the Christian Church. These are the words of the apostle Paul: "Be not highminded, but fear. For if God spared not the natural branches [i.e. Israel], neither will he spare thee" [the Gentile Christians], Romans 11: 20–21. The admonitions contained in Paul's writings and in the message to the Seven Churches in the book of Revelation were literally fulfilled in the history of the Christian Church. Large geographic areas which at one time were part of Christendom were lost to Christianity not so much because of outside hostility as due to the fact that the Christians in those areas have ceased to be the "salt of the earth".

Israel's experiences contain a lesson for the world in general. There is a Divine judgment which constantly operates in world history. Whenever vested interests become unmindful of their obligations to society they invite disaster upon themselves. The American, French and Russian Revolutions—all underline the terrible relevance of this principle: "You only have I known of all the families of the earth: therefore I will visit upon you all your iniquities"; "And to whomsoever much is given, of him shall much be required. . . ."

4. THE BIBLICAL VIEW

a. *The Old Testament*

"Now therefore, if ye will obey my voice indeed, and keep my covenant, then ye shall be unto me a peculiar treasure from among all peoples: for all the earth is mine. And ye shall be unto me a kingdom of priests, and a holy nation . . .", Exodus 19: 5-6.

The above Divine message was delivered to Israel through Moses when the people of Israel arrived at Mt. Sinai on their way from Egypt. It states Israel's unique position in the sight of God ("ye shall be unto me a peculiar treasure"); it gives us the first inkling of the nature of Israel's mission in the world ("a kingdom of priests, and a holy nation"). For the first time we are told how God proposed to fulfil His promise to Abraham that in his seed all the families of the earth shall be blessed. To bring this about, to achieve this end, God had appointed Israel to be the mediator-nation between Him and the nations of the earth.

The above message delivered to Israel was, therefore, an unfolding of the purpose of the Abrahamic Covenant, and the Israelites were asked to ratify it. They had the choice either to accept it or to reject it. They accepted it, as we read: "And all the people answered together, and said, All that Jehovah hath spoken we will do . . .", Exodus 19: 8. Since the Covenant was an agreement between two parties—God and Israel—the realization of the Covenant's goal depended on the compliance by each party with the terms of the agreement. Since God was one of the two parties, and there was no question of non-compliance on His part, the attainment of the aim of the Covenant depended apparently on whether or not Israel would fulfil her part of the deal. But this is only partly true. A defensive alliance between a great and strong nation and a small and weak nation depends for its success on the stronger of the two nations. But this, as all other human illustrations, breaks down when applied to situations in which God is implicated. For human partners may fail. But God cannot fail. Certainly Israel has failed to do her part. But God must have foreknown that Israel would fail. If in view of His foreknowledge of Israel's failure He, nevertheless, entered into a covenant relationship with Israel, this fact alone is an assurance that He expected the Covenant to succeed.

That this is sound reasoning may be inferred from the certainty with which the Bible views the ultimate success of the Covenant, and the favourable outcome of Israel's mission. "And that which cometh into your mind shall not be at all, in that ye say, We will be as the nations, as the families of the countries, to serve wood and stone. As I live, saith the Lord Jehovah, surely with a mighty hand, and with an outstretched arm, and with wrath poured out, will I be king over you. And I will cause you to pass under the rod, and I will bring you into the bond of the covenant", Ezekiel 20: 32, 33, 37.*

b. The New Testament

"And after they had held their peace, James answered, saying, Brethren, hearken unto me. Symeon [i.e. Simon Peter] hath rehearsed how first God visited the Gentiles, to take out of them a people for His name. And to this agree the words of the prophets; as it is written. After these things I will return, and I will build again the tabernacle of David, which is fallen; and I will build again the ruins thereof, and I will set it up. That the residue of men may seek after the Lord, and all the Gentiles, upon whom my name is called", Acts 15: 13-17.

The above statement was made by James at the Jerusalem Council, sometimes referred to as the First Church Council, which convened to consider a weighty problem. Large members of Gentiles were being converted to the Christian faith through the labours of Paul and Barnabas. Paul did not ask of these Gentile converts to submit to circumcision, or to promise to keep the Law of Moses. He preached to them salvation through faith in the atoning death of Jesus Christ. Some of the Hebrew-Christian believers strenuously objected to Paul's position. They believed that the Gentiles are not saved, and cannot be admitted

---

* See also the Bible passages in the Chart in Part I.

into the fellowship of the believers, until they submit to circumcision and accept the Law of Moses. The Jerusalem Church met to consider this very important issue on the outcome of which the whole future of the Christian Church seemed to depend. Present at this meeting were the apostles, including Paul and Barnabas, the elders, and most likely many of the early followers of Jesus. Most of them, if not all, were Jews. After due deliberations the Council approved Paul's position, in which Peter and James, the two pillars of the Jerusalem Church, concurred. It was decided that the Gentile believers need not come to Jesus Christ by way of the Law of Moses. This was a victory for Christian liberty, for the doctrine of salvation by grace through simple faith in the redemptive work of Jesus.

It was in the course of these deliberations that James (whose Hebrew name is Jacob), the leader of the Jerusalem Church, made the statement cited above. In his brief and deeply significant declaration James outlined the highlights of the entire Christian era. An analysis of the passage of Acts 15: 13–17 reveals that James conceived of the Christian era as falling into three periods.

In the first period God gathers a people for Himself from among the Gentiles. In the second period Jesus Christ returns and causes the national restoration of the Jewish people. In the third period a nationally restored and spiritually regenerated Israel is used of God to bring about the conversion of all mankind.

(1) *The first period.* "And after they had held their peace, James answered, saying, Brethren, hearken unto me. Symeon hath rehearsed how first God visited the Gentiles, to take out of them a people for his name", Acts 15: 13–14. The first period of the Christian era is often referred to as the Church Age. "Church" in the Greek language is "ecclesia" which literally means an assembly, or a called-out body. James therefore states that in the first, or Church Age, period of the Christian era God is calling out an assembly of people from among the Gentiles. Only a partial ingathering of the Gentiles is to take place in the first period. The Gentile world as a whole—James informs us— is to be converted to God in the third period.

(2) *The second period.* "After these things I will return, and I will build again the tabernacle of David, which is fallen; and I will build again the ruins thereof, and I will set it up", Acts 15: 16. The second period of the Christian era begins with the Return

of Jesus Christ. The Church Age is terminated. God resumes His dealings with Israel. Jesus Christ causes the full and permanent national restoration and spiritual regeneration of the Jewish people. This declaration of James is in full agreement with Paul's teachings on this subject. "For I would not, brethren, have you ignorant"—Paul writes—"of this mystery, lest ye be wise in your own conceits, that a hardening in part hath befallen Israel, until the fullness of the Gentiles be come in", Romans 11: 25. In the first period of the Christian era a certain number of Jews will respond to the message of Jesus Christ ("a hardening in part hath befallen Israel"). The spiritual regeneration of all of Israel will take place only after the process of the partial ingathering of the Gentiles will have been completed: "And so all Israel shall be saved...", Romans 11: 26. James emphasizes the national restoration aspect, while Paul speaks of the spiritual regeneration aspect, of the redemption of Israel. Both these phenomena will take place in the second period of the Christian era.

(3) *The third period.* "That the residue of men may seek after the Lord, and all the Gentiles, upon whom my name is called", Acts 15: 17. This passage tells us what is the purpose of the full national restoration and spiritual regeneration of Israel which will take place in the second period with the Return of Jesus Christ. The present reconstruction of the Land of Israel by the Jewish people is preparing the way for the Return of Jesus Christ. When He comes back He will complete what they began. The Jewish people will then enter upon their God-given mission and the effect of this upon the world will, according to Paul, be equivalent to a resurrection from the dead (Romans 11: 15).

One may ask, what was the reason for this three-fold division of the Christian era? Why were not all Israel and all the Gentiles gathered in at once? The answer is that in the first century A.D. neither Israel as a nation, nor the Gentile world as a whole were ready for the Christian message. Paul declares that Jesus Christ came into the world in the fullness of time (Galatians 4: 4). By this he meant that the world into which Jesus Christ came had been prepared historically for His coming. The political subjection of Jewish Palestine to the Gentile world powers in the four hundred years between the end of the Babylonian exile and the Birth of Jesus Christ developed an unprecedented Jewish interest in the Messianic Hope, and many Jews were filled with Messianic expectations. It is from these Jews who were waiting for Israel's redemption that Jesus received many of His Jewish followers. A similar process of preparation was taking place in the Gentile world. Unified politically by the power of Rome, moulded intellectually by the Greek language and culture, the ancient world of the first century was fast becoming exhausted spiritually and morally. Neither the ancient heathen religions, nor Greek philosophy of that day, were capable of solving man's moral problems and satisfying his spiritual cravings. Yes, Jesus Christ came indeed into the world in the fullness of time.

But the world into which He came was the then known civilized world of the Mediterranean coast-lands. Beyond the frontiers of that world lay the vast stretches of the continents of Asia, Africa and Europe, with their teeming millions of Mongolian, Hindu, Negro, Germanic and Slavic races—most of them in a semi-barbaric state. Of the existence of this larger world the nations of the Mediterranean coast-lands knew little or nothing. For the peoples of this larger world to be able to respond one way or another to the Christian message required centuries of time. Similarly, while thousands of Jews rallied to the banner of Jesus Christ, the Jewish people as a whole were no more ready in the first century to enter upon their divinely appointed mission than ancient Israel in the days of the First Temple was prepared to live in accordance with the Law of Moses.

We must never lose sight of the fact that Biblical Revelation—Old and New Testament alike—aims to reach all mankind and the whole inhabited earth. "Go ye therefore, and make disciples of all the nations . . ." Matthew 28: 19. ". . . Go ye into all the world, and preach the Gospel to the whole creation", Mark 16: 15. "And that repentance and remission of sins should be preached in His name unto all the nations, beginning from Jerusalem", Luke 24: 47. Israel's main function in the ages before the Christian Church was established was to receive, write and preserve God's Revelation. The main function of the Christian Church in the days between the first and second coming of Jesus Christ—in the Church Age era—is to deliver this Revelation to all mankind.

Since primitive peoples are not in a position to receive the Biblical message of human redemption the Church Age was destined to last at least long enough for the whole unknown inhabited part of the world to be discovered, and for all nations to reach that stage in their intellectual development to be in a position to respond for or against the God of the Bible.

But this is not all. While Israel is taking, as it were, a back-seat in the Church Age period God nevertheless means for her to learn certain needful lessons. And the Church Age will last at least long enough until it is certain that Israel has learned these lessons.

And not only this. The nations of the world that are bent upon working out their salvation apart from or in opposition to God are to be given full opportunity to have their way and to find out where this will lead them. And the Church Age is to last at least long enough for the cup of the nations' wilfulness to reach its brim.

It is when all these historical processes will have attained the end of their development that the Church Age—the first period of the Christian era—will be terminated. Jesus Christ will return. Israel will be fully and permanently restored, and the nations of the earth will be converted to God. Israel's first mission—in the centuries before the Church Age—was to receive, write and preserve God's word. Israel's second mission—after the Church Age—will be the conversion of the nations unto God.

One of the most convincing proofs that this first period of the Christian era is fast drawing to a close is the culmination of the process of intellectual, moral and spiritual ripening taking place today in the whole world. Western Civilization is transforming all parts of the world into one way of life; while modern means of communication make it possible to present the Christian message to the whole human race. Thus for the first time in the world's history each nation is in a position to choose for or against the God of the Bible. This development, together with the extraordinary phenomenon of the re-establishment of the State of Israel, shows that the goals of the first period of the Christian era are rapidly being achieved.

III. Israel's Qualifications for Her Task

1. THE GEOGRAPHIC POSITION OF THE LAND OF ISRAEL

Palestine is a land bridge between three continents—Europe, Asia and Africa—which contain the bulk of the world's population. The Bible speaks of the Land of Israel as the centre of the earth, not in the geographic sense, but from the standpoint of God's dealing with mankind.[11] H. G. Wells is said to have stated that the ancient Jews were "a peculiarly stubborn little people who persisted in living in the middle of an international highway and were continually getting run over".[12] But the Jews had nothing to do with the selection of this international highway. They numbered about seventy people when, in an attempt to escape the famine which raged in the land of Canaan, they went down to Egypt and settled there. Why this small group of people was not, in the course of time, absorbed by the Egyptian nation is one of those mysteries about Israel which, outside of the Bible, are inexplicable. When they left Egypt they numbered several hundred thousand.

Judging from the Biblical records there was no great enthusiasm among the Hebrews in Egypt for the thought of leaving Egypt; while on their passage through the Wilderness large numbers rebelled against the whole idea of going to a land of which they knew nothing. Had the Jews remained in Egypt, or had they gone to a less exposed geographical area, there might not have been a Jewish nation, and world history would have been something entirely different from what it is. For as the Jerusalem Temple was considered the centre of the city of Jerusalem, and the city of Jerusalem the centre of the Land of Israel, so the Land of Israel had to be the centre in relation to the world, and the Jewish people had to live in the heart of mankind in order to fulfil their mission as the nation-priest to the nations of the earth. A Christian clergyman once said that when Israel is out of Palestine she is out of place, and when she is out of place, mankind is out of place. Israel was put in Palestine by the Will of God. There, in the centre of the earth, Israel's ears were to become attuned to the heart-beat of the peoples of the world, and made to feel the shocks and tremors convulsing the body politic of the nations of the earth.

2. THE JEWISH THEOCRATIC CONCEPT OF HISTORY

The Jewish concept of history is theocratic. The God of the Jews is the God of human destiny. He treads the highways and byways of mankind. Human history, according to the Jews, moves to a definite goal: the rule of God over all mankind. To them God is King of the whole earth, and the kingdoms of the earth are destined some day to become the Kingdom of God.

Even those Jews in Israel who have no affiliation with the Synagogue or any other religious institution feel that in rebuilding Zion they are engaged in a task of transcendent religious import not only for the Jewish people but for the whole world. The Jews have one word—Avodah—for work and Divine service. To them to serve God is to serve one's fellow-man. The Jew refuses to believe that the earth is destined to remain a place of misery, suffering and pain. He has always had a passion to attain on earth truth, justice, peace and human happiness. He has had a firm conviction that these ideals will some day find full realization right here on earth, and he has associated the fulfilment of these hopes with the coming of the Messiah. For Jesus to be born a Jew, among Jews, and in the National Homeland of the Jews, was the most natural thing to take place, aside from its theological connotation. For here only could He find the right atmosphere and the fit material with which to begin His ministry. The words which He taught His Jewish followers to say when they prayed, "Our Father who art in heaven, hallowed be Thy Name, Thy Kingdom come, Thy will be done on earth as it is in heaven", expressed—and still do—the longings of the Jewish heart.

3. THE DISPERSION OF THE JEWS

The world-wide, centuries-old, dispersion of the Jews is another important aspect of Israel's preparation for their God-given mission. One of the shortcomings of the Jewish people in the days of the Second Commonwealth was national isolationism. Jewish particularism and the universal tone of the Messianic message of Jesus met in a head-on collision. But the long dispersion of the Jews had transformed them into a cosmopolitan-minded people. The citizens of the present State of Israel have come from all over the world and brought with them the languages and way of life of their native countries. The population of the State of Israel is thus a world in miniature. The close ties between the Jewish people in and outside of Israel make it highly probable that Israel will retain this cosmopolitan complexion and orientation. The importance of this fact for a people with a world-wide message is quite obvious.

4. THE PRECARIOUSNESS OF THE INTERNATIONAL POSITION OF THE STATE OF ISRAEL

The Zionist determination to realize the age-long Jewish hope of national restoration in Palestine was motivated, among other things, by the recognition that only in the restored National Homeland can the Jewish nationality survive. The Zionist ideologists had apparently never envisioned the intense Arab hostility which Israel would be encountering; or the possibility that in the event of a nuclear war involving the Middle East, the Jewish population crowded into the small State of Israel might face total destruction. Had the Jewish people not resumed statehood in this present stage of world history they could not have appreciated to what extent modern warfare has wiped out national security. It is this recognition of the total lack of physical security in their own Homeland which will be instrumental in bringing the Jews back to their spiritual heritage. It is probably with these thoughts in mind that Prime Minister David Ben Gurion said, when addressing the Twenty-fourth World Zionist Congress convened in Jerusalem in April 1956, that "the future of the Jewish people and of Israel rested basically not in immediate security considerations but on the link between world Jews and Jewish culture and their attachment to the hope of the Messianic vision." [13]

Some Israeli leaders have expressed the hope that Jewish achievements in Palestine may spur the Arabs to undertake similar rehabilitation schemes in their own countries. It was suggested that a revival of the Middle East economy and a rise in the standard of living of the Arab peoples may bring about more friendly relations between the Arabs and Israel. That this hope is misplaced is seen from this that the Arab governments are more concerned with undermining Israel's position than with the development of their own countries. Even those Arab states which are forging ahead economically are using their increased resources to build up their military strength in preparation for war against Israel. Material progress does not necessarily produce higher moral standards. Germany, the most scientifically advanced country in Europe before World War Two, perpetrated the most barbaric crimes upon millions of Jews and other peoples. Communist Russia which is much more advanced scientifically and industrially than Tzarist Russia, is by far a greater threat to the security of the world than Tzarist Russia ever was. Thus while for the time being at least Israel must resign herself to live in a state of armed "peace", she is bound to turn to her Bible for the solution of her own ills and those of the world, and find new hope and meaning in the prophetic assurance that "Israel [and the world] shall be saved by Jehovah with an everlasting salvation", Isaiah 45:17.

NOTES TO CHAPTER 4

1. Quoted by Elias Newman in an address at a Conference on "The Jew in History and Prophecy" delivered at Moody Tabernacle, Chicago, Ill., January 22-25, 1918.
2. Nicolas Berdyaev, *The Meaning of History* (Charles Scribner's Sons: New York, 1936), pp. 86-7. By permission of Geoffrey Bles.
3. *The Pentateuch and Haftorahs*, edited by Chief Rabbi J. H. Hertz (Soncino Press: London, 1938), p. 58.
4. George Foot Moore, *Judaism in the First Century of the Christian Era* (Harvard University Press: Cambridge, Mass., 1927), vol. 1, p. 335. Copyright 1927, 1955 by the President and Fellows of Harvard College. Used by permission of the publishers.
5. Ibid., vol. 1, p. 342.
6. Bernard J. Bamberger, *Proselytism in the Talmudic Period* (Hebrew Union College Press: Cincinnati, 1939), pp. 143-4.
7. Kaufmann Kohler, *Grundriss einer systematischen Theologie des Judentums* (Leipzig, 1910), p. 6; quoted by Jakób Jocz, *The Jewish People and Jewish Christ* (S.P.C.K.: London, 1954), p. 311.
8. Ignaz Maybaum, *The Jewish Mission* (James Clarke & Co., Ltd.: London, 1949), p. 156.
9. Franz Rosenzweig, *Der Stern der Erlösung*, pp. 376f.; quoted by Jakób Jocz, op. cit., p. 311.
10. Simon A. Dolgin, "Can We Stay Jews Outside 'The Land'?", article in *Commentary* (New York), September 1953.
11. See Ezekiel 38:12. The Hebrew word Tabur means navel or highest point. Either of the two meanings has a significant connotation.
12. Quoted by Edgar A. Mowrer, "Factors in the Problem", *Problems of the Middle East* (Proceedings of a Conference held at the School of Education, New York University, June 5-6, 1947), p. 101.
13. Reported in the *Baltimore Sun* (Baltimore, Maryland), April 25, 1956. See also "Israel's Security Tied to Jewry's Fate"—by David Ben Gurion, published in *The American Zionist* (New York), May-June 1956.

CONCLUSION

From the Biblical standpoint man's separation from God has resulted from his wilfulness, from his wish to substitute his own way for God's way, from his desire to place himself, instead of God, in the centre of things. This was true of man on the individual as well as on the collective level. Adam and Eve individually accepted the tempter's evil suggestion that the purpose of God's commandment was not to benefit them but to bar certain sources of knowledge from them in order to keep them in a state of perpetual inferiority vis-à-vis God (Genesis 3: 5). Mankind collectively was, in the Tower of Babel incident, guilty of the same wilfulness. Instead of spreading out, and rebuilding and inhabiting the wide spaces laid waste by the Flood, as God commanded (Genesis 9: 1), they decided to concentrate in one region. There they proceeded to erect a powerful and imposing organization whose motive was self-exaltation ("let us make us a name", Genesis 11: 4).

God's punishment was to leave man to his own devices, and to allow him to follow his inclinations to their logical conclusion. History has been a continuous conflict between the God-centred and the man-centred way of life. The Bible teaches that human history, as we know it, will terminate in the complete breakdown of the man-centred world order. It is at this point when the kingdoms of the earth will pass under the rule of God.

The current world crisis affecting all areas of human life—religious, moral, political, economic and social—is the cumulative effect of the unspiritual, man-centred, trend in human history. The steadily deteriorating world situation since the First World War, the growing frequency and destructiveness of wars in modern times, the advent of the atomic-bomb era with its threat of world annihilation, these and many other events—all point to man's decreasing ability to cope with the situation. The re-emergence of the State of Israel at this critical juncture of world history suggests that God is moving to prepare a way to save man from himself. In the days of the First Commonwealth Israel wrote most of the Old Testament. After the exiles had returned from Babylon and established the Second Commonwealth the Israelites completed the Old Testament and gave to the world Jesus Christ. What will this present coming together between Israel and the Land of Israel produce? If this present restoration is preparatory to Israel's final and complete redemption—and all signs point in that direction—it will issue forth in the transformation of the kingdoms of this earth into the Kingdom of God. This is the teaching of the whole Bible—Old and New Testament. In the New Testament this event is associated with the return of the Lord Jesus Christ. "Even so, come, Lord Jesus", Revelation 22 : 20.

"What mean these groans that fill the air
    As from a tortured breast—
The nations like a moaning sea
    That cannot be at rest?

They are the death throes of a world
    Fast ripening in sin,
Whose culture is but Babylon,
    Whose glory, foul within—

But also birthpangs, bringing forth
    The age, so long foretold,
When heaven's healing tenderness
    Will this sad earth enfold.

Awake, O Land of Israel,
    To beauty, love, and song,
Out of the dust of long neglect
    And centuries of wrong—
Out of the being trodden down
    In mire by alien feet—
Out of thy lonely widowhood—
    Awake, no more to weep!

Behold! thy children come to thee;
    They long for thine embrace!
They come from wand'rings to and fro,
    From exile and disgrace.

.   .   .   .   .

They come to raise thy broken walls,
    Thy ruins to repair—
To change thy barren wilderness
    Into a garden fair.

.   .   .   .   .

O land where the Shekinah shone,
    Whose hills by One were trod,
Writ in the volume of the Book—
    The Promised One of God:
Rich blessings will from thee proceed
    To earth's remotest bound
When thy lost sons, at home again,
    Immanuel have found."[1]

NOTES TO CONCLUSION

1. This selection is from two poems by the late Max I. Reich, entitled "The Whole Creation In Travail", and "The Land of Israel"; see *Sweet Singer of Israel* (Moody Press: Chicago, 1948), pp. 152, 159.

GENERAL INDEX

Owing to lack of space, names mentioned in the notes to the chapters have not been incorporated in the index. R. following a name normally means Rabbi

Yetzer ha-ra and ha-tov, 184
Yiddish, 120, 296
Yohanan ben Zakkai, 134, 200
Yudgan, Judah, 61

Zechariah, 41, 46, 247, 322, 323
Zion, 165
Zion, rebuilding of, 60, 75, 77, 82, 86, 114, 158, 168, 370

Zionism, Zionists, 6, 48, 50, 73–7, 82–88, 98, 100, 106, 113f, 158, 161, 371f
Zionism and religion, 113f, 136
Zionist Congresses, 76, 77, 164, 372
Zionist Organization, 45, 50, 72–7
Zohar, 199, 220
Zunz, Leopold, 64
Zweig, Arnold, 84

INDEX OF SCRIPTURAL REFERENCES